STO 72

2-7-78

Guide to World Commodity Markets

Guide to World Commodity Markets

Consultant Editor:
Brian Reidy

Editorial Adviser:
John Edwards

With acknowledgements to:
The Federation of Commodity Associations

Editor:
Ethel de Keyser

Kogan Page, London/Nichols Publishing
Company, New York

Copyright © Kogan Page Limited 1977

First published in Great Britain in 1977 by
Kogan Page Limited, 120 Pentonville Road, London N1 9JN
ISBN 0 85038 411 7

First published in the United States of America 1977
by Nichols Publishing Company, Post Office Box 96, New York,
NY 10024

Library of Congress Cataloging in Publication Data
Main entry under title:

Guide to world commodity markets.

    Includes indexes.
    1. Commodity exchanges. I. Reidy, Brian. II. Edwards, John.
III. De Keyser, Ethel.
HG6046.G84   332.6'44   77-4858
ISBN 0-89397-002-6

Printed in Great Britain at the Alden Press, Oxford

Contents

1995900

Exchange, 192; The Board of Trade of Kansas City, Missouri, Inc, 197; Minneapolis Grain Exchange, 199; Citrus Associates of the New York Cotton Exchange, Inc, 200; Commodity Exchange Inc, 201; New York Cocoa Exchange Inc, 206; New York Cocoa Exchange, Inc, Trading in Natural Rubber Futures Contracts, 207; New York Coffee and Sugar Exchange, Inc, 208; New York Cotton Exchange, 210; New York Mercantile Exchange, 215; Petroleum Associates of the New York Cotton Exchange, Inc, 220; Wool Associates of the New York Cotton Exchange, Inc, 220

Uruguay: Agricultural Commodity Exchange, 221

Appendices

List of Tables and Price Graphs

Foreword

F F Wolff CBE, TD *Chairman of The Federation of Commodity Associations*

The publishers of this book have served a very useful function in providing such a comprehensive guide to the Commodity Markets of the World.

The aims of The Federation of Commodity Associations, of which I have the honour of being Chairman, are to promote and protect the commercial interests of commodity associations, companies and firms and I am delighted to see that the first part of the book is devoted to explaining the role and functions of Commodity Markets in international trade, together with a good description of methods of trading.

From time to time many cartels and government bodies seek to impose artificial restrictions on the laws of supply and demand and commodity markets, unfortunately, tend to become one of their targets.

Invariably, the Federation find that this is due to a lack of understanding of the markets and this book goes a long way towards explaining their evolution and development and also the extent to which they are used in countries throughout the world.

Consequently, I feel that the information it contains will be of interest and of use to business firms, financial institutions, universities and students, not to mention potential users and investors in commodities in all parts of the globe.

Preface

Commodity markets provide a centre where producers may contact the users of the commodity, directly or indirectly, and establish a price at which the raw material is bought and sold. Futures markets are an extension of the physical trade. They were established in the mid 19th century to protect buyers and sellers against price fluctuations which occured between the time the bargain was struck and the time taken to deliver the commodity. Futures markets allow for the participation of a cross section of interested parties, as well as providing price insurance for those buying and selling the actual commodity. In this volume we have included data on both futures and physical markets.

On the physical market, the exact requirements of the buyer regarding the type and location of the commodity may be met as the commodity is being purchased for immediate delivery. In a futures market an agreed quantity of a commodity is bought and/or sold at a specified time in the future. Purchase and sale contracts may be cancelled out before the delivery date.

Part 1 of this volume contains articles which detail the background of commodity markets and their usage by producers, consumers and speculators, their role as an international barometer of prices and the moves to establish commodity cartels in order to redress the balance between developing and industrialized countries. *Part 2* provides information on the commodities traded, and *Part 3* lists the markets under country and city, in alphabetical order, with detailed information on each market.

The names and addresses of trading members of the futures markets, where these have been available, are listed in *Appendix 1*.

In this first edition of the Guide to World Commodity Markets, because of pressures of time and the delay in some replies, it has not been possible to ensure that every commodity market and exchange is listed. Most of the data in *Part 3* was supplied by the commodity markets in answer to questionnaires, and every effort has been made to ensure accurate and complete information throughout. It is important however to note that in many cases arbitration rules have been summarized and that for comprehensive information in this area reference must be made to the relevant book of Rules and Regulations.

We trust that the information contained in this volume will convey the reason for and use of commodity markets and that the commodity market data will fill gaps in existing material.

Acknowledgements

In compiling a book of this nature, information and advice is required from a variety of companies and individuals in the United Kingdom and abroad. We wish to express our appreciation for all the assistance received and, in particular, to record our indebtedness to the following: the officials in the commodity markets who have taken the time and trouble to complete the questionnaires sent to them and those who subsequently checked the final copy; the Embassies and High Commissions, notably the US Embassy in the United Kingdom, the officials of which were particularly helpful; the organizations from which the numerous Tables in this book were obtained and, finally, to Eurocharts Information Services in the United Kingdom who assisted us in a number of ways and who together with the Commodity Research Bureau in the United States supplied the price graphs.

Part 1:
The Role and Function
of Commodity Markets

The Evolution of International Futures Markets

Brian Reidy

Commodity futures markets exist because they offer an indispensable form of price insurance that no sensible producer or consumer of a commodity can afford to be without.

There is a risk with commodities: that of price fluctuation. Prices are certain to rise and fall over any given period of time, and the extent to which they will do this is completely unpredictable. There are so many unknowns affecting the supply and demand for a given commodity that accurate price forecasting is impossible.

The price of a commodity, like that for any other product or service, is determined by the forces of supply and demand. These forces are constantly changing through a variety of factors. Crop disasters caused by disease, floods, frosts and drought stand out as one dramatic example affecting supply. Demand, on the other hand, is usually influenced by overall economic conditions and the price level of a given commodity.

Strong economic growth will bring forth sharply increased consumption and the re-stocking of industrial commodities such as metals or natural rubber. Increased prosperity and confidence about the future course of economic growth will also induce the private consumer and the industrialist to buy more goods or invest in new plant and buildings. During periods of recession or weak economic growth the opposite happens: fabricators and commodity merchants will rapidly run down their inventories and buy their raw material requirements on a strict hand to mouth basis. Consumers spend less and industrialists postpone capital spending programmes or curtail them.

The overall balance between supply and demand for a commodity at any given time is most vividly and accurately reflected by the behaviour of its price. It is the dynamics of the price mechanism which ultimately balances out the opposing forces of supply and demand.

To insure against the price risk in commodities, one 'hedges' on a commodities futures market. Hedging, however, cannot provide complete protection against price movement. It can only *lessen* the risk of adverse price movements. Price changes in commodities can be as sharp and sudden as they are financially damaging. It must therefore be stressed that while hedging is an essential form of insurance against price risk *it is not a complete* insurance against it.

But if price movements are so erratic and unpredictable and hedging always less than a complete insurance against them, why bother with the exercise at all?

The answer to that question is that some financial certainty is better than no financial certainty at all. By hedging it is possible to minimize greatly the risks involved on the costs of raw materials and thus to control production costs and cash flow much better. Hedging creates a position of some strength and enables one to deal more effectively with competitors. The closer the control of raw material input prices by hedging, the greater the profit margin.

The same criteria apply for the producer. To sell forward, part or all of the production now is to be assured of a guaranteed price in the future. This is particularly important if prices are high now but are likely to be lower when the crop is actually grown and ready to be harvested.

Hedging could not be carried out without having a market on which one can deal forward, that is, deal into the future, for that particular commodity. Hence, the name 'futures markets'. This term is best understood by realizing the difference between physicals and futures in commodities. Physicals are the actual commodities that are grown or mined from the ground. On a futures market, such as the United Terminal Sugar Market Association or the Chicago Grain Market, no physical sugar or grain actually changes hands at the time of a sale or purchase of a futures contract. The futures contract is simply a piece of paper. But that piece of paper is a legally binding contract on the buyer or seller to receive or deliver the actual physical commodity (the sugar or grain in this example) if he is called upon to do so at a specified time in the future.

Put another way, a futures contract is really a *temporary substitute* for a cash transaction. The futures contract transaction will eventually be made or liquidated at a later date.

It is essential to realize that the contracts on all futures markets, for whatever commodity, must reflect all the normal commercial and trade practices and standards for that particular commodity. If the contract did not reflect these standards and practices the trade would be unable to use the market because no one could be sure they were dealing in a standard grade.

Only a relatively small percentage of the futures contracts bought or sold on a futures market are ever actually delivered. The great majority of the contracts entered into are closed out (liquidated) before they fall due for delivery. They are closed out by matching a sale with a purchase or a purchase with a sale of the exact same quantity, quality, and delivery date.

Because everyone knows the futures contract can be turned into the actual physical commodity, the prices quoted on the futures market usually correspond very closely with the prices paid to buy the physical commodity from a producer. Equally there is no force majeure clause in a futures contract so a buyer or seller of a futures contract knows he is legally bound to take or make a delivery.

With the exception of the London Metal Exchange, all the world's futures markets use a clearing house system of operation. But suffice it to say for now that the clearing house is responsible for seeing that the contract is fulfilled if either of the two brokers involved in the transaction default. The LME operates on a unique 'principals contract'. This means the buyer and the seller of a contract are responsible to each other for the fulfillment of the contract at the due date. In effect this means the LME ring dealing member is guaranteeing both to his client and to other ring dealing members that the contract will be fulfilled.

In a futures market one is literally dealing for the future. One may be dealing ahead for a month's time or even for two years' time. Many of these time periods, together with contract specifications, are given under the individual markets listed in this book.

Before proceeding to the next article where the mechanics of hedging are explained, it is useful to examine the criteria needed to have a successful futures market. These are the criteria that all the markets in this book fulfil to a greater or lesser extent.

In the ideal world of the economic textbooks perfect competition exists when the following five conditions are met:

1. There is a large number of buyers and sellers in a particular market but no one buyer or seller has a dominant influence in determining prices.
2. The product is homogeneous.
3. Entry to and from the market is unhindered by rules, restrictions, etc.
4. All decisions and operations in the market are taken independently and dispassionately.
5. Information about the product's price, distribution, production and stocks position is fully and freely available to all the participants in the market.

Although these five conditions are not completely met in practice, it is, nonetheless, quite impressive how close the conditions come to being fulfilled by a mature futures market.

In an active futures market there is bound to be a large and concentrated number of buyers and sellers at any given time representing a fair cross-section of producers, fabricators, end-users, merchants, and speculators. This cross-section is likely to be international in character. American, Japanese and European wool merchants and spinners, for example, will be using the Sydney greasy wool futures market for hedging in addition to buying the physical wool at the various auctions held around Australia. There will also be arbitrage between the London and Sydney markets which will help iron out price differentials.

The international character of a futures market allows it to reflect accurately the true state of supply and demand for the commodity at any given time and this in turn determines its true price for that moment.

This price determining function of a futures market is often criticized by politicians, consumers, and producers at various times because the price action does not comply with their view of reality. But their criticisms are misplaced. It is not the market that decides the prices but the interaction between the buy and sell orders that flow into the market from all over the world. The market is merely a barometer.

It should also be stressed that the concentration of orders on one or two futures markets for a given commodity is vital if prices are to reflect faithfully the world supply and demand situation. The more fragmented the markets, the greater the chance for one party to gain dominance in one of them. This can only distort prices and leads, in the end, to the small markets atrophying from lack of trade use.

Futures markets also come close to the ideal of pure competition in their method of trading. Trading on futures markets is done at specified times by the open outcry method. All the brokers licensed to trade on that particular market's floor face one another and cry out their bids and offers for all to hear and act upon if they wish.

The trading method makes it very difficult for an individual or group to exert an undue influence on prices. Trading between market sessions, a feature of most futures markets, does not diminish the truth of this statement because the prices struck in unofficial trading simply reflect the price trend determined during the official trading periods.

The conditions of a future market's contract regarding what constitutes good delivery for the particular commodity ensures that the competition criterion of product homogeneity is also fulfilled. The contract will stipulate precisely determined quality characteristics for a commodity and the interchangeability of each contract. A futures market cannot exist unless the commodity dealt in can be graded and delivered as a standardized, precise, homogeneous unit.

Free entry into and exit from a market also comes close to being fulfilled because the commodity lot sizes are small. A 'lot' is the minimum unit of a given commodity that one can trade in on a futures market. Not only are the lot sizes small, but commission charges are low and the market user can deal on a margin deposit (usually ten per cent of the contract's value). Should the market move against the user's position he will be required to put up more money or collateral to maintain his margin deposit on the contract's current value.

But the high volume of the market's turnover, and thus its high liquidity, allows the small user to operate on the market as quickly and easily as the giant international concern.

Information on prices being made on a futures market is disseminated instantly and internationally over ticker machines. There are no secret price deals or discounts made to favoured clients. The price struck on the market is the price that anyone would have paid if he had dealt at that time.

Statistical and news information about the production of a commodity, its stocks levels, distribution and other price-affecting information is widely distributed and usually quite plentiful. While the amount and detailed nature of the information may never be sufficient to satisfy everyone, there is certainly enough information available about any given commodity at any moment to allow the producers and users of that commodity to take a view on its total supply and demand position and thus its likely price movements.

The flow of information is also so universal in its distribution that it is extremely difficult for any one party or group to have privileged information which would enable them to deal for long to their exclusive advantage. It does happen. But the scope for manipulating prices is extremely limited on an open futures market.

If futures markets are such models of as near-perfect competition as you will get in the real world, why are not more commodities traded on them?

The answer to this is threefold. It is impossible to have a successful futures market unless:
1. The commodity is durable or non-perishable enough to be capable of storage for many months without serious deterioration. If this condition cannot be met, then it is impossible to have a market which of necessity requires dealing ahead for delivery in many months' time. You cannot have a futures market in tomatoes, for example, but — if the need was there — you could create one to deal in canned tomato juice.
2. The commodity must be homogeneous and easily standardized and classified. Otherwise, it would be impossible to have the lots traded on the market absolutely interchangeable. A futures market in crude oil, iron ore, or wolfram, for example, would be extremely difficult to create because the grades of oil, iron and wolfram differ so widely.
3. Both the supply of and the demand for the commodity must be international in character and free from controls. It would be difficult, for example, to

create a futures market in uranium because it is a strategic material which can be used either to create power or nuclear weapons. Its production and usage is closely supervised by governments.

A more general way of stating the conditions for this third criterion is that a significant percentage of the commodity's production and consumption internationally must be free from government control or control by blocks of producers or consumers.

Without this freedom in supply and demand, market forces cannot operate. Prices would be largely dictated by those groups who control the bulk of the commodity's production. If this were the case there would be little or no uncertainty about price levels. And if there is little or no price uncertainty then there is no need for a futures market. A futures market exists for hedging, the object of which is to lessen the price risk a producer or consumer runs in a given commodity. Equally, if demand is small then there is no need for a futures market even if a significant price risk exists.

Futures markets have been established which largely satisfy the three criteria above but have, nonetheless, failed. Their failure is due to one or more of the following reasons:

1. The market did not satisfy an economic need and thus did not attract a sufficient volume of hedging and speculative business.

   Again, one can only generalize here and point out that this is a chicken and egg situation. Historically, a market develops out of a need to spread and lessen price risks. Its ultimate size, and thus its viability, will be determined by the volume of hedging that is done on the market. This volume of hedging cannot be maximized unless a sufficient volume of producer, consumer, and speculator funds can be attracted. If one or two of these three vital parties takes an insufficient interest in the market, then the market will not have the depth and liquidity to remain viable. And thus it withers away as fewer and fewer parties use its facilities.

   One moral here is: do not knock the speculator. Hedging cannot be maximized unless a sufficient volume of speculative funds are attracted to a market. The speculative funds give the market the extra depth and liquidity that it needs if hedging positions are to be evenly balanced out. If there were no speculators willing to take an opposite market view from that prevailing in many producer or consumer quarters, one would have a very volatile and uneven market.

2. The market is simply boycotted by fabricator, merchant, and/or producer interests with the result — as above — that the market withers away. This boycott usually reflects a hostility on the part of the producer and/or fabricator interests to the increased price competition that a viable futures market will bring.

   This boycott usually occurs in commodities where production is controlled by a relatively small number of big producers and the fabricators (those consumers who convert the commodity into a usable product) are accustomed to receiving regular supplies at discounts or can fairly easily pass on higher prices to the final consumer.

   Two metals which fall into this category are nickel and aluminium. Attempts in the past to create futures markets in these metals have failed because the producers are unwilling to see their price structures disrupted.

3. Finally, the market failure occurs when contract terms for the commodity concerned prove to be out of line with the needs of the trade. Hedging, in this case, proves to be fairly pointless because anyone taking delivery of the commodity would find it unsuited to real-life commercial practice. This happened with a turkey futures market in the United States. The contract allowed for the delivery of packaged and branded birds. These packaged and branded birds were difficult for anyone but a large packer to dispose of through the trade. The result was that interest in the market waned and the market turned into a dumping ground for birds surplus to the needs of the packers.

Use of the Markets
by Producer and Consumer
Brian Reidy

Although the speculative, or more euphemistically, the investment side of the commodity markets, tends to make news — particularly when prices are rising — the prime objective of the system is to offer protection against excessive price fluctuations to both producers and users of commodities.

This protection is known as hedging and its bedrock principle is to maintain a balanced book by offsetting a vulnerable position in a raw material already held, by making a temporary purchase or sale on the futures market. The table below shows a typical commodity market table for cocoa, as published daily from Tuesday to Saturday in the *Financial Times* of London. It will be seen that the positions quoted extend to 17 months ahead with the first position, March, being the 'spot' month, or the first deliverable month for which a quotation is available on the futures market.

COCOA No 5 Contract	Yesterday's close	+ or −	Business Done
March	2173.0—75.0	−38.0	2240.0—173.0
May	2140.0—42.0	−40.5	2209.5—135.0
July	2082.0—83.0	−45.0	2145.0—078.0
September	2015.0—17.0	−41.0	2070.0— 20.0
December	1815.0—25.0	−32.5	1870.0— 15.0
March	1765.0—68.0	−35.0	1800.0—760.0
May	1721.0—30.0	−33.5	— —

In each of these positions it is possible to take out a contract either to buy or to sell at the quoted price. In market jargon, to go 'short' is to take up a contract to *sell* several months hence (no physical commodity need change hands) and to go 'long' is to take up a contract to *buy* at a future date.

The risks which the hedger seeks to cover are borne by those who, due to the nature of their business, have an opposite interest in the market, and also by the oft-maligned speculator whose activities play a valuable part in assuming the risks which the trade is attempting to avoid.

Hedging involves insuring against price changes in a physical commodity such as stocks of cocoa held in a company's warehouse (whether held by producer or user) by a simultaneous, but opposite, transaction in futures.

To the holder of the stocks of any raw material the risks are very real. The market value of this vital part of his company's assets changes almost daily due to forces beyond his control. News of a sudden crop disaster, such as the devastating frost which hit the main coffee growing areas of Brazil in 1975, will precipitate a rapid rise in prices which will be to his advantage. But bumper harvests in a commodity, and sugar has been a good example, coupled with a heavy overhang of world stocks, will cause a gradual and dangerous erosion in values.

The commodity markets provide the safeguard against two ever-present basic risks for both the manufacturer of a finished product, such as chocolates, and the grower of cocoa beans if he has part of his crop to dispose of not covered by a governmental or similar contract. One risk is that the value of unsold products will depreciate if commodity prices fall; another is that contracts made in advance for the forward sales of goods will show losses if commodity prices rise.

Before looking at the mechanics of the operation needed to cover each of the basic risks mentioned above, let us examine a simple example of hedging. If a trader bought a commodity for cash on 1 January at £200 a tonne and sold it on 31 March for £190 a tonne — because the market had gone against him — he would have made a loss of £10 a tonne. But if he had sold futures on 1 January at, say, £220 a tonne, and then closed out his futures commitments on 31 March by buying at £210 a tonne, his profit on the futures deal would have balanced out loss on the spot, or cash, deal. By taking the reverse action on the futures market, the seller of the commodity could have achieved a similar hedge.

To return to the question of the first basic risk — that the value of unsold products will depreciate if commodity prices fall — the action needed in this situation is to effect a forward sale on the futures market by means of a 'short' hedge. The objective is to protect the value of existing stocks and to earn a return sufficient to cover the cost of storage and insurance if this is possible.

To insure against a price fall, our chocolate manufacturer hedges by selling short some months away. His judgement is correct and prices do decline. Consequently the value of the cocoa in his warehouse also declines. He gains, however, on his short hedge inasmuch as the lower the market price moves the less he will have to pay to buy back his contract when the time comes. This technical gain on his futures contract, if his hedge equals the tonnage of his cocoa stocks, should counterbalance exactly the loss he is incurring in his warehouse. If prices rise instead of falling during the time of the contract, then the increase in the value of his stock means that it can be sold for a sum large enough to offset the loss he has suffered on his short hedge. A practical example of a short hedge is as follows:

(a) On 1 March 1977 a chocolate manufacturer buys 100 tonnes of cocoa beans from an African producer for £2000 a tonne for delivery on the same date in the following year. The total capital commitment is £200,000.

(b) The manufacturer's cocoa requirements are guaranteed, and he takes no further action. His liability is £200,000, but meanwhile the world market price has fallen back to £1400 a tonne by the time he is due to take delivery. He is now faced with an inventory loss of £60,000, or £600 for each tonne of cocoa he has contracted to buy.

(c) Had the chocolate manufacturer sold an equivalent tonnage (hedged) on the cocoa futures market, at the time he purchased his cocoa from the producer, the following position would have applied:
    — Price paid to cocoa producer 1.3.77 = £2000 a tonne
    — Price obtained on future sale 1.3.77 = £2000 a tonne
    — Market price for March 1978 futures on 1.3.78 = £1400 a tonne.

The chocolate manufacturer would close out the futures sale on delivery of the cocoa beans from Africa by purchasing back the short hedge from the futures market at £1400 a tonne — thus making a profit of £60,000, sufficient to offset the potential loss.

This example serves to indicate how the commodity markets operate to the advantage of the ultimate consumer as well. Although the manufacturer is faced with the inescapable fact that he will have to process high-priced cocoa, he would not be forced to contemplate an increase in his chocolate prices because of the compensatory profit obtained from the futures market.

The second fundamental risk — that forward sales already contracted will show losses if commodity prices rise — will concern exporters of raw materials and the like who are in the position of having to give a firm price for delivery at prevailing market levels, but where shipment of the commodity is not due until several months later. He may not have the space to store the raw material and therefore does not acquire it at the time the transaction is agreed, or he does not wish to have capital tied up in stocks for any length of time. To cover himself he takes up a 'long' hedge in the relevant commodity market. If the price falls when the time comes to ship the commodity to his customer he will show a loss on the futures transaction but will be able to purchase the spot commodity for less than the agreed selling price. If the price of the commodity should rise in the interim period, he will have made an equivalent profit on his futures position to compensate for the higher price of the physical commodity. A long hedge would also be used by a manufacturer who fixes his selling price for future delivery at current costs and would suffer if raw material costs were to rise in the meantime.

There is, in fact, a three-stage procedure which needs to be strictly adhered to for the satisfactory conclusion of each hedging operation: (i) the tonnage of the hedge should balance the tonnage of the material at risk; (ii) as soon as the original risk is eliminated the hedging party must give immediate orders to the broker to close out the hedge — if this is not done simultaneously the hedger is at once reassuming the very price risk that the initial action was directed at avoiding; (iii) final accounting should show the result of physical trading together with that of the hedging transaction so that the net outcome of the operation is clearly established on the books.

Apart from the hedging operation, the futures markets provide the basis for a world pricing system for commodities as well as ensuring strict standardization of the raw materials for delivery.

Speculation on the Commodity Market

John Edwards

Speculative interest and investment in commodities and the futures market has grown considerably in recent years. This is because investors, worried by inflation and changes in international exchange rates, particularly sterling, have sought protection for their funds in raw materials, which have an intrinsic basic value whatever may happen to 'paper' money. There is always a need for raw materials and foodstuffs, and the cost of producing these, taking into account inflation and monetary changes, must inevitably be reflected in the market price.

Certainly a look at historical trends in raw material prices shows conclusively that, over the years, these have generally moved up to reflect the inflation in production costs and monetary values. This has occurred despite improvements in production techniques, substitution by synthetic competitors and changes in consumer buying habits.

Although company shares can provide, to a certain extent, a 'hedge' against inflation, the stock markets are not subject to the same international influences as commodities and are, therefore, of little use in seeking protection against the erosion in value of local currencies. The disadvantage of commodity speculation is that no dividends, or interest rates, are payable. This distinguishes commodity speculation from other forms of investment. In addition, if the physical commodity itself is bought, there is the cost and the problems of storage and insurance, as well as quality deterioration in the case of perishable raw materials. The advantages include the prospect of a much greater capital gain than is usually possible with shares. This is particularly the case if the investment is made on the futures market where the investor involved in a forward transaction normally has to deposit only about ten per cent of the total outlay. This high gearing, with £1000 for example representing an investment of £10,000, allied to the violent price fluctuations that occur on occasion often through unpredictable events such as crop setbacks or mine disasters, are the prime reasons why commodity speculation has a reputation for being very risky.

Nevertheless, the rewards can be very profitable indeed and losses may be limited by careful trading. The futures market in particular offers very flexible opportunities as much to sell a commodity one does not own as to buy a commodity with no intention of taking delivery. In both cases the commitment is cancelled out by a matching sale or purchase long before the delivery date falls due. For example, a speculator may decide in January that the price of sugar is going to rise later in the year and would then buy 50 tonnes of sugar on the futures market for delivery ten months later in October. He would put up ten per cent of the cost involved with the commodity broker of his choice — as with shares there are a host of brokers, merchants and dealers who handle speculative business as members of the futures markets. Any time during that ten month period the speculator can decide to cancel his purchase by a matching sale of 50 tonnes of October sugar, and he must do so before the delivery date in October to avoid being forced to take actual delivery of the sugar he does not want. Most of the transactions on the futures markets are 'paper' deals of this kind, cancelled before the delivery date falls due. A speculator seldom gets involved with the actual commodity. Even if he is careless or forgetful, he will soon be reminded by his broker or the market warehouse of the impending delivery. Only on occasions does a buyer, usually from the trade itself, decide to take actual delivery, although the London Metal Exchange does include a much higher proportion of physical transactions than the other futures markets because of its historical role as a residual, price-fixing, market.

It is, in fact, just as easy to 'sell' a commodity one does not have, if market prices are considered likely to fall in the future, as it is to 'buy' a commodity one does not want. The danger of selling, however, is that if the market changes direction suddenly, or if the speculator does not cancel his sale early enough before the due delivery date, the losses that can be suffered are without limit. For a buyer the commodity he owns always retains some value, at least on paper, even though this might be severely reduced, but a commitment to supply a commodity may be of little value and in times of scarcity the speculator who has to cancel a sale commitment by a matching purchase can be held to ransom by holders of the actual commodity. It is this danger, and the general difficulty of visualizing the ability to sell something one does not own, which results in 'short' selling as it is known being confined mainly to professional speculators or the trade which owns the actual commodity.

There are, however, ample opportunities for the average speculator who wishes to use the commodity markets to protect his funds. There is nothing, for example, to prevent any individual from buying the physical commodity itself and storing it until such time as the price has risen sufficiently to make it attractive to sell. Because of storage problems with perishable commodities, metals are usually the favourite for this type of investment. Historically, gold and other precious metals such as silver and platinum have been most popular with investors, but recently base metals, such as copper, tin, lead and zinc, have also been bought for what is called 'long-term' investment purposes. The idea is that inflation on mine production costs, and shortages of supply as the world's higher living standards increase demand for base metals, must bring much higher prices eventually. Individuals, and some big financial syndicates and institutions, have considered it worthwhile locking up quite considerable sums of money in buying and storing metals with the intention of holding them until prices move up to yield a capital profit, which it is hoped will be far in excess of what could have been earned by investment in other areas. The added attraction is the built-in protection of raw materials against the erosion of inflation and currency changes on monetary values.

However, physical investment of this kind often requires large sums, which are tied up for many years with no return on the investment; it is also a gamble on the price rising sufficiently to offset the loss of these earnings. Thus the bulk of commodity speculation comes in the futures market, where funds can be moved about more freely and used to much greater purpose, although the risks can be greater. Futures markets can also be used for a variety of purposes, including tax straddles or spreads. Losses can be limited by the use of options — an increasingly popular form of investment with speculators. The flexibility of the futures markets enables speculators to take advantage of special opportunities or developments that have a quick impact on the price of the raw material. The severe frost in Brazil in July 1975, which doubled the price of coffee in a very short time and within two years had raised prices to ten times the previous level, is a good example.

In London, speculation in commodities is officially frowned upon, because the general public opinion, echoed by Government, is that the prices of raw materials and foodstuffs, vital to the nation, should not be influenced by outside speculators taking advantage of changes in supply and demand patterns to make money. In other commodity futures markets, however, notably in the United States, there is a different attitude. Speculation is actively encouraged — although sometimes attacked by Government officials — on the grounds that it is an essential ingredient in providing the funds for a viable market in which the trade can protect itself against price fluctuations by 'hedging'. It is argued that without speculation the trade would often be unable to find someone prepared to do business 'on the other side', and the extra flow of funds ensures a healthy, proper market. It is also claimed that on the whole the speculators put more into the futures market in the long run than they take out, and this is to the benefit of the trade and the consumer or producer. It is agreed, however, that excessive speculation can artificially distort price trends for a period of time.

Concerned at the growth in commodity speculation during recent years, with its potential effect on prices coupled with the frauds and scandals that have been perpetrated as a result of the huge extra sums involved, the US Government set up in 1975 the Commodity Futures Trading Commission (CFTC) to supervise the markets and introduce extra rules and regulations where this is considered necessary. The establishment of this body may well set the trend for other countries.

Prospects for Commodity Cartels

John Edwards

The success of the Organization of Petroleum Exporting Countries (OPEC) in controlling oil prices and supplies has inevitably led to speculation whether producers of other vital raw materials can adopt similar tactics.

Developing countries in the third world, many of whom are dependent on raw materials as a major, and often only, source of export earnings, generally feel they have been exploited by the industrialized world buying up non-renewable resources at a cheap price. They are, therefore, anxious to redress the balance not only by obtaining what they consider a fair price for their raw materials but also by retaining more of the processing and manufacturing of primary products in their own countries. It is argued that more processing, or at least semi-processing, in the countries producing the raw materials would mean a fairer distribution of wealth world-wide. It would provide extra employment opportunities where these are most needed and also help poorer countries develop a higher standard of living through greater industrialization. Not surprisingly, the industrialized countries generally do not agree with the prospect of having to pay more for their raw material imports, nor with a policy of removing processing away from the main consuming areas. It is, however, recognized that something has to be done to stop the trend of the rich countries becoming richer at the expense of the poor countries becoming poorer.

The developing countries see their best hope for making the most of their raw material resources in the future either from forming producer cartels where possible, or by concluding special international commodity agreements with the consuming countries aimed at ensuring equitable prices. A consistent supporter of commodity agreements on behalf of the developing countries has been the United Nations Conference on Trade and Development (UNCTAD). Together with the sister United Nations body — the Food and Agriculture Organization (FAO) — it has actively promoted the formation of commodity pacts. But the initiative which started at the Havana conference, which took place after the Second World War, was pursued with little success until the emergence of OPEC. The role of the Organization of Petroleum Exporting Countries in the oil crisis created a new awareness of the importance of raw materials to the world as a whole.

The only commodity pact which has operated consistently over 20 years has been the International Tin Agreement, and the Fifth Agreement in tin — lasting for five years — came into effect provisionally from 1 January 1977. Other international agreements which have been operational for a period cover several commodities, including cocoa, coffee, sugar and wheat. Regular informal meetings are also held by producers and consumers of bananas, cotton, copper, lead and zinc, jute, sisal and tea to exchange statistical information and in some cases to set target price levels. On balance, the success of international commodity agreements has been extremely limited and very unsatisfactory for the developing world.

A new initiative aimed at setting up an integrated commodity price stabilization programme through a series of consumer-producer pacts, backed by a multi-buffer stock fund to finance the requirements of 18 specified commodities, received official approval at the UNCTAD Nairobi conference in 1976 after a long and heated debate. The basic idea is that international agreements should be negotiated for the individual commodities concerned, narrowed down to ten 'core' commodities in the beginning. These are coffee, copper, cocoa, cotton, jute, hard fibres (such as sisal), rubber, sugar, tea and tin. Where necessary, the agreements would include provisions for a buffer stock which would buy up surplus supplies when prices threatened to fall below a specified 'floor' level and sell any surpluses held if prices go above an agreed 'ceiling' level.

The new concept is that the finance for the buffer stock should be provided from a central pool supplied with funds from all countries and not just producing countries, as has been the case in the past with the tin and cocoa agreements. The bulk of the contributions to this central buffer stock would almost certainly come from the richer, consumer countries who have expressed grave doubts about the integrated programme. These countries argue that a case-by-case approach is needed to solve the special problems of each commodity and that lumping them together will hinder rather than help the establishment of agreements. Despite these reservations consuming countries undoubtedly wish to co-operate in plans for regulating supplies and prices of raw materials to a greater extent than in the past, bearing in mind the example set by oil in highlighting the dependence of the industrialized nations in ensuring adequate supplies of primary products.

Whilst the debate continues on whether international commodity agreements can be negotiated to stabilize effectively primary producers' earnings and whether buffer stocks are the right mechanism to use, alternative methods of achieving a similar objective are being tried and investigated.

Some producing countries have formed their own associations and this trend could gain momentum if the moves to create effective international agreements between producers and consumers are unsuccessful. The International Bauxite Association has managed to lift the prices paid by aluminium companies following an interchange of information between the member countries, which include Australia — not usually associated with the developing world. But the Australians have made it plain that they will not participate in any moves to impose higher prices by 'blackmail' in the form of co-operative action by the producers in the style of OPEC. Other producer associations are the Iron Ore Producers' Association and the Tungsten Producers' Association. The Council of Copper Exporting Countries (known as CIPEC after its initials in French) is the oldest existing producers' association, formed in the 1960s by four developing countries — Chile, Peru, Zaire and Zambia — with the intention of finding ways to stabilize the violent fluctuations in the copper market. But over the years political differences and disputes between the member countries, plus the many problems involved in controlling copper prices, have prevented CIPEC from taking any positive action or making meaningful decisions despite a considerable amount of debate. In recent years CIPEC has widened its membership to include several include several other copper-producing nations, and has changed its basic philosophy of hostility to consumers. Instead it has adopted a more conciliatory approach to consuming countries both independently and through the United Nations Conference on Trade and Development. The major problem for copper producers is that much of the world's copper is produced in the industrialized areas. The United States and the Soviet Union are the world's two biggest producers of copper, while plentiful supplies of scrap copper are produced in industrialized areas and account for some 40 per cent of total copper supplies available. There are similar difficulties in relation to cotton, sugar and grain producers since a large proportion of the world's supplies is produced in industrialized areas where aims and ambitions might be contrary to those of the developing world.

Oil is one of the few raw materials over which producers have sustained control of supplies and prices for a lengthy period of time. In other cases, such as coffee, producers have managed to control the market for a period during times of scarcity but this control has dissipated once a surplus emerges. One exception is wool, where the Governments of Australia, New Zealand and South Africa have managed to stop prices from falling too low by buying up surplus stocks when the market falls to a specified level. But this is a unilateral action by each of the Governments concerned, although they have consulted each other, with Australia, as the leading producer, setting the pattern. Malaysia has also taken unilateral action in buying up surplus supplies of natural rubber on occasions when prices threatened to fall too low. But it is an expensive operation and the support of other rubber-producing countries has been enlisted for the future through the Association of Natural Rubber Producing Countries (ANRPC). The aim is to create a buffer stock to buy up surplus stocks when prices threaten to fall below a specified 'floor' level and possibly implement production cutbacks if and when this is necessary.

The success or otherwise of all these producer attempts to obtain higher prices, or at least a more stabilized market, appears to depend very much on the changes in economic conditions and could well be a source of friction throughout the world.

An alternative approach has been tried by the European Economic Community with the Lome Convention governing imports from 46 developing countries. This covers a wide range of commodities but includes a special fund, called Stabex, that is used to make up the earnings of the developing countries if and when their export earnings fall drastically, either because of a drop in market prices or a setback in their production not being compensated for by higher prices. The Stabex fund is too small at present to be able to make up any sizeable shortfall, but its advocates hope it will set a precedent for the future and spread to a much wider range of products and countries. The basic principle is that the guarantee of stabilized earnings is of much more value to the poorer producing countries concerned and will encourage them to increase production without the fear of surplus supplies making it unprofitable to do so. In this way the industrialized countries also hope to ensure a regular flow of raw materials from the primary producers, instead of relying on high prices that often benefit producers in rich countries as much as, if not more than, those in the developing countries.

Built into the Lome Convention is a continuation of the Commonwealth Sugar Agreement, generally reckoned to be one of the most successful and progressive commodity agreements. Under the Commonwealth Agreement cane sugar producers in the Commonwealth countries were provided with a guaranteed price — agreed after negotiations between both sides to be a fair and reasonable price for producers — for a specified quantity of sugar supplied to Britain each year. As part and parcel of the Agreement, Britain controlled its production of beet sugar so as not to create a surfeit of supplies. After considerable opposition from the beet growers on the Continent, the EEC finally agreed to import 1.3 million tonnes of cane sugar each year from African, Caribbean and Pacific countries (the so-called ACP group) at a price linked to the Community price for beet sugar. Although cane producers have complained about the price being too low for them, they have obtained a form of indexation reflecting the inflation in the EEC linked to the returns paid to European beet growers, who form a powerful lobby within the Community.

Nevertheless, despite these hesitant steps towards greater stabilization in the world commodity markets, through UNCTAD, through the producers, or by international agreements, there is still a considerable way to go in meeting producers' hopes for a better deal in future.

The Role of the Markets in Reflecting World Prices and Trade
John Edwards

Commodity futures markets play two main roles. One is to provide the facility for hedging against price fluctuations to enable trading in the commodity to take place without excessive risk — in other words to provide an insurance policy. The other equally important function is to give an indication of prices for the particular commodity for the future, as well as the present. In order to establish a fair and reasonable price, reflecting all the relevant influences, it is necessary to have a central meeting point where buying and selling of the commodity is carried out, if only on paper. The true test of a commodity price is the sum that someone is prepared to pay for it — it is the only 'real' price, taking into account all the factors that influence a decision on whether to buy or sell. These factors include not only whether the commodity is in adequate supply to meet demand, or in surplus or shortage, but also the economic influences that can affect the attitude of a buyer or seller. Fears of inflation or changes in international exchange rates; a possible need to sell or reluctance to buy because of outside circumstances and, most important, expectations of what is likely to happen in the future taking into account the general economic climate, are the influencing elements. A buyer, for example, may be keen to make purchases at a good price, even though the commodity is currently in gross surplus supply to demand, because of fears of a major strike in the months ahead that might cripple future output of the commodity. A seller too may be prepared to sell a commodity in short supply quite cheaply anticipating a big future surge in production and the need to keep demand at a healthy level.

At the same time commodity futures markets play a vital role in indicating the level of prices obtainable many months ahead. These forward prices give producers and consumers an invaluable guide in planning their future actions. The spot (or current) price is often very different from the price prevailing a year later when the crops planted, or the production planned, have to be sold. The futures markets provide an indication of the likely trend and can also be used to 'fix' the price obtainable for future sales or purchases by 'paper' transactions allied to the actual physical transactions. As with 'hedging', the profit or loss on futures can be used to balance the profit or loss on physical transactions so that the buyer or seller knows the price terms involved many months in advance of the actual delivery date.

In other words some of the gambling element inherent in producing crops which are subject to unpredictable weather conditions, or mining materials which may be hit by an industrial recession, is lessened by the futures market.

At one stage in recent years it was thought that the financial risk involved in planning future production could be offset by the use of long-term supply contracts, which would be agreed in advance, so that the producers need not be concerned about disposing of output. But events have proved that supply contracts of this kind are not worth a great deal. Currency changes, and inflation, have in many cases made a nonsense of the price clauses carefully negotiated to ensure the producer a fair, if not generous, profit. Experience also shows that in times of surplus production, the buyer is in an immensely powerful position to 'renegotiate' the contracts in his favour in order to remain competitive with his rivals who were obtaining raw material supplies at lower prices. The producers, of course, could also not guarantee meeting their supply commitments in the event of an unavoidable production setback, through natural causes or strikes. So-called long-term contracts have, therefore, deteriorated to the point where they now constitute the initial negotiating position for both sides. When there is a change of government with a new regime frequently anxious to repudiate all the actions and commitments of its predecessor, this is of particular importance.

Some of these disadvantages also apply to the 'producer price' system — widely used by base metal producers, particularly in North America — to sell their products without having recourse to the world commodity and futures markets. The basic idea is that the producers fix a price at which it is considered that sufficient quantities can be sold to provide a reasonable profit. The price is then periodically adjusted, when this is absolutely necessary, to meet changing circumstances. The underlying trend is, of course, upwards, bearing in mind the general rise in production costs through inflation and the gradual exhaustion of the world's non-renewable resources, such as metals and minerals. On occasions the producer price is officially lowered to take account of a fall in demand or a surge in production generally.

Over the years the producer price system has revealed several inherent faults. To begin with it requires agreement amongst the bulk of producers to charge the same price. In addition the producers also have to show restraint in exploiting a co-operative price since if it is pushed too high consumers will either turn to alternative materials, where this is possible, or petition for government action to stop being overcharged. Producers in the industrialized world can no longer control markets as they did in the past. Nowadays they have to bow to all kinds of pressures, including competition from other producers not willing, or able, to participate in a producer pricing system. Selling by Communist bloc countries more concerned with obtaining 'hard' currency than a profitable price provides a good example.

For this reason producer price systems have become increasingly difficult to sustain except in cases where the producers are integrated in such a way as to be the major consumers of the raw material — aluminium is a prime example here. Alternatively where available supplies are concentrated into a relatively few companies, informal if not official agreements not to indulge in competitive pricing can be made.

In all cases producers these days have to take account of overall market forces when attempting to fix prices.

The inherent weakness of the producer price system is that it can cause stagnation in the industry, providing too little incentive for the producer to expand output by seeking out new markets, and in the same way discouraging consumers from developing the kind of techniques stimulated by shortages or high prices. In other words there is not the stimulation of market forces to encourage greater efficiency and technological advance. While the violent fluctuations in commodity futures markets come under severe criticism from producers when prices are low, and from consumers when prices are high, these movements regulate indirectly the flow of supplies and demand world-wide bringing them back into balance whenever they get out of line. High prices stimulate output and discourage demand in times of shortage and low prices do the reverse during times of surplus.

The existence of commodity futures markets, where the prices are openly quoted and published for all to see, also evens out the flow of supplies internationally. If one market moves out of line with another in a different country, commodity dealers are quick to spot the difference as an opportunity to make money. For instance, if copper prices in New York move to a significantly higher level than those in London it encourages dealers to switch supplies to New York to take advantage of the higher price and this continues until prices on the two markets are close enough together to make it no longer attractive. In this way prices are equalized throughout the world as much as import regulations and currency changes will permit. The existence of protective trading blocs, like the European Common Market, make this difficult to achieve on occasions because of import duties and quotas. Equally important in influencing prices is the role of the commodity futures market as a central collecting house for receiving and disseminating information on a world-wide basis. To survive, dealers and speculators using the futures markets have to be well informed and therefore institute the best possible information collecting service drawing on customers and 'contacts' throughout the world. This information is then passed on to the rest of the world even if only by the behaviour of the market price.

An unexpected move in the price, for no apparent reason, usually means that one dealer or another has obtained advance information of some development. The news has to be imparted to the dealer's customers to explain his actions or to ensure that they do not miss an opportunity and thereby become dissatisfied customers. The information is then inevitably disseminated. This market grapevine is a very important influence in deciding the trend of prices over and above normal supply-demand considerations. False rumours may have a short-term effect on prices but normally market sentiment — a consensus of opinion amongst the dealers and main traders — is an invaluable guide to the likely trend in values.

For most of the time dealers are, of course, only reflecting the attitude of their customers, both buyers and sellers. They bring two frequently conflicting views together — the consumer's desire to pay as little as possible and the producer's ambition to obtain the highest return — and this is eventually expressed in the market price at which business is done. It is only through this procedure that a 'true' price can be reached bearing in mind the many diverse forces that are at work. The much criticized speculator is just another cog in the system, providing finance and opinions often not properly reflected in purely industrial transactions.

Speculative interest in the commodity futures markets is a good indication of uncertainty about the economic system. It expresses the desire to seek safety in buying basic raw materials which have an intrinsic value. The speculator frequently discerns the trend of developments well in advance of those in the actual trade who are unable to take a detached view. It is this mixture of views from all quarters that makes the commodity futures markets such a good guide to price trends and in turn an important influence in regulating trade and production of the raw materials throughout the world.

Part 2:
Commodities

A brief background on the major commodities traded

John Edwards

Cocoa

Cocoa is the raw material used in the manufacture of chocolate and chocolate products. Cocoa bean trees require a tropical or sub-tropical climate, with adequate rainfall at the right times — a combination that restricts the growing areas throughout the world. The main producing area is West Africa, where Ghana is the biggest world producer, but large crops are also grown in Nigeria, Ivory Coast and the Camerouns. Cocoa is grown in various other parts of the world, but the only significant producing country outside West Africa at present is Brazil, where output which is concentrated in the Bahia state has risen rapidly in recent years. It is believed that cocoa was first cultivated in South America in the 16th century by the Spaniards but West Africa, notably Ghana, later became the dominant producing area while Brazil tended to rely on coffee for its main export earnings.

The cocoa tree takes some years to reach full maturity and production yields are dependent on the extent of farming attention given, particularly in relation to pesticides since the crop is vulnerable to various diseases. In most countries there are two crops per year — a mid or light crop (Temporao in Brazil) and the main crop. When picked the bean is either sold in its raw state to chocolate manufacturers or processed into cocoa butter, liquor or into powder form. Its most common form is as a type of vegetable fat which is blended with other ingredients, especially sugar, to produce the finished product.

Demand for chocolate tends to be linked with improved living standards and therefore has a strong underlying growth rate. In recent years consumption has tended to outstrip production following a continual series of crop setbacks as a result of poor weather conditions. Countries like Ghana have also tended to diversify their crops and so decrease their reliance on cocoa for export earnings. However, consumption of cocoa is price sensitive, with demand being affected by the general economic climate in consuming countries and resistance against rising chocolate prices. In the past cocoa prices have fluctuated wildly with periods of shortages and high prices followed by times of surpluses which have driven prices down to depressed levels. Since cocoa is almost entirely produced in developing countries and sold to the main consuming areas in North America and Europe, great efforts have been made to seek protection for countries relying on cocoa exports for their foreign exchange earnings. After some 15 years of negotiations the International Cocoa Agreement was concluded between the main producing and consuming countries, with the notable exception of the United States, which refused to participate. The intention of the Agreement is to keep cocoa prices within an agreed range and in particular to prevent values falling below a 'floor' level through support buying by a buffer stock, financed by a levy on exports and imports, and a system of export quotas triggered off by price movements, However, the Agreement, which was renewed for a second period of three years in 1976, has not as yet become operative because market prices have remained well above the agreed price range due to a scarcity of supplies.

One method to protect the farmers against price fluctuations employed by the West African countries in particular, is for all sales to be channelled through government-controlled marketing boards, which pay a fixed price to the producer whatever the situation on the world market. But this method prevents, to a large extent, the normal free market control of production by price influence, favoured by Brazil, in which indirect control is exercised by export taxes and quotas when this is required. The two major world markets are centred in London and New York. In London cocoa is the most active of the 'soft' (non-metal) commodity futures markets and is used extensively by producers, chocolate manufacturers and the many merchants in the trade.

Cocoa Beans: World Production 1967/68 to 1975/76

Country	1967/ 68	1968/ 69	1969/ 70	1970/ 71	1971/ 72	1972/ 73	1973/ 74	1974/ 75	1975/[1] 76
					Thousand tonnes				
Africa									
Angola	0.4	0.5	0.3	0.4	0.5	0.6	0.7	0.5	0.5
Cameroon	92.0	103.9	108.3	112.0	123.0	106.9	110.0	118.0	100.0
Congo	1.8	1.1	1.3	2.0	2.0	2.1	2.1	2.1	2.0
Equatorial Guinea	33.6	32.0	24.0	30.0	22.0	10.0	12.0	12.0	12.0
Gabon	4.1	4.5	4.7	5.0	5.3	5.0	5.0	5.0	4.5
Ghana	423.5	327.0	414.3	406.0	470.0	415.7	343.0	381.6	396.2
Ivory Coast	146.6	144.5	180.7	179.6	225.8	185.4	210.0	241.0	220.0
Liberia	1.9	1.7	1.9	2.2	2.6	3.0	3.1	3.0	3.0
Madagascar	0.5	0.5	0.9	0.9	0.9	0.7	1.2	1.0	1.0
Nigeria	238.0	191.8	220.8	304.8	256.6	241.1	215.0	214.0	215.0
São Tomé and Príncipe	10.6	9.1	9.7	10.4	10.4	11.3	10.4	7.9	8.3
Sierra Leone	4.1	2.2	4.0	5.3	6.3	6.6	7.7	6.0	6.0
Tanzania	0.2	0.4	0.4	0.5	0.5	0.6	0.6	1.5	1.5
Togo	18.3	20.0	23.6	27.9	29.0	18.6	16.5	15.0	17.0
Zaire	4.9	4.5	4.9	5.6	6.4	5.0	5.0	2.0	5.0
Others[2]	–	5.0	11.0	15.0	10.0	22.0	5.0	2.0	2.0
Total	981	849	1,011	1,108	1,171	1,035	948	1,013	994
North, Central and South America									
Brazil	143.6	165.2	200.6	182.4	164.3	158.7	242.4	265.5	250.0
Bolivia	1.2	1.3	1.3	1.3	1.4	1.4	1.4	1.4	1.4
Colombia	18.0	18.5	19.0	21.0	22.0	23.0	24.5	26.0	26.0
Costa Rica	7.2	9.1	4.8	4.2	7.3	5.0	6.0	6.0	6.0
Cuba	1.9	1.2	1.3	1.4	2.0	2.0	2.0	2.0	2.0
Dominica	0.1	0.1	0.1	0.1	0.1	0.1	0.1	0.1	0.1
Dominican Rep.	30.7	33.6	23.9	34.6	45.0	31.3	40.7	33.2	35.0
Ecuador	85.1	50.9	55.0	71.6	64.9	54.0	71.3	75.3	60.0
Grenada	2.1	3.8	2.5	3.0	2.3	2.4	2.6	2.7	2.5
Guatemala	0.5	0.5	0.5	0.8	0.6	0.6	0.7	0.4	1.0
Haiti	3.9	2.0	4.0	3.7	3.0	3.5	3.5	3.5	3.5
Honduras	0.2	0.3	0.3	0.3	0.3	0.3	0.3	0.1	0.3
Jamaica	1.7	1.5	1.8	1.9	2.4	2.5	1.7	1.8	1.7
Mexico	26.7	26.7	24.0	25.0	30.0	29.6	28.1	32.0	33.0
Nicaragua	0.6	0.7	0.6	0.6	0.6	0.6	0.6	0.6	0.6
Panama	0.5	0.5	0.6	0.6	0.5	0.6	0.5	0.6	0.6
Peru	1.8	2.0	2.0	2.0	2.0	2.0	2.0	2.0	3.0
Surinam	0.1	0.1	0.1	–	–	–	–	–	–
St. Lucia	0.1	0.1	0.1	0.1	0.1	0.1	0.1	0.1	0.1
St. Vincent	–	–	–	–	–	0.1	0.1	0.1	0.1
Trinidad and Tobago	6.4	4.5	5.4	4.1	4.5	4.8	3.4	4.7	3.5
Venezuela	19.3	18.3	18.9	19.0	19.0	16.0	16.4	19.0	16.0
Total	351	341	367	378	373	339	449	477	447
Asia and Oceania									
Fiji	0.1	0.1	0.1	0.1	0.1	0.1	0.1	0.1	0.1
Indonesia	1.2	1.5	1.6	1.7	2.0	2.0	3.0	3.0	4.0
Malaysia	1.9	1.8	2.3	3.5	5.0	7.0	10.0	12.0	14.0
New Hebrides	0.7	0.9	0.6	0.7	0.3	0.8	0.7	0.7	0.7
Papua New Guinea	23.7	27.1	22.3	28.0	29.9	23.1	30.0	36.0	35.0
Philippines	4.2	4.4	4.3	3.6	3.0	3.5	4.0	4.0	3.7
Solomon Islands	0.1	0.1	0.1	0.1	0.2	0.2	0.2	0.2	0.1
Sri Lanka	2.2	1.8	2.3	2.2	2.0	1.3	2.0	2.0	2.0
Western Samoa	2.0	3.0	2.6	2.3	2.4	0.9	1.6	1.5	1.5
Total	36	41	36	42	45	39	52	59	61
World Total	1,368	1,231	1,414	1,528	1,589	1,413	1,449	1,549	1,502

(1) *Estimates by Statistics Committee of ICCO, 30 September 1976.* (2) *Includes exports from non-members not accounted for elsewhere in the production estimates of specified countries.*

By courtesy of the International Cocoa Organization.

Cocoa Beans: World Imports 1967/71 to 1975/76

Country	1967-1971[1]	1972	1973	1973/74	1974/75	1975/76 Oct-Dec	1975/76 Jan-Mar	1975/76 Apr-Jun	1975/76 Jul-Sep
					Tonnes				
Western Europe									
Austria	13,020	14,940	13,563	11,112	12,160	2,595	3,192	2,206	3,130
Belgium/Luxembourg	17,605	21,401	19,013	16,277	17,797	4,105	4,849	3,673	3,446
Denmark	4,153	5,155	3,513	2,311	3,151	916	940	813	1,019
Finland	2,045	2,760	2,389	2,789	2,985	255	612	612	703
France	42,599	45,321	42,047	39,583	36,960	10,259	16,178	9,650	6,911
Germany F.R.	135,120	142,286	151,605	145,251	162,040	41,149	46,107	30,452	26,524
Greece	4,753	5,750	5,453	4,580	4,057	1,465	1,638	887	–
Iceland	37	90	81	76	–	–	–	–	–
Ireland	9,610	8,325	11,831	10.775	7,547	56	2,970	2,488	1,154
Italy	42,068	40,573	42,928	35,998	30,948	8,491	8,628	9,022	7,838
Netherlands	113,723	122,365	119,083	110,980	120,499	32,055	31,754	35,506	27,687
Norway	5,035	6,187	4,824	4,407	5,137	629	1,983	1,365	1,455
Portugal	2,632	3,641	3,585	3,531	3,100	212	1,022	311	657
Spain	32,299	35,376	35,301	34,315	41,177	6,440	4,858	5,731	5,285
Sweden	6,618	7,441	5,138	4,462	5,188	1,056	2,387	1,441	1,237
Switzerland	15,866	16,065	18,291	15,584	14,259	2,159	4,980	3,402	2,896
United Kingdom	87,060	110,735	94,996	101,806	71,321	24,093	25,355	21,799	27,206
Yugoslavia	10,613	13,100	10,235	17,503	14,924	2,487	2,688	2,074	3,346
Total	544,860	601,510	583,870	561,340	553,350	138,460	160,150	131,450	121,540
Eastern Europe									
Bulgaria	9,143	11,766	8,302	*10,000	12,402	3,326	3,040	2,352	–
Czechoslovakia	17,139	20,255	18,845	17,900	21,581	5,311	7,310	4,102	2,949
German D.R.	13,672	21,726	19,216	21,335	20,239	7,817	6,525	4,833	4,408
Hungary	10,275	13,230	11,406	13,005	13,670	2,218	6,074	2,225	–
Poland	20,254	31,842	29,009	29,050	32,068	8,606	9,987	7,633	7,404
Romania	5,844	7,830	8,913	10,343	11,006	2,060	3,790	2,032	2,795
USSR	105,500	132,000	119,100	135,000	164,681	8,574	46,777	56,797	11,067
Total	181,830	238,650	214,790	236,630	275,640	37,920	83,510	79,970	34,160
Africa									
Algeria	603	811	387	*400	395	–	*400	–	–
Egypt	1,078	218	111	*800	1,346	–	–	–	–
Morocco	312	307	*240	–	304	–	–	..	–
South Africa	5,260	6,756	5,105	6,276	6,504	1,654	1,816	788	–
Tunisia	328	475	300	501	–	–	–	–	–
Total	7,580	8,570	6,140	7,550	9,000	2,000	2,500	*1,500	*1,100
North, Central and South America									
Argentina	7,453	6,905	6,734	*8,000	8,491	2,852	1,174	2,549	–
Canada	16,787	21,240	15,789	12,386	10,318	2,970	3,458	2,840	3,154
Chile	738	999	*1,170	*1,000	–	–	–	–	–
Colombia	12,119	8,640	5,979	8,120	–	–	–	–	–
Cuba	–	–	–	501	–	–	–	–	–
El Salvador	373	391	*390	*350	335	–	–	–	–
Guatemala	66	48	73	–	–	8	30	–	–
Nicaragua	53	191	150	–	–	–	–	–	–
Peru	1,305	2,697	–	968	453	985	–	–	–
United States	269,134	286,702	251,943	228,479	200,994	74,230	80,330	64,250	57,734
Uruguay	581	*550	*550	*550	*600	92	–	–	–
Total	308,610	328,370	284,680	260,570	230,600	83,200	89,000	72,100	64,200
Asia and Oceania									
Australia	14,101	17,176	13,064	19,052	12,989	1,158	3,300	4,074	4,390
China	871	1,640	8,460	*6,000	*8,000	–	–	–	–
India	819	658	988	787	–	–	–	–	–
Iran	*50	205	197	74	30	49	–	–	–
Israel	1,143	1,391	524	1,666	–	–	–	–	–
Japan	34,665	35,894	38,930	28,675	30,194	4,076	10,824	6,127	10,367
Korea, Rep of	*150	309	494	343	–	70	–	206	–
Lebanon	393	474	391	–	–	–	–	–	–
Malaysia	*900	1,033	1,909	691	29	1	1	27	–
New Zealand	3,982	5,125	3,374	5,906	3,988	121	1,184	724	–
Philippines	4,123	4,795	2,684	2,972	2,458	1,848	2,330	–	–
Singapore	1,805	5,042	5,306	4,806	3,089	1,359	362	1,108	1,065
Turkey	1,029	1,830	1,191	843	1,703	515	490	331	453
Total	64,030	75,580	77,510	72,170	65,630	10,700	20,010	14,930	21,110
World Total	1,106,910	1,252,680	1,166,999	1,138,260	1,134,220	272,280	355,170	299,950	242,110

(1) *Average.*   * *Unofficial or estimate.*
By courtesy of the International Cocoa Organization.

Cocoa: London

COCOA,3RD MONTH CONT..MONTHLY

By courtesy of Eurocharts Information Service

Cocoa: New York

(MONTHLY HIGH, LOW & CLOSE OF NEAREST FUTURES)   CENTS PER POUND

By courtesy of Commodity Research Bureau Incorporated

41

Coffee

Coffee is one of the most widely traded agricultural commodities in the world. The bulk of production is concentrated in South America and Africa and from these continents it is exported to the United States and Europe. It is known to have had a long history as a beverage, starting in the Middle Eastern countries and spreading to Europe via the Turks. The Portuguese are said to have taken the coffee plant (or tree) to South America, where it flourished, particularly in Brazil where it has provided the largest source of export earnings for many years.

Other important producing countries on the South American continent are Colombia, Mexico, Guatemala and El Salvador. In recent years African countries — Ivory Coast, Angola, Uganda, the Camerouns and Ethiopia — have expanded their share of the growing world market, mainly with supplies of the Robusta type coffee used for manufacturing 'instant' or soluble coffee. Indonesia and India are also significant producers.

However, the international coffee trade is dominated by Brazil which has the capacity to produce around a third of the total world output and in the early 1950s built up huge surplus stocks that depressed prices to very low levels. But the Brazilian coffee-growing areas are vulnerable to severe frosts, normally in July, which have caused considerable crop setbacks on unpredictable occasions and consequently resulted in wild price fluctuations.

Coffee production can also be affected by general climatic conditions, ranging from drought to coffee rust disease, which in the past eliminated Sri Lanka as a producer and is now attacking several coffee-growing areas in South America. The amount of attention given to the plants in the form of fertilizers, pesticides and general farming husbandry can also affect production. But any deliberate moves to stimulate output tend to take time since trees do not attain full yields until four to seven years after being planted. Therefore high prices are slow to affect production. Once the investment and effort is made there is little room for manoeuvre in controlling output, except by destroying old trees, should the market situation have changed in the period between planting and actual production.

The huge stocks of surplus coffee built up in Brazil in particular put considerable pressure on the poorer countries which rely on coffee export earnings. As a result an International Coffee Agreement between producers and consumers was formulated, in an attempt to stabilize market prices by the use of export quotas linked to agreed price levels. This worked quite well for some ten years, during which producers were encouraged to diversify out of coffee into other crops. But a shortage of supplies, created by production setbacks in Brazil, led to the temporary breakdown of the Agreement and it has only been renegotiated by omitting the all-important price provisions and quota regulations. These are to be decided later when market equilibrium is restored and supplies are more plentiful.

Coffee consumption is price sensitive, since the end (consumer) product is raw material intensive involving only the roasting and processing of the raw (green) coffee bean, packaging and distribution. It is also subject to competition from a wide range of other beverages. Demand in the industrialized nations, with the United States the biggest single consumer, appears to have reached its maximum and is tending to decline in line with the rise in prices. But this is being offset to an extent by growing demand in developing countries, particularly in Brazil itself, which has developed its own soluble coffee manufacturing industry to boost export earnings and provide increased domestic employment opportunities.

Coffee-producing countries have special government-owned or -controlled marketing boards to handle exports, either working directly with buyers or regulating the activities of private traders selling on the world markets.

The two main coffee futures markets are in London and New York, but there are also forward markets in Paris, Le Havre and Hamburg. These markets reflect not only the prices paid for coffee passing through the market warehouses, but also trade and outside influences.

Coffee, Green: Production — Average 1967/68 to 1971/72, Annual 1972/73 to 1976/77[1]

Region and Country	Average 1967/68- 1971/72	1972/73	1973/74	1974/75	1975/76	1976/77
North America:			*Thousands of 60 kilogram bags*			
Costa Rica	1,322	1,335	1,570	1,390	1,305	1,500
Cuba	477	475	500	450	415	415
Dominican Republic	646	750	845	880	1,020	800
El Salvador	2,314	2,100	2,378	3,300	2,010	3,200
Guatemala	1,856	2,250	2,200	2,540	2,150	2,550
Haiti	514	525	550	520	660	600
Honduras	550	850	775	815	830	950
Jamaica	20	22	30	21	31	18
Mexico	3,085	3,700	3,300	3,900	4,100	4,300
Nicaragua	601	570	610	700	810	850
Panama	81	82	72	75	75	75
Trinidad & Tobago	60	50	30	65	42	57
U.S.—Hawaii	31	22	19	17	11	10
U.S.—Puerto Rico	233	200	220	200	200	200
Total	11,790	12,931	13,099	14,873	13,659	15,525
South America:						
Bolivia	127	95	95	90	100	105
Brazil	18,370	24,000	14,500	27,500	23,000	9,500
Colombia	7,870	8,800	7,800	9,000	8,700	9,000
Ecuador[3]	1,047	1,100	870	1,270	1,170	1,200
Guyana	16	12	10	15	15	15
Paraguay	49	50	50	42	40	20
Peru	940	1,030	1,000	900	900	1,000
Venezuela	872	1,100	960	765	1,075	835
Total	29,291	36,187	25,285	39,582	35,000	21,675
Africa:						
Angola	3,300	3,500	3,200	3,000	1,200	1,200
Benin[4]	16	15	13	14	14	14
Burundi	316	355	350	450	285	350
Cameroon	1,160	1,578	1,260	1,816	1,332	1,580
Central African Rep.	174	180	190	175	165	165
Congo, Brazzaville	15	14	10	10	10	10
Equatorial Guinea	125	115	105	110	90	90
Ethiopia	2,009	2,100	1,700	2,050	2,100	2,100
Gabon	16	15	9	10	10	10
Ghana	85	80	45	50	65	50
Guinea	160	125	105	100	90	90
Ivory Coast	4,195	5,050	3,285	4,500	5,080	5,300
Kenya	870	1,265	1,100	1,100	1,240	1,135
Liberia	71	85	65	75	75	75
Malagasy Republic	1,019	1,000	1,000	1,300	1,200	1,200
Nigeria	63	70	38	40	65	50
Rwanda	209	186	266	256	235	235
Sierra Leone	97	135	67	125	75	120
Tanzania	853	800	700	865	900	900

Coffee, Green: Production — Average 1967/68 to 1971/72, Annual 1972/73 to 1976/77[1] — continued

Region and Country	Average 1967/68- 1971/72	1972/73	1973/74	1974/75	1975/76	1976/77
Africa cont.						
Togo	215	200	180	200	195	190
Uganda	3,047	3,300	3,100	3,000	2,800	2,700
Zaire (Congo, Kinshasa)	1,150	1,380	1,317	1,150	1,383	1,433
Total	19,164	21,548	18,105	20,396	18,609	18,997
Asia:						
India	1,320	1,580	1,535	1,630	1,480	1,715
Indonesia	2,190	2,700	2,750	2,675	2,700	2,800
Malaysia	91	65	67	70	100	100
Philippines	785	850	865	1,035	1,080	1,150
Portuguese Timor	54	65	60	75	75	65
Vietnam	52	55	55	60	60	60
Yemen	57	45	25	35	35	35
Total	4,549	5,360	5,357	5,580	5,530	5,925
Oceania:						
New Caledonia	28	25	25	25	25	25
Papua New Guinea	389	560	588	633	667	600
Total	418	585	613	658	692	625
WORLD TOTAL	65,212	76,611	62,459	81,089	73,490	62,747

1. *Coffee marketing year begins about July in some countries and in others about October.* 2. *132,276 lbs.*
3. *As indicated in footnote 1, the coffee marketing year begins in some countries as early as July. Ecuador is one of these countries. Hence, the crop harvested principally during June—October 1976 in that country is shown as production for the 1976/77 marketing year. In Ecuador, however, this is referred to as the 1975/76 crop.* 4. *Formerly Dahomey.*
Note: *Production estimates for some countries include cross-border movements.*
By courtesy of the U.S. Department of Agriculture.

Coffee, Green: Imports, January—December 1970 to 1976

	1970	1971	1972	1973	1974	1975	1976*
	Thousands of 60 kilogram bags						
Total	50,756	52,823	54,327	58,052	53,861	56,488	58,214
Imports	50,744	52,807	54,313	58,043	53,785	56,451	58,205
U.S.A.	20,649	22,692	22,309	23,695	21,059	21,721	21,712
E.E.C.	18,428	20,019	20,368	21,821	20,890	22,233	23,112
Belgium	1,116	1,302	1,295	1,428	1,352	1,553	1,508
Denmark	1,037	1,043	1,087	1,046	1,008	1,119	1,103
France	4,103	4,385	4,529	4,772	5,015	5,295	5,267
Germany, Federal Rep. of	5,448	5,733	5,877	5,867	5,517	5,836	6,524
Ireland	34	28	40	38	34	41	62
Italy	2,761	2,984	2,985	3,376	3,396	3,399	3,565[1]
Netherlands	2,015	2,218	2,349	2,475	2,440	2,791	2,741[1/3]
United Kingdom	1,914	2,326	2,206	2,819	2,128	2,199	2,342
Others	11,667	10,096	11,636	12,527	11,836	12,497	13,381
Australia	381	389	378	438	478	442	533
Austria	395	487	549	499	510	620	665
Canada	1,501	1,567	1,552	1,591	1,564	1,778	1,706[3]
Cyprus	23	21	28	39	14	25	26[1]
Finland	1,342	381	912	1,005	1,003	1,003	1,174
Hong Kong	575	285	146	453	244	293	213[3]
Israel	135	114	116	142	189	157[3]	163[3]
Japan	1,491	1,276	1,756	2,239	1,614	2,034	2,658
New Zealand	113	101	121	69	109	90	81[1]
Norway	653	554	685	643	655	648	688
Portugal	292	344	380	361	346	255	352[3]
Spain	1,309	1,109	1,357	1,338	1,467	1,296	1,566

Coffee, Green: Imports, January—December 1970 to 1976 — continued

	1970	1971	1972	1973	1974	1975	1976*
	Thousands of 60 kilogram bags						
Sweden	1,813	1,764	1,837	1,913	1,762	1,931	2,009[1]
Switzerland	1,056	1,098	1,198	1,089	1,034	1,151	1,017
Yugoslavia	588	606	621	708	847	774	530[3]

* *Preliminary.* 1. *Includes estimates.* 2. *Excludes imports from Belgium.* 3. *Estimated.*
By courtsey of the International Coffee Organization.

Coffee, Green: Exports, January—December 1970 to 1976

	1970	1971	1972	1973	1974	1975	1976*
	Thousands of 60 kilogram bags						
Total	52,722	53,489	57,866	62,584	54,823	57,882	58,285
Colombian Milds	8,172	8,114	8,504	8,998	8,777	10,132	8,493
Colombia	6,509	6,569	6,528	6,766	6,906	8,175	6,290
Kenya	894	935	1,044	1,242	1,183	1,104	1,249
Tanzania	769	610	932	990	688	853	954
Other Milds	11,088	11,301	12,982	15,155	14,230	15,668	16,367
Burundi	333	318	403	378	354	421	366
Costa Rica	1,142	1,035	1,277	1,394	1,488	1,274	1,086
Dominican Republic	487	421	526	668	584	533	678
Ecuador	879	777	904	1,162	988	1,072	1,494
El Salvador	1,865	1,689	2,083	2,489	2,554	3,062	2,692
Guatemala	1,599	1,685	1,856	1,919	2,215	2,158	2,105
Haiti	260	394	403	327	306	315	421
Honduras	423	419	544	664	515	812	723
India	507	610	742	968	843	993	831
Jamaica	14	18	16	15	16	21	18
Mexico	1,413	1,621	1,724	2,327	1,992	2,392	2,735
Nicaragua	503	530	580	622	557	674	790
Panama	29	29	41	30	24	26	21
Papua New Guinea	390	462	498	614	597	595	799
Peru	734	710	915	973	442	720	703
Rwanda	237	254	177	359	478	371	607
Venezuela	273	329	293	246	277	229	298
Unwashed Arabicas	18,449	19,891	20,709	21,342	14,337	15,703	16,916
Bolivia	62	64	69	74	54	86	78
Brazil	17,085	18,399	19,215	19,817	13,280	14,604	15,602
Ethiopia	1,283	1,403	1,356	1,403	936	914	1,162
Paraguay	19	25	69	48	67	99	74[1]
Robustas	15,013	14,183	15,671	17,089	17,479	16,379	16,509
Angola	3,013	3,035	2,985	3,648	3,730	2,724	1,395
Ghana	55	50	74	54	47	44	61
Guinea	185	103	74	124	17	56	18
Indonesia	1,438	1,139	1,398	1,632	1,797	2,168	2,110
Liberia	79	77	88	93	59	69	70
Nigeria	45	56	73	42	4	20	34[1]
OAMCAF	(5,739)	(5,528)	(6,034)	(6,533)	(7,444)	(7,170)	(8,766)
Benin	1	21	38	9[1]	28[1]	37[1]	31[1]
Cameroon	1,084	980	1,116	1,422	1,669	1,623	1,641
Central African Emp.	221	197	205	161	144	179	145
Congo	14	12	29	13	8	12	29[1]
Gabon	6	8	21	6[1]	3[1]	2[1]	3
Ivory Coast	3,353	3,306	3,504	3,567	4,346	4,095	5,527
Malagasy Republic	860	856	932	1,090	1,069	1,089	1,211
Togo	200	148	189	265	177	133	179
Sierra Leone	109	69	238	192	53	106	52
Trinidad and Tobago	41	69	52	43	18	55	44
Uganda	3,226	2,725	3,307	3,632	3,121	2,943	2,600
Zaire	1,083	1,332	1,348	1,096	1,189	1,024	1,359[1]

* *Preliminary.* 1. *Estimated.*
By courtsey of the International Coffee Organization.

Guide to World Commodity Markets

Coffee: London

COFFEE, 3RD MONTH CONT., MONTHLY

By courtesy of Eurocharts Information Service

Coffee: New York

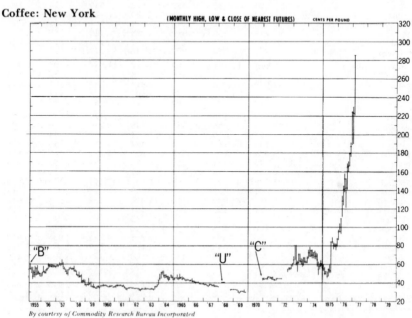

(MONTHLY HIGH, LOW & CLOSE OF NEAREST FUTURES) CENTS PER POUND

By courtesy of Commodity Research Bureau Incorporated

46

Copper

Copper is one of the oldest non-ferrous metals known to man with reports of its mining dating back to earliest times. It is used to make bronze (when blended with tin) and brass (when alloyed with zinc). Nowadays it is widely used throughout industry, although its main outlet is in electrical uses becauses of its high conductivity. But the 'red metal', as it is often known, has big markets in non-electrical industries too — such as transport, construction and consumer durables — because of its anti-corrosive nature, good heat transference, malleability and tensile strength. It is also blended with nickel for cupro-nickel coins and is an important military metal, as brass used in cartridges and in electrical equipment used in armaments.

Copper is obtained by mining (either open cast or underground) deposits found all over the world, which are often mixed with a variety of other metals ranging from silver to lead and zinc. The largest individual producing country is the United States, followed by the Soviet Union. However, these two countries use most, if not all, of their domestic production (the United States is normally a net importer) and the rest of the world, especially the big consuming areas in Western Europe and Japan, relies upon exports from the African continent (Zambia, Zaire and South Africa), South America (Chile and Peru), Canada, Australia (including Papua/New Guinea) and the Philippines. In Europe — Poland, Yugoslavia, Finland and Sweden are significant producers.

At the same time, in the industrialized areas, notably in Western Europe and the United States, an increasingly large proportion of copper supplies — up to 40 per cent of the total — comes from secondary or scrap sources. There are two main sorts of secondary metal: 'new' scrap that is generated when the original primary copper is being manufactured into a particular product, and 'old' scrap which is the reclamation of a product using copper that is no longer required for its original use. 'Old' scrap includes pure reclaimed copper that can be refined back into its original state, and products — such as alloys like brass or bronze — that can be used again.

Since most copper is reclaimable in some form or other after use, except for oxides used for chemical purposes, the 'mine' above the ground is increasing all the time in line with the increased output of primary metal. The primary metal is first processed from the mine in ore concentrates, which quality varies according to the orebody of the mine. It is then smelted to separate the 'impurities' or other metals in the ore and then refined, mainly into cathodes (the oblong shape of the mould), or into wirebars, from which wire can be drawn.

The cost of producing primary copper varies widely according to the orebody and the location of the mine, but in recent years it has become very much more expensive because of the lower-grade deposits being exploited as the rich reserves become exhausted. Although it is estimated that there is ample copper in the earth's crust to last for an indefinite period, the difficulty involved and new technology needed in exploiting these reserves is expected to bring shortages for periods during which the price incentive to provide sufficient financial resources is created. Strong moves are afoot for price stabilization agreements to be made to iron out the wild fluctuations in the price of copper that can be so damaging to the economies of developing countries which rely on copper as the main source of their export earnings.

Spurred on by the example of the oil-producing countries, the intergovernmental Council of Copper Exporting Countries (known as CIPEC) was formed several years ago by Chile, Peru, Zaire (Congo) and Zambia, which have since been joined by several other copper-exporting nations. But internal divisions within CIPEC, and the formidable problem of imposing price controls when so much of the world's primary and scrap supplies are in the consumer countries, has thwarted any positive action being taken except for some voluntary production cutbacks that did not prevent the biggest-ever world surplus of copper building up in 1976/77. New moves are being made by the United Nations Conference on Trade and Development (UNCTAD) to create a multi-buffer stock to support the 'floor' price of 'core' commodities, of which copper is one. Meanwhile, the world price of copper is based mainly on the daily prices quoted on the London Metal Exchange.

The price at which copper is sold is based on two systems. One, in North America (Canada and the United States), is the so-called producer price system where the producers fix a price charged to consumers who contract to buy certain tonnages on a regular basis. This price is changed as infrequently as possible but is raised and lowered according to the supply-demand situation, including the cost and availability of imported copper. But in the rest of the non-communist world, copper prices in direct supply contracts between consumers and producers are based on the daily prices quoted on the London Metal Exchange. A sizeable amount of 'merchant' copper is also traded at the Metal Exchange or the New York copper market price. Thus, although only a small proportion of copper actually passes through the London Metal Exchange, and even less through the New York market, the Exchange prices influence the cost of copper throughout the world.

Copper: World Mine Production 1971 to 1976

THOUSAND METRIC TONS

	1971	1972	1973	1974	1975	1976 Jan-Mar	Apr	May	June	July
EUROPE										
Austria	2·6	2·3	2·7	2·6	1·9	0·4	0·1	0·1	0·1	
Finland	28·5	34·8	38·2	36·7	38·7	10·6	3·7	4·1	2·9	3·1
France	0·3	0·5	0·4	0·4	0·4	0·1				
Germany, Federal Republic ..	1·4	1·3	1·4	1·7	2·0	0·5	0·1			
Greece	–	–	–	–	–	–		–	–	–
Italy..	1·5	1·0	0·9	0·8	0·8	0·4	0·1	0·1	0·2	0·1
Irish Republic[2]	11·8	13·6	13·0	12·6	11·0	1·2	0·4	0·4	0·4	0·4
Norway	22·6	25·4	29·9	23·1	27·3	9·2	2·5	3·0	2·8	
Portugal	4·0	3·9	3·8	4·0	5·0	1·2	0·4	0·4	0·4	0·4
Spain	35·2	39·9	43·0	44·5	42·5	11·0				
Sweden	30·2	30·6	44·8	40·5	40·7	12·1	5·5	4·5	3·7	
Yugoslavia	107·3	123·9	147·7	155·2	151·6	44·5	15·0	15·7	14·7	
Total ..	245·4	277·2	325·8	322·1	321·9	91·2				
AFRICA										
Algeria	0·5	0·4	0·4	0·4	0·5	0·1			0·1	0·1
Botswana	–	–	0·6	1·6	5·5	1·5	0·5	0·5	0·5	0·5
Congo (Brazzaville) ..	0·5	1·4	1·4	–	1·5	0·4	0·1	0·2	0·1	0·1
Mauritania	4·0	14·9	21·8	20·2	21·0	5·2	1·7	1·8	1·7	1·7
Morocco	3·7	3·8	4·1	5·0	5·2	1·4				
Mozambique	1·6	2·3	2·5	2·5	2·5	0·8	0·2	0·3	0·2	0·2
Rhodesia	23·3	31·8	32·0	32·0	24·0	6·0	2·0	2·0	2·0	2·0
South African Republic ..	148·4	161·9	175·8	179·1	178·9	47·5	16·2	15·7	14·4	
South West Africa ..	25·9	21·5	28·3	26·1	25·3	9·0	3·4	3·2		
Uganda	15·9	14·5	14·2	11·6	8·5	2·5				
Zaire	405·8	437·3	490·2	496·0	494·8	120·0	40·0	40·0	40·0	40·0
Zambia	651·4	717·7	706·6	698·0	676·9	183·2	55·7	62·7	67·5	
Total ..	1 281·0	1 407·5	1 477·9	1 472·5	1 444·6	377·6				
ASIA										
Burma	0·1	0·1	0·2	0·2	1·0	0·3	0·1	0·1	0·1	0·1
Cyprus	16·4	16·4	15·4	11·9	8·0	2·1	0·7	0·7	0·7	0·7
India	11·2	14·6	22·4	20·1	24·0	6·0	2·0	2·0	2·0	2·0
Indonesia[2]	–	5·0	37·9	64·6	62·1	18·6				
Iran	1·0	1·2	3·0	6·5	7·0	1·8	0·6	0·6	0·6	0·6
Israel	10·7	12·2	10·5	10·0	10·0	2·5	0·8	0·9	0·8	0·8
Japan	121·0	112·1	91·3	82·1	84·6	20·8	6·5	6·6	6·5	
Malaysia	–	–	–	–	3·8	4·9	1·6	1·7	1·6	1·6
Philippine Republic ..	197·4	213·7	221·2	225·5	226·7	56·0	19·6	19·6	19·6	
South Korea	1·0	0·8	1·0	1·3	1·5	0·4	0·1	0·1		
Taiwan	3·8	2·5	2·4	2·5	2·5	0·6	0·2	0·2	0·2	0·2
Turkey	22·2	22·1	30·2	40·7	38·0	16·5				
Total ..	384·8	400·7	435·5	465·4	469·2	130·5				
AMERICA										
Canada	654·5	719·7	823·9	826·2	712·9	178·3	57·4	66·5	57·1	
U.S.A.	1 380·9	1 510·3	1 558·5	1 448·8	1 280·0	336·5	123·5	124·0	117·3	
Bolivia	7·7	8·4	8·2	7·9	8·5	2·1	0·7	0·7	0·7	0·7
Brazil	5·3	4·8	4·2	3·5	1·7	–				
Chile[1]	708·3	716·8	735·4	902·1	828·3	235·6				
Cuba	–	1·8	2·1	6·0	5·0	1·5	0·5	0·5	0·5	0·5
Haiti	5·6	–	–	–	–	–				
Mexico	63·2	78·7	80·5	82·7	80·0	20·0				
Nicaragua	3·6	2·5	2·7	2·5	0·6	–	–	–	–	
Peru	207·4	219·1	215·0	211·3	176·0	49·1	18·5			
Total ..	3 036·5	3 262·1	3 430·5	3 491·0	3 093·0	823·1				
OCEANIA										
Australia	177·3	185·8	220·3	251·3	221·0	57·8	15·6			
Papua New Guinea[2] ..	–	124·0	182·9	184·1	172·5	47·9	13·2	13·2	13·2	
Total ..	177·3	309·8	403·2	435·4	393·5	105·7	30·1			
TOTAL ..	5 125·0	5 657·3	6 072·9	6 186·4	5 722·2	1 528·1				
Monthly Average ..	427·1	471·4	506·1	515·5	476·9	509·4				
OTHER COUNTRIES										
Albania	6·5	6·7	7·0	7·0	8·0	2·0	0·8	0·8	0·8	0·8
Bulgaria	35·0	38·0	48·0	50·0	48·0	12·0	4·0	4·0	4·0	4·0
Czechoslovakia	4·7	4·7	4·3	4·5	4·5	1·3	0·4	0·4	0·4	0·4
Germany D.R.	15·0	20·0	18·0	18·0	18·0	4·5	1·5	1·5	1·5	1·5
Hungary	1·0	1·0	1·0	1·2	1·0	0·2	0·1	0·1	0·1	0·1
Poland	122·2	135·0	155·0	198·0	270·0	75·0	25·0	25·0	25·0	25·0
Romania	25·0	30·0	40·0	40·0	40·0	10·0	3·4	3·4	3·4	3·4
U.S.S.R.	990·0	1 030·0	1 100·0	1 200·0	1 200·0	325·0	108·3	108·3	108·3	108·3
China and other Asia*	130·0	135·0	140·0	150·0	155·0	39·0	13·0	13·0	13·0	13·0
Total ..	1 329·4	1 400·4	1 513·3	1 668·7	1 744·5	469·0	156·5	156·5	156·5	156·5
WORLD TOTAL	6 454·4	7 057·7	7 586·2	7 855·1	7 466·7	1 997·1				
Monthly Average	537·8	588·1	632·2	654·6	622·2	665·7				

This table shows the recoverable copper content of ores and concentrates produced. Some of the data for the latest months are provisional

Notes (1) Production of blister and refined copper plus production of ores and concentrates, for export as such
(2) Figures shown for individual months are estimates based on actual quarterly statistics

By courtesy of the World Bureau of Metal Statistics.

Copper: World Smelter Production 1971 to 1976

THOUSAND METRIC TONS

	1971	1972	1973	1974	1975	1976 Jan-Mar	Apr	May	June	July
EUROPE										
Austria	11·0	11·0	11·0	11·0	11·0	3·0	1·0	1·0	1·0	1·0
Belgium	65·1	66·0	66·0	78·5	66·0	16·5	5·5	5·5	5·5	5·5
Finland	32·3	41·5	48·1	48·4	44·7	11·9	4·1	3·8	2·4	3·9
France	6·8	6·5	8·8	9·3	2·8	1·1				
Germany, Federal Republic	161·5	203·5	232·5	244·7	215·8	55·1				
Norway	34·5	33·0	34·6	31·4	26·3	4·9	1·8	1·8	1·9	
Portugal	4·5	3·8	4·0	4·0	4·0	1·0	0·3	0·4	0·3	0·3
Spain	70·0	84·5	86·3	99·0	107·1	27·0				
Sweden	58·2	55·4	61·8	59·9	57·0	15·5	5·6	5·6	5·2	
Yugoslavia	93·5	131·3	138·1	151·5	146·2	30·1	13·1	13·0	12·3	
Total	537·4	636·5	691·2	737·7	680·9	166·1				
AFRICA										
Botswana	–	–	–	1·6	12·0	3·0	1·0	1·0	1·0	1·0
Rhodesia	23·3	30·0	30·0	30·0	30·0	7·5	2·5	2·5	2·5	2·5
South Africa Republic	152·3	167·8	150·4	147·8	149·7	38·8	12·6	12·1		
South West Africa	28·1	26·1	35·4	45·8	35·7	7·0	2·3	2·2		
Uganda	15·7	14·1	9·6	8·9	8·0	2·0				
Zaire(1)(2)	404·6	428·2	450·0	453·8	440·0	105·0	35·0	35·0	35·0	35·0
Zambia(2)	643·7	697·3	688·6	709·3	659·0	184·5	56·2	55·7	59·5	
Total	1 267·7	1 363·5	1 364·0	1 397·2	1 334·4	347·8				
ASIA										
India	9·5	10·5	11·0	11·0	22·0	9·1	1·5	1·9		
Iran	0·6	0·6	2·0	6·5	6·0	1·5	0·5	0·5	0·5	0·5
Japan	661·2	777·7	1 000·5	1 008·9	850·0	258·7	72·6	76·4	73·4	83·3
South Korea	5·7	3·5	7·7	12·4	21·0	7·4	2·2			
Taiwan	3·7	3·5	3·6	4·0	4·0	1·0	0·4	0·3	0·3	0·3
Turkey	17·5	17·1	25·0	29·6	18·0	4·5	1·5	1·5	1·5	1·5
Total	698·2	812·9	1 049·8	1 072·4	921·0	282·2	78·7			
AMERICA										
Canada	462·3	473·7	495·0	537·0	500·0	123·4	42·8	43·2	40·3	
U.S.A.	1 421·0	1 596·1	1 652·7	1 496·3	1 357·6	350·6	119·1	126·3	115·0	
Brazil	5·1	4·8	4·2	3·5	1·7	–	–	–	–	
Chile	625·1	630·6	589·9	724·3	724·4	197·3				
Mexico	59·2	72·3	73·0	78·0	76·0	19·0				
Peru	166·4	176·2	176·0	177·4	144·7	35·3	13·5	13·3	13·6	
Total	2 739·1	2 953·7	2 990·8	3 016·5	2 804·4	725·6				
AUSTRALIA	149·8	149·5	165·8	200·6	185·3	45·0	12·7			
TOTAL	5 392·2	5 916·1	6 261·6	6 424·4	5 926·0	1 566·7				
Monthly Average	449·3	493·0	521·8	535·3	493·8	522·2				
OTHER COUNTRIES(3)										
Albania	6·5	6·7	7·0	6·0	8·0	2·0	0·7	0·7	0·7	0·7
Bulgaria	45·0	48·0	53·0	48·0	56·0	14·0	4·8	4·8	4·8	4·8
Czechoslovakia	7·0	7·0	7·0	6·0	6·0	1·2	0·5	0·5	0·5	0·5
Germany D.R.	48·0	47·0	45·0	48·0	48·0	12·0	4·0	4·0	4·0	4·0
Hungary	1·0	1·0	1·0	1·0	1·0	0·3	0·1	0·1	0·1	0·1
Poland	87·8	134·0	155·0	195·0	250·0	70·0	23·3	23·3	23·3	23·3
Romania	25·0	35·0	40·0	40·0	40·0	10·0	3·3	3·3	3·3	3·3
U.S.S.R.	990·0	1 050·0	1 100·0	1 200·0	1 200·0	325·0	108·3	108·3	108·3	108·3
China P.R. and other Asia*	130·0	135·0	140·0	150·0	155·0	39·0	13·0	13·0	13·0	13·0
Total	1 340·3	1 463·7	1 548·0	1 694·0	1 764·0	473·5	158·0	158·0	158·0	158·0
WORLD TOTAL	6 732·5	7 379·8	7 809·6	8 118·4	7 690·0	2 040·7				
Monthly Average	561·0	615·0	650·8	676·5	640·8	680·2				

The basis of this table is metal produced in the form of blister and anodes from ores, concentrates, other primary materials and secondary blister produced from scrap. The figures are in terms of recoverable copper content wherever possible. The figures shown for each country represent output of the smelters as defined, though some part of this may be exported for refining. Some of the data for the latest months are provisional.

Notes (1) Production of refined copper plus production of blister for export as such
(2) Includes leach cathodes, i.e. refined copper produced direct from concentrates without being treated in the smelter
(3) Primary production only

By courtesy of the World Bureau of Metal Statistics.

Copper: World Refined Production 1971 to 1976

THOUSAND METRIC TONS

	1971	1972	1973	1974	1975	1976 Jan-Mar	Apr	May	June	July
EUROPE										
Austria	21·3	22·7	22·8	26·7	26·9	6·9	2·4	2·5		
Belgium	312·8	314·4	367·5	378·7	346·4	91·6	32·3P			
Finland	32·3	38·4	42·9	38·3	35·8	9·5	3·3	3·1	1·9	3·1
France	29·3	29·2	30·1	43·9	39·5	9·9	2·8	2·8		
Germany, Federal Republic	400·1	398·5	406·7	423·6	422·2	108·0	36·3	37·8	37·7	36·6
Italy	9·5	9·0	12·2	13·7	13·2	3·8	1·2	1·3	1·3	1·3
Norway	27·7	26·4	25·8	24·8	19·7	3·0	1·2	1·0	1·0	
Portugal	4·2	3·8	3·7	3·6	3·2	0·6	–	0·1	0·3	0·3
Spain	79·3	87·0	93·8	123·5	121·3	30·0				
Sweden	50·1	51·6	59·5	59·9	56·2	13·9	5·1	5·1	5·1	
United Kingdom	177·6	162·0	170·8	160·1	151·5	43·8	10·5	10·6	11·5	
Yugoslavia	92·6	130·0	137·5	150·0	137·9	28·4	12·3	12·3	11·6	
Total	1 236·8	1 273·0	1 373·3	1 446·8	1 373·8	349·4				
AFRICA										
Egypt	1·8	2·0	2·0	2·0	2·0	0·5	0·2	0·2	0·2	0·2
Rhodesia	23·3	30·0	30·0	30·0	30·0	7·5	2·5	2·5	2·5	2·5
South Africa	79·2	79·3	90·6	88·5	86·4	20·2	7·4	6·6	6·2	6·0
Zaïre	207·8	216·2	230·2	254·5	225·9	57·0	19·0	19·0	19·0	19·0
Zambia	534·3	615·2	638·5	676·8	629·1	178·9	57·0			
Total	846·4	942·7	991·3	1 051·8	973·4	264·1				
ASIA										
India	9·6	10·5	11·7	11·8	12·3	2·9	0·9	0·8		
Iran	6·0	6·0	7·0	7·0	7·0	1·8	0·6	0·3	0·6	0·6
Japan	713·3	810·0	950·8	996·0	818·9	207·8	66·7	66·3	73·3	77·2
South Korea	6·8	9·1	9·2	12·4	20·9	7·4	2·2	2·1P		
Taiwan	3·7	4·8	6·6	9·9	8·5	2·4	1·0			
Turkey	17·5	17·1	15·0	29·6	16·0	4·0				
Total	756·9	857·5	1 000·3	1 066·7	883·6	226·3				
AMERICA										
Canada	477·5	495·9	497·6	559·1	529·2	121·8	42·2	43·9	45·5P	
U.S.A.	1 780·3	2 048·9	2 098·0	1 940·1	1 608·8	403·7	147·2	141·3	128·5P	144·0P
Brazil	23·1	26·8	29·7	37·3	28·8	7·2				
Chile	467·8	461·4	414·8	538·1	535·2	143·1				
Mexico	59·7	64·0	61·9	74·3	70·2	19·5	6·7	7·5	7·8	7·7
Peru	32·6	39·2	39·0	39·0	53·7	18·7	8·2	7·7	9·4	
Total	2 841·0	3 136·2	3 141·0	3 187·9	2 825·9	714·0				
AUSTRALIA	161·8	156·1	159·1	195·8	195·4	45·0	12·8			
TOTAL	5 842·9	6 365·5	6 665·0	6 949·0	6 252·1	1 598·8				
Monthly Average	486·9	530·5	555·4	579·1	521·0	532·9				
OTHER COUNTRIES										
Albania*	5·0	5·0	6·0	6·0	6·0	1·5	0·5	0·5	0·5	0·5
Bulgaria	41·0	45·0	48·0	48·0	48·0	12·0	4·0	4·0	4·0	4·0
Czechoslovakia	17·2	18·1	17·8	18·0	18·0	4·5	1·5	1·5	1·5	1·5
Germany, D.R.*	48·0	47·0	45·0	48·0	50·0	12·0	4·0	4·0	4·0	4·0
Hungary	11·8	7·0	9·5	10·0	11·5	2·5	1·0	1·0	1·0	1·0
Poland	92·7	131·0	156·4	194·5	248·0	69·0	23·0	23·0	23·0	23·0
Roumania	25·0	35·0	40·0	40·0	40·0	10·0	3·3	3·3	3·3	3·3
U.S.S.R.*	1 150·0	1 225·0	1 300·0	1 350·0	1 350·0	375·0	125·0	125·0	125·0	125·0
China P.R. and other Asia*	150·0	175·0	190·0	200·0	200·0	50·0	16·7	16·7	16·7	16·7
Total	1 540·7	1 688·1	1 812·7	1 914·5	1 971·5	536·5	179·0	179·0	179·0	179·0
WORLD TOTAL	7 383·6	8 053·6	8 477·7	8 863·5	8 223·6	2 135·3				
Monthly Average	615·3	671·1	706·5	738·6	685·3	711·8				

This table indicates total production of refined copper, whether electrolytic or fire refined. It includes production from blister, anodes and other primary materials, together with secondary production from scrap and other similar materials. It does not include copper recovered from secondary materials by simple remelting. Some data for the latest months are provisional.

By courtesy of the World Bureau of Metal Statistics.

Copper: World Refined Consumption 1971 to 1976

THOUSAND METRIC TONS

	1971	1972	1973	1974	1975	1976				
						Jan-Mar	Apr	May	June	July
EUROPE										
Austria	42·2	46·9	38·9	42·6	31·9	7·6	2·6	2·4	2·3	2·7
Belgium	147·0	153·0	164·4	178·2	174·2	50·6				
Denmark	4·7	4·1	5·5	4·7	2·5	0·6	0·2	0·2	0·2	
Finland	29·3	30·1	32·6	40·3	33·7	8·5	2·9	3·1		
France	343·6	390·3	407·8	414·2	364·5	102·2	37·2	35·0	38·4	
Germany, Federal Republic ..	630·5	672·2	727·2	731·2	620·0	203·1	65·0	63·0	63·7	
Greece	12·9	15·6	18·0	14·4	18·0	4·5	1·5	1·5	1·5	1·5
Irish Republic	0·1	0·1	0·3	0·4	0·4	0·1	–	0·1	–	–
Italy..	270·0	284·0	295·0	308·0	288·5	77·3				
Netherlands	41·6	36·7	38·2	29·6	37·5	12·5				
Norway	5·0	4·8	6·0	5·6	5·2	1·4	0·4	0·5	0·5	
Portugal	12·0	12·0	13·5	11·5	12·0	3·0	1·0	1·0	1·0	1·0
Spain	106·7	119·4	139·8	143·9	119·9	31·9	10·2	13·5	12·9	
Sweden	91·4	96·9	114·0	108·2	94·4	23·6	8·1	8·6		
Switzerland	40·5	30·1	25·5	30·2	21·3	5·4	2·0	2·0	2·0	1·3
United Kingdom	517·3	534·6	541·2	496·9	450·5	118·6	34·4	40·6	36·9	
Yugoslavia	71·4	65·1	80·2	119·3	147·8	47·3	18·0	17·9	14·3	
Total ..	2 366·2	2 495·9	2 648·1	2 679·2	2 423·3	698·2				
AFRICA										
Algeria	2·0	2·4	2·3	2·5	2·5	0·6	0·2	0·2	0·2	0·2
Egypt	6·9	7·0	8·0	10·0	10·0	2·5	0·8	0·9	0·8	0·8
Rhodesia	4·0	4·0	5·0	5·0	5·0	1·2	0·4	0·4	0·4	0·4
South Africa	42·1	47·4	62·7	66·8	64·0	16·3				
Zaire	1·3	1·5	2·5	2·5	2·5	0·6	0·2	0·2	0·2	0·2
Zambia	1·4	2·0	3·7	4·0	2·3	0·4	0·1	0·1	0·1	
Other Africa	1·5	2·0	2·5	1·0	4·0	1·0	0·3	0·4	0·3	0·3
Total ..	59·2	66·3	86·7	91·8	90·3	22·6				
ASIA										
India	61·0	59·3	62·9	49·8	48·0	15·0	5·0	5·0	5·0	5·0
Iran	10·0	10·0	10·0	12·0	12·0	3·0	1·0	1·0	1·0	1·0
Japan	805·7	951·3	1 201·8	831·0	806·2	256·5	101·5	94·5		
Philippine Republic	2·0	2·5	4·5	5·0	6·0	1·5	0·5	0·5	0·5	0·5
S. Korea	8·7	9·8	23·8	23·5	24·0	7·5	2·5	2·5	2·5	2·5
Taiwan	10·8	18·2	21·0	28·6	26·2	6·5				
Turkey	14·4	15·0	15·0	14·0	20·5	5·0				
Other Asia[1]	1·4	2·5	2·5	2·1	4·0	1·0	0·3	0·4	0·3	0·3
Total ..	914·0	1 068·6	1 341·5	966·0	946·9	296·0				
AMERICA										
Canada	220·4	223·8	248·2	270·1	196·1	57·4P	20·0P	19·9P	19·6P	
U.S.A.	1 833·4	2 029·9	P 221·1	1 994·9	1 396·8	423·6	160·0	167·4		
Argentina..	34·2	37·3	36·7	47·3	36·0	9·0	3·0	3·0	3·0	3·0
Brazil	93·5	111·6	123·7	173·9	155·2	38·5				
Chile	26·7	36·3	34·2	29·4	26·8	6·5				
Mexico	60·0	64·0	66·0	72·5	70·8	19·7	6·5	7·6	7·9	7·9
Peru	4·7	6·0	6·0	8·1	11·0	3·0	1·0	1·0	1·0	1·0
Other America	1·5	2·0	3·0	3·9	4·0	1·0	0·3	0·4	0·3	0·3
Total ..	2 274·4	2 510·9	2 738·9	2 600·1	1 896·7	558·7				
AUSTRALASIA										
Australia	110·4	102·1	121·8	121·6	103·0	24·9	8·8			
New Zealand	0·5	1·0	2·0	2·3	2·5	0·6	0·2	0·2	0·2	0·2
Total ..	110·9	103·1	123·8	123·9	105·5	25·5	9·0			
TOTAL ..	5 724·7	6 244·8	6 939·0	6 461·0	5 461·7	1 601·0				
Monthly Average ..	477·0	520·4	578·2	538·4	455·1	533·7				
OTHER COUNTRIES*										
Albania	1·2	1·2	1·5	1·5	1·5	0·3	0·1	0·1	0·1	0·1
Bulgaria	38·5	42·0	44·5	48·0	48·0	12·0	4·0	4·0	4·0	4·0
Czechoslavakia	63·1	65·0	75·0	76·0	75·0	19·0	6·2	6·2	6·2	6·2
Germany Democratic Republic	90·0	100·0	102·0	105·0	120·0	31·2	10·4	10·4	10·4	10·4
Hungary	23·0	23·0	26·0	28·0	30·0	7·5	2·5	2·5	2·5	2·5
Poland	97·1	113·0	140·0	150·0	150·0	40·0	13·4	13·4	13·4	13·4
Romania	35·0	47·0	54·0	58·0	60·0	15·0	5·0	5·0	5·0	5·0
U.S.S.R.	1 030·0	1 080·0	1 100·0	1 100·0	1 200·0	312·5	104·2	104·2	104·2	104·2
China, P.R. and other Asia ..	250·0	270·0	300·0	300·0	300·0	87·5	29·2	29·2	29·2	29·2
Total ..	1 627·9	1 741·2	1 843·0	1 936·5	1 984·5	525·0	175·0	175·0	175·0	175·0
WORLD TOTAL	7 352·6	7 986·0	8 782·0	8 397·5	7 446·2	2 126·0				
Monthly Average.. ..	612·7	665·5	731·8	699·8	620·5	708·7				

This table shows consumption of unwrought refined copper, whether refined from primary or secondary materials. The direct use of copper in scrap form is excluded. Some of the data for the latest months are provisional.
Note (1) Excludes Soviet Sphere Countries

By courtesy of the World Bureau of Metal Statistics.

Copper Wirebars: London

COPPER WIREBARS,3 MONTHS,MONTHLY

By courtesy of Eurocharts Information Service

Copper: New York

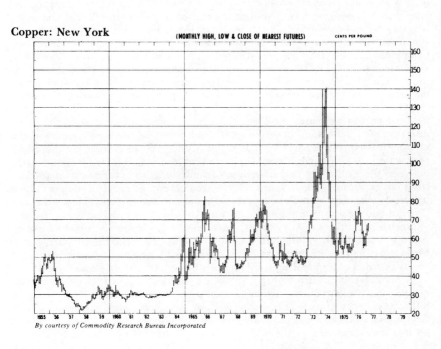

(MONTHLY HIGH, LOW & CLOSE OF NEAREST FUTURES)   CENTS PER POUND

By courtesy of Commodity Research Bureau Incorporated

Cotton and Wool

Cotton was one of the first commodities traded on the type of futures market which exists today. In the mid-19th century, when the county of Lancashire was the centre of the world cotton trade, the time taken for shipments of cotton to arrive in Liverpool from abroad, especially from the United States, meant that traders had to seek some form of price protection when pledging to supply their customers, the spinners, with their raw material requirements. So a futures market was formed. This flourished for many years until the decline in the Lancashire cotton industry, coupled with the price stability imposed by the huge surplus stocks held by the United States Government until the 1960s, resulted in the closing down of the futures market. This finally took place in 1951. In the United States, however, the New York cotton futures market survived the long period of price stability and in recent years has again become active as the world shortage of supplies, which was felt once the United States Government had disposed of its surplus cotton, sent prices soaring. These surplus stocks were acquired as a means of providing farmers with an adequate income. Now the free market forces of supply and demand have, to a large extent, been restored to normal. Cotton has survived competition from synthetic fibres, which at one stage threatened to relegate cotton — one of the oldest commodities — to obscurity.

The successful fight put up by the cotton industry against its modern competitors (who were dealt a serious blow by the steep rise in the price of oil, the raw material base for most synthetic fibres) is of great importance to many of the developing countries which rely on cotton both for export earnings and employment opportunities. Although the United States and the Soviet Union are the two biggest producers, cotton is grown throughout the world and provides the basis for many domestic textile industries. It is amongst the ten 'core' commodities, selected by the United Nations Conference on Trade and Development (UNCTAD) to be included in the integrated commodity support programme that seeks to stabilize prices and to regulate trade in certain key raw materials by agreement between the leading producing and consuming countries.

Many trade sources feel that the proposed buffer stock support for any international cotton agreement will be difficult to formulate in view of the many different qualities traded in the world. In addition the United States is no longer dominating exports in the way that it did in the past because of the increasing production in other countries. In any event there is extensive co-operation between the producing and consuming countries in the general effort to fight competition from synthetics, but the changed pattern of supply and demand has inevitably brought considerable price fluctuations as consumption ebbs and flows or bad weather conditions hit cotton crops in key producing areas.

Recognizing this new situation, an attempt was made to launch a cotton futures market in London. But this failed to attract sufficient support, partly because of the lack of domestic demand and partly because the market came in at a time when cotton trading was in a quiet period of relatively stable prices.

A more ambitious attempt to provide the world with a cotton futures market outside the United States, where prices tend to reflect mainly US domestic influences, is being made with the new Hong Kong commodity futures market. Cotton has been chosen as the first commodity to be traded on what promises to be the first important commodity futures exchange to be launched for many years. Hong Kong is especially suited for trading in cotton, since it is an area of high consumption and is also within easy distance of major producing countries. Strict rules have been drawn up by the Hong Kong Government to ensure that the new futures market will not be swamped by speculation and diverted from its prime purpose of providing the much needed hedging and price fixing facilities required by non-US cotton producers, consumers and traders.

Meanwhile another natural fibre that is also successful in fighting competition from synthetics has provided the base for the Sydney futures market in Australia. Although by no means as big as cotton in the volume of trade, wool is sold extensively throughout the world and has been subject to severe price fluctuations since demand is closely linked with the economic health of the main industrialized countries, especially Japan.

The three main wool-exporting countries — Australia, New Zealand and South Africa — have each introduced their own price support systems for domestic growers and co-operate in promoting sales through the International Wool Secretariat. But there is little that can be done to stabilize demand and wool production is not confined to these three countries alone — Argentina is also a significant exporter and many other countries with large sheep populations provide a varying proportion of their own requirements. Prices can thus vary considerably, despite the occasional buildup of stockpiles in the main exporting countries to stop values at the auctions (through which the bulk of wool exports are sold) falling too low. The Sydney futures market has proved so successful in attracting support that further attempts have been made to relaunch the wool futures market in London to provide a hedging facility for European traders nearer to home. So far these attempts have not been too successful, as was the case with the New York wool futures market, but trading volume now appears to be finally building up.

Cotton: World Production 1967/68 to 1974/75

Country	1967/68	1968/69	1969/70	1970/71	1971/72	1972/73	1973/74	1974/75
North America			*1,000 bales[4]*					
Br. W. Indies	1	1	1	—	—	1	1	2
Costa Rica	20	17	10	6	—	1	3	2
Cuba	5	5	5	5	5	5	5	5
El Salvador	160	203	210	252	315	323	345	345
Guatemala	360	380	260	265	375	430	555	485
Honduras	38	35	15	9	11	20	25	24
Mexico	2,000	2,450	1,750	1,440	1,715	1,780	1,500	2,230
Nicaragua	470	420	310	360	480	485	660	560
United States[1/2]	7,215	11,030	9,950	10,269	10,270	13,890	13,300	11,525
Others	3	3	3	3	3	3	3	3
Total	10,272	14,544	12,514	12,609	13,174	16,938	16,397	15,181
South America								
Argentina	340	520	670	390	400	575	585	790
Bolivia	15	20	17	45	70	115	110	90
Brazil	2,750	3,320	3,100	2,300	3,100	2,950	2,600	2,375
Colombia	465	640	590	540	590	630	620	730
Ecuador	20	25	25	21	18	25	26	55
Paraguay	40	60	60	30	60	105	110	120
Peru[2]	390	515	393	410	400	315	410	335
Uruguay	1	1	1	1	1	—	1	2
Venezuela	56	71	66	76	98	95	125	200
Total	4,077	5,172	4,922	3,813	4,737	4,810	4,587	4,697

Cotton: World Production 1967/68 to 1974/75 — continued

Country	1967/ 68	1968/ 69	1969/ 70	1970/ 71	1971/ 72	1972/ 73	1973/ 74	1974/ 75
				1,000 bales[4]				
Western Europe								
Greece	443	338	515	508	537	640	500	583
Italy	11	8	9	5	6	4	4	4
Spain	300	355	270	250	200	260	210	270
Yugoslavia	15	18	19	20	16	12	11	11
Total	769	719	813	783	759	916	725	868
Eastern Europe								
Albania	30	20	25	30	30	30	30	30
Bulgaria	100	80	60	70	60	75	75	55
Total	130	100	85	100	90	105	105	85
U.S.S.R.	9,370	9,200	8,850	10,800	11,000	11,400	12,000	13,000
Asia and Oceania								
Afghanistan	105	110	130	100	105	115	150	150
Australia	150	154	128	89	201	147	140	150
China, Peop. Rep.[3]	8,900	8,300	8,100	9,200	10,200	9,800	11,700	11,500
India	5,300	4,900	4,850	4,400	5,800	5,370	5,530	5,950
Iran	545	770	760	710	680	955	920	1,095
Iraq	55	60	65	65	65	65	70	70
Israel	131	154	183	163	169	186	173	230
Rep. of Korea	18	20	20	20	19	18	21	14
Pakistan	2,387	2,433	2,470	2,502	3,263	3,237	3,037	2,925
Syria	585	710	690	690	725	750	720	670
Thailand	125	200	200	85	150	95	75	90
Turkey	1,825	2,005	1,845	1,845	2,420	2,505	2,365	2,760
Yemen, Rep.	5	3	2	2	3	3	5	12
Yemen, P.D.R.	8	30	23	26	20	21	16	30
Others	28	29	31	21	27	25	25	33
Total	20,242	19,928	19,547	19,983	23,912	23,357	25,012	25,714
Africa								
Algeria	4	6	8	5	1	2	3	3
Angola	55	75	108	142	145	83	140	175
Benin	21	40	42	65	85	88	80	57
Burundi	10	10	10	10	10	10	10	10
Cameroon, U.R.	84	116	157	65	73	77	48	70
Central Afr. Rep.	81	100	102	91	78	88	76	80
Chad	180	260	200	160	190	180	200	245
Egypt	2,014	2,013	2,497	2,346	2,351	2,369	2,258	2,018
Ethiopia	45	55	65	65	75	80	100	110
Ivory Coast	61	78	61	54	91	99	108	110
Kenya	17	19	23	25	25	25	25	25
Madagascar	16	20	29	37	43	43	54	60
Malawi	18	25	30	33	33	25	32	30
Mali	57	75	80	92	117	112	88	106
Morocco	25	30	31	28	40	40	27	24
Mozambique	195	205	215	162	218	225	175	180
Niger	10	11	17	16	14	9	6	13
Nigeria	125	260	425	180	175	220	140	240
Rhodesia	80	200	200	200	200	160	150	200
Senegal	7	16	18	19	36	39	55	71
South Africa	70	125	90	85	92	82	185	215
Sudan	900	1,050	1,135	1,130	1,125	920	1,090	930
Tanzania	325	240	330	345	300	355	310	320
Togo	17	9	9	10	14	10	15	18
Uganda	285	355	390	345	345	360	245	150

Cotton: World Production 1967/68 to 1974/75 — continued

Country	1967/ 68	1968/ 69	1969/ 70	1970/ 71	1971/ 72	1972/ 73	1973/ 74	1974/ 75
				1,000 bales[4]				
Africa cont.								
Upper Volta	29	53	61	39	48	55	45	52
Zaire	40	75	80	90	95	110	85	80
Zambia	7	10	10	18	20	13	8	5
Others	2	1	1	1	1	–	5	5
Total	4,780	5,532	6,424	5,858	6,040	5,879	5,763	5,602
World total	49,640	55,195	53,155	53,946	59,712	63,405	64,589	65,147
Socialist countries	18,415	17,615	17,050	20,115	21,305	21,320	23,820	24,600
Elsewhere	31,225	37,580	36,105	33,831	38,407	42,085	40,769	40,547

(1) *Running bales adjusted for ginnings within season, city crop, etc. except that beginning with 1972/73, data are in bales of 478 lbs, net.* (2) *Based on ginnings within season.* (3) *Revised series.* (4) *Year beginning August 1st.*
By courtesy of the Secretariat of the International Cotton Advisory Committee.

Cotton: World Consumption 1967/68 to 1974/75

Country	1967/ 68	1968/ 69	1969/ 70	1970/ 71	1971/ 72	1972/ 73	1973/ 74	1974/ 75
				1,000 bales				
North America								
Canada	390	390	360	350	365	345	330	250
Costa Rica	5	5	5	5	5	5	5	5
Cuba	90	90	90	90	90	90	100	100
El Salvador	53	47	50	52	60	65	65	70
Guatemala	40	35	43	37	40	40	65	65
Honduras	6	6	8	8	8	9	13	13
Jamaica	5	5	5	5	5	5	5	5
Mexico	710	685	685	675	750	800	830	800
Nicaragua	13	13	15	18	22	20	23	23
United States[1]	8,982	8,242	7,991	8,068	8,039	7,800	7,500	5,885
Others	8	8	8	7	6	6	6	6
Total	10,302	9,526	9,260	9,315	9,390	9,185	8,942	7,222
South America								
Argentina	433	475	477	492	500	465	530	525
Bolivia	12	15	15	20	20	20	20	20
Brazil	1,250	1,330	1,350	1,380	1,500	1,700	1,750	1,700
Chile	130	130	132	130	132	110	140	140
Colombia	300	310	325	345	360	405	480	430
Ecuador	33	35	34	35	34	40	46	50
Paraguay	18	17	17	17	18	18	22	22
Peru	77	80	90	120	140	145	145	130
Uruguay	34	27	26	31	24	22	33	28
Venezuela	80	95	95	100	115	125	160	130
Total	2,367	2,514	2,561	2,670	2,843	3,050	3,326	3,175
Western Europe								
Austria	97	104	108	107	107	102	104	88
Belgium	301	305	322	305	286	264	268	213
Denmark	31	17	12	11	12	11	12	8
Finland	73	72	62	65	64	59	58	53
France	1,120	1,123	1,143	1,095	1,085	1,064	1,077	932
Germany, F.R.	1,189	1,177	1,170	1,078	1,109	1,074	1,096	962

Cotton: World Consumption from 1967/68 to 1974/75 — continued

Country	1967/ 68	1968/ 68	1969/ 70	1970/ 71	1971/ 72	1972/ 73	1973/ 74	1974/ 75
				1,000 bales				
Western Europe cont.								
Greece	202	210	224	243	281	355	380	415
Ireland	30	30	25	22	22	23	25	22
Italy	1,028	1,021	1,021	925	924	862	898	828
Malta	4	4	4	4	5	5	5	5
Netherlands	285	288	271	253	239	217	211	172
Norway	20	16	17	15	13	12	12	11
Portugal	368	392	415	428	482	505	552	474
Spain	450	550	520	510	550	570	550	530
Sweden	78	70	65	55	43	42	41	35
Switzerland	182	187	195	197	197	190	190	175
United Kingdom	831	816	792	741	638	650	560	510
Yugoslavia	415	420	425	415	415	425	435	440
Total	6,704	6,802	6,791	6,469	6,472	6,430	6,474	5,873
Eastern Europe								
Albania	32	30	32	32	35	35	35	35
Bulgaria	330	340	345	350	370	375	380	385
Czechoslovakia	510	500	510	530	550	550	565	575
Germany, D.R.	410	410	430	425	420	420	425	430
Hungary	340	320	330	350	330	340	345	365
Poland	660	650	670	690	700	690	700	690
Rumania	350	370	370	380	380	390	400	420
Total	2,632	2,620	2,687	2,757	2,785	2,800	2,850	2,900
U.S.S.R.	7,800	7,900	8,100	8,500	8,800	8,850	9,000	9,300
Asia and Oceania								
Afghanistan	50	50	50	50	50	55	55	55
Australia	142	140	140	140	130	135	150	130
Bangladesh	—	—	—	—	125	220	190	190
Burma	65	55	60	70	65	65	65	55
China, Peop. Rep.[2]	8,700	8,700	8,700	9,300	10,600	11,300	12,000	12,500
China (Taiwan)	440	455	510	630	610	530	720	740
Hong Kong	774	776	771	801	694	689	831	798
India	5,335	5,370	5,520	5,200	5,500	5,700	6,000	5,925
Indonesia	100	125	175	200	235	220	250	300
Iran	270	300	300	280	275	340	410	450
Iraq	35	40	55	55	55	70	85	110
Israel	112	125	113	100	108	110	95	103
Japan	3,350	3,476	3,392	3,541	3,614	3,724	3,650	2,900
Korea, Rep.	415	445	480	540	530	525	740	730
Lebanon	25	25	25	25	25	25	25	25
Malaysia/Singapore	20	25	35	55	70	100	150	140
Pakistan[2]	1,560	1,775	2,120	1,985	2,020	2,490	2,485	2,120
Philippines	170	180	165	155	150	147	170	135
Sri Lanka	9	10	10	12	20	30	30	30
Syria	110	109	110	120	155	170	150	180
Thailand	235	240	300	300	325	380	450	335
Turkey	740	785	830	830	850	950	1,150	1,150
Vietnam, Rep.	30	55	85	100	110	110	90	70
Others[2]	107	123	133	156	175	173	181	180
Total	22,794	23,384	24,079	24,645	26,491	28,258	30,122	29,351
Africa								
Algeria	12	10	15	25	30	35	35	40
Cameroon	5	5	7	8	11	15	20	25
Central African Rep.	10	12	12	11	12	9	10	8

Cotton: World Consumption from 1967/68 to 1974/75 — continued

Country	1967/68	1968/69	1969/70	1970/71	1971/72	1972/73	1973/74	1974/75
				1,000 bales				
Africa cont.								
Egypt	850	850	875	935	970	1,000	1,030	1,020
Ethiopia	60	75	75	75	80	90	90	90
Ghana	12	15	25	35	35	40	40	45
Ivory Coast	15	14	12	20	17	20	35	40
Kenya	15	20	25	33	33	37	43	43
Madagascar	20	25	25	29	40	38	53	55
Mali	2	10	10	10	10	17	17	20
Morocco	35	35	33	35	45	45	57	53
Mozambique	15	15	15	15	15	25	34	35
Nigeria	100	125	175	190	190	170	230	250
Rhodesia	40	45	50	50	50	50	50	50
Senegal	10	13	13	13	16	17	20	21
South Africa	200	210	210	225	240	250	280	250
Sudan	65	70	70	60	60	60	70	90
Tanzania	20	30	33	35	40	50	55	65
Tunisia	20	20	23	23	27	30	35	35
Uganda	40	50	50	55	55	50	45	40
Zaire	50	50	50	50	65	70	65	80
Others[2]	33	41	45	53	62	70	74	79
Total	1,629	1,740	1,848	1,985	2,103	2,188	2,388	2,434
World total	54,228	54,486	55,326	56,341	58,884	60,761	63,102	60,255
Socialist countries	19,317	19,420	19,697	20,792	22,435	23,200	24,120	24,970
Elsewhere	34,911	35,066	35,629	35,549	36,443	37,561	38,982	35,285

(1) *1,000 running bales through 1971/72.* (2) *Revised series.*
By courtesy of the Secretariat of the International Cotton Advisory Committee.

Cotton: New York

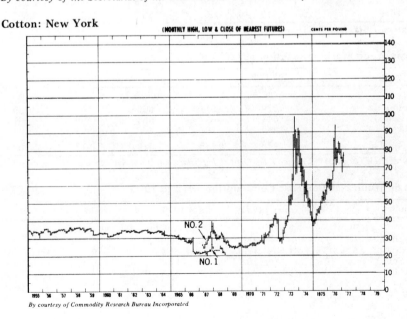

By courtesy of Commodity Research Bureau Incorporated

Guide to World Commodity Markets

Greasy Wool: World Production 1972/73 to 1976/77

Country	1972/73	1973/74	1974/75	1975/76	1976/77p
			million kg		
Argentina	177	180	184	190	191
Australia	736	703	792	747	725
Brazil	33	33	34	34	34
Bulgaria	32	32	31	31	31
Canada	2	2	2	2	2
Chile	16	16	16	16	16
France	21	21	22	21	—
Greece	8	9	9	9	9
India	35	35	35	35	35
Iran	44	48	49	50	50
Iraq	17	17	17	17	17
Irish Republic	10	10	10	10	10
Italy	12	11	11	12	—
Lesotho	4	3	3	3	3
Mongolia	20	20	20	20	20
Morocco	18	18	18	18	18
New Zealand	309	285	294	312	315
Pakistan	20	20	20	20	20
Peru	12	12	12	12	12
Portugal	12	14	14	14	—
Rumania	31	31	31	31	31
South Africa	114	113	115	114	116
Soviet Union	420	433	462	463	—
Spain	32	32	31	31	—
Turkey	48	48	48	47	—
United Kingdom	48	49	49	51	52
United States	80	72	65	57	52
Uruguay	60	60	63	68	68
Yugoslavia	10	10	10	10	10
Other	161	164	166	166	—
Total	2,542	2,501	2,633	2,613	2,590

Sources: IWTO and IWS.

Clean Wool: World Production 1972/73 to 1976/77

Description	1972/73	1973/74	1974/75	1975/76	1976/77p
			million kg		
Merino	529	511	560	544	539
Crossbred	644	627	663	668	661
Other	299	297	306	305	302
Total	1,472	1,435	1,529	1,517	1,502

Sources: IWTO and IWS. By courtesy of the International Wool Secretariat. p — provisional.

Virgin Wool: Net Domestic Consumption 1972 to 1975

Country	1972	1973	1974	1975p
		million kg clean		
Australia	25.7	25.9	24.9	20.0
Austria	12.8	11.4	9.1	8.6
Belgium	16.4	17.4	16.9	15.9
Canada	23.2	20.4	17.3	17.2
Denmark	8.3	7.2	5.6	7.0
Finland	6.3	6.1	5.9	4.9

Virgin Wool: Net Domestic Consumption 1972 to 1975 — continued

Country	1972	1973	1974	1975p
	million kg clean			
France	54.0	48.7	44.5	49.6
German F.R.	169.6	140.6	125.2	130.9
Greece	11.8	12.7	7.7	12.6
India	14.7	10.7	9.7	10.6
Iran	28.0	27.2	30.2	33.6
Irish Republic	4.1	6.6	6.0	4.7
Israel	4.0	1.7	1.5p	1.5
Italy	72.6	61.2	60.1	56.8
Japan	175.9	174.3	170.5	163.6
Korea	7.7	6.8	6.7	4.6
Mexico	6.8	4.4	4.1	4.2
Netherlands	25.3	22.8	20.9	21.0
New Zealand	13.0	11.1	15.4	15.1
Norway	7.0	6.7	6.4	5.3
Portugal	9.1	8.5	7.3	5.7
South Africa	8.7	8.4	10.2	9.5
Spain	25.5	26.0	22.7	25.0
Sweden	11.6	10.4	9.6	8.9
Switzerland	16.0	14.9	13.5	12.9
Taiwan	5.5	4.3	2.3	3.2
Turkey	19.5	15.3	15.4	16.2
United Kingdom	120.6	104.1	91.8	88.8
United States	141.0	106.8	86.5	75.2
Total	1,044.7	922.6	850.2	837.4
Eastern Europe (Raw Wool Supply)				
Bulgaria	16.8	17.5	17.1	—
Czechoslovakia	18.6	16.9	18.6	—
German D.R.	21.6	18.4	17.2	—
Hungary	4.5	6.4	6.2	—
Poland	25.2	23.2	21.4	—
Rumania	19.1	20.2	21.0	—
Soviet Union	259.5	283.4	302.4	—
Yugoslavia	16.6	17.7	23.6	—
Grand Total	1,426.6	1,326.3	1,277.7	—

The virgin wool content of all products purchased by consumers, including the virgin wool content of blended products.   p — *provisional.*
By courtesy of the International Wool Secretariat.

Wool: UK

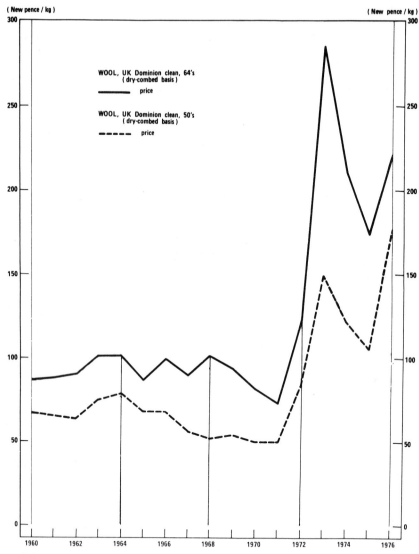

(New pence / kg)

WOOL, UK Dominion clean, 64's
(dry-combed basis)
———— price

WOOL, UK Dominion clean, 50's
(dry-combed basis)
– – – – price

a/ Nominal prices divided by the United Nations index of export unit values of manufactured goods (see table 6, page 3).

By courtesy of UNCTAD Commodities Division

Grains

Commodity markets dealing in grains are the biggest and most important of all markets, regulating supplies and prices of staple foodstuffs grown throughout the world. The grains can be roughly divided into two main sectors: wheat used for human consumption in flour products and the grains such as corn (maize) and barley used for animal foodstuffs. As living standards rise throughout the world, countries where rice has been the traditional staple diet tend to move away from rice towards flour-based products and livestock fed on grains. With the world's population constantly increasing a crop disaster in any one of the main producing areas, notably the Soviet Union — the biggest single producer — can threaten starvation in the poorest areas as grain prices are forced up. In recent years, however, there has been great pressure on feed grain and protein (soya bean) supplies following a general rise in the world's livestock population in line with the increasing popularity of meat. There are serious doubts whether future grain supplies will be sufficient to be used in this 'wasteful' way as compared with processing the grains directly into human foodstuffs; animals are poor converters of grain into protein.

While grains are grown all over the world, the main exporting countries are relatively few in number — first and foremost is the United States, then Canada, Australia, Argentina and France. The European Community is on balance a net importer with its purchases of grains. Its imports of hard wheat (notably by Britain for bread manufacture), corn and soya beans exceed by far its exports of soft wheat and flour. Japan is also a regular large-scale importer. In recent years the Soviet Union has become a net importer since it has had to purchase large quantities of grain whenever crops have failed to reach target levels. This has occurred more frequently in recent times since it has also found it increasingly difficult to produce the extra quantities required to feed its growing human and livestock population with a relatively short growing season in most grain-producing areas. The Soviet Union used to be a net exporter to the Western world as well as supplying Eastern European countries, but it has been forced to sign a long-term (five-year) agreement with the United States guaranteeing the purchase of a minimum quantity of grain each year. China has also become a more active buyer of grain on world markets, relying particularly on Canada and Australia for the bulk of its supplies.

The key to the world grain supply-demand balance often lies with the crops in the Indian sub-continent where a constant battle is fought to produce crops of sufficient size to meet the needs of growing populations. Any setback in the Asian rice crops also brings urgent import demand for grains, with the United States often the only country with adequate and available supplies. It should be noted, however, that the United States has now used up all the reserve grain acreages that farmers were paid not to use.

Plans to build up an international emergency reserve stock, as proposed by the United Nations Food and Agriculture Organization (FAO), have so far foundered on the problems of where and how to carry the stocks and more particularly which country is to finance them. The International Wheat Agreement, set up to stabilize prices and supplies, collapsed several years ago and now only provides a central point for collating information on market trends and helping to channel food aid supplies from the richer countries to the areas most in need. With the world so dependent on the United States for supplies, the

63

views of the Americans, who in the past have been hostile to international commodity agreements distorting the 'free' markets, are crucial to any further moves for creating an international stockpile of world price agreements.

At present world market prices for wheat, corn and soya beans are decided daily on the huge Chicago Board of Trade futures market, by far the biggest and most active commodity market in the world. There are separate trading 'pits' in Chicago for wheat, corn and soya beans, soya bean meal and soya bean oil, and these are used extensively by the domestic and international grain trade as well as by a huge army of regular or occasional speculators. Prices fluctuate continually in accordance with the changing supply-demand situation, particularly in the United States itself. Although farmers in the United States nowadays receive a guaranteed minimum price, they rely heavily on Chicago to indicate trends in order to decide on their planting intentions and sale programmes.

The European Community farmers are protected by the Common Agricultural Policy that fixes minimum prices for grains. They are also protected against competition from imports by a complicated system of import levies. On most occasions EEC grain prices tend to be above world market levels but they can be at a discount if there is a world shortage of grain — the EEC price levels are fixed, in theory at least, to provide growers with a reasonable return and encourage as much self-sufficiency within the Community as possible. Efforts to step up corn production in the Community, mainly in France, have been badly hampered so far by unsuitable weather conditions and yields of corn are much lower in Europe than in the United States, although wheat yields are more than competitive.

In London there are grain futures markets for barley and wheat. Although turnover has increased in recent years, these tend to be rather specialized domestic markets badly restricted by the EEC grain price system that gives producers little incentive to hedge and offers few attractions for speculators, except in special times of shortage when prices can move sharply.

World Coarse Grains 1972/73 to 1976/77

Country	1972/73	1973/74	1974/75	1975/76	1976/77 Dec 15	1976/77 Feb 1
		Trade years beginning 1 July				
Exports: [1]			*Millions of metric tons*			
Canada	4.2	2.9	2.8	4.9	4.6	4.7
Australia	1.6	1.9	2.9	3.2	3.2	3.1
Argentina	4.2	8.4	8.5	5.3	6.1	6.4
S. Africa	3.3	0.5	3.5	3.3	2.0	1.9
Thailand	1.1	2.3	2.2	2.6	2.2	2.2
Brazil	0.5	0.4	1.5	1.4	1.4	1.4
Sub-Total	15.0	16.3	21.4	20.6	19.6	19.8
West Europe	4.8	3.8	2.9	4.5	1.1	1.3
U.S.S.R.	0.4	0.9	1.0	0.0	3.0	3.0
Others	3.2	4.0	2.4	4.4	3.4	3.6
Total Non-U.S.	23.4	24.9	27.8	29.6	27.1	27.7
U.S. [2]	35.6	44.5	34.3	46.5	50.8	51.0
World Total	59.0	69.4	62.1	76.0	77.9	78.7
Imports:						
West Europe	21.7	25.1	25.2	23.9	36.5	36.8
U.S.S.R.	6.9	7.1	2.7	15.5	6.0	6.0
Japan	12.0	14.1	13.1	13.5	14.5	14.6
East Europe	5.1	3.7	6.4	6.9	7.6	7.3
Others	13.3	19.4	14.7	16.2	13.2	14.0
World Total	59.0	69.4	62.1	76.0	77.9	78.7
(+ Intra EC-9)	65.3	79.5	70.5	84.8	84.0	84.8
Production: [4/5]						
Canada	20.9	20.4	17.4	20.0	20.9	21.2
Australia	3.7	4.7	4.5	5.5	5.5	5.1
Argentina	16.0	17.9	13.8	12.4	15.8	14.9
S. Africa	4.5	11.9	9.7	7.8	9.7	9.7
Thailand	1.4	2.5	2.7	3.3	3.0	3.0
Brazil	14.3	15.6	16.9	18.0	19.7	19.8
West Europe	81.6	84.0	85.0	81.5	72.7	73.0
U.S.S.R. [6]	72.5	101.0	99.7	65.8	115.0	113.3
East Europe	56.7	55.7	57.3	59.5	57.9	58.3
Others	148.7	159.2	163.0	174.5	173.6	175.7
Total Non-U.S.	420.3	473.0	470.0	448.3	493.6	493.8
U.S.	182.1	186.6	150.5	184.9	189.4	193.1
World Total	602.4	659.6	620.5	633.3	683.0	686.9
Consumption [4/7]						
U.S.	158.0	155.6	121.4	133.2	139.3	137.7 [3]
U.S.S.R. [6]	80.0	104.1	101.4	83.4	116.0	110.3
PRC	54.0	59.1	61.4	62.1	61.9	61.9
Others	329.2	343.0	342.1	356.0	361.0	360.4
World Total	621.2	661.9	626.3	634.7	678.2	670.4
End Stocks [4/8]						
Total Foreign [9]	25.9	33.4	33.9	30.5	32.6	39.6
(U.S.S.R.: Stks Chg)	(+0.0)	(+5.0)	(−2.0)	(−2.0)	(+6.0)	(+7.0)
U.S.	31.7	21.8	15.4	17.4	19.7	24.8 [3]
World Total [9]	57.6	55.2	49.3	47.9	52.3	64.4

1. *Corn, barley, oats, sorghum, and rye, excluding products.* 2. *Adjusted for transshipments through Canadian ports; excludes products.* 3. *U.S. supply-use estimates are midpoints of the official range estimates.* 4. *Rye, corn, barley, oats, sorghum, millet and mixed grains.*

World Coarse Grains 1972/73 to 1976/77 — continued

5. *Production data include all harvests occurring within the July-June year indicated, except that small grain crops from the early harvesting Northern Hemisphere areas are "moved forward" i.e., the May 1976 harvests in areas such as India, North Africa, and southern United States are actually included in "1976/77" accounting period that begins July 1, 1976.*
6. *"Bunker weight" basis: not discounted for excess moisture and foreign material.*
7. *Consumption data are based on an aggregate of differing local marketing years. For countries for which stocks data are not available (excluding the U.S.S.R.), consumption estimates represent "apparent" consumption, i.e., they are inclusive of annual stock level adjustments. 8. Stocks data are based on an aggregate of differing local marketing years and should not be construed as representing world stock levels at a fixed point in time. Stocks data are not available for all countries and exclude those such as the People's Republic of China and parts of Eastern Europe; the world stock levels have been adjusted for estimated year-to-year changes in U.S.S.R. grain stocks, but do not purport to include the entire absolute level of U.S.S.R. stocks. 9. Inclusive of Soviet stock changes; see footnote 8.*
By courtesy of the U.S. Department of Agriculture.

World Wheat and Wheat Flour 1972/73 to 1976/77

Country	1972/73	1973/74	1974/75	1975/76	1976/77 Dec 15	1976/77 Feb 1
		Trade years beginning 1 July				
Exports:			*Millions of metric tons*			
Canada	15.6	11.5	11.2	12.1	12.0	12.0
Australia	5.6	5.4	8.2	7.9	7.8	7.8
Argentina	3.4	1.1	2.2	3.2	4.6	4.8
Sub-Total	24.6	18.0	21.6	23.2	24.4	24.6
West Europe	6.9	5.8	8.8	9.0	5.6	4.9
U.S.S.R.	1.3	5.0	4.0	0.5	1.0	1.0
Others	2.8	2.7	2.0	1.4	1.0	1.9
Total Non-U.S.	35.7	31.5	36.4	34.1	32.0	32.4
U.S.[1]	31.8	31.1	28.0	31.5	26.9	26.3
World Total	67.4	62.6	64.4	65.6	58.9	58.6
Imports:						
West Europe	8.2	6.4	6.7	6.7	6.3	5.3
U.S.S.R.	14.9	4.4	2.5	10.1	5.5	5.5
Japan	5.5	5.4	5.4	5.9	5.7	5.7
East Europe	4.6	5.6	4.7	4.9	5.7	5.7
PRC	5.3	5.6	5.7	2.2	2.5	3.5
Others	28.9	35.1	39.5	35.8	33.1	32.9
World Total	67.4	62.6	64.4	65.6	58.9	58.6
(+ Intra EC-9)	72.7	69.1	68.6	71.9	64.9	64.6
Production:[3]						
Canada	14.5	16.2	13.3	17.1	23.5	23.5
Australia	6.6	12.0	11.4	12.0	10.0	11.6
Argentina	6.9	6.6	6.0	8.6	12.0	11.0
West Europe	51.3	50.8	56.7	48.6	50.5	50.6
U.S.S.R.[4]	86.0	109.8	83.8	66.2	95.0	96.9
East Europe	30.7	31.5	34.0	28.5	33.5	33.7
India	26.4	24.7	21.8	24.2	28.0	28.3
Others	79.0	73.7	80.5	86.0	92.6	92.7
Total Non-U.S.	301.4	325.2	307.5	291.2	345.1	348.3
U.S.	42.0	46.4	48.9	58.1	58.4	58.4
World Total	343.4	371.6	356.4	349.3	403.6	406.8

World Wheat and Wheat Flour 1972/73 to 1976/77 — continued

Country	1972/73	1973/74	1974/75	1975/76	1976/77 Dec 15	1976/77 Feb 1
	Trade years beginning 1 July					
Consumption: [5]	*Millions of metric tons*					
U.S.	21.7	20.4	18.8	19.8	21.6	20.2[2]
U.S.S.R.[4]	99.6	99.2	90.3	81.8	84.0	87.9
PRC	41.2	40.0	42.7	41.2	41.5	42.0
Others	200.7	207.8	207.9	204.1	215.2	216.4
World Total	363.2	367.5	359.7	346.9	362.3	366.5
Ending Stocks: [6]						
Total Foreign[7]	43.5	54.8	49.1	45.1	76.1	73.7
U.S.S.R.: Stks Chg	(+0.0)	(+10.0)	(−8.0)	(−6.0)	(+15.0)	(+13.0)
U.S.	16.3	9.2	11.7	18.1	27.7	29.8[2]
World Total[7]	59.8	64.0	60.8	63.2	103.8	103.5

1. *Adjusted for transshipments through Canadian ports; excludes products other than flour.*
2. *U.S. supply-use estimates are midpoints of the official range estimates.* 3. *Production data include all harvests occurring within the July-June year shown, except that small grain crops for the early harvesting are "moved forward"; ie, the May 1976 harvests in areas such as India, North Africa, and Southern United States are actually included in "1976/77" accounting period which begins July 1, 1976.* 4. *"Bunker weight" basis; not discounted for excess moisture and foreign material.* 5. *Consumption data are based on an aggregate of differing local marketing years. For countries for which stocks data are not available (excluding the U.S.S.R.), consumption estimates represent "apparent" consumption, ie, they are inclusive of annual stock level adjustments.* 6. *Stocks data are based on an aggregate of differing local marketing years and should not be construed as representing world stock levels at a fixed point in time. Stocks data are not available for all countries and exclude those such as the People's Republic of China and parts of Eastern Europe; the world stock levels have been adjusted for estimated year-to-year changes in U.S.S.R. grain stocks, but do not purport to include the entire absolute level of U.S.S.R. stocks.* 7. *Inclusive of Soviet stock changes; see footnote 6.*

By courtesy of the U.S. Department of Agriculture.

Soya Beans: Production and Exports 1965 to 1976

Item and Year	United States Seed	United States Oil	Brazil Seed	Brazil Oil	China, P. Rep. Seed	China, P. Rep. Oil[1]	Argentina Seed	Argentina Oil	Paraguay Seed	Paraguay Oil	Sub-total as oil	Other	Total as oil
					1,000 metric tons								
Production:[2]													
1965	19,076	3,174	523	83	6,940	553	17	3	18	3	3,816	118	3,934
1966	23,014	3,829	595	95	6,840	545	18	3	12	2	4,473	151	4,624
1967	25,269	4,204	716	114	6,800	542	20	3	18	3	4,866	190	5,056
1968	26,575	4,422	654	104	6,950	554	22	4	14	2	5,085	190	5,275
1969	30,127	5,013	1,057	168	6,480	516	32	5	45	7	5,709	216	5,925
1970	30,839	5,131	1,509	246	6,200	494	27	4	52	8	5,883	206	6,089
1971	30,675	5,104	2,077	338	6,900	550	59	10	75	12	6,013	253	6,266
1972	32,006	5,325	3,666	597	6,700	534	78	13	97	16	6,484	261	6,745
1973	34,581	5,754	5,000	814	6,500	518	272	44	122	20	7,150	261	7,411
1974	42,108	7,006	7,876	1,296	8,000	637	496	81	185	30	9,050	331	9,381
1975[3]	33,062	5,501	9,892	1,628	9,500	757	485	79	218	35	8,000	313	8,313
1976[4]	41,406	6,889	11,344	1,867	10,000	796	695	113	253	41	9,706	419	10,125
Exports:[5]													
1965	1,097	553	13	—	101	2	—	—	—	—	1,766	3	1,769
1966	1,195	394	21	—	99	4	—	—	1	—	1,714	4	1,718
1967	1,269	515	54	—	101	4	—	—	—	—	1,943	6	1,949
1968	1,419	434	12	—	100	3	—	—	1	—	1,969	8	1,977
1969	1,499	403	55	—	85	3	—	—	—	—	2,045	13	2,058
1970	2,116	681	51	3	75	2	—	—	—	1	2,929	9	2,938
1971	2,042	784	38	7	81	2	—	—	2	1	2,957	15	2,972
1972	2,123	595	184	60	65	—	—	—	7	—	3,034	20	3,054
1973	2,340	439	316	91	—	—	9	15	9	3	3,222	24	3,246
1974	2,467	762	483	2	—	—	13	29	18	1	3,775	23	3,798
1975[3]	2,212	356	590	264	40	—	13	19	18	—	3,512	23	3,535
1976[4]	2,675	495	710	480	10	—	27	35	27	2	4,461	24	4,485

1. Net exports. 2. Seed harvested in previous calendar year except Brazil. Oil Production estimated on the basis of average assumed extraction rates and crushings as indicated, and therefore represent potential rather than actual oil production. 3. Preliminary. 4. Forecast. 5. Exports of seed expressed as oil using assumed extraction rates as indicated. 6. 92 per cent beginning in 1970. 7. 93 per cent beginning in 1974.
Note: Totals computed from unrounded data.

By courtesy of the U.S. Department of Agriculture

Corn: Chicago

(MONTHLY HIGH, LOW & CLOSE OF NEAREST FUTURES)   CENTS PER BUSHEL

By courtesy of Commodity Research Bureau Incorporated

Wheat: Chicago

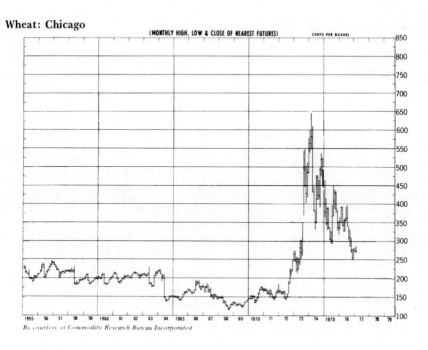

(MONTHLY HIGH, LOW & CLOSE OF NEAREST FUTURES)   CENTS PER BUSHEL

By courtesy of Commodity Research Bureau Incorporated

69

Soybeans: Chicago

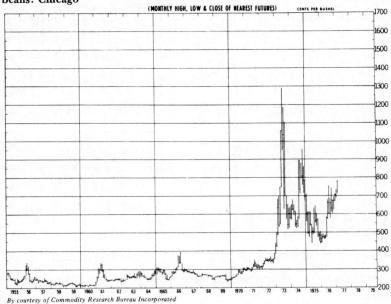

(MONTHLY HIGH, LOW & CLOSE OF NEAREST FUTURES)   CENTS PER BUSHEL

By courtesy of Commodity Research Bureau Incorporated

Soybean Meal: Chicago

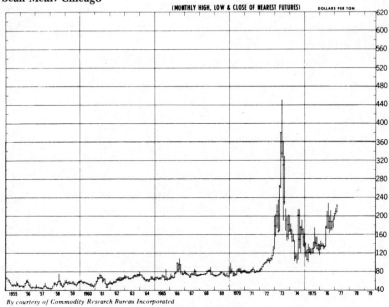

(MONTHLY HIGH, LOW & CLOSE OF NEAREST FUTURES)   DOLLARS PER TON

By courtesy of Commodity Research Bureau Incorporated

70

Soybean Oil: Chicago

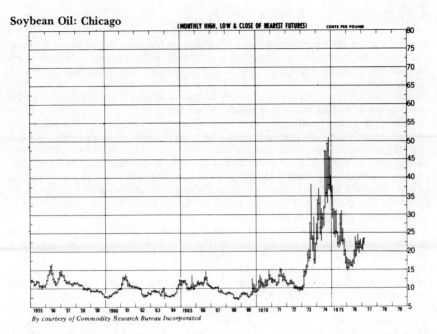

(MONTHLY HIGH, LOW & CLOSE OF NEAREST FUTURES)   CENTS PER POUND

By courtesy of Commodity Research Bureau Incorporated

Note:
Soya Beans have also been spelt as Soybeans, Soya Bean Oil as Soybean Oil and Soya Bean Meal as Soybean Meal as relating to different markets.

Lead

Lead is one of the earliest metals used by man. It has been found in the form of lead pans for plants in the hanging gardens of Babylon and was also used extensively in water piping by the Romans. It is a soft, easily worked metal, bluish grey in colour, which is manufactured by roasting the ore (galena) in a furnace. It has little mechanical strength and is almost without elasticity. Its most valued component is its resistance to corrosion.

Lead has a wide and varied range of uses. It is used in the chemical and pigment industries, in printing type, X-ray and nuclear work, some alloys, sheeting and cable sheathing, but its major use is in batteries. Some 40 per cent of the total consumption of refined lead is used for the manufacture of electric storage batteries. An additional 12 per cent is used in tetraethyl lead which is added to petrol to give it a higher octane rating. In the United States, however, from 1973 to the end of 1975, as a result of the Clean Air Act, the use of lead in petrol fell by some 25 per cent.

Competition has also been felt in certain areas, eg plumbing, where plastics and aluminium have been substituted for lead. Lead producers have made efforts to counter this substitution by promotion which includes new uses for lead. These have concentrated on lead-bonded materials for reducing noise levels; on television tubes and battery systems for peak power supply. Lead compounds are also used in the plastics industry.

The United States, the Soviet Union, Australia, Canada, Mexico and Peru are the primary lead-producing countries and account for more than 60 per cent of total world output. Mine production overall has risen by 15 per cent since 1967 but consumption has outstripped production and the deficit has been met from scrap recycling, mostly from batteries. Scrap recovery is very high, at times accounting for as much as 60 per cent of total supplies.

World consumption of lead has risen by 3.6 per cent since 1958 and by 4.8 per cent from 1968 to 1973. This increase is accounted for by battery usage, since the demand for lead in other areas has remained more or less constant. Canada and Australia are the two leading exporters of lead. In the United States approximately 80 per cent self-sufficiency in lead production has now been achieved and mine output has risen 85 per cent since 1967. This is largely due to the development of the lead belt in Missouri. These deposits are unusual in that lead has been found with no silver, zinc or other such economic by-products. Lead is more often discovered in combination with zinc ores, and zinc and lead are therefore mined together.

The producer price system is the dominant one in North America but the pricing policies of primary producers are greatly influenced by fluctuations of the secondary market. Producers such as Peru, Mexico and Zambia which have difficulties in cutting back on production in times of oversupply contribute towards the difficulties in maintaining price stability, but the main problem arises from the preponderance of scrap lead from producers primarily concerned with their profit margins and not with the market price.

The London Metal Exchange provides the basis for prices outside the US as well as influencing the US producer price. Active participation by lead producers on the Metal Exchange assists in maintaining price stability while allowing the market to reflect supply-demand trends.

Lead: World Mine Production 1971 to 1976

THOUSAND METRIC TONS

	1971	1972	1973	1974	1975	1976				
						Jan-Mar	Mar	Apr	May	June
EUROPE										
Austria	6·4	5·7	5·2	5·8	4·8	1·3	0·6	0·3	0·4	0·4
Finland	4·7	3·8	2·1	1·5	0·9	0·3	0·1	0·1	0·2	0·1
France	29·8	26·6	25·0	23·5	21·9	7·3	2·5	2·5	2·2	2·5
Germany, Federal Republic ..	50·1	46·2	45·4	42·7	43·4	11·6	3·9	3·6	3·4	
Greece	12·2	16·3	18·8	22·6	24·0	4·8	1·6	1·6	1·6	1·6
Greenland	–	–	5·7	24·1	24·3	6·4	2·2	2·4	2·3	2·4
Irish Republic	51·6	59·6	56·2	37·7	36·3	9·0	3·0	3·0	3·0	3·0
Italy	31·6	33·7	25·9	22·7	26·8	6·2	2·2	2·2	2·5	
Norway	3·2	3·2	3·3	3·1	3·2	1·0	0·4	0·3	0·3	
Portugal	1·4	1·2	0·5	1·1	1·2	0·3	0·1	0·1	0·1	0·1
Spain	69·5	69·0	63·9	60·7	57·8	13·5	4·3	5·4	4·6	
Sweden	79·5	75·8	75·8	72·7	68·8	19·4	6·2	6·8	7·3	
United Kingdom	1·5	0·4	0·2	4·0	0·2	–	–	–	–	–
Yugoslavia	124·3	120·2	119·3	119·8	132·0	33·0	11·0	11·0	11·0	11·0
Total ..	465·8	461·7	447·3	442·0	445·6	114·1	38·1	39·3	38·9	
AFRICA										
Algeria	4·7	5·0	3·9	3·1	4·8	0·9	0·3	0·3	0·3	0·3
Morocco	78·5	86·1	93·2	86·3	69·9	24·0	8·0	8·0	8·0	8·0
South Africa	–	–	1·3	2·5	2·7	–	–	–	–	
South West Africa	73·2	59·0	63·3	51·3	48·8	11·6	3·7	3·2	3·0	
Tunisia	18·8	18·7	14·8	12·5	18·0	3·9	1·3	1·3	1·3	1·3
Zambia	33·9	31·4	25·3	25·2	19·4	4·6	1·7	1·8	1·3	0·5
Congo Brazzaville	–	0·5	1·3	1·7	1·2	0·3	0·1	0·1	0·1	0·1
Total ..	209·1	200·7	203·1	182·6	164·8	45·3	15·1	14·7	14·0	
ASIA										
Burma	8·9	7·6	9·8	10·0	12·0	3·0	1·0	1·0	1·0	1·0
India	3·3	3·7	7·3	8·9	9·7	2·4	0·8	0·8	0·8	0·8
Iran	24·0	33·0	37·5	47·5	42·0	10·5	3·5	3·5	3·5	3·5
Japan	70·6	63·4	52·9	44·2	50·6	12·7	4·5	4·4	4·1	4·6
South Korea	10·6	9·4	12·9	10·6	10·1	1·8	0·6	0·7	0·7	
Turkey	7·0	6·8	9·3	4·7	6·0	1·5	0·5	0·5	0·5	
Thailand	2·3	3·0	3·7	1·6	3·6	0·9	0·3	0·3	0·3	0·3
Other	–	–	0·2	1·8	–					
Total ..	126·7	126·9	133·6	129·3	134·0	32·8	11·2	11·2	10·9	
AMERICA										
Canada	394·8	376·3	387·8	301·4	352·5	70·8	26·7	20·2	29·1	20·7
U.S.A.	546·7	584·9	569·8	615·8	575·4	148·5	53·8	46·8	47·1	
Argentina	36·0	38·4	35·0	35·0	36·0	9·0	3·0	3·0	3·0	3·0
Bolivia[(1)]	23·2	20·4	20·2	19·4	20·4	4·5	1·5	1·5	1·5	1·5
Brazil	27·0	29·9	26·9	27·4	30·0	7·5	2·5	2·5	2·5	2·5
Mexico	173·7	161·4	179·3	218·0	180·0	51·0	17·0	17·0	17·0	17·0
Peru	147·4	189·0	198·6	193·0	165·6	45·0	15·0	15·0	15·0	15·0
Other	27·0	20·6	21·9	25·5	24·0	6·0	2·0	2·0	2·0	2·0
Total ..	1 375·8	1 420·9	1 439·5	1 435·5	1 383·9	342·3	121·5	108·0	117·2	
AUSTRALASIA										
Australia	403·6	396·0	402·8	375·3	408·6	86·4	32·8	29·9	30·0	
New Zealand	1·0	1·6	0·6	–	–	–	–	–	–	
Total ..	404·6	397·6	403·4	375·3	408·6	86·4	32·8	29·9	30·0	
TOTAL ..	**2 582·0**	**2 607·8**	**2 626·9**	**2 564·7**	**2 536·9**	**620·9**	**218·7**	**203·1**	**211·0**	
Monthly Average ..	*215·2*	*217·3*	*218·9*	*213·7*	*211·4*	*206·7*				
OTHER COUNTRIES										
Bulgaria	100·0	102·0	105·0	110·0	108·0	27·0	9·0	9·0	9·0	9·0
Czechoslovakia*	5·8	5·6	5·3	5·0	6·0	1·5	0·5	0·5	0·5	0·5
Germany, Democratic Republic* ..	5·0	5·0	3·0	–	3·6	0·9	0·3	0·3	0·3	0·3
Hungary	2·5	2·4	3·0	3·0	3·6	0·9	0·3	0·3	0·3	0·3
Poland	65·0	68·0	69·5	70·0	72·0	18·0	6·0	6·0	6·0	6·0
Roumania*	40·0	45·0	45·0	45·0	42·0	10·5	3·5	3·5	3·5	3·5
U.S.S.R.*	500·0	530·0	570·0	590·0	504·0	150·0	50·0	50·0	50·0	50·0
China P.R.*	120·0	125·0	130·0	140·0	132·0	36·0	12·0	12·0	12·0	12·0
North Korea*	80·0	80·0	90·0	100·0	100·8	25·2	8·4	8·4	8·4	8·4
Total ..	918·3	963·0	1 020·8	1 063·0	972·0	270·0	90·0	90·0	90·0	90·0
WORLD TOTAL	**3 500·3**	**3 570·8**	**3 647·7**	**3 627·7**	**3 508·9**	**890·9**	**308·7**	**293·1**	**301·0**	
Monthly Average	*291·7*	*297·6*	*304·0*	*302·3*	*292·4*	*296·7*				

In this table the accounting is based on the lead content by analysis of lead ores and concentrates plus the lead content of mixed ores and concentrates known to be intended for treatment for lead recovery. Some of the data for the latest months are provisional.

Notes (1) Exports

By courtesy of the World Bureau of Metal Statistics.

Lead: World Refined Production 1971 to 1976

THOUSAND METRIC TONS

	1971	1972	1973	1974	1975	1976 Jan-Mar	Mar	Apr	May	June
EUROPE										
Austria	14·0	15·5	14·7	15·6	15·1	3·8	1·4	1·4	1·6	1·4
Belgium	84·1	97·4	103·0	99·6	103·0	20·0	10·8	10·5	9·1	9·1
Denmark	11·4	12·0	13·4	14·9	13·0	4·5	1·9	1·6	1·5	1·5
France	158·5	186·9	186·4	177·7	150·7	47·7	17·3	16·8	16·7	16·6
Germany, Federal Republic	302·0	273·4	302·6	321·4	260·2	63·7	23·1	22·3	24·4	23·3
Greece	19·8	20·4	24·0	14·6	12·8	4·0	1·5	1·5	1·5	1·5
Italy	75·8	69·2	50·4	74·0	77·8	22·0	8·0	7·0	6·0	6·0
Netherlands	23·6	22·0	25·3	26·4	23·9	6·0	2·1	1·8	2·1	1·0
Norway	1·0	0·7	0·9	1·2	1·2	0·3	0·1	0·1	0·1	0·1
Portugal	1·2	1·2	1·0	1·1	1·2	0·3	0·1	0·1	0·1	0·1
Spain	75·4	84·4	90·7	82·0	80·1	19·7	6·9	5·0	4·9	5·0
Sweden	44·8	45·3	42·4	40·9	36·9	10·0	3·3	3·4	2·0	4·6
United Kingdom	263·6	270·6	265·1	276·9	228·5	53·5	22·6	18·9	21·8	20·1
Yugoslavia	99·1	87·5	98·0	113·9	126·1	28·3	11·3	9·7	10·5	9·8
Total	1 174·3	1 186·5	1 217·9	1 260·2	1 130·5	283·8	110·4	100·1	102·3	100·1
AFRICA										
Morocco	18·7	–	–	–	–	3·0	1·0	1·0	1·0	1·0
South West Africa	69·8	64·7	66·7	64·2	44·3	8·6	3·2	2·7	4·6	
Tunisia	18·8	25·9	26·9	27·5	23·7	6·0				
Zambia	28·3	30·2	25·4	24·7	18·9	4·5	1·6	1·8	1·3	0·5
Total	135·6	120·8	119·0	116·4	86·9	22·1				
ASIA										
Burma	8·9	7·6	9·8	10·0	12·0	3·0	1·0	1·0	1·0	1·0
India	2·4	2·7	2·6	4·0	4·8	1·4	0·5	0·3	0·4	0·5
Iran	–	–	–	0·3	0·4	0·1	0·1	–	–	0·1
Japan	215·1	223·2	228·0	227·9	194·2	53·3	18·0	19·6	17·8	18·5
Turkey	3·2	2·4	5·5	5·6	2·2	0·6	0·2	0·2	0·2	0·2
South Korea	3·3	3·8	4·6	4·8	4·8	1·2	0·4	0·4	0·4	0·4
Total	232·9	239·7	250·5	252·6	218·4	59·6	20·2	21·5	19·8	20·7
AMERICA										
Canada	168·3	186·9	187·0	126·4	171·5	50·9	17·1	16·0	16·0	16·3
U.S.A.	715·9	766·2	759·3	751·5	751·5	194·4	63·9	67·4		
Argentina	43·8	35·3	32·2	35·0	39·6	9·9	3·3	3·3	3·3	3·3
Brazil	45·7	47·0	58·8	62·8	76·0	15·0	5·0	5·0	5·0	5·0
Mexico	154·7	161·3	188·9	201·9	178·0	45·0				
Peru	68·0	85·5	82·9	80·6	71·0	18·0				
Total	1 196·4	1 282·2	1 309·1	1 258·2	1 287·6	333·2				
AUSTRALIA	193·4	208·8	220·9	224·8	189·8	47·2	16·0	15·5		
TOTAL	2 932·6	3 038·0	3 117·4	3 112·2	2 913·2	745·9				
Monthly Average	244·4	253·2	259·8	259·4	242·8	248·6				
OTHER COUNTRIES										
Bulgaria	102·2	102·0	100·0	105·0	108·0	27·0	9·0	9·0	9·0	9·0
Czechoslovakia*	17·6	18·2	16·7	18·0	18·0	4·5	1·5	1·5	1·5	1·5
Germany, Democratic Repbulic*	32·0	33·0	35·6	35·0	36·0	9·0	3·0	3·0	3·0	3·0
Poland	60·2	65·3	68·4	70·0	66·0	16·5	5·5	5·5	5·5	5·5
Roumania*	40·0	45·0	45·0	45·0	42·0	10·5	3·5	3·5	3·5	3·5
U.S.S.R.*	580·0	600·0	640·0	660·0	600·0	150·0	50·0	50·0	50·0	50·0
China P.R.*	120·0	125·0	130·0	140·0	132·0	33·0	11·0	11·0	11·0	11·0
North Korea*	55·0	60·0	60·0	65·0	60·0	15·0	5·0	5·0	5·0	5·0
Total	1 007·0	1 048·5	1 095·7	1 138·0	1 062·0	265·5	88·5	88·5	88·5	88·5
WORLD TOTAL	3 939·6	4 086·5	4 213·1	4 250·2	3 975·2	1 011·4				
Monthly Average	328·3	340·5	351·1	354·2	331·3	337·1				

In this table accounting is based on production of refined pig lead including the lead content of primary antimonial lead and excluding remelted pig lead and secondary antimonial lead. Some of the data for the latest months are provisional.

By courtesy of The World Bureau of Metal Statistics.

Lead: World Refined Consumption 1971 to 1976

THOUSAND METRIC TONS

	1971	1972	1973	1974	1975	1976 Jan-Mar	Feb	Mar	Apr	May
EUROPE										
Austria	26·6	29·5	29·9	34·9	29·1	9·4				
Belgium	49·2	48·1	52·4	63·5	49·9	12·0				
Denmark	23·3	20·4	18·9	22·9	17·7	5·2				
Finland	9·8	12·0	13·0	13·4	13·9	4·0				
France	188·4	202·0	213·7	199·4	188·5	53·6				
Germany, Federal Republic ..	286·5	273·5	293·7	265·2	221·4	64·2				
Greece	27·0	39·1	43·6	26·5	30·0	7·5	2·5	2·5	2·5	2·5
Irish Republic	1·0	2·3	2·0	1·7	2·4	0·9	0·3	0·3	0·3	0·3
Italy	178·0	186·0	184·0	204·0	195·0	36·0	17·0			
Netherlands	49·2	41·4	37·9	39·2	42·0	10·5	3·5	3·5	3·5	3·5
Norway	12·5	12·5	14·0	14·5	14·8	3·7				
Portugal .. .. .. ,.	10·0	11·2	11·5	12·0	12·0	3·0	1·0	1·0	1·0	1·0
Spain	79·7	87·8	100·4	96·3	73·5	20·0				
Sweden	42·9	33·5	33·7	34·2	32·9	11·0				
Switzerland	22·3	20·8	15·7	21·0	12·6	4·0				
United Kingdom	276·7	278·4	282·2	266·4	237·8	65·2	22·1	20·8	21·0	20·7
Yugoslavia	53·2	55·0	69·6	72·0	72·0	18·0	6·0	6·0	6·0	6·0
Other Europe	0·1	0·1	0·1	0·1	0·1	–	–	–	–	–
Total ..	1 336·4	1 353·6	1 416·3	1 387·2	1 245·6	328·2				
AFRICA										
South Africa	27·0	25·8	26·7	30·5	37·0	8·2	3·3	3·0	3·0	2·6
Zambia	6·0	6·0	6·0	5·9	6·0	1·5	0·5	0·5	0·5	0·5
Other	13·0	17·0	15·9	13·8	20·0	6·0	2·0	2·0	2·0	2·0
Total ..	46·0	48·8	48·6	50·2	63·0	15·7	5·8	5·5	5·5	5·1
ASIA										
India	33·0	41·0	41·4	42·7	48·0	12·0	4·0	4·0	4·0	4·0
Japan	209·7	231·0	267·3	224·2	189·4	55·2	18·5	19·9	18·2	17·8
Turkey	6·5	8·0	10·0	14·2	12·0	3·0	1·0	1·0	1·0	1·0
Other	40·0	40·0	53·8	58·3	54·0	12·0	4·0	4·0	4·0	4·0
Total ..	289·2	320·0	372·5	339·4	303·4	82·2	27·5	28·9	27·2	26·8
AMERICA										
Canada	54·7	63·8	69·1	71·1	57·5	25·3				
U.S.A.	938·9	1 016·3	1 093·2	1 032·8	811·0	225·0				
Argentina	44·0	37·2	32·9	38·0	42·0	10·5	3·5	3·5	3·5	3·5
Brazil	54·0	52·5	54·5	61·8	79·0	15·0	5·0	5·0	5·0	5·0
Mexico	93·2	92·0	99·6	94·0	102·0	25·5	8·5	8·5	8·5	8·5
Peru	6·9	7·9	10·4	10·0	7·8	2·1	0·7	0·7	0·7	0·7
Other	12·0	10·0	13·2	11·9	15·6	3·9	1·3	1·3	1·3	1·3
Total ..	1 203·7	1 279·7	1 372·9	1 319·6	1 114·9	307·3				
AUSTRALASIA										
Australia	63·0	63·3	73·7	71·5	67·5	18·6	7·1	7·9	9·8	4·1
New Zealand	5·0	7·2	6·0	8·1	7·0	1·5	0·5	0·5	0·5	0·5
Total ..	68·0	70·5	79·7	79·6	74·5	20·1	7·6	8·4	10·3	4·6
TOTAL	2 943·3	3 072·6	3 290·0	3 176·0	2 801·4	753·5				
Monthly Average ..	*245·3*	*256·1*	*274·2*	*264·7*	*233·5*	*251·2*				
OTHER COUNTRIES*										
Albania	2·0	2·0	2·0	2·0	2·4	0·6	0·2	0·2	0·2	0·2
Bulgaria	80·0	80·0	80·0	85·0	84·0	21·0	7·0	7·0	7·0	7·0
Czechoslavakia	44·6	48·8	48·7	53·0	54·0	13·5	4·5	4·5	4·5	4·5
Germany, Democratic Republic	80·0	80·0	85·0	88·0	102·0	22·5	7·5	7·5	7·5	7·5
Hungary	14·8	15·0	13·6	15·0	15·6	3·9	1·3	1·3	1·3	1·3
Poland	78·8	81·8	87·0	90·0	84·0	22·5	7·5	7·5	7·5	7·5
Roumania	35·0	40·0	40·0	45·0	39·6	10·5	3·5	3·5	3·5	3·5
U.S.S.R.	530·0	560·0	600·0	620·0	546·0	156·0	52·0	52·0	52·0	52·0
China P.R.	170·0	180·0	170·0	175·0	180·0	45·0	15·0	15·0	15·0	15·0
North Korea	20·0	20·0	20·0	20·0	20·4	5·1	1·7	1·7	1·7	1·7
Total ..	1 055·2	1 107·6	1 146·3	1 193·0	1 128·0	300·6	100·2	100·2	100·2	100·2
WORLD TOTAL	3 998·5	4 180·2	4 436·3	4 369·0	3 929·4	1 054·1				
Monthly Average	*333·2*	*348·4*	*369·7*	*364·1*	*327·5*	*351·4*				

In this table the accounting is based on the consumption of refined pig lead and the lead content of antimonial lead. Remelted pig lead and remelted antimonial lead are excluded. Some of the data for the latest months are provisional.

By courtesy of the World Bureau of Metal Statistics.

Lead: London

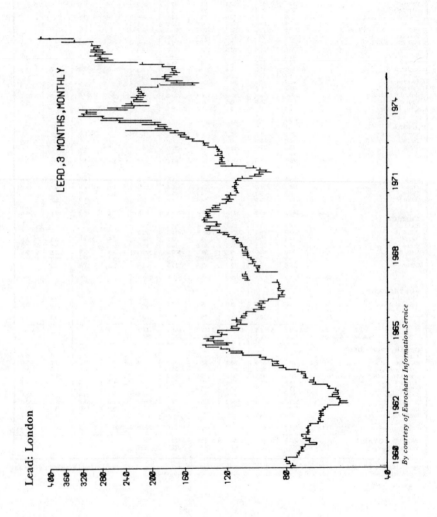

LEAD, 3 MONTHS, MONTHLY

By courtesy of Eurocharts Information Service

Rubber

Natural rubber production is dominated by Malaysia, which produces nearly half the world's total output. Other important producing countries are Indonesia (the second biggest producer), Thailand, Sri Lanka and India. Rubber trees were first introduced into Malaysia from plants smuggled from the Amazon when Brazil was the leading world producer many years ago. An interesting feature of Malaysian rubber production is that in recent years the main expansion in output has come from smallholdings, with the active encouragement of Government, and these now produce considerably more than the estates, which used to be the dominant producing sector.

Rubber is obtained by 'tapping' the tree for the liquid that drips into a bowl and coagulates. It is then treated in various ways to produce the different types required for a wide range of uses. The manufacture of tyres is the biggest market. Apart from a short 'wintering' period, the tree produces all the year round and supplies can only be controlled to a limited extent in the short term by halting 'tapping' or by not using the chemical stimulants that help to improve yields. In the longer term, output depends on the number of trees planted. Market prices move strongly in line with the economies in industrialized areas that are the main buyers and demand is especially influenced by the state of the motor industry and tyre trade.

There is another problem in respect of rubber in that synthetically produced rubber can be tailored close to the consumers' requirements and therefore presents competition. Synthetic rubber production has grown enormously over the years and world output is now more than double that of natural rubber. However, the oil crisis has presented synthetic rubber manufacturers with considerable problems about future expansion, and natural rubber has continued to expand the markets where it has a special advantage, such as in radial tyres where natural rubber is an essential ingredient. Over the years Malaysia has played a leading role in keeping up natural rubber prices during periods of depressed demand by buying up surplus stocks and selling them later when prices have recovered. However, it is now seeking to share this burden with other producers, and UNCTAD is anxious to include rubber in its integrated programme for commodity stabilization.

London has the main futures market for rubber, with the market in New York inactive. But the price is largely set in Kuala Lumpur and Singapore where the bulk of trading in physical supplies is centred.

Natural Rubber: World Production 1965 to 1975

	Malaysia	Indonesia	Thailand[1]	Sri Lanka	Viet-nam	Cam-bodia	India	Africa[2]	Brazil	Others[3]	Total Estates	Total Small-holders	Grand Total[4]
	In '000 tons										*In '000 tons*		
1965	916,935	716,466	216,405	118,311	60,963	48,917	49,387	159,250	29,291	31,750	1,067.5	1,285.0	2,352.5
1966	972,837	736,675	207,535	131,015	48,841	51,330	53,195	176,500	24,347	31,000	1,087.5	1,305.0	2,392.5
1967	990,446	700,834	216,119	143,204	40,631	53,663	62,339	163,000	21,494	32,250	1,102.5	1,420.0	2,522.5
1968	1,100,284	793,910	259,221	148,719	29,696	51,332	68,845	169,000	22,958	40,750	1,145.0	1,540.0	2,685.0
1969	1,268,014	880,426	283,381	150,834	26,151	51,836	79,951	182,000	23,950	43,500	1,205.0	1,790.0	2,995.0
1970	1,269,203	815,161	287,163	159,158	28,458	12,763	89,905	213,000	24,976	44,506	1,227.5	1,875.0	3,102.5
1971	1,318,518	819,311	316,323	141,409	34,533	1,147	98,884	203,750	24,231	53,500	1,245.0	1,840.0	3,085.0
1972	1,304,147	773,655	336,919	140,371	20,294	15,312	109,137	208,500	25,818	58,500	1,250.0	1,870.0	3,120.0
1973	1,542,323	885,802	381,954	154,675	20,619	16,500	123,232	224,500	23,402	68,000	1,292.5	2,212.5	3,505.0
1974	1,549,298	854,964	379,188	132,008	21,979	17,750	128,351	232,750	18,606	84,000	1,300.0	2,140.0	3,440.0
1975	1,477,582	825,000	348,737	148,751	20,000	10,000	136,019	211,000	19,348	93,500	1,200.0	2,100.0	3,300.0

1. Exports plus consumption. 2. Equivalent to net exports plus local consumption. 3. See following Table. 4. Including allowances for apparent discrepancies in officially reported statistics.

By courtesy of the Rubber Statistical Bulletin.

Natural Rubber: Production in Other Countries 1965 to 1975

	Brunei[2]	Burma[1]	China	Papua New Guinea[2]	Philip-pines[3]	Singa-pore	Portuguese Timor	Other Latin America	Total
1965	801	10,520	—	5,697	6,150	1,309	243	7,000	31,750
1966	680	9,338	—	5,743	6,450	1,498	204	7,000	31,000
1967	400	6,851	—	5,696	10,400	1,660	150	7,000	32,250
1968	136	9,800	—	5,689	16,350	1,734	140	7,000	40,750
1969	320	10,000	—	5,966	18,800	1,347	148	7,000	44,500
1970	314	9,641	—	6,460	20,100	1,000	123	7,000	44,500
1971	166	11,887	5,000	5,966	21,300	1,066	152	8,000	53,500
1972	70	10,000	10,000	5,932	22,400	949	100	9,000	58,500
1973	362	10,000	15,000	5,885	25,850	942	150	10,000	68,000
1974	515	14,914	20,000	5,553	31,550	274	150	11,000	84,000
1975	—	15,750	25,000	5,532	35,000	66	—	12,000	93,500

1. Up to 1973: Exports, plus local consumption. 2. Has been taken as equivalent to exports.
3. Estimated on the basis of reported production for crop years, ending June 30th.

By courtesy of the Rubber Statistical Bulletin.

Natural Rubber: World Consumption 1965 to 1975

Year	United States of America	United Kingdom	France	Germany, Federal Republic	Italy	Nether-lands	Total E.E.C.[1]	Other Western Europe[2]	Eastern Europe
1965	522,966	186,700	122,515	157,861	87,000	20,800	602,500	135,000	425,000
1966	554,435	183,900	125,987	157,604	91,400	22,550	607,500	142,500	430,000
1967	496,693	178,500	127,821	141,338	100,000	19,700	595,000	137,500	445,000
1968	591,201	194,100	128,810	170,000	100,000	20,566	645,000	150,000	460,000
1969	607,872	191,400	149,511	191,241	102,000	20,357	687,500	160,000	465,000
1970	568,290	188,200	158,229	200,725	113,000	22,000	717,500	177,500	465,000
1971	587,080	187,200	159,203	198,247	121,000	22,000	720,000	195,000	475,000
1972	650,878	174,000	160,154	192,997	118,000	23,200	698,750	202,500	485,000
1973	697,961	173,100	162,265	205,592	120,000	23,353	717,250	205,000	490,000
1974	733,126	166,500	162,367	193,938	125,000	24,750	707,500	222,500	500,000
1975	669,966	170,500	156,204	197,101	118,000	24,104	695,750	212,500	450,000

Year	China	Australia	Brazil	Canada	India	Japan	Others[2]	Total Rest of World[4]	Grand Total[3]
1965	140,000	38,970	26,554	43,480	64,675	201,500	236,500	611,750	2,447,500
1966	155,000	37,630	30,862	47,268	66,693	216,000	248,500	646,000	2,542,500
1967	165,000	37,280	32,133	46,113	72,516	243,000	257,500	788,500	2,535,000
1968	180,000	43,960	38,156	45,477	84,206	255,000	289,750	756,500	2,780,000
1969	195,000	42,030	35,072	49,664	86,692	268,000	317,500	799,000	2,910,000
1970	210,000	40,170	36,739	50,616	86,469	283,000	345,000	842,000	2,992,500
1971	212,500	40,500	41,761	52,030	93,125	295,000	382,500	905,000	3,095,000
1972	215,000	46,330	44,219	60,355	101,100	312,000	420,000	984,000	3,235,000
1973	217,500	52,090	51,156	60,446	123,298	335,000	452,500	1,074,500	3,402,500
1974	220,000	59,360	57,945	63,306	133,538	312,000	505,000	1,131,250	3,515,000
1975	220,000	49,878	58,704	72,295	129,138	285,200	480,000	1,075,250	3,322,500

1. The figures from 1965, include estimates for consumption in Belgium, Denmark, the Republic of Ireland and Luxemburg. 2. Estimated consumption arrived at by correcting net Imports to allow for working stocks at 1.5 months' consumption. 3. Including allowances for discrepancies in officially reported statistics. 4. Excluding Eastern Europe and China.

By courtesy of the Rubber Statistical Bulletin.

Rubber: London

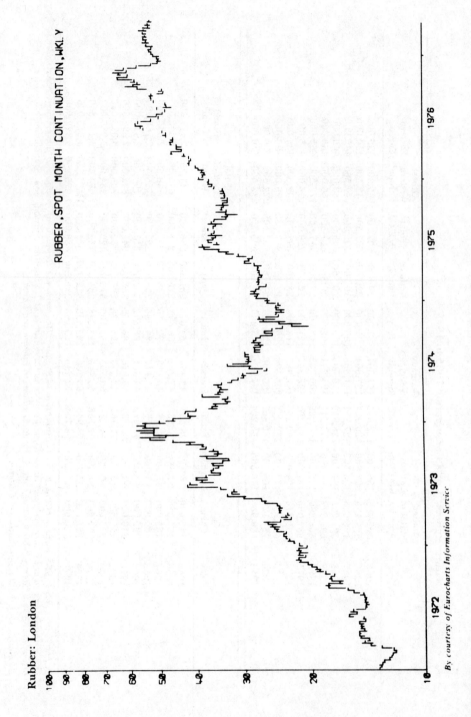

RUBBER.SPOT MONTH CONTINUATION.WKLY

By courtesy of Eurocharts Information Service

Rubber: Singapore

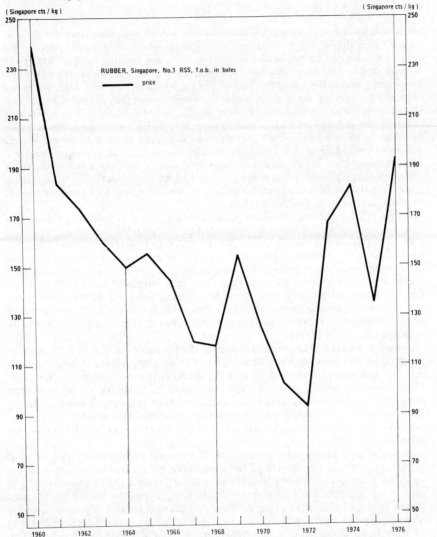

(Singapore cts / kg)

RUBBER, Singapore, No.1 RSS, f.o.b. in bales
—— price

a/ Nominal prices divided by the United Nations index of export unit values of manufactured goods (see table 6, page 3).
By courtesy of UNCTAD Commodities Division

Silver

Silver has been valued as a precious metal for a very long time, but it is only in recent times that it has become one of the most active and popular commodity futures markets — traded in Chicago, New York and London. Its past history in coinage and in jewellery, and its close links with gold, have classified silver as a 'monetary' metal for a lengthy period during which prices were kept stable by large stocks held by the United States Treasury that it was prepared to sell at a known price. But the disposal of these stocks, and the gradual disappearance of silver in the coinage of most countries because of its increasing value as a raw material, have to a large extent cut its links with gold and the monetary system and transformed silver into a commodity like the base metals — copper, lead and zinc. In fact, silver is very much an industrial metal, used for a wide variety of products ranging from photography — its biggest single outlet — to electrical goods, sterling ware and alloys, as well as in jewellery and by a growing market in commemorative and collection sets.

Silver is an excellent conductor of electricity, very resistant to corrosion and light sensitive in its silver nitrate form. It has all the attributes of an important base metal as well as being valued for its pleasing appearance. These elements have assisted in elevating silver into the role of a precious metal. Its links are even closer with base metals, since these days the bulk of new silver production comes as a by-product when mining copper, lead, zinc and other metals. There are still mines where large quantities of silver are produced as the main metal, but the cost of mining pure silver ore bodies tends to be very high. As a result of being produced for the most part as a by-product, silver output is less price sensitive than other metals.

Another unusual feature about silver is the fundamental deficit between new production and consumption. This varies year by year, largely through the rise and fall in demand, but each year a big shortfall in new production has to be filled from the 'mine' above the ground — that is, reclaimed supplies of silver already used plus the vast quantities that have been mined and hoarded during the past centuries. Silver price behaviour is, therefore, important in persuading holders of these surplus stocks that it is worth selling them to help fill the supply shortfall.

Silver is as a result very sensitive to the general confidence in the value of 'paper' money and the effects of inflation. Like gold it has been used over the years as a means of storing wealth in a handy, convenient form against the ravages of war, currency changes and inflation. There are known to be large stocks held in India, for example, which are exported either legally or illegally when prices rise sufficiently to make the holders think it worthwhile selling and possibly exchanging for gold. Apart from steady industrial usage, which fluctuates year by year depending on economic activity, there is a constant interest in silver from a large body of speculators, gambling on whether the price has risen too fast and is due for a fall, or whether further price increases are likely. Reflecting the increasing concern about inflation, and the breakdown on the international exchange rate system, silver prices in recent years have moved strongly upwards despite some notable setbacks. The biggest volume markets are in New York and Chicago, but there is also extensive trading activity in London via the bullion market, which handles the bulk of physical transactions, and the London Metal Exchange where the silver futures market opened in 1968 in response to the changed situation of this metal.

Silver: World Supplies 1972 to 1976 (excluding Communist dominated areas)

	1972	1973	1974	1975	1976
New Production:		*Millions of ounces*			
Western Hemisphere:					
Mexico	37.5	38.8	37.5	42.0	42.1
United States	37.2	37.5	33.8	34.1	34.0
Canada	44.8	47.5	42.8	39.1	41.0
Peru	40.2	42.0	41.0	38.0	40.0
Other South and Central Amercian countries	18.2	17.2	18.9	18.0	18.4
Total	177.9	183.0	174.0	171.2	175.5
Outside the Western Hemisphere:					
Australia	21.9	22.4	21.6	22.0	23.0
Other Countries	45.9	49.7	45.9	45.0	45.5
Total	67.8	72.1	67.5	67.0	68.5
Total new production	245.7	255.1	241.5	238.2	244.0
Other sources of supply:					
From U.S. Treasury	2.3	0.9	1.0	2.7	1.3
From stocks of foreign governments	10.0	50.0	20.0	10.0	10.0
From demonetized coin	15.0	15.0	35.0	20.0	50.0
From Indian stocks	19.0	39.0	42.0	53.0	55.0
Salvage and other misc. sources	45.3	60.5	55.6	70.6	71.7
Liquidation of (additions to) private bullion stocks	90.0	80.0	50.0	—	(10.0)
Total other supplies	181.6	245.4	203.6	156.3	178.0
Available for world consumption	427.3	500.5	445.1	394.5	422.0

Note: *Figures for 1976 are preliminary.*　　　　　　　　*By courtesy of Handy & Harman.*

Silver: World Consumption 1972 to 1976 (excluding Communist dominated areas)

	1972	1973	1974	1975	1976
		Millions of ounces			
Industrial uses:					
United States	151.7	196.4	177.0	157.7	167.5
Canada	7.4	9.6	8.6	7.7	6.5
Mexico	7.0	11.8	6.5	6.0	7.0
United Kingdom	27.0	31.0	35.0	27.5	28.0
France	16.5	14.3	13.2	18.0	19.0
West Germany	60.0	64.7	49.4	44.0	42.0
Italy	32.0	33.5	30.0	26.0	28.0
Japan	54.3	69.0	57.7	46.4	56.0
India	13.0	13.0	15.0	13.0	18.0
Other countries	20.0	28.0	25.0	19.0	23.0
Total industrial uses	388.9	471.3	417.4	365.3	395.0
Coinage:					
United States	2.3	0.9	1.0	2.7	1.3
Canada	0.1	1.4	8.6	10.0	6.0
Austria	5.8	6.6	5.6	5.0	5.5
France	0.3	0.1	3.6	3.0	5.8
West Germany	22.6	9.5	8.8	5.5	1.8
Other countries	7.3	10.7	0.1	3.0	6.6
Total coinage	38.4	29.2	27.7	29.2	27.0
Total consumption	427.3	500.5	445.1	394.5	422.0

Note: *Figures for 1976 are preliminary.*　　　　　　　　*By courtesy of Handy & Harman.*

Silver: London

By courtesy of Eurocharts Information Service

Silver: New York

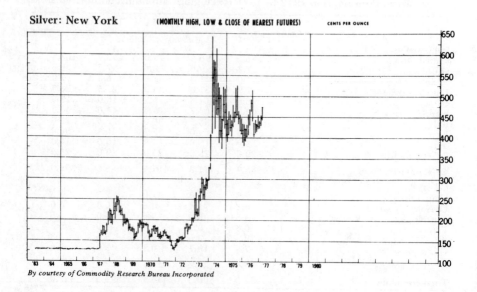

By courtesy of Commodity Research Bureau Incorporated

Sugar

Sugar is produced in either one or both of two forms — beet and cane — virtually in every country throughout the world. Cane sugar production takes place in the tropical or semi-tropical countries, including many developing nations. The sugar is obtained by crushing the cane in sugar mills to squeeze out the raw sugar that is later refined into the product, used either by the consumer in various forms ranging from cubes to icing sugar, or by industry, particularly the confectionery and catering trades where it is often supplied in liquid form as well for easier usage, storage and transportation. By-products of cane sugar include bagasse (the crushed cane) and molasses, as well as rum, syrup and treacle.

Beet sugar is a totally different product in that it is a root crop, somewhat similar to turnips, grown in temperate climates including the leading industrialized nations in Europe, and in the Soviet Union and the United States. It is an annually planted crop, favoured by farmers not only for the quick cash return but also as a 'break' crop used to 'clean' up fields planted with grains on a rotational basis.

The sugar squeezed out of the beet by the processor and later refined is virtually indistinguishable, even by experts, from cane sugar in the end product. The remnants of the beet, once crushed, provide a valuable source of animal feed as an addition to farm incomes.

Production of beet and cane varies each year, according to weather conditions in the main producing areas, but on average cane accounts for between 55 and 60 per cent of total world output that in 1976 was around 85m tonnes — double the world crop about 20 years ago.

The growth in consumption of sugar is associated with the general rise in the standard of living world-wide. But there have been extreme price fluctuations on the world market, ranging from a low of £12 a long ton to over £650 a tonne within a ten-year period. This is because world trade in sugar is restricted by the growth in domestic production, especially in the European Community, and by special trade deals and agreements between groups of countries that leave only a relatively small percentage to be traded on the so-called world 'free' market, represented by the terminal markets in London, Paris and New York. For example, out of a total world output of cane and beet sugar of 81.6m tonnes in 1975, it is estimated that only about 13m tonnes was exported via the 'free' market. The bulk of these exports were cane sugar made up of roughly 3.6m tonnes from Central America (of which Cuba supplied 1.6m tonnes); 2.8m tonnes from South America (with Brazil as the world's biggest single exporter with 1.7m tonnes); 3.1m tonnes from Asia; 2m tonnes from Oceania; and 1.1m tonnes from Africa.

White sugar beet exports come occasionally from the European Community, which is now more than self-sufficient in production, and from some Eastern European countries.

Centrifugal Sugar: World Production 1970 to 1975

Countries		1970	1971	1972	1973	1974	1975
				Calendar Year			
Europe				*Tonnes — Raw Value*			
Albania	b	18,161	15,221	17,500	18,300	18,500	18,000
Austria	b	330,979	278,124	406,813	371,096	402,660	523,180
Bulgaria	b	230,000	240,000	230,000	210,000	230,000	215,000
Czechoslovakia	b	735,000	730,000	770,000	730,000	750,000	780,000
E.E.C.	b	8,663,644	9,898,296	9,578,649	9,768,460	8,879,998	10,418,079
	c	422,950	388,957	357,115	408,398	357,251	400,000
	b+c	(9,086,594)	(10,287,253)	(9.935,764)	(10,176,858)	(9,237,249)	(10,818,079)
Finland	b	59,700	64,639	91,064	80,989	82,435	88,300
German Dem. Rep.	b	400,000	450,000	600,000	500,000	570,000	682,500
Greece	b	187,880	154,690	139,802	172,174	202,066	307,600
Hungary	b	303,831	261,874	323,481	326,449	290,126	334,640
Poland	b	1,542,068	1,761,157	1,845,594	1,823,040	1,600,000	1,720,000
Portugal:							
Azores	b	7,138	6,825	8,132	8,030	6,323	11,008
Madeira	c	3,224	3,083	2,971	2,039	2,345	1,874
Roumania	b	409,499	526,087	565,000	611,000	600,000	583,000
Spain	b	845,550	939,728	857,619	861,013	638,305	774,120
	c	41,882	44,059	33,203	30,463	28,740	25,725
	b+c	(887,432)	(983,787)	(890,822)	(891,476)	(667,045)	(799,845)
Sweden	b	219,522	269,217	292,471	262,234	301,481	277,668
Switzerland	b	58,184	74,220	66,937	77,802	72,267	64,605
Turkey	b	643,087	910,233	811,366	735,975	833,658	757,875
U.S.S.R.	b	8,847,000	8,402,000	9,674,000	9,600,000	8,526,000	8,200,000
Yugoslavia	b	384,902	380,000	373,818	425,000	560,000	500,000
Total	b	23,886,145	25,362,311	26,652,246	26,581,562	24,563,819	26,255,575
Total	c	468,056	436,099	393,289	440,900	388,338	427,599
Total	b+c	24,354,201	25,798,410	27,045,535	27,022,462	24,952,155	26,683,174
North America							
Canada:	b	112,131	141,499	132.952	117,304	98,230	120,269
U.S.A.—Mainland	b	3,185,200	3,110,647	3,206,048	3,041,188	2,921,988	3,150,360
	c	1,087,980	1,048,427	1,235,530	1,431,197	1,267,704	1,524,371
	b+c	(4,273,180)	(4,159,074)	(4,441,578)	(4,472,385)	(4,189,692)	(4,674,731)
Total	b	3,297,331	3,252,146	3,339,000	3,158,492	3,020,218	3,270,629
Total	c	1,087,980	1,048,427	1,235,530	1,431,197	1,267,704	1,524,371
Total	b+c	4,385,311	4,300,573	4,574,530	4,589,689	4,287,922	4,795,000
Central America							
Bahamas	c	18,768	0	0	0	0	0
Barbados	c	160,420	140,451	116,500	120,839	112,680	101,967
Belize	c	69,753	64,756	73,002	73,689	91,884	85,684
Costa Rica	c	150,000	172,795	200,190	203,000	193,230	205,000
Cuba	c	7,558,569	5,950,029	4,687,802	5,382,548	5,925,850	6,427,382
Dominican Rep.	c	1,014,075	1,132,491	1,173,208	1,178,049	1,229,933	1,169,725
El Salvador	c	117,054	157,963	187,473	231,979	260,760	244,009
Guatemala	c	184,905	209,048	263,813	272,305	365,948	384,146
Haiti	c	66,000	68,000	70,000	60,000	68,000	69,000
Honduras	c	53,000	55,000	65,000	55,000	67,000	75,000
Jamaica	c	382,294	393,632	387,441	339,086	378,445	366,441
Leeward and							
Windward Isl	c	32,500	37,587	27,053	24,463	26,732	25,855
Mexico	c	2,402,015	2,489,173	2,586,819	2,809,761	2,838,178	2,724,121
Nicaragua	c	140,904	169,641	165,839	172,000	165,000	210,000
Panama	c	76,275	86,865	85,531	86,820	115,000	130,000
Puerto Rico	c	407,000	295,584	266,955	230,605	263,404	274,308
Trinidad and Tobago	c	221,543	220,177	237,898	185,544	186,815	163,040
Total	c	13,055,075	11,643,192	10,594,515	11,425,688	12,288,859	12,655,678

Centrifugal Sugar: World Production 1970 to 1975 — continued

Countries		1970	1971	Calendar Year 1972	1973	1974	1975
South America				*Tonnes — Raw Value*			
Argentina	c	976,327	996,124	1,303,044	1,638,279	1,513,625	1,367,180
Bolivia	c	131,285	90,661	132,427	165,000	165,199	212,772
Brazil	c	5,019,219	5,297,747	6,150,759	6,937,176	6,930,876	6,298,594
Chile	b	228,000	192,000	152,000	79,824	116,489	219,181
Colombia	c	676,174	743,974	823,681	809,891	894,820	969,701
Ecuador	c	235,000	249,253	265,686	307,109	280,000	292,100
Guyana	c	332,826	394,540	335,338	280,283	352,740	310,859
Paraguay	c	52,355	61,306	57,446	69,000	76,381	70,000
Peru	c	770,764	882,496	899,415	897,634	992,464	963,657
Surinam	c	13,056	10,956	12,051	9,495	11,000	10,500
Uruguay	b	38,611	49,225	51,842	52,000	67,253	70,000
	c	14,024	17,533	28,382	28,000	22,715	25,000
	b+c	(52,635)	(66,758)	(80,224)	(80,000)	(89,968)	(95,000)
Venezuela	c	455,128	511,986	539,722	476,564	551,413	535,000
Total	b	266,611	241,225	203,842	131,824	183,742	289,181
Total	c	8,676,158	9,256,576	10,547,951	11,618,431	11,791,233	11,055,363
Total	b+c	8,942,769	9,497,801	10,751,793	11,750,255	11,974,975	11,344,544
Asia							
Afghanistan	b	5,348	4,696	5,000	5,500	5,000	5,500
	c	4,000	4,000	4,000	4,000	4,000	4,500
	b+c	(9,348)	(8,696)	(9,000)	(9,500)	(9,000)	(10,000)
Bangladesh	c	*	*	27,300	34,762	108,045	94,579
Burma	c	90,000	95,000	100,000	100,000	80,000	82,000
China	b	700,000	750,000	800,000	850,000	1,000,000	1,000,000
	c	2,200,000	2,300,000	2,350,000	2,450,000	2,900,000	3,000,000
	b+c	(2,900,000)	(3,050,000)	(3,150,000)	(3,300,000)	(3,900,000)	(4,000,000)
(Taiwan Province)	c	687,810	759,568	783,989	832,275	830,000	800,000
India	c	4,634,226	3,958,789	3,706,734	3,987,669	4,488,694	5,047,579
Indonesia	c	708,315	834,100	889,300	875,000	935,000	1,000,000
Iran	b	557,215	566,726	547,826	580,000	433,308	515,000
	c	59,568	70,000	50,000	70,000	90,455	85,000
	b+c	(616,783)	(636,726)	(597,826)	(650,000)	(523,763)	(600,000)
Iraq	b	3,200	4,200	4,500	8,000	8,000	9,000
	c	7,975	11,249	12,000	12,000	12,000	12,000
	b+c	(11,175)	(15,449)	(16,500)	(20,000)	(20,000)	(21,000)
Israel	b	29,329	31,526	28,261	25,652	20,000	30,000
Japan	b	342,682	395,074	374,366	380,083	373,997	258,226
	c	303,350	300,833	220,271	243,859	252,149	200,448
	b+c	(646,032)	(695,907)	(594,637)	(623,942)	(626,146)	(458,674)
Lebanon	b	12,890	19,000	24,000	11,000	11,000	10,000
Malaysia	c	0	0	0	15,954	20,000	59,000
Nepal	c	10,000	9,000	10,000	10,000	9,000	10,000
Pakistan	b	30,000	17,000	17,000	10,000	10,000	20,000
	c	740,000	573,000	383,000	528,436	510,000	520,000
	b+c	(770,000)	(590,000)	(400,000)	(538,436)	(520,000)	(540,000)
Philippines	c	1,980,004	2,170,979	2,098,801	2,092,609	2,655,810	2,672,316
Sri Lanka	c	15,684	10,870	7,126	10,000	20,839	19,845
Syrian Arab Rep.	b	26,222	32,000	35,000	18,052	18,000	21,659
Thailand	c	494,815	640,235	701,936	839,324	985,486	1,215,750
Total	b	1,706,886	1,820,222	1,835,953	1,888,287	1,879,305	1,869,385
Total	c	11,935,747	11,737,623	11,344,457	12,105,888	13,901,478	14,823,017
Total	b+c	13,642,633	13,557,845	13,180,410	13,994,175	15,780,783	16,692,402
Africa							
Algeria	b	5,273	18,800	20,000	25,000	25,000	18,000
Angola	c	78,765	76,073	84,213	81,903	70,000	30,000
Cameroon	c	9,633	11,676	12,000	12,000	14,000	14,500
Congo (Brazzaville)	c	85,000	70,000	39,957	37,492	28,623	29,007
Egypt, Arab Rep. of	c	520,000	550,000	550,000	571,909	534,000	537,000
Ethiopia	c	103,214	120,000	130,548	139,695	130,435	135,000
Ghana	c	8,000	8,000	10,000	10,000	5,217	8,000
Ivory Coast	c	0	0	0	0	0	32,000
Kenya	c	141,323	140,146	99,707	150,000	178,596	165,000

Centrifugal Sugar: World Production 1970 to 1975 — continued

Countries		1970	1971	1972	1973	1974	1975
				Calendar Year			
Africa cont:—				*Tonnes — Raw Value*			
Malagasy Rep.	c	108,000	99,038	110,162	105,076	121,887	120,867
Malawi	c	33,484	33,213	34,416	49,994	47,384	68,520
Mali	c	6,167	5,547	8,000	10,000	15,000	13,500
Mauritius	c	610,776	657,296	727,410	760,782	737,966	496,164
Morocco	b	153,000	226,740	245,000	230,132	260,000	268,000
Mozambique	c	286,586	325,548	327,596	299,171	300,000	260,000
Nigeria	c	26,639	31,337	28,000	30,000	40,000	40,000
Rhodesia	c	135,000	200,000	200,000	225,000	255,000	257,000
Rwanda	c	326	300	300	300	521	500
Somalia	c	49,949	49,232	40,876	50,000	32,965	42,000
South Africa	c	1,648,698	1,720,428	2,110,755	1,953,100	1,970,104	1,968,441
Sudan	c	81,845	78,895	99,321	100,000	130,000	139,434
Swaziland	c	180,417	178,249	191,633	176,125	204,778	223,693
Tanzania	c	87,254	95,787	88,483	114,278	105,422	120,000
Tunisia	b	5,792	2,738	4,327	4,500	4,359	4,900
Uganda	c	154,065	152,327	131,207	73,800	43,933	50,000
Zaire, Republic of	c	46,238	48,188	48,000	50,000	67,512	62,100
Zambia	c	40,098	41,546	51,119	58,184	64,782	95,000
Total	b	164,065	248,278	269,327	259,632	289,359	290,900
Total	c	4,441,477	4,692,826	5,123,703	5,058,809	5,098,125	4,907,726
Total	b+c	4,605,542	4,941,104	5,393,030	5,318,441	5,387,484	5,198,626
Oceania							
Australia	c	2,506,853	2,732,084	2,868,880	2,582,754	2,937,868	2,930,196
Fiji	c	349,541	372,609	320,639	303,227	297,596	283,684
Hawaii	c	1,054,213	1,115,816	1,015,028	1,026,195	945,752	1,005,685
Total	c	3,910,607	4,220,509	4,204,547	3,912,176	4,181,216	4,219,565
World							
Total	b	29,321,038	30,924,182	32,300,368	32,019,797	29,936,443	31,975,670
Total	c	43,575,100	43,035,252	43,443,992	45,993,089	48,916,951	49,613,319
Total	b+c	72,896,138	73,959,434	75,744,360	78,012,886	78,853,394	81,588,989
Beet Sugar as % of Total Production		40.2	41.8	42.6	41.0	38.0	39.2
Cane Sugar as % of Total Production		59.8	58.2	57.4	59.0	62.0	60.8

b = *beet sugar.*   c = *cane sugar.*   * = *included under Pakistan.*
By courtesy of the International Sugar Organization.

Centrifugal Sugar: World Consumption 1970 to 1975

Countries	1970	1971	1972	1973	1974	1975
			Tonnes — Raw Value			
Europe						
Albania	34,000	35,000	35,500	36,000	36,200	35,000
Austria	325,200	329,015	346,448	394,948	384,321	334,326
Bulgaria	530,000	550,000	570,000	550,000	510,000	520,000
Cyprus	18,172	18,564	17,883	20,135	12,840	19,802
Czechoslovakia	630,000	630,000	640,000	650,000	653,000	655,000
E.E.C.	10,692,070	10,460,719	10,474,683	11,116,435	11,698,412	9,540,851
Finland	223,776	220,446	234,108	229,846	215,724	200,000
Fr. Overseas Territories	22,500	23,000	23,500	23,500	20,500	20,750
German, Dem. Rep.	639,677	670,000	700,000	730,000	750,000	700,400
Gibraltar	1,330	1,147	1,150	1,100	1,100	1,000
Greece	187,187	209,010	234,022	276,740	287,392	253,800
Hungary	421,291	440,438	466,264	501,079	499,610	535,690
Iceland	11,000	10,500	10,000	10,000	10,200	9,252
Malta	11,732	19,884	18,000	19,000	18,000	18,500
Norway	174,705	185,052	183,060	166,162	143,596	101,475
Poland	1,418,108	1,441,745	1,503,545	1,549,173	1,550,000	1,600,000
Portugal: Mainland	222,428	227,099	252,475	269,991	271,339	261,888
Azores & Madeira	16,787	17,437	17,422	17,612	17,964	18,364
Roumania	440,000	530,000	555,000	575,000	600,000	600,000
Spain: Peninsular & Balearic Isls.	930,000	955,905	980,000	1,000,000	1,000,000	1,062,440
Canary Islands	42,000	45,000	50,000	55,000	50,000	30,000
Sweden	369,657	373,864	373,251	375,177	381,941	368,721
Switzerland	318,130	306,162	319,530	335,382	286,833	219,369
Turkey	662,005	707,185	787,627	924,611	898,088	937,489
U.S.S.R.	10,247,000	10,350,000	10,750,000	11,200,000	11,250,000	11,304,000
Yugoslavia	565,000	584,000	602,305	620,000	630,000	650,000
Total	29,153,755	29,341,172	30,145,773	31,646,891	32,177,060	29,998,117
North America						
Canada	1,073,870	1,054,107	1,036,504	1,211,765	984,107	1,056,756
U.S.A. Mainland	10,401,236	10,377,081	10,456,842	10,463,528	10,165,204	8,989,394
Total	11,475,106	11,431,188	11,493,346	11,675,293	11,149,311	10,046,150
Central America						
Bahamas	4,633	5,354	6,000	6,500	7,250	7,500
Barbados	12,993	13,637	13,361	13,624	17,256	15,093
Belize	5,975	4,962	4,936	5,772	6,351	5,777
Bermuda	2,700	2,600	2,700	2,800	2,700	2,500
Costa Rica	80,000	86,000	95,200	100,000	104,326	110,000
Cuba	619,376	616,089	470,890	463,742	522,162	499,313
Dominican Republic	124,300	136,285	145,669	170,205	171,972	166,030
El Salvador	70,559	74,385	82,604	90,434	102,708	118,138
Guatemala	123,416	137,804	148,924	162,346	173,403	193,906
Haiti	44,000	46,000	48,000	50,000	53,000	54,000
Honduras	47,000	50,000	54,000	58,000	60,000	65,000
Jamaica	83,575	91,047	94,780	95,017	103,433	104,846
Leeward and Windward Islands*	16,800	17,000	17,000	18,000	16,000	16,000
Mexico	1,992,482	1,919,999	2,075,354	2,298,475	2,343,632	2,557,712
Netherlands Antilles	6,851	7,500	8,000	8,500	7,500	7,500
Nicaragua	69,100	72,600	79,063	85,000	90,000	100,000
Panama	38,067	43,777	50,947	44,000	55,000	46,000
Panama Canal Zone	2,500	2,600	2,650	2,650	2,500	2,600
Puerto Rico and Virgin Islands (U.S.)	113,000	121,151	126,185	129,786	125,456	120,911
Trinidad and Tobago	49,400	53,440	52,874	52,377	46,116	45,195
Virgin Islands (U.K.)	362	400	450	475	450	500
Total	3,507,089	3,502,630	3,579,587	3,857,703	4,011,215	4,238,521

Centrifugal Sugar: World Consumption 1970 to 1975 — continued

Countries	1970	1971	1972	1973	1974	1975
South America			*Tonnes — Raw Value*			
Argentina	951,593	1,057,199	1,026,105	957,802	1,100,269	1,086,317
Bolivia	117,425	122,071	130,612	130,000	117,935	143,166
Brazil	3,495,185	3,796,552	4,125,278	4,266,325	4,576,549	4,989,878
Chile	337,000	380,000	402,000	365,326	293,570	321,879
Colombia	545,692	602,081	625,574	690,223	749,716	771,461
Ecuador	145,000	160,756	192,584	206,172	220,500	233,680
Guyana	26,031	31,776	32,150	34,664	33,154	30,321
Paraguay	49,000	51,155	57,383	57,325	54,687	55,000
Peru	380,860	418,133	459,252	484,084	523,986	551,061
Surinam	11,372	11,634	11,580	11,344	11,000	11,000
Uruguay	119,173	122,186	121,550	120,000	112,200	113,000
Venezuela	414,137	426,771	462,226	499,363	519,859	540,000
Total	6,592,468	7,180,314	7,646,294	7,822,628	8,313,425	8,846,763
Asia						
Afghanistan	60,000	63,000	60,000	55,000	60,000	60,000
Bangladesh	*	*	90,927	115,104	102,279	105,941
Brunei	4,350	4,500	5,000	5,500	6,000	6,000
Burma	95,000	97,000	100,000	102,000	80,000	80,000
China	3,150,000	3,340,000	3,550,000	3,800,000	4,200,000	4,200,000
(Taiwan Province)	236,475	242,999	255,421	309,684	305,000	308,000
Hong Kong	79,985	92,059	75,951	97,109	85,694	85,000
India	3,766,641	4,437,817	3,911,114	3,826,601	3,790,295	3,861,698
Indonesia	886,747	872,021	960,676	1,000,000	1,050,000	1,100,000
Iran	706,524	804,000	869,565	900,000	886,854	910,000
Iraq	315,000	320,000	325,000	350,000	400,000	430,000
Israel	175,946	194,118	199,293	232,487	200,000	190,000
Japan	3,028,594	3,101,093	3,248,843	3,293,713	3,336,060	2,796,390
Jordan	71,000	75,000	80,000	50,000	50,882	46,229
Khmer Republic	8,822	12,000	14,000	13,000	11,500	10,000
Korea (North)	180,000	200,000	180,000	170,000	100,000	135,000
Korea, Republic of	212,247	247,656	213,680	259,260	241,414	245,000
Kuwait	26,000	29,232	30,922	32,144	34,000	35,000
Laos	6,000	4,000	4,000	4,000	3,500	3,500
Lebanon	60,673	73,589	76,725	78,936	83,000	80,000
Macao	3,538	3,277	3,317	3,020	2,923	2,500
Malaysia	401,924	389,428	350,000	339,562	340,000	370,000
Maldives, Republic of	3,700	3,800	3,900	3,950	3,500	3,600
Mongolia	22,000	22,000	25,000	28,000	28,000	28,500
Nepal	16,304	17,000	19,680	20,000	18,000	19,000
Pakistan	625,000	640,000	669,113	578,630	525,000	550,000
Persian Gulf	40,000	42,000	43,500	45,000	50,000	50,000
Philippines	612,715	663,377	749,298	792,274	949,058	852,650
Saudi Arabia	90,000	100,000	130,000	114,076	130,000	157,609
Singapore	106,415	132,902	126,948	87,408	91,456	90,253
Southern Yemen Rep.	38,000	39,000	40,000	42,000	40,000	35,000
Sri Lanka	311,029	299,085	242,023	177,181	103,587	69,606
Syrian Arab Republic	140,000	160,000	180,000	200,000	220,000	214,137
Thailand	371,901	403,902	412,504	433,027	499,630	547,524
Timor	950	635	684	839	850	790
Vietnam (North)	57,000	62,000	67,000	72,000	77,000	80,000
Vietnam (South)	365,000	279,704	222,242	204,522	150,000	155,000
Yemen	52,000	50,000	50,000	48,000	28,000	36,000
Total	16,327,480	17,518,194	17,586,326	17,884,027	18,283,482	17,949,927
Africa						
Algeria	240,000	245,000	255,000	280,000	330,000	340,000
Angola	60,186	66,140	75,980	78,048	80,000	45,000
Benin	10,300	10,500	9,000	9,000	8,200	8,300
Botswana	11,000	11,500	11,700	11,800	12,000	12,000
Burundi	3,000	3,300	3,000	3,200	3,000	2,820
Cameroon	20,000	21,000	23,000	28,000	30,000	30,000
Cape Verde Islands	4,733	4,707	5,263	4,853	4,159	4,200
Central African Rep.	4,000	4,000	3,800	4,000	3,400	3,500
Chad	22,000	23,000	25,000	27,000	25,000	23,000
Congo (Brazzaville)	7,500	7,335	6,618	8,414	8,466	9,627

Centrifugal Sugar: World Consumption 1970 to 1975 — continued

Countries	1970	1971	1972	1973	1974	1975
Africa cont.—			*Tonnes — Raw Value*			
Egypt, Arab Rep. of	520,000	557,786	580,000	600,800	637,400	715,600
Equatorial Guinea	875	890	900	950	800	800
Ethiopia	95,674	100,000	100,551	114,579	119,376	120,000
Gabon	2,000	2,000	3,000	2,870	3,907	4,500
Gambia	8,000	7,500	5,000	4,000	1,900	2,800
Ghana	90,000	95,000	90,000	85,000	51,226	65,000
Guinea	13,500	14,000	14,000	13,000	13,000	13,500
Guinea Bissau	2,018	2,134	2,352	2,347	2,300	2,300
Ivory Coast	51,579	56,387	67,995	67,750	54,457	55,000
Kenya	172,937	213,633	210,265	236,282	243,056	250,000
Lesotho	← - - - - - - - -		Included under South Africa		- - - - - - - →	
Liberia	5,500	6,500	6,800	7,937	8,000	7,500
Libya	66,000	70,000	75,000	85,000	95,000	97,000
Malagasy Republic	56,761	57,024	62,956	71,742	74,595	77,484
Malawi	32,249	36,379	33,666	37,828	35,660	33,608
Mali	37,804	38,000	36,000	37,000	25,000	35,000
Mauritania	20,000	17,500	16,500	20,000	22,305	18,067
Mauritius	33,796	35,403	35,304	37,485	34,982	38,660
Morocco	411,000	439,200	460,000	480,000	480,000	500,000
Mozambique	88,714	107,666	117,190	139,448	130,000	135,000
Niger	9,780	8,500	11,001	12,543	11,500	11,700
Nigeria	100,000	120,000	140,000	160,000	180,000	185,000
Rhodesia	90,000	100,000	105,000	115,000	125,000	128,000
Rwanda	3,496	3,000	3,000	3,000	3,000	3,000
St. Helena	210	223	210	225	220	200
Sao Tomé and Principé	1,045	960	1,065	1,105	790	1,000
Senegal	68,500	75,000	80,000	85,000	78,000	79,000
Seychelles	2,100	2,200	2,300	2,400	2,500	2,300
Sierra Leone, Rep. of	28,000	29,000	29,500	28,500	24,500	25,000
Somalia	53,509	55,753	59,299	62,500	48,174	52,000
South Africa†	916,180	958,905	1,000,297	1,068,110	1,139,555	1,215,102
Spanish Possessions in North Africa	6,500	7,000	7,200	7,500	7,000	7,200
Spanish Sahara	300	350	375	390	360	360
Sudan	245,915	272,601	277,174	285,000	270,000	283,567
Swaziland	13,538	13,799	13,865	15,589	16,468	19,344
Tanzania	107,617	125,349	136,592	140,400	133,965	129,000
Togo	9,000	8,500	7,500	8,000	5,000	5,000
Tunisia	100,000	108,629	120,490	130,000	138,069	136,000
Uganda	143,478	164,069	133,219	71,553	48,968	49,000
Upper Volta	12,865	13,500	14,500	14,000	9,000	9,500
Zaire, Republic of	60,870	65,000	70,000	72,000	80,000	84,000
Zambia	50,294	63,139	67,449	74,738	86,070	90,000
Total	4,114,323	4,448,961	4,615,876	4,855,886	4,945,328	5,165,539
Oceania						
Australia	702,542	716,828	716,826	756,656	763,859	792,224
British Oceania	4,679	4,890	5,000	5,150	4,000	5,000
Fiji	25,745	28,469	25,531	28,177	30,120	27,941
Hawaii	32,842	31,648	35,476	37,043	34,083	31,304
New Zealand	157,599	156,340	161,247	162,202	183,362	164,200
Papua New Guinea	18,000	17,000	17,000	21,000	20,000	20,000
U.S. Administration Oceania	5,350	5,400	5,450	5,500	5,500	5,500
Western Samoa	3,691	3,953	3,900	3,400	3,000	3,623
Total	950,448	964,528	970,430	1,019,128	1,043,924	1,049,792
WORLD TOTAL	72,120,669	74,386,987	76,037,632	78,761,556	79,923,745	77,294,809

* *Included under Pakistan.*
† *Figures include Lesotho.*
By courtesy of the International Sugar Organization.

Sugar: London

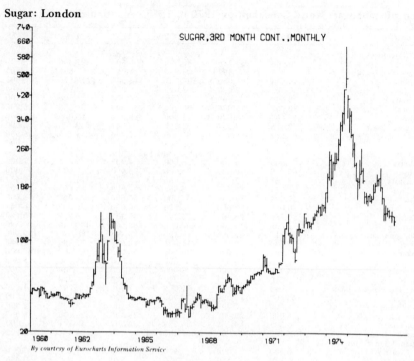

SUGAR,3RD MONTH CONT.,MONTHLY

By courtesy of Eurocharts Information Service

Sugar: World

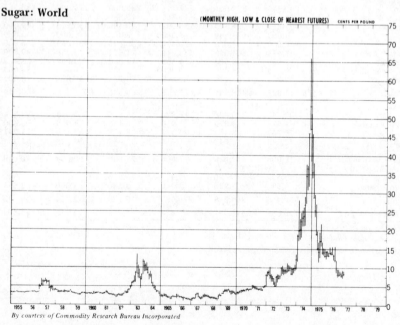

(MONTHLY HIGH, LOW & CLOSE OF NEAREST FUTURES)   CENTS PER POUND

By courtesy of Commodity Research Bureau Incorporated

92

Tin

The Bronze Age resulted from the discovery that if tin was alloyed with copper, weapons, tools and other implements were given much greater hardness and a sharper cutting edge. The Phoenicians were the earliest international traders in tin, obtaining most of their supplies from Cornwall, which for some time gave Britain a dominant role as world producer.

Although tin is still being produced in Cornwall, mainly from slag heaps that were not originally considered rich enough to be profitable, the vast majority of the world's tin supplies — nearly 80 per cent — comes from four countries: Malaysia, Bolivia, Thailand and Indonesia. China and the Soviet Union are also significant producers; so are Australia, Nigeria and Zaire. It is believed that rich deposits exist in Brazil's Amazon basin, but so far the cost of exploiting these is considered to be too high. There are believed to be other unexploited reserves in China and Zaire, as well as offshore Malaysia, Thailand and Indonesia. Of special importance is the fact that tin is one of the few metals not found in the United States, which is therefore totally dependent on imports for supplies of this strategic metal.

The main use of tin is in providing a protective coating for steel in order to produce tinplate for cans (tins) especially for food and beverages. As a chemically inert, non-toxic metal, only a thin coating is needed on the steel to give the required protection.

Tin is also alloyed with other metals, notably lead, to produce solder used throughout industry, and with copper to produce bronze. Its purest form is pewter. An expanding market for tin is in the manufacture of chemical compounds for fungicides and pesticides.

In view of its uses, there is very little scrap recovery. Consumption has tended to increase slowly and tinplate in particular is subject to competition from other materials such as aluminium and plastic or the so-called 'tin-free steel' that incorporates other metals to provide the required protection.

Demand for tin is dependent on economic activity in the main industrialized countries and the supply situation tends to move rapidly from periods of shortages to surpluses, causing wild price fluctuations. In view of this and in view of the concentration of production in developing countries, tin has a long history of price control pacts, first amongst producers themselves and subsequently in the only long-lasting and successful commodity pact between consumers and producers, the International Tin Agreement. The Agreement has lasted for 20 years and was provisionally renewed for a further five years with effect from January 1977. When possible, it uses a buffer stock mechanism to keep prices within a 'floor' and 'ceiling' range agreed by consumers and producers on the International Tin Council. Further protection is given to the 'floor' price by the use of export quotas when these are considered necessary to help out the buffer stock.

Little can be done to stop the 'ceiling' price being breached in times of shortage. However, the United States has in the past filled shortfalls by releases from its strategic stockpile of tin, acquired in the 1950s after the Korean War. This stockpile has now been reduced to around 200,000 tonnes — about a year's world consumption — and there are increasing doubts in the United States about how much more should be released.

World prices of tin, which the International Agreement seeks to control, are decided on the Penang market in Malaysia and the London Metal Exchange. Penang is the main physical market where buyers bid for supplies from the smelters, and the prices paid there are also used to fix the prices in direct shipments from producers to consumers. However, many supply contracts use the prices quoted on the London Metal Exchange as well, which at present provides the only hedging facilities and forward prices available. Regular tin supplies also pass through the Metal Exchange warehouses.

Tin: World Production 1971 to 1976

THOUSAND METRIC TONS

	1971	1972	1973	1974	1975 Jan-Dec	1975 July-Sept	1975 Oct-Dec	1976 Jan-Mar
Mine								
EUROPE								
Portugal	0.6	0.5	0.5	0.4	0.4	0.1	0.1	0.1
Spain	0.4	0.4	0.5	0.6	0.7	0.1	0.1	0.2
United Kingdom	1.8	3.3	3.6	3.8	3.3	0.7	0.9	0.9
Other Europe	0.3	0.4	0.4	0.2	0.1	0.1	–	–
Total	3.1	4.7	5.0	5.0	4.5	1.0	1.1	1.2
AFRICA								
Nigeria	7.3	6.7	5.8	5.5	4.7	1.0	1.2	1.2
Ruanda Burundi	1.3	1.4	1.4	1.4	1.2	0.3	0.3	0.3
South Africa Republic	2.0	2.1	2.6	2.6	2.6	0.7	0.7	0.6
South West Africa	1.0	0.9	0.7	0.7	0.7	0.1	0.2	0.2
Zaire	6.5	6.0	5.4	4.8	4.2	1.0	1.0	1.0
Other Africa	1.0	0.9	0.9	1.0	1.0	0.3	0.2	0.2
Total	19.1	18.0	16.8	16.0	14.4	3.4	3.6	3.5
ASIA								
Burma	0.5	0.5	0.6	0.6	0.6	0.2	0.2	0.1
Indonesia	19.8	21.8	22.5	25.0	24.4	7.2	5.9	5.0
Japan	0.8	0.9	0.8	0.7	0.7	0.1	0.2	0.2
Malaysia	75.4	76.8	72.3	68.1	64.4	15.6	15.9	15.6
Thailand	21.7	22.1	20.9	20.3	16.4	3.7	3.6	5.0
Other Asia	1.6	0.8	0.8	0.7	0.6	1.6	1.5	0.1
Total	119.8	122.9	117.9	115.2	107.1	28.4	27.3	26.0
AMERICA								
Bolivia	30.3	32.4	28.4	28.9	28.3	6.7	6.6	6.6
Mexico	0.5	0.4	0.3	0.4	0.2	0.1	–	–
Other America	4.3	4.9	4.3	4.1	5.0	1.4	1.4	1.4
Total	35.1	37.7	33.0	33.4	33.5	8.2	8.0	8.0
AUSTRALIA	9.4	12.0	10.8	10.5	9.7	2.2	2.2	2.2
TOTAL	186.5	195.3	183.7	180.1	169.2	43.2	42.2	40.9
OTHER COUNTRIES*								
China P.R.	23.0	23.0	22.8	23.0	23.0			
Czechoslovakia	0.2	0.2	0.2	0.1	0.2	0.1		0.1
Germany, Democratic Republic	1.0	1.0	0.8	1.0	1.1			
U.S.S.R.	12.0	12.0	13.0	14.0	14.0			
Total	36.2	36.2	36.8	38.1	38.3			
WORLD TOTAL	222.7	231.5	220.5	218.2	207.5	43.3	42.2	41.0
Refined								
EUROPE								
Belgium	4.1	4.0	3.7	3.4	4.6	1.3	1.4	1.2
Germany, Federal Republic	2.3	2.4	2.1	2.5	2.3	0.4	0.6	0.6
Netherlands	0.8	–	–	–	–	–	–	–
Portugal	0.5	0.6	0.5	0.6	0.6	0.1	0.2	0.1
Spain	4.5	4.8	6.1	6.2	8.0	1.5	1.0	1.2
United Kingdom	25.2	26.3	23.1	15.3	16.8	3.6	4.2	4.5
Other Europe	–	–	–	0.2	–	–	–	–
Total	37.4	38.1	35.5	28.3	32.3	6.9	7.4	7.6
AFRICA								
Nigeria	7.3	6.7	6.0	5.6	4.7	1.2	1.5	1.1
South Africa Republic	1.4	1.6	1.8	2.0	2.4	0.6	0.6	0.6
Zaire	1.4	1.4	1.0	0.6	0.6	0.2	0.1	0.1
Other Africa	0.6	0.6	0.6	0.6	0.6	0.2	0.2	0.2
Total	10.7	10.3	9.4	8.8	8.3	2.2	2.4	2.0
ASIA								
Indonesia	9.2	12.0	14.6	15.1	17.8	3.6	6.6	5.0
Japan	1.5	1.5	1.4	1.3	1.3	0.3	0.3	0.3
Malaysia	87.1	91.0	82.5	84.4	83.1	20.6	21.4	19.0
Thailand	21.7	22.3	22.9	19.8	16.6	4.0	3.9	4.8
Other Asia	0.1	0.1	0.1	–	–	–	–	–
Total	119.6	126.9	121.5	120.6	118.8	28.5	32.2	29.1
AMERICA								
Bolivia	6.8	6.5	6.9	7.0	7.5	1.6	1.9	2.1
Brazil	3.7	3.8	3.8	6.2	5.6	1.6	1.3	1.6
Mexico	0.5	0.9	2.2	1.7	1.5	0.3	0.2	0.3
U.S.A.	7.6	4.4	6.6	6.0	7.9	1.9	2.2	1.9
Other America	0.3	0.3	0.3	0.1	0.3	–	0.1	–
Total	18.9	15.9	19.8	21.0	22.8	5.4	5.7	5.9
AUSTRALIA	7.0	7.4	7.4	7.4	5.7	1.5	1.5	1.3
TOTAL	193.6	198.6	193.6	185.9	187.9	44.5	49.2	45.9
of which, approximately:								
Primary	185.3	190.6	185.8	178.9	180.7	42.7	47.0	43.4
Secondary	8.3	8.0	7.8	7.0	7.2	1.8	2.2	2.5
OTHER COUNTRIES*								
China P.R.	23.0	23.0	22.8	23.0	23.0			
Czechoslovakia	0.1	0.1	0.1	0.1	0.1			
Germany, Democratic Republic	1.1	1.1	1.2	1.1	1.1			
U.S.S.R.	12.0	12.0	12.0	15.0	15.0			
Total	36.2	36.2	36.1	39.2	39.2			
WORLD TOTAL	229.8	234.8	229.7	225.1	227.1	44.5	49.2	45.9

By courtesy of the World Bureau of Metal Statistics.

Tin: World Refined Consumption 1971 to 1976

THOUSAND METRIC TONS

	1971	1972	1973	1974	1975 Jan-Dec	1975 July-Sept	1975 Oct-Dec	1976 Jan-Mar
EUROPE								
Austria	0·6	0·6	0·6	0·6	0·4	0·1	0·1	0·1
Belgium	3·0	3·5	3·7	4·3	4·8	0·9	1·3	0·7
Denmark	0·7	0·6	0·6	0·6	0·6	0·1	0·1	0·1
Finland	0·2	0·2	0·2	0·3	0·2	0·1	0·1	0·1
France	10·5	11·0	11·7	11·3	10·0	2·2	2·1	2·6
Germany, Federal Republic	15·4	15·9	16·9	15·7	13·0	2·7	3·2	4·1
Greece	0·2	0·4	0·4	0·4	0·6	0·1	0·1	0·1
Italy	7·2	7·5	8·4	9·3	8·0	2·0	2·0	2·0
Netherlands	5·1	5·0	5·0	4·4	3·9	0·8	0·9	0·9
Norway	0·6	0·6	0·6	0·4	0·8	0·1	0·2	0·2
Portugal	0·4	0·4	0·4	0·4	0·5	0·1	0·1	0·1
Spain	3·9	3·2	3·8	4·5	6·6	1·1	1·1	1·1
Sweden	0·4	0·4	0·4	0·5	0·6	0·1	0·1	0·1
Switzerland	0·9	0·8	0·8	0·7	0·7	0·2	0·1	0·2
United Kingdom	18·1	17·9	16·4	16·7	14·4	2·9	3·1	3·3
Yugoslavia	0·8	0·8	0·8	1·6	1·0	0·4	0·4	0·4
Other Europe	0·1	0·1	0·2	0·1	0·1	0·1	0·1	–
Total	68·1	68·9	72·9	71·8	66·2	14·0	15·1	16·1
AFRICA								
Egypt	0·3	0·6	0·5	1·0	0·5	0·1	0·1	0·1
Morocco	0·2	0·2	0·2	0·2	0·2	0·1	0·1	0·1
South Africa Republic	2·0	2·2	2·3	2·3	2·2	0·6	0·6	0·6
Other Africa	0·5	0·6	0·6	0·6	1·0	0·1	0·1	0·1
Total	3·0	3·6	3·6	4·1	3·9	0·9	0·9	0·9
ASIA								
India	4·0	5·5	4·7	1·8	1·5	0·7	0·7	0·7
Indonesia	0·3	0·3	0·4	0·3	0·4	0·1	0·1	0·1
Iran	0·3	0·3	0·5	0·5	0·5	0·1	0·1	0·1
Japan	29·5	32·5	38·8	33·6	28·2	6·9	7·5	7·5
Pakistan	0·4	0·4	0·4	0·4	0·3	0·1	0·1	0·1
Philippine Rep.	0·8	0·7	0·8	1·0	1·1	0·2	0·3	0·2
South Korea	0·6	0·5	1·0	0·6	0·6	0·2	0·1	0·2
Taiwan	0·5	0·5	0·4	0·7	0·9	0·1	0·1	0·1
Turkey	1·2	1·3	1·4	1·4	1·2	0·4	0·4	0·3
Other Asia	1·3	1·2	1·2	1·3	0·8	0·3	0·3	0·3
Total	38·7	43·2	49·6	41·6	35·5	9·1	9·7	9·6
AMERICA								
Argentina	1·8	1·6	1·5	1·6	1·1	0·4	0·4	0·5
Brazil	2·5	2·6	3·9	3·5	3·3	1·1	1·1	1·1
Canada	5·0	5·5	5·3	5·7	4·4	1·1	1·0	1·1
Chile	0·8	0·7	0·7	0·7	0·4	0·1	0·2	0·2
Mexico	1·6	1·6	0·5	2·2	1·8	0·4	0·4	0·4
U.S.A.	56·0	56·6	61·1	53·6	55·3	10·7	11·0	12·7
Venezuela	0·2	0·2	0·2	–	–	–	–	–
Other America	0·5	0·4	0·5	0·4	0·6	0·1	0·1	0·1
Total	68·4	69·2	73·7	67·7	66·9	13·9	14·2	16·1
AUSTRALASIA								
Australia	4·6	3·9	4·7	4·6	3·6	0·6	0·7	0·8
New Zealand	0·4	0·4	0·4	0·7	0·4	0·1	0·1	0·1
Total	5·0	4·3	5·1	5·3	4·0	0·7	0·8	0·9
TOTAL	183·2	189·2	204·9	190·5	176·5	38·6	40·7	43·4
OTHER COUNTRIES*								
Czechoslovakia	3·5	3·5	3·5	3·8	3·4	0·9	0·8	0·9
German Democratic Republic	2·2	2·2	2·5	2·5	2·5	–	–	–
Hungary	1·5	1·3	1·5	1·7	1·7	0·3	0·3	0·3
Poland	4·7	4·2	4·8	4·5	4·5	1·1	1·0	1·0
Roumania	2·5	2·9	3·3	3·1	2·7	0·7	0·7	0·7
U.S.S.R.	17·0	17·5	18·0	19·0	21·0	–	–	–
Other Eastern Europe	0·9	0·9	0·9	2·2	1·2	0·2	0·2	0·2
China P.R.	13·0	13·5	14·0	14·0	14·0	–	–	–
Total	45·3	46·0	48·5	50·8	51·0	3·2	3·0	3·1
WORLD TOTAL	228·5	235·2	253·4	241·3	227·5	41·8	43·7	46·5

This table shows consumption of unwrought refined tin, whether refined from primary or secondary materials; the direct use of scrap tin and scrap alloys is excluded. For some countries a small unknown consumption of secondary refined tin may be omitted.

By courtesy of the World Bureau of Metal Statistics.

Standard Tin: London

STANDARD TIN,3 MONTHS,MONTHLY

By courtesy of Eurocharts Information Service

Zinc

Zinc is a metal which has been used by man since prehistoric times. Deposits are distributed over 50 countries with Canada as the major producer supplying a quarter of the total world production in 1974 (4.8 million tonnes). The USSR, USA, Australia and Peru are the other major producers. The two largest exporting countries are Canada and Australia while Western Europe, the United States and Japan are the biggest consumers, accounting for some 82 per cent of world consumption. Both the EEC and Japan encourage the import of concentrates to assist their smelting industries and are thus only small importers of refined zinc metals. However, a sharp cutback in US zinc smelting capacity in the early 1970s means that it now imports a far greater percentage of its zinc requirements in metal form.

Zinc has a high consumption rate amongst non-ferrous metals in volume terms with annual sales of around 6 million tonnes. This is exceeded only by aluminium and copper. The major uses of zinc are in galvanizing steel, in zinc strip and sheet, in zinc oxide, in brass and die casting. Its uses in galvanizing and in oxide have, until now, made recovery uneconomic. The biggest single use of zinc is in galvanizing steel, where its anti-corrosion properties help protect the steel. In recent years die-casting has become an increasingly important market, and there is more scope for scrap recovery in this area. Zinc is constantly under competitive attack from alternative products, such as aluminium and plastics, and these have made major inroads when zinc has been in short supply or prices have been too high.

Supplies of zinc come from two different sources — the custom smelters who process ore concentrates bought from the mines which is then resold in refined form to the fabricators and the integrated producer. The custom smelters' profit margin comes from the difference between the purchase price of the concentrates and the price at which the processed zinc is sold. He is therefore less concerned with the overall price affecting both concentrates and processed zinc, than with maintaining an adequate profit margin.

Integrated producers, who both mine the concentrates and own captive smelters to process it, are more affected by price fluctuations.

Within the United States, zinc producers set a fixed price, based on output costs and the state of the market, for direct supply contracts with consumers. Outside the USA primary producers and custom smelters established a European producer price in 1964 which is agreed informally between themselves although each company announces its own price and in times of surplus supplies there is considerable competitive discounting.

At the same time, the London Metal Exchange zinc market which provided the basis for world prices outside the US prior to 1964 still has an important influence in highlighting shifts in supply-demand patterns and outside factors not reflected in the more inflexible producer prices. As a residual market the Metal Exchange zinc contract tends to play a more important role in times of surplus, since for the bulk of its supplies it usually relies on re-selling by consumers, and shipments from Communist bloc countries not participating in the producer price system. In view of the growing dependence of the US on imports there are plans for the introduction of a zinc futures market on the New York Commodity Exchange (Comex).

Zinc: World Mine Production 1971 to 1976

THOUSAND METRIC TONS

	1971	1972	1973	1974	1975	1976 Jan.-Mar	Mar	Apr	May	June
EUROPE										
Austria	18.6	19.9	21.9	21.0	16.9	4.8	1.9	2.6	2.9	1.5
Finland	50.9	49.9	58.6	59.3	52.8	14.0	4.9	4.8	6.6	4.6
France	15.1	13.3	13.3	14.3	13.9	3.6	1.3	2.9	3.2	2.8
Germany, Federal Republic	164.9	151.7	151.9	144.5	147.0	36.5	12.6	11.4	12.2	
Greece	10.2	17.0	20.0	20.0	14.4	5.4	1.8	1.8	1.8	1.8
Greenland	–	–	27.2	88.5	84.7	23.1	7.4	8.1	7.0	6.2
Irish Republic	87.5	95.0	64.1	66.3	66.6	18.0	6.0	6.0	6.0	6.0
Italy	106.0	102.6	78.6	78.6	76.5	18.3	6.3	6.5	6.0	
Norway	11.0	15.6	19.0	22.0	24.2	7.4	2.9	2.0	2.2	
Portugal	2.1	1.8	0.7	1.6	–	–	–	–	–	–
Spain	92.0	89.0	94.0	93.6	84.2	22.0				
Sweden	95.6	109.8	114.8	113.7	107.1	31.3	11.6	10.7	10.7	
Yugoslavia	76.8	74.3	97.4	94.7	100.9	22.5	7.5	7.5	7.5	7.5
Total	730.7	739.9	761.5	818.1	790.4	206.9				
AFRICA										
Algeria	15.8	17.0	14.4	10.2	13.2	4.0				
Congo	0.9	2.7	3.3	3.3	4.0	0.9	0.3	0.3	0.3	0.3
Morocco	12.5	22.9	20.5	14.0	18.0	4.5	1.5	1.5	1.5	1.5
South Africa	–	2.4	18.7	37.4	67.0	23.6	7.4	6.4	6.4	
South West Africa	48.9	41.9	33.9	44.9	45.6	12.0	4.0	4.0	4.0	4.0
Tunisia	11.8	10.2	8.6	6.9	6.3	1.5	0.5	0.5	0.5	0.5
Zaire	109.0	100.0	88.0	81.3	80.4	22.5	7.5	7.5	7.5	7.5
Zambia	68.9	70.5	73.2	80.5	67.6	17.3	6.3	5.6	5.8	
Total	267.8	267.6	260.6	278.5	302.1	86.3				
ASIA										
Burma	3.4	3.6	3.6	4.0	2.2	0.6	0.2	0.2	0.2	0.2
India	8.5	9.6	13.6	16.4	6.6	2.2				
Iran	25.9	47.5	32.5	42.5	95.0	9.0				
Japan	294.4	281.1	264.0	240.8	254.4	65.1	23.2	21.4	18.6	22.1
Philippines	3.9	4.6	5.4	7.8	10.5	2.7	1.0			
South Korea	30.1	37.3	48.3	42.3	45.7	13.5	4.6	4.7	4.6	
Thailand	0.9	1.0	0.1	33.5	5.6	4.5				
Turkey	24.0	19.2	24.7	31.6	26.6	7.5	2.5	2.5	2.5	2.5
Total	391.1	403.9	392.2	418.9	461.7	109.5				
AMERICA										
Argentina	40.0	44.5	40.6	37.2	34.9	8.5				
Bolivia(1)	46.0	40.0	48.9	49.0	49.5	12.0	4.0	4.0	4.0	4.0
Brazil	16.9	19.0	25.0	37.8	37.4	9.0	3.0	3.0	3.0	3.0
Canada	1 270.3	1 271.6	1 350.4	1 206.9	1 194.5	300.0	105.4	93.9	108.1	92.6
Honduras	22.1	24.1	25.5	24.3	26.0	7.5	2.5	2.5	2.5	2.5
Mexico	261.2	271.8	271.4	262.7	220.8	55.0				
Nicaragua	3.4	14.8	18.7	14.2	10.6	3.0	1.0	1.0	1.0	1.0
Peru	311.4	320.0	412.0	397.2	383.2	90.0	30.0	30.0	30.0	30.0
United States	501.0	476.8	477.4	498.3	470.1	124.4	42.7	41.1	41.6	
Other	2.0	2.5	2.5	3.2	2.0	0.6	0.2	0.2	0.2	0.2
Total	2 474.3	2 485.1	2 672.4	2 530.8	2 429.0	610.0				
AUSTRALASIA										
Australia	452.6	507.1	480.5	457.1	496.6	99.7	38.6	34.9		
New Zealand	2.0	1.7	0.6	–	–	–	–	–	–	–
Total	454.6	508.8	481.1	457.1	496.6	99.7	38.6	34.9		
TOTAL	4 318.5	4 405.3	4 567.8	4 503.4	4 479.8	1 112.4				
Monthly Average	359.9	367.1	380.7	375.3	373.3	370.8				
OTHER COUNTRIES										
U.S.S.R.*	750.0	800.0	900.0	950.0	1 030.0	240.0	80.0	80.0	80.0	80.0
Germany, Democratic Republic*	5.0	5.0	3.0	–	–	–				
Bulgaria	80.0	80.0	60.0	80.0	80.0	21.0	7.0	7.0	7.0	7.0
Czechoslovakia	8.5	9.3	9.0	9.3	9.5	3.0	1.0	1.0	1.0	1.0
Hungary	3.5	3.5	4.0	2.7	2.2	0.6	0.2	0.2	0.2	0.2
Poland	236.4	222.4	210.0	200.0	190.0	54.0	18.0	18.0	18.0	18.0
Roumania	50.0	55.0	60.0	60.0	60.0	15.0	5.0	5.0	5.0	5.0
China*	110.0	110.0	110.0	130.0	135.0	33.0	11.0	11.0	11.0	11.0
North Korea*	140.0	150.0	160.0	162.0	160.0	42.0	14.0	14.0	14.0	14.0
Total	1 383.4	1 435.2	1 536.0	1 594.0	1 666.7	408.6	136.2	136.2	136.2	136.2
WORLD TOTAL	5 701.9	5 840.5	6 103.8	6 097.4	6 146.5	1 521.0				
Monthly Average	475.2	486.7	508.7	508.1	512.2	507.0				

In this table the accounting is based on the zinc content by analysis of zinc ores and concentrates plus the zinc content of mixed ores and concentrates known to be intended for treatment for zinc recovery. Some of the data for latest months are estimated.

Notes (1) Exports

By courtesy of the World Bureau of Metal Statistics.

Zinc: World Slab Production 1971 to 1976

THOUSAND METRIC TONS

	1971	1972	1973	1974	1975	1976 Jan-Mar	1976 Mar	1976 Apr	1976 May	1976 June
EUROPE										
Austria	16·0	16·9	17·0	16·5	16·3	3·9	1·2	1·3	1·4	1·3
Belgium	209·1	255·6	277·7	288·8	218·2	54·3	17·6	18·4	18·6	21·2
Finland	62·7	81·1	80·7	91·8	109·9	24·8	9·5	7·4	7·7	7·9
France	218·7	261·5	259·4	276·7	181·1	51·4	17·9	19·6	20·5	20·6
Germany, Federal Republic ..	262·6	358·7	395·0	400·0	294·7	69·2	23·0	22·3	24·7	26·7
Italy	138·9	155·9	182·0	196·4	179·7	37·0	13·0	12·0	13·0	14·0
Netherlands	44·0	48·3	30·5	78·2	116·0	29·0	9·0	12·0	11·2	11·0
Norway	62·4	73·3	81·0	72·4	60·6	12·7	4·0	4·0	4·2	4·0
Spain	85·7	99·7	106·4	130·0	135·1	38·2	12·9	13·4	13·2	13·0
United Kingdom	116·5	73·8	83·8	84·4	53·4	2·6	2·6	3·8	2·6	3·8
Yugoslavia	45·5	48·7	55·3	86·4	97·9	38·5	14·2	6·3	10·6	13·1
Total ..	1 262·1	1 473·5	1 568·8	1 721·6	1 462·9	361·6	124·9	120·5	127·7	136·6
AFRICA										
Algeria	–	–	–	8·0	20·0	6·0	2·0	2·0	2·0	2·0
South Africa	43·4	47·2	53·1	65·4	63·7	17·6		6·2	5·8	
Zaire	63·0	67·0	68·0	68·7	65·6	16·5	5·5	5·5	5·5	5·5
Zambia	57·1	56·2	53·4	58·3	46·9	11·6	3·9	3·4	3·9	2·3
Other Africa					30·0					
Total ..	163·5	170·4	174·5	200·4	226·2	51·7				
ASIA										
Japan	719·8	809·0	844·0	850·8	701·9	170·1	48·5	57·6	61·5	63·5
India	21·2	25·2	20·8	21·1	25·7	5·4	1·8	1·8	1·8	1·8
S. Korea	9·2	10·5	12·6	11·5	20·9	6·8	2·4	2·4		
Total ..	750·2	844·7	877·4	883·4	748·5	182·3	52·7	61·8		
AMERICA										
Canada	372·5	476·2	532·6	426·3	426·9	110·6	36·6	42·1	40·5	43·0
U.S.A.	768·7	641·3	570·4	495·5	449·9	113·2	38·8	37·4	37·8	
Argentina	31·9	36·5	33·3	37·2	39·6	10·0				
Brazil	16·3	15·6	22·3	30·5	31·8	7·5	2·5	2·5	2·5	2·5
Mexico	83·4	83·8	67·2	133·4	149·0	36·0	12·0	12·0	12·0	12·0
Peru	57·4	67·5	67·1	70·7	63·7	18·0				
Total ..	1 330·2	1 320·9	1 292·9	1 193·6	1 160·9	295·3				
AUSTRALIA	265·7	303·7	306·4	283·8	193·3	50·4	18·1	19·1		
TOTAL ..	3 771·7	4 113·2	4 220·0	4 282·8	3 791·8	941·3				
Monthly Average ..	*314·3*	*342·8*	*351·7*	*356·9*	*316·0*	*313·8*				
OTHER COUNTRIES										
Bulgaria	78·4	80·0	80·0	80·0	80·0	22·5	7·5	7·5	7·5	7·5
Germany, Democratic Republic* ..	15·0	13·6	14·6	15·0	15·0	4·5	1·5	1·5	1·5	1·5
Hungary					0·7	0·3	0·1	0·1	0·1	0·1
Poland	220·1	228·3	224·0	233·0	230·0	60·0	20·0	20·0	20·0	20·0
Roumania	60·0	60·0	65·0	70·0	70·0	18·0	6·0	6·0	6·0	6·0
U.S.S.R.*	770·0	820·0	940·0	980·0	1 030·0	246·0	82·0	82·0	82·0	82·0
China P.R.*	110·0	120·0	120·0	130·0	130·0	33·0	11·0	11·0	11·0	11·0
North Korea	100·0	120·0	130·0	130·0	140·0	34·5	11·5	11·5	11·5	11·5
Total ..	1 353·5	1 441·9	1 573·6	1 638·0	1 695·7	418·8	139·6	139·6	139·6	139·6
WORLD TOTAL	5 125·2	5 555·1	5 793·6	5 920·8	5 487·5	1 360·1				
Monthly Average	*427·1*	*462·9*	*482·8*	*493·4*	*457·3*	*453·4*				

This table is based on the total production of slab zinc by smelters and refineries, including production on toll in the reporting country, regardless of the type of source material, i.e. whether ores, concentrates, residues, slag or scrap. Remelted zinc and zinc dust are excluded. Some of the data for the latest months are provisional.

By courtesy of the World Bureau of Metal Statistics.

Zinc: World Slab Consumption 1971 to 1976

THOUSAND METRIC TONS

	1971	1972	1973	1974	1975	1976 Jan-Mar	Feb	Mar	Apr	May
EUROPE										
Austria	19·8	20·9	21·4	25·2	24·4	5·4				
Belgium	130·9	139·2	180·1	194·9	103·3	30·0				
Denmark	9·9	12·8	12·8	13·0	11·9	3·8				
Finland	7·8	11·0	16·0	19·0	16·0	4·0				
France	225·4	264·1	290·4	306·1	222·5	66·5				
Germany, Federal Republic	387·5	413·1	438·2	389·1	297·4	105·7				
Greece	8·0	10·0	14·7	15·6	11·7	4·2	1·4	1·4	1·4	1·4
Irish Republic	6·0	3·0	6·2	4·9	4·8	1·5	0·5	0·5	0·5	0·5
Italy	170·0	203·0	220·0	202·0	150·2	45·0				
Netherlands	36·0	35·0	32·3	32·7	28·6	7·2				
Norway	25·0	26·0	26·0	26·0	30·0	7·5				
Portugal	10·0	11·0	10·0	11·5	8·0	3·0	1·0	1·0	1·0	1·0
Spain	86·0	101·0	111·6	119·6	92·1	21·5				
Sweden	32·9	38·5	43·3	35·6	43·5	11·0				
Switzerland	25·7	32·7	28·0	24·3	16·2	3·9				
United Kingdom	273·7	279·3	305·4	268·5	208·7	59·9	19·1	23·0	19·1	21·1
Yugoslavia	53·5	51·7	62·5	67·1	65·0	16·5	5·5	5·5	5·5	5·5
Total	1 508·1	1 652·3	1 818·9	1 755·1	1 334·3	396·6				
AFRICA										
South and South West Africa	53·9	51·0	62·1	69·5	63·2	15·8				
Other	24·0	38·0	25·0	29·2	18·3	7·5	2·5	2·5	2·5	2·5
Total	77·9	89·0	87·1	98·7	81·5	23·3				
ASIA										
Hong Kong	9·0	9·0	11·1	13·7	5·9	3·0	1·0	1·0	1·0	1·0
India	90·0	102·8	77·9	77·5	55·0	21·0	7·0	7·0	7·0	7·0
Japan	624·1	708·3	814·9	695·4	541·3	163·5	54·6	57·6	56·0	58·4
Philippines	20·0	20·0	10·2	8·8	9·3	5·1	1·7	1·7	1·7	1·7
South Korea	13·6	15·0	23·1	25·4	24·1	4·5	1·5	1·5	1·5	1·5
Taiwan	15·0	15·0	23·6	22·3	12·3	5·4	1·8	1·8	1·8	1·8
Thailand	17·0	18·0	21·4	23·3	17·1	6·0	2·0	2·0	2·0	2·0
Turkey	10·0	10·0	10·0	15·0	12·1	3·0	1·0	1·0	1·0	1·0
Other	9·0	9·0	53·7	48·4	53·5	12·0	4·0	4·0	4·0	4·0
Total	807·7	907·1	1 045·9	929·8	730·6	223·5	74·6	77·6	76·0	78·4
AMERICA										
Canada	114·5	136·3	153·3	141·4	149·9	30·8	9·3	12·8		
U.S.A.	1 136·9	1 285·7	1 363·9	1 167·4	838·9	252·3	79·5	96·7	89·6	93·1
Argentina	34·0	38·4	36·6	38·9	42·0	11·1	3·7	3·7	3·7	3·7
Brazil	66·9	74·4	104·2	93·4	83·0	24·0	8·0	8·0	8·0	8·0
Chile	6·0	6·0	5·4	5·1	6·0	1·5	0·5	0·5	0·5	0·5
Columbia	7·6	7·5	7·3	8·5	5·8	1·8	0·6	0·6	0·6	0·6
Mexico	42·4	48·8	61·0	59·8	62·7	18·0	6·0	6·0	6·0	6·0
Peru	5·0	6·0	← 27·3	30·0	25·0	9·0	3·0	3·0	3·0	3·0
Venezeula	10·1	10·2	5·8	10·9	8·0	3·0	1·0	1·0	1·0	1·0
Other	6·3	8·0	9·5	8·1	2·9	3·0	1·0	1·0	1·0	1·0
Total	1 429·7	1 621·3	1 774·7	1 563·5	1 224·2	354·5	112·6	133·3		
AUSTRALASIA										
Australia	108·9	114·1	112·5	120·6	80·0	24·0				
New Zealand	13·0	22·0	22·0	21·0	14·9	6·0	2·0	2·0	2·0	2·0
Total	121·9	136·1	134·5	141·6	94·9	30·0				
TOTAL	3 945·3	4 415·4	4 861·1	4 488·7	3 465·5	1 027·9				
Monthly Average	*328·8*	*367·9*	*405·1*	*374·1*	*288·8*	*342·6*				
OTHER COUNTRIES*										
Bulgaria	28·0	35·0	40·0	40·0	40·0	10·5	3·5	3·5	3·5	3·5
Czechoslovakia	45·0	55·0	55·0	60·0	62·0	15·0	5·0	5·0	5·0	5·0
Germany, Democratic Republic	60·0	60·0	55·0	62·0	61·0	15·0	5·0	5·0	5·0	5·0
Hungary	20·9	19·2	21·9	23·0	25·5	6·0	2·0	2·0	2·0	2·0
Poland	140·3	140·0	148·7	141·5	145·0	40·5	13·5	13·5	13·5	13·5
Roumania	35·0	35·0	40·0	40·0	45·0	10·5	3·5	3·5	3·5	3·5
U.S.S.R.	700·0	760·0	840·0	900·0	950·0	222·0	74·0	74·0	74·0	74·0
China P.R.	170·0	170·0	190·0	200·0	220·0	51·0	17·0	17·0	17·0	17·0
North Korea	15·0	15·0	20·0	20·0	20·0	6·0	2·0	2·0	2·0	2·0
Other Asia	5·0	5·0	5·0	5·0	5·0	1·5	0·5	0·5	0·5	0·5
Total	1 219·2	1 294·2	1 415·6	1 491·5	1 573·5	378·0	126·0	126·0	126·0	126·0
WORLD TOTAL	5 164·5	5 709·6	6 276·7	5 980·2	5 039·0	1 405·9				
Monthly Average	*430·4*	*475·8*	*523·1*	*498·4*	*419·9*	*468·6*				

In this table the accounting is based on the consumption of slab zinc. Remelted zinc and zinc dust are excluded. Some of the data for latest months are provisional.

By courtesy of the World Bureau of Metal Statistics.

Zinc: London

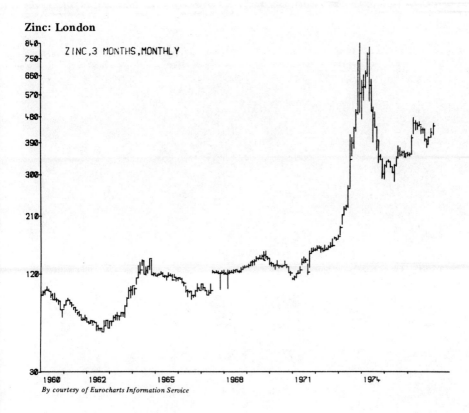

ZINC,3 MONTHS,MONTHLY

By courtesy of Eurocharts Information Service

Part 3:
Commodity Market Data

Australia

Sydney Futures Exchange Ltd

7th Level, Australia Square Tower, Sydney 2000

Telephone: 2-241 1077; **Telex:** AA 26713; **Cable address:** Woolfutures Sydney

Commodities: Greasy Wool, Live Cattle

Titles of appointments: Chairman, Vice-Chairman and Manager/Secretary

Name of Manager/Secretary: T E Graves

Hours of trading: 10.45 to 12.30, 14.15 to 16.00. There are five minute calls at 10.45 and 14.15 for Live Cattle and ten minute calls at 11.00, 14.30 and 15.50 for Wool.

Trading unit: Wool — 1,500 kg clean weight, Cattle — 10,000 kg liveweight ie from 24-32 steer

Trading limits: None

Contract particulars:
Quality:
Wool — The standard type of wool traded is 64s' quality Good Topmaking Merino Fleece Wool of Good to Average length. Other Merino Wools may be delivered from 70s' quality down to 60s' and these are subject to a premium and discount against the value for standard wool.
Cattle — Live Steers and each showing no more than two permanent incisor teeth, weighing 360 kg liveweight, with a fat thickness of 5-10mm at the eye muscle measured between the 12th and 13th rib, and dressing 56 per cent.

Delivery points:
Wool contracts for delivery shall be made up from wool submitted to auction at any recognized wool selling centre in Australia and sold through members of the National Council of Wool Selling Brokers of Australia or such affiliates of such Council or to approved auctions from time to time.
Steers shall be delivered to Homebush Bay Saleyards (NSW) in good order and condition, where the steers will be slaughtered and delivered to the Buyer in dressed carcass form.

Are rules and regulations available? Yes — Memorandum and Articles of Association and By-Laws

Can they be purchased? Yes, by Floor Members and Associate Members

Arbitration rules: In the event of a dispute or undesirable situation the Clearing House shall refer the matter to a special Sub-Committee appointed by and including a representative of the Clearing House of not fewer than three and not more than six persons (who need not be members of Sydney Futures Exchange). If in the opinion of the Sub-Committee an undesirable situation or practice affecting a market has developed or is developing the Sub-Committee shall notify the Board of the Exchange and the Board of the Clearing House. The Board of the Exchange may on receipt of such notice take any steps to correct such situation or practice and may give direction to Members accordingly.

Is there an appeal? No

Currency dealt in: Australian dollars

Average volume of trading over past two years: Wool Contract — Monthly average $51,417,500. Live Cattle — average monthly since inception $669,467

Recommended commission rates and margins: Minimum brokerage rates for business transacted on the Exchange: Non-Member — per contract bought $20; per contract sold $20; per round turn $40. (Straddle) Non-Member — per opening contract bought $20; per opening contract sold $20; per closing contract of the above nil; per straddle round turn $40. An Associate Member of a market shall be charged by a Floor Member half the above non-member rates for business executed in the market for which he is an associate. Floor Member transacting business through another Floor Member — per contract bought $5; per contract sold $5; maximum per day $150. Give-up order — payable to the executing Floor Member; per contract bought or sold $6.50.

Membership, types of: The membership of the Exchange comprises Floor Members and Associate Members. Floor Membership is only granted to persons resident in or firms registered and/or corporations incorporated in or registered in the Commonwealth of Australia and conducting business in the Commonwealth of Australia. The number of Associate Members are determined by the Board from time to time. The numbers at present are limited to 114 Wool and 18 Live Cattle Associates.

Trading members, as at December 1975: *See Appendix 1 (page 225).*

Date of establishment of market: May 1960

Austria

Vienna Commodity Exchange

(Wiener Börsekammer)
Wipplingerstr 34, A-1011 Vienna

Telephone: 222-63 37 66; **Telex:** 07-4693; **Cable address:** Stock Exchange, Wien

Commodities: A variety of goods, especially: Timber, Colonial Products and Foods, Textiles, Chemicals, Skins, Leather and Technical Leather

Titles of appointments: President, Vice-Presidents, Secretary General

Names of Chief Executives: DDr Franz Ockermüller — President, Dr Franz Josef Mayer-Gunthof — Vice-President (for the Commodity Exchange), Dr Harald Eichler — Secretary General

Hours of trading: Skins, Leather and Technical Leather — every Tuesday from 12.00 to 13.00; Timber — every Wednesday from 11.00 to 13.00; Colonial Products, Textiles and Chemicals — every Thursday from 11.00 to 13.00

Trading limits: None

Are rules and regulations available? Yes

Can they be purchased? Yes

Arbitration rules: As decided in 1966 the Court of Arbitration is competent (a) without an arbitration contract, for Commodity Exchange transactions; (b) on grounds of an arbitration contract; (c) for business transactions concluded outside the Commodity Exchange. The Court of Arbitration is made up of three arbitrators, one of which is selected by each party, and the third one is jointly appointed by these two arbitrators. The arbitrators must be selected from the list of arbitrators. A secretary qualified to hold judicial office has to be present at the Court of Arbitration. The procedure is opened by an action and after a verbal hearing it will be closed by an award. The reasons for the award have to be given. If the defendant fails to appear the Court of Arbitration may pronounce an award in default. There are no strict rules for the procedure and there is no obligation to consult a lawyer. The most important duty of the Court of Arbitration is to settle a litigation by way of arrangement. In Austria arbitral awards constitute an execution title like the verdict by the law court.

Is there an appeal? No

Currency dealt in: Austrian schilling

Average volume of trading over past two years: The Vienna Commodity Exchange is chiefly a place for negotiation and the establishment of business connections.

Recommended commission rates and margins: 2 per cent; for other agreements each party has to pay half

Date of establishment of market: 1875

Canada

The Winnipeg Commodity Exchange
678-167 Lombard Ave, Winnipeg, Manitoba R3B 0V7

Telephone: 204-942 6401 (Office), 204-943 0661 (Trading Floor);
Telex: 07-587778

Commodities: Flaxseed, Rapeseed, Rye, Barley, Oats, Wheat and Gold

Titles of appointments: Board of Governors (15 elected) who elect a Chairman, two Vice-Chairmen and three Public Governors; appointed: one Secretary-Treasurer, one President and executive employees

Names of Chief Executives: R S Ennis — President, P K Huffman — Secretary

Hours of trading: Gold — 08.15 to 13.30 Central Time; Grain — 09.30 to 13.15 Central Time

Trading units:

	Board Lot (tonnes)	Job Lot (tonnes)
Domestic Feed Wheet	100	20
Domestic Feed Oats	100	20
Domestic Feed Barley	100	20
Rye	100	20
Flaxseed	100	20
Rapeseed	100	20
Gold	Standard (400 oz)	
	Centum (100 oz)	

Trading limits:

	Price fluctuation units (cents per tonne)	Daily limits up or down from previous close (dollars per tonne)
Domestic Feed Wheat	10	5
Domestic Feed Oats	10	5
Domestic Feed Barley	10	5
Rye	10	5
Flaxseed	10	10
Rapeseed	10	10
	(per oz)	
Gold	Regular 5	Normal 10
	Fast market — to 20	Last trading day — none

109

Contract particulars:

Quality:

Domestic Feed Wheat	— No 3 CWRS, or No 3 CU $7.50/t
Domestic Feed Oats	— No 1 Feed, or Higher 50¢/t, or No 2 Feed $3.50/t
Domestic Feed Barley	— No 1 Feed, or Higher 50¢/t, or No 2 Feed $2/t
Rye	— No 2 CW, or No 1 CW, or No 3 CW $2/t
Flaxseed	— No 1 CW, or No 2 CW $2/t
Rapeseed	— No 1 CR, or No 2 CR $13/t
Gold	— .995 and Serial No by Melter/Assayer acceptable for good London delivery

Delivery points:

Domestic Feed Wheat	— Thunder Bay; October, December, May, July
Domestic Feed Oats	— Thunder Bay; October, December, May, July
Domestic Feed Barley	— Thunder Bay; October, December, May, July
Rye	— Thunder Bay; October, November*, December, May, July
Flaxseed	— Thunder Bay; October, November*, December, May, July
Rapeseed	— Thunder Bay; October, November*, December, May, July
	— Vancouver — ADP; September, November, January, March, June
Gold	— Toronto all US dollars: Standard — October, January, April, July plus one of the following months in the forward year: October, January, April, July Centum — August, November, February, May plus one of the following months in the forward year: November, February, May, August

* Thunder Bay November delivery point month only to 20th (approx)
ADP — alternative delivery points: Saskatoon, Edmonton, Calgary to 13th (approx) of delivery month

Are rules and regulations available? Yes

Can they be purchased? Yes

Arbitration rules: Members can demand arbitration of commercial disputes between each other, and proceedings are subject to Exchange By-Laws. Non-members may request arbitration with a member, but this is subject to consent. Arbitration is normally conducted by the Committee of Arbitration.

Is there an appeal? Yes, under Exchange By-Laws, to Committee on Appeals

Currency dealt in: Grains and Oilseeds — Canadian dollars
Gold — US dollars

Average volume of trading over past two years:

Total volume, 1973—4 and 1974—5 crop years
1 August — 31 July

Flaxseed	91,696,000 bu
Rapeseed	334,314,000 bu
Rye	165,438,000 bu
Barley	275,544,000 bu
Oats	150,888,000 bu
Wheat	126,358,000 bu
Gold	79,449 contracts, 400 oz
	31,835 contracts, 100 oz
	(commenced trading June 1974)

Recommended commission rates and margins:

	Customer minimum maintenance margins*			*Exchange minimum commissions: non-member*		
				Regular round turn	Spread all four sides	Day-trade round turn
	(dollars per unit of trade)			*(dollars per unit of trade)*		
Domestic Feed Wheat	80		B	25	7	3.50
			J	5.50		
Domestic Feed Oats	80		B	25	7	3.50
			J	5.50		
Domestic Feed Barley	80		B	25	7	3.50
			J	5.50		
Rye	80		B	25	7	3.50
			J	5.50		
Flaxseed	160		B	30	9	4.50
			J	6.50		
Rapeseed	180		B	30	9	4.50
			J	6.50		

		Regular	*Hedge*	*Spread*			
Gold — Standard	I	$4,000	$2,000	$400	$75	$100	$50
	M	$2,000	$2,000	$200			
— Centum	I	$1,000	$500	$100	$35	$50	$25
	M	$500	$250	$50			

*The minimum rate of margin to be maintained by a customer shall be no less than the rate of margin required by Winnipeg Commodity Clearing Ltd

B—Board Lot; J—Job Lot; I—June, forward year; M—June, current year

Membership: Exchange is a voluntary, unincorporated, non-profit association of persons. Each member has one vote. Firms and corporations may be registered annually for trading privileges.

Date of establishment of markets:

Futures

Domestic Feed Barley	1974 (3)
Domestic Feed Oats	1974 (2)
Domestic Feed Wheat	1974 (1)
Flaxseed	1904
Gold — 400 oz	1972
— 200 oz	1974
Rye	1917
Thunder Bay Rapeseed	1970
Vancouver Rapeseed	1963
Cash Grains —	1887
(1) All Wheat	1903—1943
(2) All Oats	1904—1973
(3) All Barley	1913—1973

Membership of other organizations:

In Exchange, by others — Winnipeg Commodity Clearing Ltd, Lake Shippers Clearance Association Ltd

In others, by Exchange — Canada Grains Council, Rapeseed Association of Canada, Palliser Wheat Growers Association

Associated — The Shippers & Exporters Association of the Winnipeg Commodity Exchange, The Futures Brokers Association

France

International Market of Robusta Coffees

Bourse de Commerce, Place Jules Ferry, 76600 Le Havre
Bourse de Commerce, 2 rue de Viarmes, 75040 Paris Cedex 01

Telephone: Le Havre — 35-421027, Paris — 1-5088450/5088460; **Telex:** Le Havre
190 713, 220 270 Comagre Paris

Commodity: Robusta Coffee

Titles of appointments: President, Vice-President

Names of Chief Executives: Le Havre — Robert Le Fur — President, Association
of Authorized Coffee Brokers (President du Syndicat des Courtiers Assermentes
en Cafe); Paris — Jean-Jacques Fricquenon — President, Technical Committee,
Jacques Dumont — Vice-President of the Technical Committee

Hours of trading: Monday to Friday 10.20 to 13.00, 15.00 to 18.30

Trading unit: 10 tonnes. Quotations are per 100 kg net weight of Robusta
Coffee CIF Le Havre.

Trading Limits: 70 francs per 100 kg for a price between 1001 and 1700 francs;
105 francs per 100 kg for a price between 1701 and 2500 francs; 135 francs per
100 kg for a price between 2501 and 3000 francs; 165 francs per 100 kg for a
price between 3001 and 3500 francs; 180 francs per 100 kg for a price between
3501 and 4000 francs

Contract particulars:
Quality: Robusta Coffee from Ivory Coast, Angola, Uganda, Cameroun, Togo,
Zaire, Central African Republic, Malagasy, Indonesia — based on samples of
300 grams containing a max of 60 imperfections. The size of the bean to
correspond with 14 screen coffee and having a weight allowance of not more
than 8 per cent. Coffee must be free from disease, correct with respect to origin,
comply with current regulations concerning admission to delivery ports. Each
consignment must be homogeneous and accompanied by a certificate of quality
and grading. It must be contained in the original bags, be of good quality, have
no spoilage and be stored in approved warehouses under customs control.

Delivery points: Marseilles, Le Havre, Bordeaux, Rotterdam, Amsterdam

Are rules and regulations available? Yes — the regulations of the International
Market of Robusta Coffees of Commercial Exchanges of Paris and Le Havre
became law by ministerial order of 4 November 1975.

Can they be purchased? Yes

Arbitration rules: Rules of 'Chambre Arbitrale' or rules of French Code du Commerce implemented by Tribunal de Commerce de Paris

Is there an appeal? Yes, before the Cour d'Appel de Paris

Currency dealt in: French francs

Average volume of trading over past two years: 1975 — 64,390 tonnes; 1976 — 93,580 tonnes

Recommended commission rates and margins: Commission rates are determined by ministerial 'arrete' with discount in favour of overseas associates and home associates.

Trading members, as at October 1976: *See Appendix 1 (page 225).*

Date of establishment of market: Originally opened in Le Havre in 1882; closed down on 2 September 1939; after the war it reopened on 16 November 1954 and was replaced by the new Coffee Robusta market on 4 November 1975.

PARIS

Cocoa Terminal Market on the Paris Commodity Exchange

Bourse de Commerce, 2 rue de Viarmes, 75040 Paris Cedex 01

Telephone: 1-5088450/5088460; **Telex:** 220 270 Comagre Paris

Commodity: Cocoa Beans

Title of appointments: President, Vice-President

Names of Chief Executives: M Rene des Cloizeaux — President, M Pierre Duclau — Vice-President

Hours of trading: Monday to Friday 10.00 to 13.00, 15.00 to 18.30

Trading unit: 10 tonnes. The quotations are to be understood basis CIF the ports determined by the technical committee, per 100 kg net weight.

Trading limits: The max fluctuation up or down allowed during a session is 90 francs per 100 kg as against the previous margin call.

Contract particulars:
Quality: The regulated market of cocoa beans is based on good fermented main crop cocoa beans from Ivory Coast. Cocoa from other origins may be admitted for delivery by the technical committee. The technical committee determines the differentials applicable to the different qualities, origins and campaigns.

Conditions of admission: To be delivered to the Paris Market the merchandise must be: (a) of sound, loyal and merchantable quality without bad smell or bad taste; (b) the quality 'good fermented' must not contain more than 5 per cent defective beans and 5 per cent slaty beans. The quality 'fair fermented' must not contain more than 10 per cent defective beans and 10 per cent slaty beans;

(c) packed in usual bags from origin in good condition, bags free; (d) stored in a bonded warehouse approved by the technical committee, in France or abroad; (e) must have the object of a tender accepted by the Clearing House. Every tendered lot must be homogeneous and of one mark and be accompanied by a quality certificate.

Delivery points: Marseilles, Sete, Bordeaux, Le Havre, Dunkirk, Amsterdam, Hamburg

Are rules and regulations available? Yes. The regulations of the Cocoa Terminal Market on the Paris Commodity Exchange became law by ministerial order of 4 November 1975.

Can they be purchased? Yes

Arbitration rules: Rules of 'Chambre Arbitrale' or rules of French Code du Commerce implemented by Tribunal de Commerce de Paris

Is there an appeal? Yes, before the Cour d'Appel de Paris

Currency dealt in: French francs

Average volume of trading over past two years: 1975 — 917,340 tonnes, 1976 — 607,920 tonnes

Recommended commission rates and margins: Commission rates are determined by ministerial 'arrete' with discount in favour of overseas associated and home associates.

Date of establishment of market: February 1963

Trading members, as at October 1976: *See Appendix 1 (page 225).*

International Market of White Sugar of Paris

Bourse de Commerce, 2 rue de Viarmes, Paris Cedex 01

Telephone: 1-5088450/5088460; **Telex:** 220 270 Comagre Paris

Commodity: White Sugar

Titles of appointments: President, Vice-President

Names of Chief Executives: M Maurice Varsano — President, M Jacques Boucher — Vice-President

Hours of trading: Monday to Friday 10.00 to 13.00, 15.00 to 18.30

Trading unit: 50 tonnes

Trading limits: 200 francs for a price (1000 kg) up to 2000 francs; 300 francs for a price (1000 kg) between 2001 and 4000 francs; 400 francs for a price (1000 kg) between 4001 and 6000 francs

Contract particulars:

Quality: Basis — white beet or cane crystal sugar of any origin. Max humidity — 0.08 per cent, min polarization — 99.7 degrees. The colour shall not be inferior to type colour No 6 of the Brunswick Institute. Free running, sound, merchantable quality, dry and well-blended of regular size grains

Delivery points: The delivery is made in the harbour indicated in the 'notification de livraison'. Allowed harbours — Odessa, Constanta, Varna, Mersin, Rijeka, Koper, Trieste, Marseilles, Alicante, Cadiz, Gijon, Bilbao, Bordeaux, Nantes, Dublin, Greenock, Birkenhead, London, Kingston-upon-Hull, Le Havre, Rouen, Dunkirk, Antwerp, Rotterdam, Amsterdam, Bremen, Hamburg, Copenhagen, Rostock, Szczecin, Gdansk and Gdynia. Porkala and Helsinki will be allowed from July 1978.

Are rules and regulations available? Yes — the regulations of the International Market of White Sugar of Paris of the Commercial Exchanges of Paris became law by Ministerial order of 4 November 1975.

Can they be purchased? Yes

Arbitration rules: Rules of 'Chambre Arbitrale' or rules of French Code du Commerce implemented by Tribunal de Commerce de Paris.

Is there an appeal? Yes, before the Cour d'Appel de Paris

Currency dealt in: French francs

Average volume of trading over past year: 1976 — 2,376,900 tonnes

Recommended commission rates and margins: Commission rates are determined by ministerial 'arrete' with discount in favour of overseas associates and home associates.

Trading members, as at October 1976: *See Appendix 1 (page 225).*

Date of establishment of market: The Market was opened in May 1964.

Paris Toasted Soya Beans International Market

Bourse de Commerce, 2 rue de Viarmes, Paris Cedex 01

Telephone: 1-5088450/5088460; **Telex:** 220 270 Comagre Paris

Commodity: Soya Beans

Titles of appointments: President, Vice-President

Names of Chief Executives: M Andre Hurtebize — President, M Alain Chenut — Vice-President

Hours of trading: Monday to Friday 11.00 to 13.00, 15.00 to 18.30

Trading unit: 55 tonnes

Trading limits: The max fluctuation up or down allowed during a session is 9 francs per 100 kg as against the previous margin call.

Contract particulars:

Quality: Based on toasted Soya Beans in bulk from any origin approved by the technical committee, CIF ship's tackle Rotterdam.

Conditions of admission: To be delivered on the Paris Market the merchandise must be of sound, loyal and merchantable quality, it must contain a min of 44 per cent of proteins and grease, and a max of 8.5 per cent of cellulose.

Delivery point: Rotterdam

Are rules and regulations available? Yes — the regulations of the Paris Toasted Soya Beans International Market became law by Ministerial order of 11 March 1976.

Can they be purchased? Yes

Arbitration rules: Rules of 'Chambre Arbitrale' or rules of French Code du Commerce implemented by Tribunal de Commerce de Paris

Is there an appeal? Yes, before the Cour d'Appel de Paris

Currency dealt in: French francs

Average volume of trading over past year: 1976 — 506,990 tonnes

Recommended commission rates and margins: Commission rates are determined by ministerial 'arrete' with discount in favour of overseas associates and home associates.

Trading members, as at October 1976: *See Appendix 1 (page 225).*

Date of establishment of market: Established in March 1967 and reopened on 9 June 1976.

Germany (West)

Berlin Produce Exchange

(Berliner Produktenbörse)
Hardenbergstr 16-18, 1000 Berlin 12

Telephone: 30-31 07 21 (IHK Berlin); **Telex:** 1 83 663 (IHK with suffix Börse)

Commodities: Grain, Milling Products (Flour and Bran), Fodder and similar products

Titles of appointments: Chairman of Executive, first and second Deputy Chairman, eight Members of Executive, Syndic

Name of Syndic of Exchange: Hans Joachim Schwarze

Hours of trading: Every Friday 16.30 to 18.00

Trading unit: Per 100 kg

Trading limits: None

Contract particulars:
Quality: Berlin Mill Products
Delivery points: Berlin (West) or by arrangement

Are rules and regulations available? Yes

Can they be purchased? Yes

Arbitration rules: These are the special arbitration regulations of the Association of Berlin Corn and Produce Traders. Agreement may also be reached in other Arbitration Courts.

Is there an appeal? No

Currency dealt in: Deutsche mark

Recommended commission rates and margins: By agreement

Membership, types of: Wholesalers, Mills, Insurers, Forwarding Agents and Agents

Date of establishment of market: 1685 — founding of Berlin Exchange; from 1900 special section; since 1975 Berlin Produce Exchange

Membership of other organizations: European Commodities Exchange, Luxembourg

BREMEN

Bremen Cotton Exchange

(Bremer Baumwollbörse)
Wachtstr 17-24, PO Box 10 67 27, D-2800 Bremen 1

Telephone: 421-321901/3; **Telex:** 024 4623; **Cable address:** baumwolle

Commodities: Raw Cotton, Linters, Cotton Waste

Titles of appointments: Board of Directors, consisting of 20 members including one president, two vice-presidents and two associated members

Name of Managing Director: Karl E Klopfer

Are rules and regulations available? Yes — German and English editions for physical trading of raw cotton, cotton waste and linters are available.

Can they be purchased? Yes, from the Secretariat of the Bremer Baumwollbörse

Arbitration rules: See Rules of the Bremer Baumwollbörse, Section VIII for technical arbitration; Section V for quality arbitration and Section VI for fibre testing.

Is there an appeal? Yes, see Rules of the Bremer Baumwollbörse, Sections as above.

Currency dealt in: Usually in US dollars and/or Deutsche marks

Average volume of trading over past two years: 1-1.2 million bales of cotton (of approx 480 lb per bale) annually

Membership, types of: Ordinary members with voting rights — (a) private companies and (b) individuals, both with residence in the Federal Republic of Germany; and associated members (not entitled to vote) — private companies and state marketing organizations with residence outside Federal Republic of Germany

Members, as at December 1975: Approx 300 members

Date of establishment of market: 1 October 1872. Up to 1970 physical and futures market; since 1971 physical market only. The Bremer Baumwollbörse is now an organization offering facilities for physical commodity trading by providing internationally recognized trading rules for raw cotton, linters and cotton waste, including arbitration machinery. It serves the interests of all engaged in the cotton business, in particular cotton traders, spinning mills, cotton shippers, brokers, forwarding agents, etc.

Membership of other organizations: CICCA, Liverpool (Committee for International Cooperation between Cotton Associations); IFCATI, Zurich (International Federation of Cotton and Allied Textile Industries); International Chamber of Commerce, German National Committee, Cologne, among others.

DUISBURG
Grain and Commodity Exchange Rhein-Ruhr Duisburg-Essen
incorporated at Duisburg

(Getreide und Warenbörse Rhein-Ruhr Duisburg-Essen eV zu Duisburg)
Mercatorstr 22-24, Postfach 10 11 23, 4100 Duisburg 1

Commodity: Bread grains, Milling products, Fodder and Industrial grains, Feeding stuff

Telephone: 2131-28211 (Chamber of Industry and Commerce); **Telex:** 0855 820

Titles of appointments: Chairman, four Vice-Chairmen (comprising Inner Committee) and ten Committee Members

Name of Chief Executive: Dr Heinz Nohlen

Hours of trading: Every second and fourth Monday, from 15.30 to 17.30

Trading unit: None

Trading limits: None

Contract particulars:
Quality: By sample or average quality of commodity

Are rules and regulations available? Yes — standard conditions in the German Grain Trade

Can they be purchased? Yes — from Strothe Verlag, Hanover

Arbitration rules: Arbitration Rules of the Grain Exchange at Duisburg

Is there an appeal? Yes — appeal to the Higher Arbitration Court of the Exchange

Currency dealt in: Deutsche marks

Membership, types of: No different types within the membership

Date of establishment of market: 1893

FRANKFURT
Frankfurt Corn and Produce Exchange
(Frankfurter Getreide und Produktenbörse)
Börsenplatz 2, D 6000 Frankfurt/Main

Telephone: 611-2197218; **Telex:** 0412516 getrb d

Commodities: Home-grown/foreign Grain, Milling Products, home-grown and foreign Fodder, Potatoes, Coarse Fodder, Peat, Eggs, Specially Light Fuel Oil

Titles of appointments: Chairman, Deputy Chairman, eight to ten Executive Members, Syndic, Secretariat

Name of Chief Executive: Richard Speich

Branches and affiliates: Quotation Commission for Specially Light Fuel Oil at the Chamber of Industry and Commerce, Wiesbaden

Hours of trading: Every Wednesday, 15.00 to 17.00

Trading unit: Corn, Milling Products, Potatoes, Coarse Fodder, Peat — 100 kg or 1000 kg; Eggs — 100 cartons (= 3600 eggs); Specially Light Fuel Oil — 100 litres

Contract particulars:
Quality: The qualities traded are basically determined by the appropriate regulations of the German Federal Republic as well as by EEC standards.
Delivery point: Frankfurt

Are rules and regulations available? No

Arbitration rules: Arbitration Rules of the Frankfurt Corn and Produce Exchange and of the Potato Board

Is there an appeal? Yes, to the High Court of Arbitration

Membership, types of: (a) Principals, managers or persons who according to law, statute or contract are appointed to carry out business transactions and are entitled to conclude business transactions independently at the Exchange; (b) employees who are not entitled to conclude business transactions independently

Date of establishment of market: 1862

Membership of other organizations: Study Group of the South German Produce Exchanges, Study Group of the German Produce Exchanges, Consortium of European Commodity Exchanges

HANOVER
Lower Saxony Grain and Produce Exchange
incorporated at Hanover
(Niedersächsische Getreide und Produktenbörse eV zu Hannover)
Rathenaustr 2, 3000 Hanover

Telephone: 511-3 27661; **Cable address:** Getreidebörse Hannover

Commodities: Grain, Feeding Stuff, Fertilizers, Flour, Potatoes

Titles of appointments: Chairman, Vice-Chairman, Syndic

Name of Syndic of the Exchange: Dr Hans Litten

Hours of trading: Every Tuesday 14.30 to 16.30

Trading unit: 100 kg; 1000 kg

Rules and regulations: These are the Standard Conditions in the German Grain Trade.

Arbitration rules: These are implemented by the Arbitration Court of the Exchange.

Membership, types of: Import Trade, Wholesale Trade, Producers, Milling Contractors, Shipping and Forwarding Agents

Members as at December 1975: 150 Member Firms

WORMS

Worms Grain and Produce Exchange

(Wormser Getreide und Produktenbörse eV)

Mälzerei Schill, 6522 Osthofen, Postfach

Telephone: 4925-06242 833/860; **Telex:** 04 67839; **Cable address:** brauko

Commodities: Grain and Fodder, Mill Products, Agricultural Products, Fertilizers, Seeds

Titles of appointments: Chairman, two Deputy Chairmen, seven Committee Members

Name of Chief Executive: Rolf Eller

Hours of trading: Every Friday 16.30 to 18.00

Date of establishment of market: 1907

Hong Kong

Hong Kong Commodity Exchange

Hutchison House, Murray Rd, Hong Kong Central

Telephone: 5-243059/243050

Commodity: Raw Cotton

Titles of appointments: Chairman, two Deputy Chairmen, President Management Committee

Name of Chairman: P O Scales

Trading unit: 25,000 lb

Contract particulars: Contracts are for cotton of any origin. The quality of the cotton shall be in accordance with the following specifications:
(i) Cotton other than Saw Ginned shall not be tenderable.
(ii) If American or American-type cotton of any origin (excluding Pakistan) is tendered the following specifications apply: (a) Grade — Middling (Universal Standard) but failing bales classing Strict Low Middling (Universal Standard) or, if off colour or spotted, Middling Light Spotted (Universal Standard) shall be tenderable at allowances as quoted by the LCA (b) Staple — One inch, but failing bales not less than 31/32 of an inch shall be tenderable at allowances, as quoted by The Liverpool Cotton Association Ltd (c) Micronaire — Min 3.5 No Control Limit, max 4.9 No Control Limit. If any bales are below 3.5 NCL but not lower than 3.2 NCL, the buyer shall accept these inferior bales at allowances as per the LCS/ACSA Micronaire Agreement in force on the day of tender; plus a penalty of 5 per cent of the official quotation on the day of tender of these bales.
Delivery point: In approved Godown, Hong Kong

Are rules and regulations available? Yes — from President of the Management Committee, Hong Kong Exchange

Currency dealt in: US dollars

Membership: Full membership is reserved to individuals, partnerships or corporations resident or incorporated in Hong Kong. Affiliated membership available to those whose interests are specifically related to the commodity.

Date of establishment of market: Summer 1977

India

ANDHRA PRADESH
Tobacco Board
Guntur, Andhra Pradesh

Chairman: N K Muralidhara Rao

BANGALORE
Coffee Board
No 1 Vidhana Veedhi, Bangalore

Chairman: M Venkataratnam

BOMBAY
Central Silk Board
'Meghdoot', 95-B Marine Drive, Bombay 400002

Chairman: S Muni Raju

CALCUTTA
Tea Board of India
14 Brabourne Rd, PB No 2172, Calcutta

Chairman: T S Brocca

COCHIN
Cardamom Board
XLV/448 Chittur Rd, Ernakulam, Cochin 18

Chairman: M Venkataraman

Coir Board
MG Rd, Ernakulam, Cochin 16

Chairman: J Alexander

KERALA STATE
Rubber Board
PO Kottayam-9, Kerala State

Chairman: Prof K T Chandy

Italy

Bari Commodity Exchange
(Borsa Merci)
Corso Cavour 2, 70121 Bari

Telephone: 80-216600

Commodity Exchange of Bologna
(Borsa Merci di Bologna)
Associazione Granaria Emiliana Romagnola, Piazza Costituzione 8, Bologna

Telephone: 51-50 19 51/51 90 51 (14 lines); Telex: 51240; Cable address: AGER

Commodities: Cereals, Flour and by-products, Poultry Feed, Dry Vegetables

Name of President: Emilio Vandini

Hours of trading: Every Friday 08.00 to 17.30

Contract particulars:
Quality: Contract No 1 Home Produced 'Soft Wheat'; Contract No 2 Home
Produced 'Hard Wheat'; Contract No 3 Home Produced 'Large Wheat'; Contract
No 4 Home Produced Rye, Barley, Oats; Contract No 5 Animal Feeds; Contract
No 6 Home Produced 'Oil-Seeds'; Contract No 7 Ground Soft Wheat; Contract
No 8 Dry Vegetables; Contract No 9 Plain Fodder for Animal Use

Are rules and regulations available? Yes

Can they be purchased? Yes

Arbitration rules: Arbitration is provided for in the model contract issued by the
AGER and in the rules of the Market of Bologna, and is, save where other
agreements have been entered into, subject to the present rules. Disputes arising
from dealings, commission and brokerage or otherwise in cereals and their by-
products, flours, rices, vegetables, oil-seed, pasture-seed, cattle food in general
must be decided on the basis of the Usages and Customs of the Market of
Bologna.
The arbitrators nominated by the parties must be chosen from among the

members of the Association. Each party to an arbitration may nominate only one arbitrator. The official arbitrators must be chosen from those included in the special Register.

The arbitration may be set in motion by the deposition with the Secretariat of the AGER of the relevant Certificate of Contract which the parties to the case must present, duly signed and set out in the appropriate form of the Association. When agreement has been reached and the Deed of Agreement signed, the Deed itself must be deposited with the Secretariat of the Association together with the payment of a deposit to the Secretariat for anticipated expenses and arbitral fees. Both parties to the case are responsible in equal proportions for the payment within five days of the deposit. The deposit is to accrue to the Association even if the arbitration does not take place.

The methods of procedure are laid down by the Arbitral College which alone has the power to lay down the terms of presentation of documents and correspondence. The Arbitral College shall also be empowered to hear the parties and eventual intermediaries. All skilled professional judgments or analyses must be paid for by the interested party who requests these. If during the course of the arbitral judgment the parties should come to an understanding regarding the controversy, the President may order the annulment of the proceedings. The arbitrators are charged to proceed to the publication of the arbitration award within 45 days of the date of the deposition of the Agreement with the Secretariat of the Association. In the case of failure to pay expenses and dues on the part of either of the parties in arbitration, the Association may have recourse to legal action against one or both of the parties to the dispute.

Is there an appeal? No

Currency dealt in: Lire

FLORENCE
Florence Commodity Exchange
(**La Borsa Merci di Firenze**)
Florence

Commodities: Principal commodities traded are Vegetable Oil, Flour, Wheat, Cereal, Fertilizer, plus products common to particular areas such as Wine.

Titles of appointments: President, a Delegation of seven members and a Committee of five members

Hours of trading: The market is open on Tuesday and Friday each week.

Rules and regulations: The Exchange was established on 16 July 1951 by decree of the President of the Republic. Additional regulations were approved by a Ministerial decree of 28 August 1954.

NAPLES

Naples Commodity Exchange

(Borsa Merci di Napoli)
Via Mercato dei Grani, 80133 Naples

Telephone: 81-321969

PADUA

Padua Commodity Exchange

(Borsa Merci di Padova)
Piazza Insurrezione, 35100 Padua

Telephone: 49-655 611; **Telex:** 43047 Camcompd; **Cable address:** Camcommercio Padova

Commodities: Grain, Beans, Animal Foodstuffs, Olive Oil, Wheat Oil, Beasts for slaughter, Eggs, Poultry and Rabbits, Chickens and Brood Eggs, Forage and Straw, Dairy Produce, Fruits — fresh and tinned, Tinned Meat, Pasta, Sugar, Alcoholic Beverages, Fertilizers, Skins, Solid Fuel, Petrol by-products, Timber, Quarrying materials, Fabricated Concrete and Cement

Titles of appointments: President of Board of Deputies, President and Vice-President of Committee, Secretary

Name of Secretary: Chiavegato Arch Adriano

Hours of trading: Every Thursday 08.00 to 13.00, principal market; every Saturday 08.00 to 13.00, ordinary market

Are rules and regulations available? Yes

Can they be purchased? By all members of the Exchange

Arbitration rules: When a dispute arises relating to contracts, it shall be deferred to the Board of Deputies or the Committee to attempt an amicable settlement. In the event of this attempt proving unsuccessful the dispute shall be heard by an arbitration committee which is nominated from time to time under the appropriate arbitration rule approved by the Chamber of Commerce, Industry and Agriculture.

Currency dealt in: Lire

Recommended commission rates and margins: None

Date of establishment of market: 14 December 1875

PARMA
Parma Board of Trade
(La Borsa Merci di Parma)
Camera di Commercio Industria ed Agricoltura, Parma

Telephone: 521-44341/2/3/4/5; **Telex:** Parmatel 51059

Commodities: Cured Hams and Salami, Dairy Produce, Tomato Extract, Cereal, Flour and by-products, Potatoes, Grapes, Vegetables, Pork, Poultry, Eggs

Title of appointments: The market is run by the Chamber of Commerce. This elects a Committee of seven members each year to implement the rules and regulations and to oversee prices and trading. Every commodity traded has, in addition, its own committee which is composed of brokers, dealers, farmers and producers, among others.

Hours of trading: The market is open on Wednesday and Saturday of each week.

Rules and regulations: A number of laws govern the operations of the market. These include Law 272 passed 20 March 1913, and Law 1068 passed 4 August 1913; these have since been modified on a number of occasions.

Currency dealt in: Lire

Date founded: 14 June 1970

Japan

Hokkaido Grain Exchange
3, Odori Nishi 5-chome, Chuo-ku, 060, Sapporo, Hokkaido

Telephone: 11-221 9131

Commodity: Grain

Kobe Grain Exchange
31, Toba-machi, Hyogo-ku, 652, Kobe

Telephone: 78-671 2901

Commodity: Grain

Kobe Raw Silk Exchange
126, Higashi-machi, Ikuta-ku, 650, Kobe

Telephone: 78-331 7141/5

Commodity: Raw Silk

Kobe Rubber Exchange
Exchange Building, 49, Harima-machi, Ikuta-ku, 650, Kobe

Telephone: 78-331 4211

Commodity: Rubber

MAEBASHI
Maebashi Dried Cocoon Exchange
10-2, Sumiyoshi-machi, 2-chome, 371, Maebashi City

Telephone: 272-31 4401

Commodity: Dried Cocoons

NAGOYA
Nagoya Grain Exchange
4, Kako-cho 1-chome, Nakamura-ku, 450, Nagoya

Telephone: 52-571 8161

Commodity: Grain

Nagoya Textile Exchange
2-15, Nishiki 3-chome, Naka-ku, 460, Nagoya City

Telephone: 52-951 2171

Commodity: Chemical Textiles

OSAKA
Osaka Chemical Textile Exchange
45, Kita Kyutaro-machi, 2-chome, Higashi-ku, 541, Osaka

Telephone: 6-261 2551

Commodity: Chemical Textiles

Osaka Grain Exchange
14, Awazaminami-dori 2-chome, Nishi-ku, 550, Osaka

Telephone: 6-531 7931/5

Commodity: Grain

Osaka Sampin Exchange

32-1 Kita-Kyutaro-Machi, 3-chome, Higashi-ku, Osaka

Telephone: 6-253 0031

Commodity: Cotton Yarn, 20's single Z-twist and 40's single Z-twist

Titles of appointments: President, 17 to 22 Directors and two to four Auditors

Name of Director: Yoshiro Aso

Hours of trading:
Cotton Yarn 20's — morning, first session 09.35, second session 10.45;
afternoon, first session 13.35, second session 14.35
Cotton Yarn 40's — morning, first session 10.05, second session 11.00;
afternoon, first session 14.05, second session 14.50

Trading unit: 907.18 kg (2,000 lb)

Trading limits: (1) Price: less than ten per cent above or below the last price of
the preceding day; (2) Quantity: As for long or short open interest for one
trading month. Member 600 contracts, Non-member 300 contracts

Contract particulars:
Quality: Pure cotton yarn qualified by the Japan spinners' inspecting foundation
Delivery points: Osaka Prefecture and Kobe City

Are rules and regulations available? Only to members

Arbitration rules: If any dispute arises between members or between members
and clients in connection with transactions on the commodity market of this
Exchange, the party concerned applies to this Exchange for arbitration.
The application for arbitration shall be made to the President and will include
the following particulars: (a) Name or trade name, profession and address of
applicant; (b) name or trade name, profession and address of the other party to
the dispute; (c) gist of plea; (d) reference documents; (e) date of plea. On
receipt of the application the President shall immediately convene the
Arbitration Committee, and shall summon the party concerned and/or witnesses.
The Arbitration Committee shall investigate the gist of the plea on the statement
of the above summoned or on making suitable examinations. On the conclusion
of the investigation, the Committee shall make the award and forward it to the
President. The President shall then advise the party concerned of the award.
Once accepted the President shall sign the award.

Is there an appeal? No

Currency dealt in: Yen

Average volume of trading over past two years:

	1975	1976
	(1 January to 31 December)	
20's	150,916	811,682
40's	243,857	490,774
Total Contracts	394,773	1,302,456

Recommended commission rates and margins:
Min rates of commission per one contract: Members ¥1,400, Non-members ¥2,400

Min margin per contract:

	20's	40's
Members	¥20,000	¥27,500
Non-members	¥40,000	¥55,000

Trading members, as at April 1977: *See Appendix 1 (page 226).*

Date of establishment of market: Founded 1893, closed 1941, and reopened 1951

Osaka Sugar Exchange

15, Andojibashi-dori 3-chome, Minami-ku, 542, Osaka

Telephone: 6-252 2021

Commodity: Sugar

SHIMONOSECKI

Kanmon Commodities Exchange

5, Nanbu-cho 1-chome, Shimonosecki, 751, Shimonosecki City

Telephone: 832-31 1313

Commodities: Miscellaneous

TOKYO

Tokyo Grain Exchange

1-12-5 Kakigara-cho, Nihonbashi, Chuo-ku, Tokyo, Japan 103

Telephone: 3-668 9311

Commodities: Soya Beans (domestic), Red Beans, White Beans, Potato Starch, Soya Beans (imported)

Titles of appointments: President, Executive Director, Managing Director, 13 additional Directors, and two Auditors

Name of President: Hajime Suzuki

Hours of trading:
Morning: first session 09.00, second session 10.00, third session 11.00
Afternoon: first session 13.00, second session 14.00, third session 15.00
On half holidays: morning: first session 09.00, second session 10.00, third session 11.00

Trading unit:
Soya Beans (domestic) 2,400 kg, Red Beans 2,400 kg, White Beans 2,400 kg, Potato Starch 2,500 kg, Soya Beans (imported) 15,000 kg

Trading limits: For the closing price on the previous business day:
Soya Beans (domestic) — five per cent
Red Beans — seven per cent between ¥700 and ¥350 per bag (60 kg)
White Beans — seven per cent between ¥500 and ¥350 per bag (60 kg)
Potato Starch — five per cent
Soya Beans (imported) — less than ¥180 per bag (60 kg) defined by the governing board (¥150 per bag as of 1 April 1977)

Contract particulars:
Quality:
Soya Beans (domestic) — No 2 small soya beans produced in Hokkaido under the Grain Inspection Law, and substitutions at differentials established by the Exchange
Read Beans — No 2 polished red beans produced in Hokkaido under the Grain Inspection Law, and substitutions at differentials; and red beans imported from China, Korea and Columbia which are established by the Exchange
White Beans — No 2 white beans produced in Hokkaido under the Grain Inspection Law, and substitutions at differentials; and Pea Beans and Great Northern Beans imported from the United States which are established by the Exchange
Potato Starch — No 1 refined powder produced in Hokkaido under the Grain Inspection Law, and substitutions at differentials established by the Exchange
Soya Beans (imported) — Non-screened yellow soya beans imported from the People's Republic of China, and substitutions at No 2 yellow soya beans imported from the United States

Delivery points: Warehouses located in Tokyo metropolis, Kanagawa prefecture, Chiba prefecture and Saitama prefecture which are specified by the Exchange

Are rules and regulations available? Only to members

Arbitration rules: The articles concerning Arbitration of Disputes occurring between members mutually and between a Commodity Commission Merchant and his customer are as follows:
Article 144: When there is a dispute between members or between a Commodity Commission Merchant and a customer concerning purchase or sale transactions in a commodity market of the Exchange, any party to the said dispute may apply to the Exchange for arbitration, provided that no application shall be made unless the said customer agrees to submit to arbitration by the Exchange, in the case of a dispute between a Commodity Commission Merchant and his customer.

Article 145: Application as described in the preceding article shall, as a rule, be made by a written document showing the following information: (1) the name or trade name of the applicant, and his occupation and address; (2) the name or trade name of the other party, and his occupation and address; (3) the reason for the application; (4) actual nature of the dispute; (5) names of documents which may serve as reference; (6) the date of the application.

Article 146: (1) When the Exchange has received an application for arbitration pursuant to article 144, the Exchange shall mediate between the parties of the dispute, confirm the gist of their claims, and then make an effort for settlement of such dispute. (2) If the above mediation has not been settled, the Exchange shall, without delay, refer such case to the Dispute Arbitration Committee, then prepare an arbitration plan and present it to both parties concerned, and advise as to acceptance of the plan.

Article 147: When an application for arbitration is presented by one party, a member who is the other party pursuant to article 144 shall submit to arbitration by the Exchange.

Article 148: Any such member of the Dispute Arbitration Committee who is a party to the dispute shall not participate in arbitration of the said dispute.

Article 149: (1) When a member of the Dispute Arbitration Committee has an interest concerned with the said dispute, any party to the dispute shall be able to challenge him. (2) Adoption or rejection of the above motion for challenge shall be decided by the Board of Directors.

Article 150: If a Commodity Commission Merchant refuses, without justifiable reasons, to accept an arbitration plan which the Exchange has prepared in accordance with the provision of Paragraph 2 of Article 146 concerning a dispute between the said Commodity Commission Merchant and his customer, in spite of acceptance by the customer thereof, the Exchange may give the necessary instructions to the said Commodity Commission Merchant to accept the arbitration plan concerned.

Is there an appeal? No

Currency dealt in: Yen

Average volume of trading over past two years: 1975 (January to December) 5,063,232 units, 1976 (January to December) 4,521,730 units

Recommended commission rates and margins:
Commission of trading and delivery per unit: (See table)

Margins: (See table)

Membership, types of: There are two types of members — 54 Commodity Commission Merchants, who are permitted to deal for their customers by the Ministry of Agriculture and Forestry upon the application from members, and 60 General Members who are admitted to affiliation by the Board of Directors of the Exchange and able to deal only on their own account.

Floor members, who can execute the transaction on the trading floor, are restricted to members only and floor representatives who are employees of the members and registered by the Exchange.

Date of establishment of market: Established 24 September 1952, opened 10 October 1952

Commission of Trading and Delivery per Unit

Commodity	Contracted Price		Commission for Customer	Commission for as CCM	Commission for as Member
Soya Beans (domestic)	Less than	¥ 5,000	¥ 800	¥ 400	¥ 480
	More than	¥ 5,000	¥ 900	¥ 450	¥ 540
Red Beans and White Beans	Less than	¥18,000	¥2,900	¥1,450	¥1,740
	Less than	¥20,000	¥3,100	¥1,550	¥1,860
	Less than	¥22,000	¥3,300	¥1,650	¥1,980
	Less than	¥24,000	¥3,500	¥1,750	¥2,100
	Less than	¥26,000	¥3,700	¥1,850	¥2,220
	Less than	¥28,000	¥3,900	¥1,950	¥2,340
	More than	¥28,000	¥4,100	¥2,050	¥2,460
Potato Starch	Regardless of price		¥ 700	¥ 350	¥ 420
Soya Beans (imported)	Commission of trading		¥3,500	¥1,750	¥2,100
	Commission of delivery		¥1,500	¥ 750	¥ 900

Note: 1. *CCM stands for the Commodity Commission Merchant*
2. *Member means, in this case, only General Member excluding CCM*

Margins:

Commodity	Level of Price		Initial Margin
Soya Beans (domestic)	Less than	¥ 3,000	¥ 8,000
	More than	¥ 3,000	¥10,000
	Less than	¥ 4,000	
	More than	¥ 4,000	¥12,000
Red Beans	Less than	¥25,000	¥70,000
	More than	¥25,000	¥80,000
	Less than	¥30,000	
	More than	¥30,000	¥90,000
White Beans	Less than	¥13,000	¥60,000
	More than	¥13,000	¥70,000
	Less than	¥18,000	
	More than	¥18,000	¥80,000
Potato Starch	Less than	¥ 1,500	¥ 8,000
	More than	¥ 1,500	¥10,000
	Less than	¥ 2,000	
	More than	¥ 2,000	¥12,000
Soya Beans (imported)	Less than	¥ 5,000	¥60,000
	More than	¥ 5,000	¥70,000
	Less than	¥ 6,000	
	More than	¥ 6,000	¥80,000

Tokyo Rubber Exchange

c/o Totori Building, 4, Nihonbashi Koami-cho, 9-chome, Chuo-ku, 103, Tokyo

Telephone: 3-668 0831

Commodity: Rubber

Tokyo Sugar Exchange

4, Nihonbashi Koami-cho 9-chome, Chuo-ku, 103, Tokyo

Telephone: 3-666 0201

Commodity: Sugar

Tokyo Textile Exchange

9, Nihonbashi Horidome 1-chome, Chuo-ku, 103, Tokyo

Telephone: 3-661 7561

Commodity: Chemical Textiles

TOYOHASHI

Toyohashi Dried Cocoon Exchange

52, Ekimae-odori 2-chome, 440, Toyohashi City

Telephone: 532-52 6231/5

Commodity: Dried Cocoons

YOKOHAMA

Yokohama Raw Silk Exchange

c/o Silk Center, 1, Yamashita-cho, 23, Naka-ku, Yokohama

Telephone: 45-641 1341

Commodity: Raw Silk

Kenya

Coffee Board of Kenya

PO Box 30566, Haile Selassie Ave, Plantation House, Nairobi

Telephone: Nairobi 332 896/7/8; **Telex:** 22190; **Cable address:** COBOK

Commodity: Coffee

Titles of appointments: Chairman, Vice-Chairman, Board Members, Secretary

Name of General Manager and Secretary: Simon Kanyoko

Hours of trading: Every Tuesday 09.30 to 13.00

Trading unit: 60 kg bags of Green Coffee

Trading limits: None

Contract particulars:
Quality: The Board offers in the auctions coffee of all our grades viz: PB, AA, AB, C, E, T, TT and of classes 1-10.

Are rules and regulations available? Only to licenced exporters

Arbitration rules: Not applicable

Currency dealt in: Kenya shilling

Average volume of trading over past two years: 25,000 bags per week

Membership, types of: Auctions are attended by licenced coffee exporters who must also be members of the 'Mild Coffee Trade Association of East Africa'.

Date of establishment of market: 1936

Coffee Lint and Seed Marketing Board

Uchumi House, Nkrumah Rd, Lugard Lane, PO Box 30477, Nairobi

Telephone: Nairobi 331006

Commodities: Cotton Lint, Cotton Seed

Titles of appointments: Chairman, Vice-Chairman, and 11 Members of the

Board one of whom shall be the Secretary to Board Meetings

Name of Chief Executive: John Githii Kigunda

Branches and affiliates:
Branches — Mombasa, Kisumu, Embu, Busia and Machakos
Sub-branches — Homa Bay, Voi
Owned ginneries — Mwea Cotton Ginnery Ltd, Nambare Ginnery Ltd, Kibos Ginnery Ltd
Private ginneries — Lamu Ginnery Co, Malindi Ginneries Ltd, Kitui Ginneries Ltd
Co-operative Societies/Union Ginneries — Kendu Bay, Homa Bay, Samia, Ndere, Malakisi, Hola, Meru

Hours of trading: Monday to Friday 08.15 to 12.30 and 14.00 to 16.30; Saturday 08.15 to 12.15

Trading unit: Cotton Lint — in lots of 50 bales each; Cotton Seed — in lots of 100 tonnes each

Contract particulars:
Quality: Lint is acceptable from all cotton ginneries as per samples drawn and submitted to the Chief Cotton Classifier/Examiner to determine quality. The grading is done at the buying centres before seed cotton is delivered to the ginneries for ginning. Lint which does not correspond to sample attracts a quality claim from the buyer. Seed may also attract a quality claim if it is decayed or destroyed in any other way before being delivered to the buyer and the defect is discovered during crushing.

Delivery points: Lint ex-Ginnery for up-country ginned lint and ex-Warehouse for Malindi, Lamu and Hola crop; Seed all ex-Ginnery. Exports — FOB Mombasa Port

Are rules and regulations available? No

Arbitration rules: Any dispute arising out of the quality of lint sold to a buyer shall be settled at an Executive Committee Meeting held between the buyer, the ginner and the Executive Committee of the Board. As regards seed, disputes are settled between the miller, the Board and the ginner.

Is there an appeal? No

Currency dealt in: Kenya shilling

Average volume of trading over past two years: K Shs 60 million per year

Date of establishment of market: The Board was established in 1964 by Legal Notice No 115/1966 section 3.

Membership of other organizations: International Cotton Advisory Council, Liverpool Cotton Exchange, Kenya National Chamber of Commerce

East African Tea Trade Association

PO Box 42281, Nairobi

Telephone: Nairobi 337521/2; **Telex:** 22070; **Cable address:** ROGAM NAIROBI

Commodity: Black Tea

Titles of appointments: Chairman, Vice-Chairman and 11 Members of Management Committee

Hours of trading: Auctions every Monday 08.50 in Mombasa, Private Contracts 5 days a week 08.30 to 16.30, auctions trading conducted by broker member, Africa Tea Brokers, Mombasa

Trading unit: Ten chests on auctions

Trading limits: Bidding to advance by not less than 5 cents a kg up to 8 shillings and 10 cents a kg thereafter

Contract particulars:
Quality: Buyers shall have the right to compare the Teas purchased by them with the sample on which they bid, but no claim for difference will be entertained unless notified in writing to the selling Broker within seven working days from Prompt day for Teas lying in other East Coast ports, nor will any such claim be considered after the Tea has been taken from the Sellers' warehouse.
Buyers shall pay the price of all lots purchased by them to the Brokers by 16.00 East African time on the tenth working day from the date of sale which shall be Prompt Day.

Delivery points: As required by Overseas buyer dependant on Overseas Sale or Contract and availability of Shipping

Are rules and regulations available: Only to members

Arbitration rules: Any dispute or difference which may arise, failing amicable settlement, shall be referred to two arbitrators, one to be chosen by each disputant, from a panel selected by the Association. Such Arbitrators shall appoint an umpire from the same panel in case of disagreement between them. The fees payable shall be 100 shillings to each Arbitrator and 100 shillings to the umpire and shall be deposited by the party claiming Arbitration. The decision as to who shall bear the cost as a result of the Arbitration shall be made by the Arbitrators or, if any umpire is called upon, the umpire, and included in the award.

Is there an appeal? No

Currency dealt in: Kenya shilling

Average volume of trading over past two years: 1974/5 — 24,958,344 kg on auctions, 1975/6 — 25,543,105 kg on auctions

Recommended commission rates and margins: Brokerage charged one per cent to seller, one-half of one per cent to buyer. Buyer at liberty to fix own selling price to Overseas client.

Membership, types of: Producer, Buyer and Broker

Floor Members, as at December 1975: Total membership of above classes 183, but not all active.

Date of establishment of market: 1958

Kenya Tea Development Authority

Commonwealth House, Government Rd, PO Box 30213, Nairobi

Telephone: Nairobi 21441/4; **Telex:** 22645 'CROPS'; **Cable address:** 'CROPS' Nairobi

Commodity: Tea

Titles of appointments: Chairman, Board

Name of General Manager: Charles K Karanja

Branches and affiliates: Ragati Tea Factory Co Ltd, Kambaa Tea Factory Co Ltd, Kanyenya Tea Factory Co Ltd, Siongo Tea Factory Co Ltd, Thumaita Tea Factory Co Ltd, Githongo Tea Factory Co Ltd, Kapko Tea Factory Co Ltd, Mokama Tea Factory Co Ltd, Chinga Tea Factory Co Ltd, Mataara Tea Factory Co Ltd, Ikumbi Tea Factory Co Ltd, Gittambo Tea Factory Co Ltd, Gathuthi Tea Factory Co Ltd

Hours of trading: Monday to Friday 08.30 to 16.30, Saturday 08.30 to 12.30

Trading unit: One kg

Trading limits: None

Contract particulars:
Quality: As per rules of the EATTA (East African Tea Trade Association)

Delivery points: Mombasa, London, Dublin, New York and other points on order

Are rules and regulations available? From EATTA, PO Box 42281, Nairobi

Can they be purchased? Yes

Arbitration rules: Obtainable from EATTA

Currency dealt in: Kenya shilling, sterling, USA and Canadian dollars

Average volume of trading over past two years: June 1974–June 1975, 20 million kg

Recommended commission rates and margins: One to two per cent

Malaysia

Malaysian Rubber Exchange and Licensing Board

Tingkat 6 and 7, Bangunan Hong Leong, Jalan Cheng Lock, Kuala Lumpur

Telephone: Kuala Lumpur 87961/4; **Telex:** MA 30220; **Cable address:** Pasgetah, Kuala Lumpur

Commodity: Rubber

Titles of appointments: Chairman, Deputy Chairman and Chief Executive, and 14 members of the Board

Name of Chief Executive: Tuan Haji Abu Bakar bin Pawanchee

Hours of trading: The market is open from 10.00 to 13.00 and 16.00 to 18.00 daily. Rubber prices are set by the Malaysian Rubber Exchange (MRE) — the regulatory and supervisory body for the proper conduct of the trade domestically and internationally — twice daily, ie at 12.00 and at 17.00. These are referred to as the official noon and closing prices respectively. In addition there is the unofficial 13.00 price quotation. Operating concurrently with the above is a continuous price and volume reporting system giving details of transactions concluded for prompt, current month and forward positions, together with the time the transactions took place, buyers' and sellers' prices and the volume of rubber transacted. This information is available to all members of the MRE and to the market.

Trading unit: One lot (25 tonnes) of rubber

Trading limits: None

Contract particulars:
Quality: The MRE regulates the conduct of guarantee and non-guarantee business, registers FOB tenders on behalf of its members and ensures that payments on contracts arising therefrom are made promptly in accordance with its Rules and By-Laws. The MRE also handles the sale and purchase contracts of the following: International 1-5 RSS; International 1 Thin Pale Crepe; No 1 Air Dried Sheet; International Thin Brown Crepe 2X. The above grades are considered to be visually graded rubber and the following general prohibitions apply: (1) Rubber that is wet, unbleached, under-cured, virgin rubber and rubber that is not completely visually dry at the time of buyer's inspection is not acceptable (except slightly under-cured rubber as specified for No 5 RSS);

(2) Skim rubber made of skim latex shall not be used in whole or in part in the production of any grade. In addition to the aforementioned grades, MRE also handles SMR (Standard Malaysian Rubber) which are graded by precise technical standards and not by usual characteristics. Some of the SMR grades are 5 CV, 5L, 5, 10, 20 and 50. They are graded to technical standards, typically for dirt, ash, copper, manganese, nitrogen and volatile matter contents. The Seller shall be responsible for all the loss in weight during transit excluding theft and pilferage — (i) exceeding ½ per cent for all grades of RSS, and (ii) exceeding 1 per cent for all other types and grades provided that if the loss exceeds ½ per cent but no more than 1 per cent the Seller shall be responsible only for the excess loss over ½ per cent. Any loss in weight shall be invoiced back at buyer's contract price.

Delivery points: Port Klang, Malacca, Johore Bahru, Penang

Delivery months quoted: Two years forward. However, in the last quarter of the second year there may be deliveries due for the coming year.

Are rules and regulations available? Only to members

Arbitration rules: In cases where a dispute arising out of the MRE Contract is referred to the MRE, it is empowered to appoint arbitrators from an Arbitration Panel to settle the matter. All arbitrations are to be held in Malaysia. The panel of arbitrators shall consist of 20 experienced members of the rubber trade of whom ten shall be ordinary members elected annually by the Board and the remaining ten shall be persons nominated by the Singapore Chamber of Commerce Rubber Association. In submitting a case for arbitration each disputant shall forward the necessary particulars in an appropriate form and forward a copy of it to his appointed arbitrator and to the other disputant. A member may enter into an arbitration with a non-member provided that the latter consents in writing to such arbitration and agrees to be bound by the Rules and By-Laws of the Corporation pertaining to arbitration. Every arbitration award shall be signed by the arbitrators and forwarded by them together with a copy of the case submitted for arbitration to the Secretary who shall seal, sign, date and file the name with the records of the MRE. The Secretary shall thereafter serve notice to the disputants that the award is ready for delivery upon payment of the prescribed fees.

Is there an appeal? Yes. An appeal must be lodged with the Secretary together with a deposit within seven working days from the date of notification by the Secretary that an arbitration award is ready for delivery. The Appeal Tribunal shall consist of all members of the Board whose decision shall be final. The Appeal Tribunal shall elect a Chairman for the hearing of each appeal but the Chairman shall not have a second or casting vote and, in the event of equality of votes, the award appealed against shall stand. The Appeal Tribunal shall have full power to: (a) discuss the appeal; (b) allow the appeal in full and where necessary to discuss the original claim brought before the arbitrators; (c) vary the award either by increasing or reducing the amount awarded; (d) vary the same by allowing a rejection and replacement instead of cash penalty and vice-versa. The Appeal Tribunal need not entertain an appeal from non-members. In all disputes in respect of an FOB Contract arising after shipment where the destination is in the USA or Canada, arbitration shall take place in New York under the Regulations of the RTANY and where the destination is a port in the UK or Europe, in London under the Regulations of the Rubber Trade Association of London. If facilities for such arbitration are not available to the parties concerned, arbitration shall take place in Malaysia in accordance with the MRE Rules and By-Laws.

Currency dealt in: Malaysian dollars. (The FOB Settlement Contract is used for the sale and purchase of International 1 RSS and other grades of rubber and as may be decided from time to time by the Board.)

Average volume of trading over past two years: 1975 (6 February—31 December) — 18,430 lots; 1976 (1 January—31 July) — 14,803 lots

Recommended commission rates and margins: A broker charges a fee of M$2.80 per tonne, leviable on both the buyer and seller for a guarantee contract and M$1.40 per tonne if it is a non-guarantee contract.

Membership, types of: The MRE does not operate an open outcry system. It maintains a Settlement House for members of the MRE in order to facilitate the clearing and settlement of contracts for the purchase and sale of rubber. Membership of the MRE shall be confined to persons carrying on or intending to carry on business in the rubber trade or industry as may from time to time be prescribed by the Rules of the MRE. There are two categories of membership: (1) Ordinary Members; (2) Associate Members. Only Ordinary members have voting rights and can hold office. All members shall be registered in one of the following classes: (a) Producers; (b) Manufacturers' Buying Agents; (c) Brokers; (d) Dealers, consisting of those members who carry on business as dealers, packers, millers, importers, exporters, shippers or in any other capacity within the rubber trade or industry not otherwise classified above.

Trading members, as at 2 December 1975: *See Appendix 1 (page 227).*

Membership of other organizations: Association of Natural Rubber Producing Countries (ANRPC), International Rubber Quality Packing and Control (IRQPC), International Rubber Association (IRA)

Date of establishment of market: 1 September 1973; with the promulgation of the Malaysian Rubber Exchange and Licensing Board Act 1972. This Act incorporates and consolidates the functions of the former Malaysian Rubber Exchange (MRE), the Malayan Rubber Export Registration Board (MRERB) and the licensing function exercised by the various District Rubber Licensing Boards under the pre-war Rubber Supervision Enactments and the collection of registration fees under the Rubber Export Registration Act 1966.

PENANG
Datuk Keramat Smelting Sdn Berhad
as joint operators of Straits Tin Market

73 Jalan Datuk Keramat, PO Box No 280, Penang

Telephone: Penang 04 63702 (6 lines)/04 63705 (Tin Market); **Telex:** MA40037; **Cable address:** Smelter Penang

Commodity: Straits Refined Tin (Escoy Brand)

Titles of appointments: Chairman, Managing Director, Technical Director, Commercial Manager, Finance Manager, Personnel and Services Manager

Name of Chief Executive: J McKeown

Branches and affiliates: Datuk Keramat Smelting Sdn Berhad, 27 Jalan Tun Perak, Kuala Lumpur; Datuk Keramat Smelting Sdn Berhad, 75-77 Jalan Connolly, Ipoh; Datuk Keramat Smelting Sdn Berhad, 99-101 Jalan Gopeng, Kampar; Datuk Keramat Smelting Sdn Berhad, 22 Batu Gajah Rd, Pusing

Hours of trading: Monday to Saturday 08.30 to 10.30. All business is done through bids which are telexed/cabled to smelter before 10.30 each day.

Trading unit: 5 tonnes

Trading limits: No limits on priced bids but market bids limited to 25 tonnes.

Contract particulars:
Quality: Straits Refined Tin assaying typically 99.85 per cent SN min and conforming to American Grade 'A' standard

Delivery points: Ex works, delivery within 60 days

Are rules and regulations available? No

Arbitration rules: There are no arbitration rules.

Currency dealt in: Malaysian ringgit

Average volume of trading over past two years: 1975 — 33,450 tonnes; 1976 — 33,000 tonnes

Membership, types of: By application

Date of establishment of market: 1886 with the establishment of the Straits Trading Co Ltd

The Netherlands

The Egg Terminal Market

NV Nederlandse Liquidatiekas, Postbox 252, Koopmansbeurs, Damrak 62A, Amsterdam

Telephone: 20-228654; **Telex:** 16582 (NLK.NL); **Cable address:** Produktenbank

The Egg Terminal Market Foundation, Postbox 8100, Rotterdam 14

Telephone: 10-200495; **Telex:** 26617 (Aterm); **Cable address:** Eitermijn

Market Place: Koopmansbeurs (Produce Exchange), Damrak 62A, Amsterdam

The Egg Terminal Market is governed by the Egg Terminal Market Foundation (the Foundation); the NV Nederlandse Liquidatiekas (clearing house) hereafter called the Kas, is in charge of the organization of the market.

Commodity: Eggs

Titles of appointments: The Kas — Chairman, two Members, two Directors; The Foundation — Chairman, Vice-Chairman, seven Members, Secretary

Names of Chief Executives: The Kas — L W J Daendels and F Moes — Directors; The Foundation — W Muller—Chairman, J Van der Plassche—Secretary

Hours of trading: Monday to Friday 09.45 to 11.45 and 13.45 to 15.45

Trading unit: Contract quantity is 72,000 eggs.

Trading limits: There are no limits on daily price fluctuations.

Price quotation: Prices quoted are per 100 eggs in guilders and fractions thereof of five cents.

Contract particulars:
Quality: Every contract comprises 72,000 hen's eggs for consumption packed in 200 boxes of 360 eggs each; 100 boxes to contain eggs of class 3 weight and 100 boxes to contain eggs of class 4 weight; delivery free in or on a means of conveyance designated by the receiver, at the door of a packing depot admitted by the Foundation. These eggs shall meet the quality standards prescribed by the EEC.

Delivery points: Delivery can be made only at a packing depot designated by the Foundation.

Delivery months: All calendar months

Are rules and regulations available? Yes

Can they be purchased? Yes

Arbitration rules: Disputes arising between contracting parties, brokers, principals, the Kas and the Foundation in connection with contracts registered by the Kas shall, with exclusion of the ordinary Court, in the last resort be decided by three arbitrators to be appointed by the Algemene Stichting Termijnhandel, with the exception of disputes on or arising from the implementation of provisions mentioned in Article 20 of the rules and regulations. The application for arbitration shall be submitted to the Algemene Stichting Termijnhandel by registered letter, enclosing eight copies, not later than eight working days after the dispute has arisen. As soon as an application for arbitration has been submitted, the secretariat shall appoint three arbitrators from the latest list of nine persons drawn up by the Algemene Stichting Termijnhandel in conjunction with the Kas, on the understanding that among the arbitrators there shall be at least one lawyer, who shall act as Chairman, and at least one futures market expert. As provisional cover for the costs of arbitration, the applicant shall deposit with the Algemene Stichting Termijnhandel, within the period indicated by them, the amount stated to him by the arbitrators. The arbitrators shall decide the period within which the opponent has to make his statement of defence and shall decide upon the further procedures to be adopted. In their final award the arbitrators shall fix their expenses, including their fees, and shall charge such costs to either party or to both parties; in the latter case in a proportion to be established by the arbitrators. The mandate to the arbitrators continues up to and including the day on which they have deposited their final award at the district court concerned.

Is there an appeal? No

Currency dealt in: Guilders

Recommended commission rates and margins: The commission rates per contract of sale or purchase (in Dfl) are:

	Commission-agent	Floor Broker	Kas
Account holders	—	10[1]	15
Other associate members	39	—	15
Non-members	57	—	15
Commission-agents	—	10[1]	15[2]

1. *Where a floor broker is used* 2. *To be collected from principals*

When a contract is settled by making delivery and taking receipt, the same amount of charges is payable upon delivery and upon receipt. In addition, a so-called notification fee of Dfl10 per contract delivered and received is payable to the Kas. This amount has to be collected by the commission-agent from his principals.

Deposit: For every open contract a deposit is payable by the contracting party to the Kas. The amount of the deposit is Dfl1,000, but this can be changed at any time. If the contracting party is a commission-agent, he has a claim on his principal for the deposit amount. The deposit must be in the possession of the Kas before noon of the working day following the day on which the contract is concluded.

Margins: On every market day the differences are computed between the quotations fixed on that day and the prices of open contracts. In the event of an adverse change in price in respect of the price of a registered open contract, margins are required from the contracting party. The contracting party will have to pay an additional margin before noon of the working day following the day on which the Kas has demanded this payment. If the contracting party is a commission-agent, the margin will be payable, in turn, by the principal to his commission-agent.

Membership, types of: Associate members — all those who in the ordinary course of their business are engaged in the production of/or the trade in eggs or in the egg products industry, may on application be admitted as associate members of the Foundation. Other members are account holders, commission-agents and floor brokers. On conditions to be made by the Kas, associate members may be accepted as account holders, commission-agents or floor brokers with the Kas.

Trading members, as at April 1977: *See Appendix 1 (page 231).*

Date of establishment of market: 14 January 1976

The Pork Terminal Market

NV Nederlandse Liquidatiekas, Postbox 252, Koopmansbeurs, Damrak 62A, Amsterdam

Telephone: 20-228654; **Telex:** 16582 (NLK.NL); **Cable address:** Produktenbank

The Cattle and Meat Terminal Market Foundation, Postbox 8100, Rotterdam 14

Telephone: 10-200495; **Telex:** 26617 (Aterm)

Market Place: Koopmansbeurs (Produce Exchange), Damrak 62A, Amsterdam

The market is organized under a set of rules by the Cattle and Meat Terminal Market Foundation (the Foundation). The NV Nederlandse Liquidatiekas (the Kas) registers the contracts concluded in the Pork Terminal Market in accordance with its relevant rules and guarantees the due completion of those contracts.

Commodity: Pork

Titles of appointments: The Kas — Chairman, two Members, two Directors; The Foundation — Chairman, Vice-Chairman, four Members, Secretary

Names of Chief Executives: The Kas — L W J Daendels and F Moes—Directors; The Foundation — W Muller—Chairman, J Van de Plassche—Secretary

Hours of trading: Monday to Friday 10.00 to 14.00

Trading unit: The contract quantity is 5,000 kg net weight of cold slaughtered pigs.

Trading limits: There are no limits on daily price fluctuations.

Price quotations: Prices quoted are per kg in guilders and cents.

Contract particulars:
Quality: (1) The quality of the pigs must be class 1A; (2) Pigs of the quality class EAA may be delivered without price surcharge; (3) A maximum of 17 pigs may be of a lesser quality than class 1A, provided that not more than three of them are of a lesser quality than class 2A/1B. For these pigs no price reduction is allowed.

Delivery points: Delivery may be made only in the vehicle designated by the receiver on the site of the slaughterhouse, admitted by the Foundation, where the pigs have been slaughtered.

Delivery months: When the market opened in March 1977 the months of May, August, September, October, November and December 1977 and January and February 1978 were quoted. In April, quotation was made for March 1978 and so on. The number of months for which quotations are in force at the same time will not exceed ten. For the time being June and July will not be quoted.

Are rules and regulations available? Yes

Can they be purchased? Yes

Arbitration rules: Disputes arising between contracting parties, admittees, principals, the Kas and the Foundation in connection with contracts registered by the Kas shall, with the exclusion of the ordinary Court, in the last resort be decided by three arbitrators to be appointed by the Algemene Stichting Termijnhandel. Disputes on or arising from the implementation of provisions mentioned in Article 21 of the rules and regulations are excepted.
The application for arbitration shall be submitted to the Algemene Stichting Termijnhandel, by registered letter enclosing eight copies, not later than 14 days after the dispute has arisen. As soon as an application for arbitration has been submitted, the secretariat shall appoint three arbitrators from the latest list of nine persons drawn up by the Algemene Stichting Termijnhandel, in conjunction with the Kas, on the understanding that among the arbitrators there shall be at least one lawyer, who shall act as Chairman, and at least one futures market expert. As provisional cover for the costs of arbitration, the applicant shall deposit with the Algemene Stichting Termijnhandel, within the period indicated by them, the amount stated to him by the arbitrators. The arbitrators shall decide the period within which the opponent has to make his statement of defence and shall decide upon the further procedures to be adopted. In their final award the arbitrators shall fix their expenses, including their fees, and they shall charge such costs to either party or to both parties, in the latter case in a proportion to be established by the arbitrators. The mandate to the arbitrators continues up to and including the day on which they have deposited their final award at the district court concerned.

Is there an appeal? No

Currency dealt in: Guilders

Recommended commission rates and margins: For each contract of purchase or sale that is concluded, the buyer and the seller pay to the Kas a commission in favour of the Kas and a commission in favour of the admittee. For the associate members this commission is Dfl25 and Dfl50 respectively, per contract. For all other participants the commission is Dfl35 and Dfl65 respectively. Where settlement is made by delivery, the same amounts are payable, with the addition of an extra charge of Dfl10 in favour of the Kas.

Deposit: For each contract not applied in setting off against another, a cash deposit must promptly be made to the Kas. For the present, this deposit has been fixed at Dfl1,500.

Margins: On each market day a settlement price is fixed, per delivery month, to establish the difference between the price in force on that day and those of the outstanding contracts. For any adverse differences, additional margins must promptly be made with the Kas by the contracting parties concerned.

Membership, types of: Anyone who, in the ordinary course of his business, is associated with the livestock and meat industries, may, at his request, be admitted as an associate member of the Foundation.

Privileged membership: The Kas may admit participants as account holders. Such a privileged member may have contracts concluded in his own name through the intermediary of an admittee. All other participants may only have contracts concluded in the name of their admittee.

Trading members, as at April 1977: *See Appendix 1 (page 231).*

Date of establishment of market: 8 March 1977

The Potato Terminal Market

NV Nederlandse Liquidatiekas, Postbox 252, Koopmansbeurs, Damrak 62A, Amsterdam

Telephone: 20-228654; **Telex:** 16582 (NLK.NL); **Cable address:** Produktenbank

Potato Terminal Market Foundation, Postbox 8100, Rotterdam 14

Telephone: 10-200495; **Telex:** 26617 (Aterm); **Cable address:** Termijnsticht

The Potato Terminal Market is governed by the NV Nederlandse Liquidatiekas (clearing house), hereafter called 'the Kas', in conjunction with the Potato Terminal Market Foundation (the Foundation).

Market Place: Koopmansbeurs (Produce Exchange), Damrak 62A, Amsterdam

Commodity: Potatoes

Titles of appointments: The Kas — Chairman, two Members, two Directors; The Foundation — Chairman, Vice-Chairman, five Members, Secretary

Names of Chief Executives: The Kas — L W J Daendels and F Moes — Directors; The Foundation — W Muller — Chairman, J Van der Plassche — Secretary

Hours of trading: Monday 11.00 to 13.00 and 14.00 to 16.00; Tuesday to Friday 10.00 to 12.00 and 14.00 to 16.00

Trading unit: Contract quantity 15,000 kg net

Trading limits: There are no limits on daily price fluctuations.

Price quotation: Prices quoted are per 100 kg in guilders and fractions thereof of ten cents.

Contract particulars:
Quality: Basic potato grades: the contracts consist of consumption potatoes packed in 50 kg net new bags. Type, grade, crop year and type of soil are prescribed by the NV Nederlandse Liquidatiekas and the Potato Terminal Market Foundation. At present they are: Bintje 40mm upwards and 50mm upwards, of the current crop and from clay-soil.

Delivery points: Only potato warehouses appointed by the Foundation and correspondingly admitted by the Kas. These storehouses must be located in The Netherlands, but not in the offshore North Sea islands (Waddeneilanden).

Delivery months: November, February, March, April and May

Are rules and regulations available? Yes

Can they be purchased? Yes

Arbitration rules: Disputes arising between contracting parties on the one hand and the Kas on the other in connection with contracts registered by the Kas in their names, and disputes arising in connection with the rules and regulations between brokers on the one hand and the Kas on the other, shall, with the exclusion of the ordinary Court, in the last resort be decided by three arbitrators to be appointed by the secretariat of the Foundation. Disputes on or arising from a settling price as referred to in Article 22 paragraph 7, or disputes on which another arrangement has been made in Article 24, and disputes on or arising from the implementation of Articles 28, 29, 30 and 31 are excepted.
The application for arbitration shall be submitted to the secretariat of the Foundation by registered letter, with eight copies, not later than eight working days after the dispute has arisen. As soon as an application for arbitration has been submitted, the secretariat shall appoint three arbitrators from the latest list of nine persons drawn up by the Foundation in conjunction with the Kas, on the understanding that among the arbitrators there shall be at least one lawyer, who shall act as Chairman, and at least one terminal market expert. As provisional cover for the costs of arbitration, the applicant shall deposit with the arbitrators, within the period indicated by them, the amount stated to him by the arbitrators. The arbitrators shall decide the period within which the opponent has to make his statement of defence and they shall decide upon the further procedures to be adopted.
In their final award the arbitrators shall fix their expenses including their fees and shall charge such costs to either party or to both parties, in the latter case in a proportion to be established by the arbitrators.
The mandate to the arbitrators continues up to and including the day on which they have deposited their final award at the district court concerned.

Is there an appeal? No

Currency dealt in: Guilders

Average volume of trading over past two years: 60,000 contracts

Recommended commission rates and margins: The round turn rate per contract (in Dfl) is:

	Brokerage	Commission Kas	Fee	Total
Members	28	17.50	4.5	50
Non-members	35	20.00	6.0	61

These rates apply whether a contract (sale or purchase) is closed out by effecting an opposite contract (purchase or sale) or by delivery or receipt.

Deposits: The deposit required by the Kas is Dfl600 per contract, which amount must be received by the Kas not later than noon on the working day following the day of execution of the contract. The Kas may change the amount of the deposit at any time.

Margins: Margins are required whenever the quotations show an adverse change in price in respect of the price of a registered contract, deposits not included. Margins as well as deposits may be covered by banker's guarantee.

Membership, types of: Growers, dealers and other persons or firms who have established a reputation in the potato economy and are affiliated to the Foundation can be admitted by the Kas as associate members.

Broker members, as at April 1977: *See Appendix 1 (page 231).*

Date of establishment of market: 10 April 1958

Norway

Oslo Fur Auctions Ltd

(Oslo Skinnauksjoner)
Ø Slottsgate 3, Oslo 1

Telephone: 2-224150; **Telex:** 16724; **Cable address:** Osloskinn

This is an auction market primarily for the sale of Norwegian furs.

Pakistan

The Karachi Cotton Association Ltd

The Cotton Exchange, II Chundrigar Rd, Karachi

Telephone: Karachi 232570 (Secretary), 233025 (Assistant Secretary), 232580 (Office), 236497 (Clearing House); **Cable address:** 'Cotex' Karachi

The cotton ginning industry in Pakistan was nationalized on 17 July 1976. One price system was introduced and all sales of cotton are taking place ex-ginning factories.

The Government has set up a special organization in the public sector, the Cotton Trading Corp of Pakistan Ltd, which handles the marketing of raw cotton at the one price system. The Government-constituted Cotton Export Corp of Pakistan Ltd handles all cotton exports. Markets in spot cotton and futures no longer exist in the private sector.

Singapore

Rubber Association of Singapore

Rooms 604 and 606, 6th Floor, Chinese Chamber of Commerce Building, 47 Hill
St, Singapore 6

Telephone: Singapore 39724/31278/39836/39839/39323; **Cable address:**
Rasinga

Commodity: Rubber

Titles of appointments: Chairman, Deputy Chairman, 13 members of the
Management Committee and the Executive Secretary

Names of Chief Executives: Tan Eng Joo, MSc — Chairman, Gnoh Chong Hock,
LLB — Executive Secretary

Hours of trading: Monday to Friday 09.30 to 12.30 and 14.30 to 16.30,
excluding public holidays

Trading unit: 25 tonnes

Trading limits: Governed by By-Laws

Contract particulars:
Quality: In accordance with the Rules, By-Laws and Regulations
Delivery points: 'Malayan Ocean Ports' (or MOP) — Singapore, Port Kelang and
Penang

Are rules and regulations available? Yes

Can they be purchased? Yes

Arbitration rules: Arbitration facilities are provided for members and non-
members. Under reciprocal arrangements with the Malaysian Rubber Exchange,
ten members are nominated by the Malaysian Rubber Exchange and ten
ordinary members are elected annually by the Committee of the Corporation.
Disputants may appoint any one of the 20 arbitrators to authenticate (assure,
ratify, endorse, certify) their rights, duties, obligations, or liabilities under a
Contract. If an agreement on the appointment of the sole Arbitrator cannot be
reached, the two disputants may each appoint his own arbitrators from the
Panel. When these two appointed arbitrators are unable to agree, the dispute will
be referred to an umpire chosen from the Panel by these two arbitrators. In the
case where one disputant is a non-member, he is required to submit written
consent to such arbitration. In addition, he has to agree also in writing to be

bound by the By-Laws of the Corporation in this regard. An arbitration award, signed by the Arbitrators, is forwarded to the Secretary, together with a copy of the case in question. The Secretary will then seal, sign, date and file it with the records of the Corporation, after which he will advise the disputants that the award is ready for delivery upon settlement of the prescribed fees.

Provisions for arbitrations on such FOB Contracts, held to be 'further contracts' (Rubber Association of Singapore FOB Contracts which are linked with CIF contracts of the Rubber Trade Association of New York or London), are accommodated by the Corporation's By-Laws and Regulations. Under these 'further contracts', where the rubber is destined for the United States and Canada, arbitration may take place in New York subject to the Regulations of its Association; where the rubber is destined for the United Kingdom or the European Continent, arbitration may be held in London under the Regulations of the Rubber Trade Association of London.

Is there an appeal? Yes, an award is subject to appeal within seven working days from the date of notification by the Secretary to the disputants that it is ready for delivery. The Appeal is then referred to a joint RAS/MRE Appeal Tribunal whose decision is conclusive and final after hearing the appeal.

Currency dealt in: Singapore dollar

Average volume of trading over past two years: 1974 — 504,260 tonnes, 1975 — 451,857 tonnes

Recommended commission rates and margins: Guarantee Contract — $2.80 per tonne, Non-Guarantee Contract — $1.40 per tonne

Membership, types of: Ordinary members — Class A — Estates' Selling Agents, Class B — Brokers, Class C — Manufacturers' Buying Agents, Class D — Dealers — these represent agents world-wide; Associate members — 29, Overseas members — 3

Trading members, as at 1 April 1976: *See Appendix 1 (page 231).*

Date of establishment of market: 1968 (under Rubber Association of Singapore [Incorporation] Act Chapter 200)

The rubber market conducts its business under the auspices of the Rubber Association of Singapore (RAS). The RAS is, in effect, the legislative, administrating and judicial centre for the rubber trade in Singapore.

The RAS is empowered by Statute to enforce its Rules and By-Laws. Through this enforcement, the rubber trade is governed.

The RAS Rules and By-Laws and Regulations have the force of law by a Management Committee. In accordance with Section 10 of the Rubber Association of Singapore (Incorporation) Act, 1967, the Members and Alternate Members of the Management Committee are appointed by the Minister for Finance for a two-year term.

The preservation, promotion and regulation of the rubber trade and industry are not the only functions provided by the Rubber Association of Singapore. In addition, it provides the rubber trade in Singapore with many facilities. These include Clearing House, facilities for weekly auction sales of rubber, official price fixing, endorsement for Certificates of Origin for Rubber, preparation and sales of International Copy Samples and facilities for arbitration.

The Clearing House: The Corporation's FOB Contract (with or without variations) is the basis upon which all market operations in Singapore are carried out. It can also be linked to the FOB Contract of the Malaysian Rubber Exchange and the CIF Contracts of the Rubber Trade Associations of London and New York. When the RAS FOB Contracts are linked to the latter, they are treated as 'further contracts' and provisions for their enforcement and settlement are stipulated in the Corporation's Rule Book.

Auctions: Auctions take place from 10.30 to 12.30 and 14.30 to 16.30 on days determined by the Committee. Ordinary Members and Associate Members are entitled to buy and sell at these auctions. Non-members may apply for Annual Permits with a payment of $100 together with a cash deposit or bankers' guarantee for $15,000. They can only buy at auctions. The validity of such permits is left to the discretion of the Committee.

Members who wish to sell rubber at an auction have to notify the Secretary. In order to be catalogued for sale, each lot of rubber has to exceed 1,000 pounds. All rubber will be sold by the lot with each lot sold separately, at a certain price per pound. The highest bidder will be the Buyer. The Clearing House arranges for payment to the Seller when delivery of the rubber is effected.

Price Fixing: In conjunction with the Malaysian Rubber Exchange in Kuala Lumpur, the Corporation performs an important function of price fixing. With the exception of Saturdays, Sundays, and public holidays, price fixing is carried out twice daily — at 12.00 and at 17.00. Working in close connection with the Clearing House, the Price Fixing Panel, consisting of dealers and brokers, submits its prices for the RSS-1 grade of natural rubber for the various delivery dates as well as for the lower grades. Prices are obtained from three members of the Price Fixing Panel. These prices would be declared by the Clearing House Manager as Official Prices for the day if they are agreed upon by the three members. However, when varying opinions regarding prices arise, the Manager of the Clearing House will initiate special procedures with which to be complied.

Membership of other organizations: International Rubber Association (IRA), International Rubber Quality and Packing Conference (IRQPC)

Switzerland

Grain and Produce Exchange of Berne
(Getreide und Produktenborse Bern)
Bundesgasse 28, 3011 Berne

Telephone: 31-223699

Names of Chief Executives: Ernst Biedermann — President, Werner Oesch — Secretary

The Grain and Produce Exchange of Berne is not a futures market. It has the following objectives: (1) to provide a meeting place for sellers and buyers in cereals, fodder and related products; (2) to establish and implement rules and conditions as they apply to domestic trade and to provide arbitration facilities; (3) to support and defend the interests of the trade and its members.

Date of establishment of market: 1913

United Kingdom

The Liverpool Cotton Association Ltd

620 Cotton Exchange Buildings, Edmund St, Liverpool L3 9LH

Telephone: 051-236 6041; **Telex:** 627849; **Cable address:** 'Cottex' Liverpool 3

Commodity: Raw Cotton

Titles of appointments: President, Vice-President and Treasurer who are *ex-officio* members of a Board of 16 Directors

Name of Director-General: P M Raynes

Contract particulars:
Quality* Liverpool Official Standards:
South Brazilian: Types 3,4,4/5,5,5/6,6,6/7,7,7/8,8,9
Ugandan: BPA — UNWE, UNUG, SS, UNFA, UNEX/D, SATU — ANWE, ENUG, SS, INFA, ONEX/D
Greek: Grades 3,4,5,6,7
Iranian: Grades 1,2,3,4,5
Indian: M G Bengal — Extra Superfine, Superfine, Fine, Full Good, Good
Nigerian: NA1, NA2, NA3
Argentine: Grades A,B,C,D,E,F,G
Pakistan: AC134 SG Punjab — Superfine, Fine/Superfine, Fine, Fully-good/Fine; 289F SG Punjab — Superfine, Fine/Superfine, Fine, Fully-good/Fine; N T SG Sind — Superfine, Fine/Superfine, Fine, Fully-good/Fine; BHP Desi — Superfine, Fine, Fully-good/Fine; Punjab — Superfine, Fine, Fully-good/Fine; Sind Desi — Choice, Superfine, Fine/Superfine
Peruvian: TANGUIS — Grades 2,2½,3,4,5,6,7; PIMA BLANCO — Grades 1,1¼,1½
Sudan: BARAKAT — Grades 1,2,3,4,5,6,C6; VS — Grades 1,2,3,4,5,6,C6
Syrian: Saw-Ginned — Extra, zero, 1,2,3
Tanzanian: Tang, Gany, Yika
Turkish: Roller-Ginned EGE — Extra 1,2,3,4,5; Cukurova — Extra 1,2; Saw-Ginned Upland — Extra 1,2

Universal Standards:
American Upland White: Good Middling, Strict Middling, Middling, Strict Low Middling, Low Middling, Strict Good Ordinary, Good Ordinary
American Upland Spotted: Strict Middling, Strict Low Middling, Low Middling
American Upland Tinged: Strict Middling, Middling, Strict Low Middling, Low Middling

*Note: *Trading under 'Liverpool Rules' is not confined to cotton as described above. The list indicates only those Standards which have been officially adopted by the Association.*

Are rules and regulations available? Yes

Can they be purchased? Yes, current price £25 to non-members

Arbitration rules: Any differences that may arise between a Member, Associate Member or Registered Firm and any other Member, Associate Member or Registered Firm concerning anything connected with the cotton trade or any transaction shall be referred to arbitration in accordance with the Rules. In all cases the holding of such arbitration and the obtaining of an award shall be a condition precedent to the right of any Member, Associate Member or Registered Firm to commence legal proceedings in respect of any such differences, and no Member, Associate Member or Registered Firm shall have any right of action against any Member, Associate Member or Registered Firm, touching or arising out of any such matter or contract, except to enforce the award in any such arbitration. The detailed procedures applicable to arbitration are set out in the By-Laws and Rules of the Liverpool Cotton Association Ltd.

Is there any appeal? Yes

Currency dealt in: Not specified, but mostly in US dollars

Recommended commission rates and margins: When a Member is employed by another Member as a Buying Broker, the rate of Brokerage for buying cotton invoiced on Spot Terms ex a delivery point in the United Kingdom shall be as mutually agreed between them provided that: (a) the rate shall not be less than 0.125 per cent of the invoice amount plus £0.17 per 100 lb net weight; or £94 per 48,000 lb net weight, whichever is the greater (as adjusted 1 March 1977); (b) the rate per 100 lb net weight shall be adjusted annually by the Directors by £0.005 per 100 lb net weight for every movement of five points (to the nearest five points) over Index Price 100 (January 1974) in the General Index of Retail Prices; (c) the minimum Brokerage of £60 per 48,000 lb net weight shall be adjusted annually by the Directors in accordance with the actual movements of the General Index of Retail Prices as compared with Index Price 100 (January 1974) to the nearest £1. But when a Member is so employed by a non-member, the rate of Brokerage shall be calculated in accordance with the foregoing plus 0.375 per cent. The above refers only to the United Kingdom.

Membership, types of: There are two types of membership — Members and Associate Members. (1) Any individual of not less than 21 years of age engaged or about to be engaged in the cotton trade or allied textile trades as a principal or of equivalent status, and any company engaged or about to be engaged in the cotton trade or allied textile trades, shall be qualified, if approved by the directors, to stand for election as a Member of the Association. Any individual or public company or private company, if qualified as indicated, may stand for election as a Member provided that, in the case of an individual, his principal place of business is in the United Kingdom and that in the case of a company it is incorporated within the United Kingdom and at least one of its directors or (at the discretion of the directors of the Association) its senior executives is a Member.

(2) Any firm whose principal place of business is in the United Kingdom and which is primarily engaged in the spinning, weaving or manufacturing of raw cotton, or in other industry associated directly or indirectly with the textile trade, or which is a member of a commodity exchange or similar organization in the United Kingdom established primarily for dealings in commodities other

than cotton, or any individual of not less than 21 years of age, engaged or about to be engaged as a principal in such firm, shall be hereby qualified, if approved by the directors, to stand for election as an Associate Member. Any individual resident or firm established outside the United Kingdom may, if approved by the directors and at their absolute discretion, stand for election as an Associate Member. An Associate Member shall have the same rights and privileges as a Member except that he or it shall not be qualified to be President, Vice-President, Treasurer or an Ordinary Director or to be a member of any committee formed under the Articles, By-Laws or Rules or an Arbitrator or Umpire under the Articles, By-Laws or Rules or to propose or second a person for election to any such position or office; he or it shall not be entitled to receive notice of or attend any meeting of the Association or to receive notice of or take part in any ballot or vote except a meeting called or ballot or vote taken for or in connection with any amendment of the Rules or the adoption of any new Rule.

Any person elected to membership shall, within one calendar month after his election, or within such further period (if any) as the directors shall sanction, pay such entrance fee as is prescribed, and also subscribe an undertaking to observe and comply with the Articles, By-Laws and Rules for the time being in force and all such further Articles, By-Laws and Rules as may from time to time be adopted. Such undertaking shall be in such form as the directors shall from time to time prescribe. The entrance fee (if any) shall be of such amount, not exceeding in any case £500, as shall from time to time be prescribed by the Association in General Meeting. Provided always that entrance fees of different amounts may be so prescribed in the case of different classes of membership.

Trading members, as at December 1975: *See Appendix 1 (page 236).*

Date of establishment of market: 1840

Membership of other organizations: International Federation of Cotton and Allied Textile Industries (IFCATI), Zurich; The Federation of Commodity Associations, London; Merseyside Chamber of Commerce and Industry (Council and Port Users Committee); Textile Industry Support Campaign, Oldham; The Manchester Textile Exchange (Committee); Incorporated Liverpool School of Tropical Medicine (Council); CICCA (Committee for International Co-operation between Cotton Associations). A representative of the Liverpool Cotton Association is invited as a trade adviser to the UK delegation to the International Cotton Advisory Committee (Washington DC), membership of which is on a governmental basis.

LONDON
British Fur Trade Association
68 Upper Thames St, London EC4V 3AN

Telephone: 01-248 5947/8

Names of Chief Executives: A R Kenyon — Treasurer, E Lockyer — Secretary

The British Fur Trade Association represents and promotes all sections of the Fur Industry. It is neither a Terminal Market nor an Exchange. Business is transacted by Private Treaty but mainly at Public Auctions, held in the City of

London, which are attended by buyers from all fur-consuming countries. The Association offers facilities for arbitration both on spot and forward contracts.

The Coffee Terminal Market Association of London

Cereal House, 58 Mark Lane, London EC3R 7NE

Telephone: 01-488 3736; **Telex:** 884370

Commodity: Coffee (Robusta)

Titles of appointments: Chairman, Vice-Chairman, 13 members of the Committee of Management and the Secretary

Name of Secretary: P A S Rucker

Hours of trading: 10.30 to 12.30, 14.30 to 17.00. Calls are at 10.00, 12.20, 14.30, 16.50. Open outcry market

Trading unit: 5 tonnes Robusta Coffee

Trading limits: None

Contract particulars:
Quality: Coffee deliverable against the contract shall be five tonnes net weight (with a tolerance of up to three per cent more or three per cent less) of sound Robusta CTMAL Standard or other grades with allowances, or premiums in accordance with these Rules in warehouses nominated by the Association from time to time in London/Home Counties, Bristol, Amsterdam, Rotterdam, and Le Havre areas.

Delivery points: London/home Counties, Bristol, Amsterdam, Rotterdam, Le Havre

Are rules and regulations available? Yes, to members

Can they be purchased? Yes, by members

Arbitration rules: A dispute arising out of a contract shall be submitted to the Committee of the Association, which shall appoint a board of arbitration consisting of not less than three members of the Committee to act on its behalf. Either party to the contract may refer a dispute to the Committee after giving four clear days' notice of his intention to the other party. A majority decision of the board of arbitration shall prevail; in the event of equality of votes, the chairman shall have a second or casting vote. The award shall be signed by the chairman of the board of arbitration and shall be deemed to be the award of the Committee and final and binding in all cases. The party referring a dispute to arbitration shall forward, in duplicate, to the Secretary of the Association, a written statement of his case together with a copy of the contract(s) and other documentary evidence; the Secretary shall forward a copy of these documents to the other party who shall, not later than 21 days after their dispatch to him, submit to the Secretary, in duplicate, a written statement of his defence and other documentary evidence, a copy of which shall be forwarded by the

Secretary to the first party. All documents shall be seen by the board of arbitration which at its discretion may decide the case on the written statements and documents submitted or call the parties and witnesses before it. A registration fee must be paid to the Secretary on reference of a dispute to the Committee. In addition the referring party must deposit a sum with the Secretary on account of fees and expenses; the board of arbitration may call for further sums at its discretion. In the event of failure to deposit such sums, the board may postpone or discontinue its proceedings. Should a party require the arbitrators to obtain the opinion of the High Court of Justice on a question of law, a further sum must be deposited with the Secretary as security for extra fees and expenses incurred. Any balance of such sums deposited shall be returned to the depositors in such proportions as the board shall determine.

If any member refuses to participate in any reference of dispute to arbitration, or refuses to perform the decision or award of the Committee, he shall be liable to suspension or expulsion from Membership of the Association by resolution of an Extraordinary Meeting, notice of such meeting being given to the Member whose suspension or expulsion is in question. The Member shall be entitled to attend or speak at the meeting, and his suspension or expulsion must be approved by at least two-thirds of those present.

The amount of arbitration fees and of any additional expenses shall be fixed by the board of arbitration; arbitration fees and expenses shall be borne by the losing party unless otherwise specially awarded. All disputes referred to arbitration shall be settled according to the law of England, notwithstanding the domicile, residence or place of business of the parties.

Is there an appeal? No

Currency dealt in: Sterling

Volume of trading over past two years: January—December 1975, 228,284 lots; January—December 1976, 660,188 lots

Recommended commission rates and margins: Clearing Members — Associate Members £6, Non-Members £10, Non-Clearing Members — Associate Members £10, Non-Members £14

Membership, types of: Floor Members (Voting Members) limited to 35 who can deal free of commission on market floor. Home and Overseas Associate Members — unlimited membership

Trading members, as at January 1977: *See Appendix 1 (page 240).*

Date of establishment of market: 1 July 1958

Federation of Commodity Associations

Plantation House, Mincing Lane, London EC3M 3HT

Telephone: 01-626 1745

Name of Secretary: J H Farr

The main aims of the Federation are to promote and protect the commercial interests of Commodity Associations and Firms and to act as a link for the exchange of views and information with the EEC Commission, any National Government and appropriate organizations. The Federation has been granted direct access to the Directorates-General of the EEC Commission and its representatives in Brussels can make enquiries and representations by personal contact with EEC officials.

Membership: 27 trade associations and 97 commodity firms

Federation of Oils, Seeds and Fats Associations Ltd (FOSFA)

24 St Mary Axe, London EC3A 8ER

Telephone: 01-283 5511; **Telex:** 8812757; **Cable address:** Ricinus London EC3

Commodities: Vegetable and Marine Oils, Animal Fats, Oilseeds, Copra, Palm Kernels, HPS Groundnuts

Titles of appointments: President, Vice-President, Treasurer — elected from 20 Council members who are themselves elected annually from the membership

Contract particulars: FOSFA publishes 60 separate contracts, each related to a specific commodity or to a specific origin where appropriate.

Arbitration: In the event of a dispute, both parties nominate an arbitrator of their choice from among the full list of representatives of FOSFA members. The two arbitrators meet and consider the evidence presented and make their award. If they cannot agree, they appoint a third member as an umpire to make the final decision. The award is issued to both parties on payment of the appropriate fee, which varies according to the time taken and complexity of the case. Non-members making use of arbitration facilities pay an extra fee; and a further fee is charged if an official FOSFA contract form is not used. A FOSFA arbitration award is enforceable in the British courts and in most other countries.

Is there an appeal? Yes. Within a specified time from the date of the arbitration award, the party notifies FOSFA of its wish to appeal and forwards a small deposit to cover estimated expenses. An Appeal Board of five members is elected by the FOSFA Committee of Appeal and a date set for the hearing. The Board, having heard both parties to the appeal, makes its decision on a majority vote and FOSFA issues an official award. The costs of an ordinary appeal are normally in the region of £150 to £200 and the awards are enforceable in the courts in most countries.

Membership: This comprises producers, shippers, merchants, brokers, crushers, refiners and others involved in the trade.

Members: There are some 900 individual representatives from 460 companies drawn from 40 countries.

Date of establishment of association: FOSFA (formed in 1971) is an amalgamation of four associations — the Incorporated Oilseeds Association founded in 1863, the London Oil and Tallow Trades Association (1910), the

London Copra Associations (1913) and the Seed, Oil, Cake and General Produce Association (1935).

The objects of the Federation are: (a) to promote trade in Oils, Fats and Oilseeds; (b) to establish greater uniformity in commercial usages, forms of contract and the voluntary adoption of such contracts and documents by the trade internationally; (c) to provide the necessary administrative machinery for the settlement of disputes by impartial and authoritative arbitration; (d) to establish and promote internationally accepted analysis facilities for the use of the trade worldwide; (e) to introduce any reforms or arrangements commending themselves to the members for the benfit of the trade.

The Federation's contract forms cover a very large range of commodities and are used as a basis for transactions world-wide. The contracts are sometimes referred to as the rules.

The General Produce Brokers' Association of London

Cereal House, 58 Mark Lane, London EC3R 7HP

Telephone: 01-480 5388/9

Titles of appointments: President, Vice-President, Secretary

Name of President: K Ralli

Rules and regulations: These are supervised and enforced by a Committee of 14.

Arbitration: Disputes are settled by a Panel of Arbitrators consisting of 80 members.

Membership, types of: Member Firms, Associate Members, Non-Resident Associate Members

Membership, as at 1976: 30 Member Firms, 17 Associate Members, nine Non-Resident Associate Members

Date founded: 1876

International Commodities Clearing House Ltd

Roman Wall House, 1-2 Crutched Friars, London EC3N 1AN

Telephone: 01-488 3200; **Telex:** 887234; **Cable address:** Libonotus London EC3

Markets served by ICCH: The London Cocoa Terminal Market Association, The Coffee Terminal Market Association of London, The United Terminal Sugar Market Association, The London Wool Terminal Market Association, The London Vegetable Oil Terminal Market Association, The London Rubber

Terminal Market Association, The GAFTA Soya Bean Meal Futures Association, The Sydney Futures Exchange Ltd

Titles of appointments: Chairman, Deputy Chairman, Joint Managing Directors, Directors

Names of Joint Managing Directors: M Stockdale and I W T McGaw

Branches and affiliates: ICCH, Sydney — Chairman, A T Payne; Managing Director, J J Sinclair; Directors, J C Taylor, J K Westmore. ICCH Australia (Pty) Ltd — Board as above. International Commodities Clearing House (Hong Kong) Ltd — Local Directors, P J McLaren (Managing Director), A P de Guingand. Paris Representative — M Gilbert Durieux

Hours of trading: Monday to Friday 09.30 to 17.30

Are rules and regulations available? Yes, to members of ICCH

Currency dealt in: Sterling in London, Australian dollars in Sydney, US dollars in Hong Kong

Volume of trading over past 12 years:

Date	Lots	Value
1965	1,150,000	£1,179,197,000
1966	1,300,000	£1,378,802,000
1967	1,880,000	£2,356,048,000
1968	2,322,000	£3,826,648,000
1969	3,250,000	£6,117,810,000
1970	3,543,246	£5,889,538,000
1971	3,577,846	£6,485,074,600
1972	3,987,446	£9,479,378,960
1973	4,665,356	£20,019,570,235
1974	4,698,394	£38,348,692,752
1975	3,708,772	£28,034,595,028
1976	5,608,836	£57,674,308,060

Membership, type of: Clearing Membership is open to organizations resident in any part of the world and subject to approval by ICCH Board of Directors. Details available on request.

Date of establishment of company: The Company was formed in 1888 as The London Produce Clearing House Ltd, by a group of commodity merchants and bankers in the City of London. In 1973 the name was changed to International Commodities Clearing House Ltd to reflect the growing international impact of the company's business.

The London Cocoa Terminal Market

London Cocoa Terminal Market Association, Cereal House, 58 Mark Lane, London EC3R 7NE

Telephone: 01-488 3736/9; **Telex:** 884370

Commodity: Cocoa

Titles of appointments: Chairman, Vice-Chairman, eight members of the Committee of Management and the Secretary

Name of Secretary: P A S Rucker

Hours of trading: The market is open from 10.00 to 13.00 and from 14.30 to close of 16.45 Call. There are Calls at 10.00, 12.58, 15.30 and 16.45. Should the market reach £40 above or below the previous day's official closing price, the market will close for 15 minutes and re-open with a special Call. All business must be done by open outcry on the floor of the market.

Trading unit: Ten tonnes of cocoa beans

Minimum fluctuation: £0.50 per tonne (£5 per contract)

Contract particulars:
Quality: Cocoas are acceptable from countries as defined in the No 5 Cocoa Contract Rule. Cocoa deliverable against the contract shall be ten tonnes net weight of cocoa beans of a gross and quality as defined in the Rules ex warehouse approved by the Association in the United Kingdom or delivered in approved warehouse in Amsterdam, Antwerp, Hamburg and Rotterdam.

Delivery points: London, Liverpool, Avonmouth, Hull, the borough of Teesside, Amsterdam, Antwerp, Hamburg, Rotterdam

Delivery months quoted: March, May, July, September, December, March, May (seven positions)

Are rules and regulations available? Only to members

Arbitration rules: A dispute arising out of a contract shall be submitted to the Committee of the Association, which shall appoint a board of arbitration consisting of not less than three members of the Committee to act on its behalf. Either party to the contract may refer a dispute to the Committee after giving four clear days' notice of his intention so to do. A majority decision of the board of arbitration shall prevail; in the event of the equality of votes, the chairman shall have a second or casting vote. The award shall be signed by the chairman of the board of arbitration and shall be deemed to be the award of the Committee and final and binding in all cases. The party referring a dispute to arbitration shall forward, in duplicate, to the Secretary of the Association, a written statement of his case together with a copy of the contract(s) and other documentary evidence; the Secretary shall forward a copy of these documents to the other party who shall, not later than 21 days after their dispatch to him, submit to the Secretary, in duplicate, a written statement of his defence and other documentary evidence, a copy of which shall be forwarded by the Secretary to the first party. All documents shall be seen by the board of arbitration which at its discretion may decide the case on the written statements and documents submitted or call the parties and witnesses before it. A registration fee must be paid to the Secretary on reference of a dispute to the Committee. In addition the referring party must deposit a sum with the Secretary on account of fees and expenses; the board of arbitration may call for further sums at its discretion. In the event of failure to deposit such sums, the board may postpone or discontinue its proceedings. Should a party require the arbitrators to obtain the opinion of the High Court of Justice on a question of law, a further sum must be deposited with the Secretary as security for extra fees and expenses incurred. Any balance of such sums deposited shall be returned to the depositors in such proportions as the board shall determine. If any member refuses to participate in any reference of dispute to arbitration, or refuses to perform the decision or award of the Committee, he shall be liable to suspension or expulsion from Membership of the Association by resolution of an Extraordinary Meeting, notice of such meeting being given to the Member whose suspension or expulsion is in question. The Member shall be entitled to attend or speak at the meeting, and his suspension or expulsion must be approved by at least two-thirds of those present. The amount of arbitration fees and of any additional expenses shall be fixed by the board of arbitration; arbitration fees and expenses shall be borne by the losing party unless otherwise specially awarded. All disputes referred to arbitration shall be settled according to the law of England, notwithstanding the domicile, residence or place of business of the parties.

Is there an appeal? No

Currency dealt in: Sterling

Volume of trading over past two years: 1975 (1 January to 31 December) 742,388 lots, 1976 (1 January to 31 December) 1,171,706 lots

Minimum commission rates: Minimum rates of commission per tonne lot, buying or selling are:

	Normal	Day Trade	Straddle
Trade and non-trade Members	£10	£5	£5
Non-members	£16	£8	£5

Membership, types of: There are two groups of voting members — Broker Members, of which there is an upper limit of 18, and Home Members, of which there is an upper limit of 36. These are permitted to deal free of commission on the market floor. Non-voting members are divided into Trade and Non-trade and are permitted to trade at a rate of commission lower than that charged to non-members.

Trading members, as at December 1976: *See Appendix 1 (page 238).*

Date of establishment of market: 1928, following on the establishment of the Cocoa Association of London two years earlier which regulated trade in physical cocoa by setting out contract rules, recognized grades and arbitration machinery.

Membership of other organizations: London Commodity Exchange Co Ltd

London Commodity Exchange Co Ltd

Cereal House, 58 Mark Lane, London EC3R 7NE

Telephone: 01-488 3736/9, 481 2080; **Telex:** 884370

Commodities: The commodities traded on Terminal Market Associations using the Exchange are Cocoa, Coffee, Rubber, Soya Bean Meal, Sugar, Vegetable Oil, Wool

Titles of appointments: Chairman, Vice-Chairman, Executive Director

Name of Executive Director: P A S Rucker

Hours of trading: Monday to Friday 09.30 to 17.30

Are rules and regulations available? The London Commodity Exchange does not exercise control over the different markets and responsibility for rules and regulations is vested in the respective markets.

Membership, types of: Terminal Market Associations which use the Exchange and are shareholders constituting the voting membership. There is also a category of Associate Members for Commodity Associations which are not shareholders and who do not have voting rights, though both shareholding and associate members may nominate their member companies for election to the Exchange.

Date of establishment of market: 1954

The London Grain Futures Market

The Grain and Feed Trade Association, Ltd, 28 St Mary Axe, London EC3A 8EP

Telephone: 01-283 5146 (five lines) and 623 3996 (five lines); **Telex:** 886984; **Telegrams:** Consignment London EC3

Commodities: European Economic Community Barley and European Economic Community Wheat

Titles of appointments: London Grain Futures & Clearing House Committee *consisting of:* four Members of The Grain and Feed Trade Association, elected by the Market; seven Members nominated by the Council of GAFTA; two persons nominated annually by the British Association of Grain, Seed & Agricultural Merchants, Ltd

Name of Secretary: W J Englebright

Hours of trading: 11.00 to 12.30 and 14.45 to 16.00. All business is done by open outcry. There is no market price movement limit. The Clearing House Committee have powers to direct as considered necessary.

Trading unit: 100 tonnes of 1,000 kg each

Price multiples: five pence per tonne (£5 per contract)

Contract particulars:
Quality: The Barley to be of the following Standard, and the Storekeeper's Warrant of Entitlement to be final as between Seller and Buyer; (a) Barley to sound and sweet and to contain not more than three per cent heat damage; (b) Natural Weight to be not less than 62.50 kg per hectolitre; (c) Moisture content not to exceed 15½ per cent (by water over test); (d) Total admixture of seeds and/or farinaceous grain (including wild oats) and dirt not to exceed five per cent, of which the dirt content not to exceed one per cent; (e) Sprouted grains not to exceed five per cent.
The price to include insurance cover and free rent for 14 days from date of tender. Delivery free to Buyer's transport in bulk from a store registered by the Committee within the mainland of Great Britain.
The Wheat to be of the following Standard, and the Storekeeper's Warrant of

Entitlement to be final as between Seller and Buyer: (a) Wheat to be sound and sweet and to contain not more than three per cent heat damage; (b) Natural Weight to be not less than 72.50 kg per hectolitre; (c) Moisture content not to exceed 15½ per cent (by water oven test); (d) Admixture — (i) Seeds and/or farinaceous grain (including wild oats) and dirt not to exceed two per cent, of which the dirt content not to exceed one per cent; (ii) Ergot and/or garlic not to exceed 0.001 per cent; (iii) Sprouted grains not to exceed two per cent.

The price to include insurance cover and free rent for 14 days from date of tender. Delivery free to Buyer's transport in bulk from a store registered by the Committee within the mainland of Great Britain.

Delivery months: September, November, January, March and May

Contract terms: Ex Store from a registered store, at Sellers' option, from within the mainland of Great Britain

Are rules and regulations available? Yes, to members and non-members

Arbitration rules: (Note: When grain is tendered from a registered store, a Warrant of Entitlement is issued by the storekeeper — this then is a contract between him and the Warrant holder who, in the event of a dispute, proceeds under its Arbitration rules.)

1. (a) All disputes from time to time arising out of or under Warrants of Entitlement (including any question of law arising in connection therewith) shall be referred to two arbitrators, one to be appointed by the holder and one by the issuer of the Warrant, or to an umpire to be appointed by the two arbitrators if and when they disagree. (b) Every arbitrator and umpire shall reside in the United Kingdom and, at the time of appointment, shall be a member of The Grain and Feed Trade Association, or a principal or an employee of a member Firm or a member Company engaged in the business of grain merchants, millers, manufacturers or brokers, or shall be members of the British Association of Grain, Seed, Feed & Agricultural Merchants, Ltd, provided always that no award shall be impugned, questioned or invalidated on the ground of want of qualification as aforesaid of any arbitrator or umpire unless objection shall first have been taken to his so acting at the commencement of or prior to the hearing of the arbitration.

2. (a) A party claiming arbitration (otherwise than in respect of condition and/or quality) must appoint his arbitrator and must make his claim for arbitration and give notice of appointment of his arbitrator in writing to the other party within one calendar month from the date of taking delivery of the grain out of store. (b) If the Warrant holder claims arbitration in respect of condition and/or quality, he must appoint his arbitrator and make his claim for arbitration and give notice of appointment of his arbitrator in writing to the Storekeeper within five working days (excluding Saturdays) of the grain being moved out of store. In any assessment of allowances for quality against the London Grain Futures Standard, herein specified, due regard shall be given to any official Grain and Feed Trade Association tests made of the delivery. (c) Arbitration having been duly claimed by one of the parties, the other party shall appoint and instruct his arbitrator within three clear days of the receipt of written notice from the party claiming of his intention to proceed and calling upon him to appoint and instruct his arbitrator.

3. (Miscellaneous detail re arbitration procedure, etc.)

4. Every Award shall be in writing on an official form to be supplied by The Grain and Feed Trade Association at a charge to be fixed from time to time by them and every such Award under the hand of the arbitrators or the umpire (as the case may be) shall be final, conclusive and binding upon the parties hereto in respect of all matters thereby determined.

Is there an appeal? No

Currency dealt in: Sterling

Volume of trading:

October/September 1973–1974	Barley	2,430,000 tonnes (1,000 kg each)
	Wheat	2,316,200 tonnes (1,000 kg each)
October/September 1974–1975	Barley	2,398,900 tonnes (1,000 kg each)
	Wheat	3,319,000 tonnes (1,000 kg each)
October/September 1975–1976	Barley	3,090,500 tonnes (1,000 kg each)
	Wheat	4,818,900 tonnes (1,000 kg each)

Minimum Commission Rates: Full Members — £4 single transaction (name disclosed on contract); £5 single transaction (name disclosed to clearing house); £15 double transaction (name undisclosed — clearing through Broker)
Associated Members — £7 single transaction (name disclosed only to clearing house); £23 double transaction (name undisclosed, clearing through Broker); £25 single or double transaction (clearing through Broker)
Day Trades — £13 on each 100 tonnes for a round turn, contracts to be closed same day

Membership: There are two categories of membership:
Full Members — Must be a Member of The Grain and Feed Trade Association and of The Baltic Mercantile and Shipping Exchange, and must have a genuine place of business, approved by the Committee, within a radius of five miles of the registered GAFTA offices
Associate Members — Must be a Member of The Grain and Feed Trade Association and have a genuine place of business approved by the Committee within the European Economic Community
Certificate of Membership — Unless otherwise determined by the Committee, cost £500 (Associates)
Annual Subscription — £125 for Full Members, and £250 for an Associate Member
Membership Limit — Unless otherwise determined by the Committee, the maximum number of Full Members shall be 58

Trading members, as at December 1976: *See Appendix 1 (page 242).*

Date of establishment of market: 3 May 1929. Initially trading was in Canadian and Argentine Wheats, and Argentine Maize.

The London Jute Association

69 Cannon St, London EC4N 5AB

Telephone: 01-248 4444; **Telex:** Chamcom/London 888941 prefixed Lonjuass; **Cable address:** Lonjuass London EC4

Commodities: Raw Jute, Kenaf and Allied Fibres

Titles of appointments: Chairman, Vice-Chairman, a maximum of 18 Committee Members, Secretary, Assistant Secretary

Name of Secretary: E Ira Brown

Hours of trading: Monday to Friday 09.00 to 17.50. Market holidays are fixed by the Committee.

Trading units: (a) with Bangladesh, India, Nepal a bale of Pucca press-packed jute weighing about 400 lb/181 kg; (b) with Thailand a tonne of 1,000 kg

Trading limits: Certain price controls may be imposed by the governments of exporting countries.

Contract particulars:
Quality: Jute shipped under an LJA contract is guaranteed of average quality of the grade specified. If the jute is inferior an allowance is fixed either by amicable settlement or by arbitration in London.
Delivery points: World-wide, except UK

Are rules and regulations available? Yes, only to members

Arbitration rules: These are set out in the By-Laws of the Association.

Is there an appeal? Yes, either party can appeal against an arbitration award; the appeal is heard by the committee.

Currency dealt in: Until 1976 in Sterling; subsequently US dollars and other currencies

Recommended commission rates and margins: Members trade as Principals.

Membership, types of: Membership is in a personal capacity. There are three types: Full, Associate and Honorary Membership.

Date of establishment of market: The Association was established in 1875.

Membership of other organizations: Federation of Commodity Associations

The London Metal Exchange
Whittington Ave, London EC3V 1LB

Telephone: 01-626 1011; **Cable address:** Metma London EC3

Commodities: Copper, Tin, Lead, Zinc, Silver

Titles of appointments: Chairman, Vice-Chairman, Secretary of the Board; Chairman, Vice-Chairman, Executive Secretary of the Committee

Names of Chief Executives: P G Smith, CBE — Chairman of the Board, Chairman of the Committee; R Gibson-Jarvie, BA (Hons) Cantab — Resident Executive Secretary

Hours of trading: Two sessions each day. One commences at noon, the other at 15.40. Each metal is traded in separately in 5-minute rings and there are two rings in each session. Trading hours from Monday to Friday are:

Copper	12.00 to 12.05	Lead	15.35 to 15.40
Silver	12.05 to 12.10	Zinc	15.40 to 15.45
Tin	12.10 to 12.15	Copper	15.45 to 15.50
Lead	12.15 to 12.20	Tin	15.50 to 15.55
Zinc	12.20 to 12.25	Silver	15.55 to 16.00
Interval	12.25 to 12.35	Interval	16.00 to 16.05
Copper Wirebars	12.35 to 12.40	Lead	16.05 to 16.10
Copper Cathodes	12.40 to 12.45	Zinc	16.10 to 16.15
Tin	12.45 to 12.50	Copper Wirebars	16.15 to 16.20
Lead	12.50 to 12.55	Copper Cathodes	16.20 to 16.25
Zinc	12.55 to 13.00	Tin	16.25 to 16.30
Silver	13.00 to 13.05	Silver	16.30 to 16.35
Kerb Trading until	13.25	Kerb Trading until	16.50

Closing prices of the second ring in the morning are known as the Official prices. These are agreed by the Quotations Committee and announced by the Secretary. The 'Settlements' are the cash sellers' prices and it is on the basis of these that the majority of long term domestic and international contracts are concluded. Although dealings in the afternoon are transacted in the same manner as in the morning, no 'Official prices' are announced.

Kerb dealings in all the metals are permitted both in the morning and in the afternoon for 15 minutes, ie until 13.25 and 16.50 respectively.

Trading unit: In Copper, Lead and Zinc, the minimum contract is 25 tonnes and dealings are transacted in multiples thereof. Tin is traded in five tonne units and Silver in 10,000 troy oz.

Trading limits: The LME has no limit as to the amount a price may rise or fall on any market.

Contract particulars:

Quality:

Copper — (1) Electrolytic Wirebars min Purity 99.9%, min Price Movement £0.5 per tonne. Or High Conductivity Fire Refined at a deduction of £20 per tonne; (2) Electrolytic Cathodes min Purity 99.9%, min Price Movement £0.5 per tonne.

Tin — (1) Standard min Purity 99.75%, min Price Movement £1 per tonne; (2) Special Grade min Purity 99.85%, min Price Movement £1 per tonne.

Lead — (1) Refined Pig min Purity 99.97%, min Price Movement £0.25 per tonne.

Zinc — (1) Produced by Distillation or Electrolysis and must be min Purity 98%, min Price Movement £0.25 per tonne.

Silver — (1) min Fineness .999 in the form of Bars of 10,000 troy oz, min Price Movement £0.001 (.1 of a penny per troy oz)

Delivery points: For Copper, Lead, Zinc and Tin — Antwerp, Avonmouth, Birkenhead, Birmingham, Bremen, Glasgow, Hamburg, Hull, Liverpool, London, Manchester, Newcastle-on-Tyne, Rotterdam, Swansea; Silver Storage at Amsterdam, Hamburg, London, Rotterdam

(A detailed list of addresses in these centres is included in the LME book of Rules and Regulations.)

Trading positions: Cash for delivery on the following business day three months forward

Are rules and regulations available? Yes

Arbitration rules: Disputes arising out of or in relation to contracts which are subject to the Rules and Regulations of the LME shall be referred to two arbitrators, one appointed by each party from the Arbitration Panel of the LME. Appointments to the Arbitration Panel are made by the Committee of the LME and those eligible for appointment shall be members of the Exchange, their partners, co-directors or members of their staff. Every Award made pursuant to any provision of this Rule shall be conclusive and binding on the parties to the arbitration.

(The above rules are given in details in the LME book of Rules and Regulations.)

Is there an appeal? Yes. Either party has the right to appeal against the Award. The appeal shall be made in writing to the Executive Secretary of the Committee of the LME within 21 days of the date of Award.

(Rules pertaining to the appeal are given in the LME book of Rules and Regulations.)

Currency dealt in: Sterling

Membership, types of: Members of the LME are known as Subscribers and function either as Individuals transacting business on their own behalf or as Representatives of firms or companies. A Candidate for election as a Subscriber must be proposed by one Subscriber and seconded by another and election is the exclusive province of the Directors whose decision is taken by a majority of votes. Subscribers are elected until 31 December each year and in the absence of a notification to the contrary it is assumed that the Subscriber is eligible for re-election.

Ring membership is granted jointly by the Directors and the Committee of the LME and only Representative Subscribers of firms and companies are eligible. A Subscriber who wishes to become a Ring dealer must apply to both the Directors and the Committee for permission. Two sponsors who are themselves Subscribers are needed, plus two referees from persons engaged in the metal trade.

There is an entrance fee for Subscribers plus a subscription, and each candidate for election is required to purchase two qualification shares in the Company. A Subscriber is entitled to be admitted to the Exchange in accordance with the Rules and Regulations.

Trading members, as at December 1976: *See Appendix 1 (page 243).*

Date of establishment of market: The LME was established in 1877 with premises in Lombard Street. The present premises opened as a terminal market in 1882.

List of membership of other organizations: Federation of Commodity Associations, British Federation of Commodity Associations

The London Rubber Terminal Market Association

Cereal House, 58 Mark Lane, London EC3R 7NE

Telephone: 01-488 3736; **Telex:** 884370; **Cable address:** Commarserve

Commodity: Natural Rubber

Titles of appointments: Chairman, Vice-Chairman, seven members of the Committee of Management and the Secretary

Name of Secretary: P H W Salt

Hours of trading: The Market is open from 09.45 until the close of the 12.45 call and from 14.30 until the close of the 16.30 call. Calls at 09.45, 12.45, 15.15 and 16.30. Trading is permitted on the kerb during the period when the Market is closed and all business done during this time must be recorded on the market board or daily sheet before the reopening of the market.

Trading unit: The trading unit is 15 tonnes for delivery in quarterly periods, but the two most prompt months (except the current month) are traded as single months in lots of 5 tonnes.

Trading limits: £0.05 pence per kg

Trading positions: Up to 22 months ahead in: January—March, April—June, July—September, October—December (or any single month)

Contract particulars:
Quality: For all contracts for delivery up to and including March 1978 — Ribbed Smoked Sheet Certified quality International No 1. For all contracts for delivery April 1978 onwards — Ribbed Smoked Sheet Certified quality not lower than International No 2

Delivery points: For all contracts for delivery up to and including December 1977 — London, Liverpool, Avonmouth. For all contracts for delivery January 1978 onwards — London, Liverpool, Avonmouth, Rotterdam, Amsterdam, Hamburg

Are rules and regulations available? Only to members

Arbitration rules: A dispute arising out of a contract shall be submitted to the Committee of the Association, which shall appoint a board of arbitration consisting of not less than three members of the Committee to act on its behalf. Either party to the contract may refer a dispute to the Committee after giving four clear days notice of his intention to the other party. A majority decision of the board of arbitration shall prevail; in the event of the equality of votes, the chairman shall have a second or casting vote. The award shall be signed by the chairman of the board of arbitration and shall be deemed to be the award of the Committee and final and binding in all cases.
The party referring a dispute to arbitration shall forward, in duplicate, to the Secretary of the Association, a written statement of his case together with a copy of the contract(s) and other documentary evidence; the Secretary shall forward a copy of these documents to the other party who shall, not later than 21 days after their dispatch to him, submit to the Secretary, in duplicate, a written statement of his defence and other documentary evidence, a copy of which shall be forwarded by the Secretary to the first party. All documents shall be seen by the board of arbitration which at its discretion may decide the case on the written statements and documents submitted or call the parties and witnesses before it. A registration fee must be paid to the Secretary on reference of a dispute to the Committee. In addition the referring party must deposit a sum with the Secretary on account of fees and expenses; the board of

arbitration may call for further sums at its discretion. In the event of failure to deposit such sums, the board may postpone or discontinue its proceedings. Should a party require the arbitrators to obtain the opinion of the High Court of Justice on a question of law, a further sum must be deposited with the Secretary as security for extra fees and expenses incurred. Any balance of such sums deposited shall be returned to the depositors in such proportions as the board shall determine.

The amount of arbitration fees and of any additional expenses shall be fixed by the board of arbitration; arbitration fees and expenses shall be borne by the losing party unless otherwise specially awarded. All disputes referred to arbitration shall be settled according to the law of England, notwithstanding the domicile, residence or place of business of the parties.

Is there an appeal? No

Currency dealt in: Sterling

Volume of trading over past two years: Volumes traded in 1975: 15 tonnes — 33,975 lots, five tonnes — 2,219 lots; 1976: 15 tonnes — 60,474 lots, five tonnes — 2,476 lots

Recommended commission rates and margins: Clearing Clients — Broker Members £4.50 per lot; Dealer Members £6 per lot; Trade Associate Members £9 per lot; General Associate Members £10.50 per lot; Non-Members £16.50 per lot. Non-Clearing Clients — Broker Members £7.50; Dealer Members £9; Trade Associate Members £12; General Associate Members £13.50; Non-Members £19.50

Membership, types of: Voting Members — Broker Members (limit ten), Dealer Members (limit 23). These members are allowed to deal on the floor of the Market free of commission. The non-voting membership is divided into Trade Associate and General Associate Members and these members are allowed to trade at rates of commission lower than those charged to Non-Members.

Trading members, as at December 1976: *See Appendix 1 (page 241)*

Date of establishment of market: The present 'open outcry' market was established in September 1974 when it took over the terminal market operations which had been in operation since 1923 under the Rubber Settlement House administered by the Rubber Trade Association of London.

Membership of other organizations: The London Commodity Exchange Co Ltd

The London Soya Bean Meal Futures Market

GAFTA Soya Bean Meal Futures Association, 28 St Mary Axe, London EC3 8EP

Telephone: 01-283 5146 (five lines) 623 3996 (five lines); **Telex** 886984; **Telegrams:** Consignment, London EC3

Commodities: Toasted Extracted Soya Bean Meal/Pellets

Titles of appointments: Committee of Management consisting of six representatives of Floor Members elected by ballot, and three Members nominated by The Grain and Feed Trade Association

Name of Secretary: W J Englebright

Location of Market: Corn Exchange Building, Mark Lane, London EC3 8EP

Hours of trading: 10.45 to 12.00 and 14.50 to 17.10. Calls are opened by the Call Chairman at such times as determined by the Committee: the duration of each Call to be at the discretion of the Chairman, but not to exceed ten minutes. All business is by open outcry.

Trading unit: 100 tonnes of 1,000 kg each

Limit fluctuations: All offers shall be made in multiples of £0.10 per tonne and when during trading hours there is in respect of any position other than the Spot or first delivery month, an unaccepted offer at £5 below or an unaccepted bid at £5 above the official closing price of the previous day issued by the Clearing House, the Market will close for *15 minutes* (except that trading may continue in the Spot or first delivery month) and will re-open with a *Special Call* after which normal trading without limits shall be resumed until the close of the day. The closing call shall take precedence over the foregoing and shall be held without any limit on fluctuations.

At Calls, the first offer to sell or buy will take precedence over any offers made at the same price. Subsequent offers to sell at a lower or buy at a higher price shall supersede all previous offers. After a bid or offer has been made in one month all bids and offers in any other months may be withdrawn at the respective buyer's or seller's option which must be exercised promptly if challenged.

All disputes as to bids, offers, acceptances or withdrawals at Calls shall be decided immediately by the Call Chairman.

Price multiples: Ten pence per tonne (£10 per contract)

Contract particulars:
Contract basis: Ex Approved Storage

Contract quality: Toasted Extracted Soya Bean Meal/Pellets warranted to contain:

	Quality 'A'	Quality 'B'	
Minimum Protein and Fat	43.0%	43.0%	
Maximum Fibre	7.5%	8.5%	at fixed
Maximum Sand and/or Silica	2.5%	2.5%	3% discount
Maximum Moisture	12.5%	13.5%	

Trading positions: February, April, June, August, October, December, February (seven positions)

Tenderable origins: Europe, United States of America, Canada and Brazil

Tender points: Antwerp, Amsterdam, Hamburg, Rotterdam and the United Kingdom

Are rules and regulations available? Yes, to Members and Non-Members

Currency dealt in: Sterling

Average volume of trading: Approx 2,500 lots @ 100 tonnes, monthly

Minimum commission rates: Per 100 tonne lot, buying or selling:
Associate Member — Normal £8, Day Trade £4, Straddle £4 (inclusive of ICCH registration fee)
Non-Member — Normal £13, Day Trade £6.50, Straddle £6.50 (inclusive of ICCH registration fee)

Membership, types of: There are two categories of membership:
Floor Membership — Floor membership of the Market shall be limited to firms or companies who are members of The Grain and Feed Trade Association, who are carrying on business from a properly established office in London, and who satisfy the Committee that they are actively interested in the trading of soya bean meal. Firms and companies whose principal place of business is not within the member countries of the European Economic Community shall not be eligible for Floor Membership.
Associate Membership — *Trade* Associate Membership shall consist of companies or firms who have a continuing interest in the production, trading or consumption of physical soya bean meal, and who are elected by a majority of the Committee. *General* Associate Membership shall consist of other companies or firms who have a continuing trade interest in the Soya Bean Meal Futures Market and who are elected by a majority of the Committee.
Membership and Transfer fees: (i) By the first Floor Members (those whose names were originally framed) — Membership fee of £4,000; (ii) By other Floor Members (elected otherwise than by transfer) — such membership fee as may from time to time be prescribed by the Committee; (iii) By Associate Members (elected other than by transfer) — Membership fee of £2,000.
Any Floor or Associate Member subsequently elected by transfer shall pay a transfer fee of £50 to the Association.
The Committee may from time to time amend the above fees.

Trading members, as at December 1976: *See Appendix 1 (page 244).*

Date of establishment of market: 8 April 1975.

Management: On behalf of the GAFTA Soya Bean Meal Futures Association the management of the Market is by International Commodities Clearing House, Ltd, Roman Wall House, 1/2 Crutched Friars, London EC3.

Arbitration rules: Any dispute arising out of any contract that is subject to the Rules of the Association shall be referred to the Association for arbitration in accordance with the provisions laid down.
A party to a contract who wishes to refer a dispute to arbitration shall, after giving to the other party four business days' notice by registered mail, cable or teleprinter of his intention to claim arbitration, refer in writing the matter in dispute to the Committee for arbitration. The Committee shall thereupon appoint an Arbitration Tribunal which shall determine any such matter in dispute, whether such dispute arises between the parties thereto, or between one of the parties thereto and the trustee in bankruptcy, liquidator or personal representative of the other party. The Arbitration Tribunal shall have jurisdiction to determine whether a contract has been made. Should a party in dispute with another party refuse to concur in the reference to arbitration, the party referring the matter to arbitration may forthwith obtain an Award of the Arbitration Tribunal on the question in dispute. The Committee may at its discretion refuse to arbitrate on any reference made by a Member who has been suspended or expelled from the Association.

For determination of a dispute the Chairman or acting Chairman shall on behalf of the Committee appoint three persons, at least two being members of the Committee, and the third a member either of the Committee or of the Arbitration Panel maintained by the Association, who shall (notwithstanding that they may subsequently cease to be members of the Committee or of the Arbitration Panel, as the case may be) act as the Arbitration Tribunal in the dispute.
The Award of the Arbitration Tribunal shall be signed by all three members of the Tribunal and when so signed shall be final and binding in all cases.

Is there an appeal? No

The London Vegetable Oil Terminal Market Association

Cereal House, 58 Mark Lane, London EC3R 7NE

Telephone: 01-488 3736; **Telex:** 884370; **Cable address:** Commarserve

Commodities: Palm Oil, Soya Bean Oil

Titles of appointments: Chairman, Vice-Chairman, six members of the Committee of Management and the Secretary

Name of Secretary: P H W Salt

Hours of trading: The market is open from 10.15 until the close of the 12.40 call and from 14.30 until the close of the 16.50 call.

Trading unit: 50 tonnes

Trading limits: Palm Oil — £0.25 per tonne, Soya Bean Oil — £0.10 per tonne

Trading positions: Palm Oil — up to 13 months ahead; February, April, June, August, October, December. Soya Bean Oil — up to 13 months ahead; January, March, May, July, September, November

Contract particulars:
Quality: Crude unbleached Palm Oil — max five per cent Free Fatty Acid (palmitic Molecular weight 256) and max 0.5% Moisture and Impurities
Delivery points: Palm Oil — Rotterdam; Soya Bean Oil — London, Liverpool

Are rules and regulations available? Yes, for members only

Arbitration rules: A dispute arising out of a contract shall be submitted to the Committee of the Association which shall appoint a board of arbitration consisting of not less than three members of the Committee to act on its behalf. Either party to the contract may refer a dispute to the Committee after giving four clear days notice of his intention to the other party. A majority decision of the board of arbitration shall prevail; in the event of equality of votes, the chairman shall have second or casting vote. The award shall be signed by the chairman of the board of arbitration and shall be deemed to be the award of the Committee and final and binding in all cases.
The party referring a dispute to arbitration shall forward, in duplicate, to the

Secretary of the Association, a written statement of his case together with a copy of the contract(s) and other documentary evidence; the Secretary shall forward a copy of these documents to the other party who shall, not later than 21 days after their dispatch to him, submit to the Secretary, in duplicate, a written statement of his defence and other documentary evidence, a copy of which shall be forwarded by the Secretary to the first party. All documents shall be seen by the board of arbitration which at its discretion may decide the case on the written statements and documents submitted or call the parties and witnesses before it. A registration fee must be paid to the Secretary on reference of a dispute to the Committee. In addition the referring party must deposit a sum with the Secretary on account of fees and expenses; the board of arbitration may call for further sums at its discretion. In the event of failure to deposit such sums, the board may postpone or discontinue its proceedings. Should a party require the arbitrators to obtain the opinion of the High Court of Justice on a question of law, a further sum must be deposited with the Secretary as security for extra fees and expenses incurred. Any balance of such sums deposited shall be returned to the depositors in such proportions as the board shall determine. The amount of arbitration fees and of any additional expenses shall be fixed by the board of arbitration; arbitration fees and expenses shall be borne by the losing party unless otherwise specially awarded. All disputes referred to arbitration shall be settled according to the law of England, notwithstanding the domicile, residence or place of business of the parties.

Is there an appeal? No

Currency dealt in: Sterling

Volume of trading over past two years: Palm Oil — 1974—49,850 tonnes, 1975—132,900 tonnes, 1976—50,250 tonnes; Soya Bean Oil — 1974—19,990 tonnes, 1975—Nil

Recommended commission rates and margins: Palm Oil — Clearing Clients: Associate Members £4, Non-Members £10; Non-Clearing Clients: Associate Members £6, Non-Members £12

Membership, types of: The voting membership comprises 33 Floor Members. The non-voting membership comprises companies or persons who may be elected to Associate Membership.

Trading members, as at December 1976: *See Appendix 1 (page 245).*

The London Wool Terminal Market Association

International Commodities Clearing House Ltd, Roman Wall House, 1-2 Crutched Friars, London EC3N 1AN

Secretarial address: Manor Buildings, Manor Row, Bradford BD1 4NL, West Yorkshire

Telephone: 01-488 3200 (ICCH Ltd), 0274-31461 (Bradford); **Telex:** 887234 (ICCH Ltd)

Commodity: Greasy Wool

Titles of appointments: Chairman, Vice-Chairman, six members of the Committee of Management and the Secretary

Name of Secretary: N G Cowley

Hours of trading: Monday to Friday, 10.30 to 12.00, 15.00 to 16.30. There are calls at 10.30, 15.00 and 16.20. After-hours trading is allowed between 16.35 and 17.30 and business done between these times must be telephoned to the Clearing House by 17.45 and recorded on the blackboard before the commencement of the morning call at 10.30 on the next trading day.

Trading unit: The greasy equivalent of 1,500 kg of clean wool

Trading limits: Prices are quoted in new pence per kg clean wool with a minimum fluctuation of 0.1 of a penny

Contract particulars:
Quality: Standard — CWC Type 78, Good Topmaking Fleece grown and shorn in Australia. Deliverable Types — Australian wools of type groups listed in the rules and regulations. Samples are appraised by a board of appraisers in Bradford according to price differentials issued monthly by the Committee.

Delivery points: Flushing (Netherlands)

Delivery months quoted: March, May, July, October, December up to 19 months ahead

Are rules and regulations available? Yes

Can they be purchased? Yes, from the Bradford office, £3 per copy

Arbitration rules: When a dispute has arisen and either party is of the opinion that it cannot be resolved amicably, written notice shall be given by such a party to the other that he intends to submit the dispute to the Association and a copy of such notice shall be sent to the Secretary of the Association. If, after the expiry of four clear days following the date of posting or otherwise dispatching such notice, the dispute has still not been resolved, written notice that a dispute exists shall be given to the Secretary and the party giving the same shall send a copy thereof to the other party to the dispute. Each party shall within seven days appoint a representative from a list of representatives published by the Committee from time to time. The representatives so appointed shall meet together to discuss a basis for amicable settlement. If no settlement can be achieved, the representatives shall so inform the Secretary and within 14 days thereafter the party who gave notice to the Secretary of the existence of the dispute shall submit his statement of case in writing to the Secretary accompanied by such documentary evidence as he may think fit. The other party shall within 14 days after receipt from the Secretary of a copy of such statement of case and supporting documents submit his statement of defence in writing to the Secretary accompanied by such documentary evidence as he may think fit. A copy of the statement of defence and supporting documents shall be forwarded by the Secretary to the claimant and the Committee (excluding any member or alternate who is or becomes directly or indirectly interested in the subject matter of the dispute and any member or alternate who shall have been appointed the representative of either party) shall thereupon have power to arbitrate upon all matters in dispute. If either party shall fail to appoint a representative or to state his case of defence in accordance with this Rule the Committee (excluding any such person as aforesaid) shall have power to arbitrate upon the dispute and to make an award on the basis of such information and evidence as it shall think fit.

The Secretary shall notify the parties when an award has been signed and shall hold the award at the disposal of either party upon payment of the fees and expenses of the arbitration. A copy of the award shall be given to whichever party does not take up the original. The award must be honoured within ten days of its date. A note of every award made under these Rules shall be entered by the Secretary in a book to be kept for the purpose.

No person shall commence any action in any Court of Law in respect of any dispute to which the Rules in this Section apply until such dispute has been determined in accordance with such Rules and the obtaining of an arbitration award shall be a condition precedent to the right of any person to sue in respect of any of the matters in dispute.

Is there an appeal? No

Currency dealt in: Sterling

Volume of trading over past two years: New Contract started September 1974. 1974–3,871 contracts traded, 1975–4,279 contracts traded

Recommended commission rates and margins: Associate Member £8 per contract, Non-Member £13 per contract, Straddles — single commission

Membership, types of: Floor Members (upper limit of 30), Associate Members (no upper limit)

Trading members, as at December 1976: *See Appendix 1 (page 246).*

Date of establishment of market: April 1953

Membership of other organizations: London Commodity Exchange Ltd, Federation of Commodity Associations

The Rubber Trade Association of London

Cereal House, 58 Mark Lane, London EC3R 7HP

Telephone: 01-480 5388/9; **Cable address:** Rutrasol London

Commodity: Rubber

Titles of appointments: Chairman, two Vice-Chairmen, nine Members of the Committee, Secretary

Name of Secretary: M V Greene

Hours of trading: Monday to Friday 09.30 to 17.00

Trading unit: Physical market — all transactions at pence per kg

Trading limits: None

Contract particulars:

Quality: Rubber is not represented by a single standard grade. There are 35 standard international grades within eight types of natural rubber produced only from the latex of the Hevea brasiliensis tree which account for nearly all the international trade in dry natural rubber sold on a visual grading basis. There are also general purpose rubbers which are graded by precise technical standards and not by visual characteristics. Contracts traded are:
No 1 Godown Contract; No 2 FOB Contract; No 3 CIF Contract for all countries; No 4 CIF Contract for the USA or Canada; Nos 5 and 6 Spot and Delivery Contracts (London, Liverpool or Avonmouth); No 10 CIF Contract for Rubber Latex in drums; No 11 Plantation Finished Crepe Sole Rubber CIF Contract for all countries (other than USA or Canada); No 12 Plantation Finished Crepe Sole Rubber CIF Contract for the USA or Canada; Nos 13 and 14 Plantation Finished Crepe Sole Rubber Spot and Delivery Contracts (London, Liverpool or Avonmouth).

Delivery points: United Kingdom, the Continent and other destinations

Are rules and regulations available? Yes

Can they be purchased? Yes

Arbitration rules: The members of the Associations Register of Arbitrators are elected by the Committee of the Association. The Panel of Arbitrators consists of 80 members. Arbitration is conducted as per Rules and By-Laws.

Is there an appeal? Yes

Currency dealt in: Various

Recommended commission rates and margins: The scale of brokerages varies in relation to membership category and contract. Details of these are obtainable from the Association.

Membership, types of: Class 'A' — Selling agents and importers; mainly agents for the large plantation groups who themselves form the Producer membership and who market a considerable proportion of their rubber through London; Class 'B' — Brokers; these have two major functions — to introduce buyers to sellers without disclosing their identity and to guarantee the solvency of both parties. Brokers are not permitted to trade or take a market position for their own account; Class 'C' — Dealers; they may trade fully with consumers and with buyers and sellers overseas and may run a position, the size of which is limited only by their financial resources; Class 'P' — Producers; Associate Members.
Membership categories A,B,C,P, are restricted to individuals on companies domiciled in the United Kingdom.
Associate Membership is open to companies domiciled in any part of the world concerned with the rubber trade, which trades in its own name and not solely as an agent. This category is not intended to include companies engaged in the manufacturing industry.

Date of establishment of market: 1913

Tea Brokers' Association of London

Sir John Lyon House, 5 High Timber St, London EC4V 3LA

Telephone: 01-236 3368/9; **Cable address:** Teabrokas London

Commodity: Tea

Titles of appointments: Chairman, Vice-Chairman, three other committee members

Name of Secretary: D Mayne

Hours of trading: Auction sales are held each Monday from 10.00 when quantity on offer requires. Auctions are also held on Tuesdays.

Trading unit: Auction lot size may vary, minimum normally 20 chests.

Contract particulars:
Quality: Sales are against sample of each individual lot.
Delivery points: UK warehouses, but lots also occasionally offered ex-Continental warehouses.

Are rules and regulations available? Yes. Conditions of sale are issued by the London Tea Trade Committee.

Can they be purchased? Yes, from the Secretary of the Tea Brokers Association

Arbitration rules: Procedure for arbitration is covered by conditions of sale.

Is there an appeal? Procedure for arbitration includes appointment of an umpire.

Currency dealt in: Sterling

Average volume of trading over past two years: About 2,000 chests of tea of all growths are sold through the London auctions each year (each chest contains approximately 50 kg of tea). This is about half the annual UK consumption and the balance is purchased through private contracts or through primary markets in the country of origin.

Recommended commission rates and margins: Selling brokerage, 1¼ per cent; Buying brokerage ½ per cent

Membership, types of: Full Members and Associate Members

Trading members, as at December 1976: *See Appendix 1 (page 246).*

The United Terminal Sugar Market Association

Cereal House, 58 Mark Lane, London EC3R 7NE

Telephone: 01-488 3736; **Telex:** 884370; **Cable address:** Commarserve

Commodity: Raw Sugar

Titles of appointments: Chairman, Vice-Chairman, six members of the Committee of Management and a Secretary

Name of Secretary: P A S Rucker

Hours of trading: The market is open from 10.40 until the close of the 12.30 call and from 14.30 until the close of the 16.45 call. Calls at 10.40, 12.30, 14.30, 15.30, 16.45 and a kerb market then continues until 20.00.

Trading unit: 50 tonnes

Trading limits: £20 per tonne

Trading positions: Up to 15 months ahead in: March, May, August, October, December

Contract particulars:
Quality: Raw Cane Sugar — minimum 96° polarization

Delivery points: CIF London/Liverpool/Greenock

Are rules and regulations available? Yes, for members only

Can they be purchased? Yes, by members

Arbitration rules: A dispute arising out of a contract shall be submitted to the Committee of the Association which shall appoint a board of arbitration consisting of not less than three members of the Committee to act on its behalf. Either party to the contract may refer a dispute to the Committee after giving four clear days notice of his intention to the other party. A majority decision of the board of arbitration shall prevail; in the event of equality of votes, the chairman shall have a second or casting vote. The award shall be signed by the chairman of the board of arbitration and shall be deemed to be the award of the Committee and final and binding in all cases.
The party referring a dispute to arbitration shall forward, in duplicate, to the Secretary of the Association, a written statement of his case together with a copy of the contract(s) and other documentary evidence; the Secretary shall forward a copy of these documents to the other party who shall, not later than 21 days after their dispatch to him, submit to the Secretary, in duplicate, a written statement of his defence and other documentary evidence, a copy of which shall be forwarded by the Secretary to the first party. All documents shall be seen by the board of arbitration which at its discretion may decide the case on the written statements and documents submitted or call the parties and witnesses before it. A registration fee must be paid to the Secretary on reference of a dispute to the Committee. In addition the referring party must deposit a sum with the Secretary on account of fees and expenses; the board of arbitration may call for further sums at its discretion. In the event of failure to deposit such sums, the board may postpone or discontinue its proceedings. Should a party require the arbitrators to obtain the opinion of the High Court of Justice on a question of law, a further sum must be deposited with the Secretary as security for extra fees and expenses incurred. Any balance of such sums deposited shall be returned to the depositors in such proportions as the board shall determine. The amount of arbitration fees and of any additional expenses shall be fixed by the board of arbitration; arbitration fees and expenses shall be borne by the losing party unless otherwise specially awarded. All disputes referred to arbitration shall be settled according to the law of England, notwithstanding the domicile, residence or place of business of the parties.

Is there an appeal? No

Currency dealt in: Sterling

Volume of trading over past two years: 1974 — 956,598 lots, 1975 — 824,263 lots, 1976 — 856,295 lots

Recommended commission rates and margins: Clearing Clients — Non-Members £12.50, Associate Members £6.25, Affiliated Members £4.50, O/S Affiliated Members £4.50; Non-Clearing Clients — Non-Members £18, Associate Members £8

Membership, types of: The voting membership comprises 30 full members. Full membership is personal and not corporate. The non-voting membership comprises companies or persons who may be elected to Associate, Affiliated or Overseas Affiliated Membership.

Trading members, as at December 1976: *See Appendix 1 (page 246).*

Date of establishment of market: The market re-opened in 1957 after the Second World War. Earlier historical records are no longer available.

Membership of other organizations: The London Commodity Exchange Co Ltd

United States of America

Chicago Board of Trade

141 W Jackson Blvd, La Salle at Jackson, Chicago, Illinois 60604

Telephone: 312-435 3500; **Telex:** 253223

Commodities: Corn, Gold, Iced Broilers, Oats, Plywood, Silver, Soya Beans Soybean Meal, Soybean Oil, Stud Lumber, Wheat

Titles of appointments: Elected Officers: Chairman of the Board, Vice-Chairman, President. Executive Officers: President, Executive Vice-President and Treasurer, Vice-President and Secretary, Assistant Treasurer

Hours of trading:

Corn —	09.30 to 13.15 Cen Time	Soya Beans —	09.30 to 13.15 Cen. Time
Iced Broilers —	09.15 to 13.05 Cen Time	Soybean Meal —	09.30 to 13.15 Cen Time
Oats —	09.30 to 13.15 Cen Time	Soybean Oil —	09.30 to 13.15 Cen Time
Plywood —	10.00 to 13.00 Cen Time	Wheat —	09.30 to 13.15 Cen Time
Silver —	09.00 to 13.25 Cen Time		

Trading units:

Corn —	5,000 bu
Gold —	3 gross kg
Iced Broilers —	28,000 lb
Oats —	5,000 bu
Plywood —	Boxcars of 36 banded units of 66 pieces each — 2,376 pieces, 76,032 sq ft total per car
Silver —	5,000 troy oz
Soya Beans —	5,000 bu
Soybean Meal —	100 short tons of 2,000 lb each
Soybean Oil —	60,000 lb (one standard tank car)
Wheat —	5,000 bu

Trading limits:

Commodity	Price quotations and minimum fluctuations	Daily limits on price movements	Daily trading limits
Corn	Quoted in cents and quarter-cents per bushel, with a min fluctuation of ¼ cent per bu ($12.50 per contract)	Consult broker	
Gold	Quoted in dollars and cents per fine troy oz, with a min fluctuation of 10 cents per		

187

Commodity	Price quotations and minimum fluctuations	Daily limits on price movements	Daily trading limits
Gold cont	fine troy oz, basis Chicago. The min fluctuation per contract is $9.60. Max fluctuation per day is $10 per fine troy oz. Max fluctuations are governed by the Exchange's regulations on variable limits. Price limits do not apply to trading in the current month on and after the first notice day.		
Iced Broilers	Quoted in dollars and cents per hundredweight with min fluctuations of 2.5 cents per 100 lb, basis regular delivery plant in seller's truck with freight to Chicago, Illinois, included	$2 per 100 lb above or below previous day's settlement price, except on and after the first notice day of the current delivery month, when there is no limit	
Oats	Quotations in cents and quarter-cents per bu, with a min fluctuation of ¼ cent per bu ($12.50 per contract)	Consult broker	Two million bu in any one future or in all futures combined
Plywood	Quoted in units of 1,000 sq ft, with min fluctuation of 10 cents per 1,000 sq ft ($7.603 per contract), basis fob Portland, Oregon	$7 per 1,000 sq ft above or below the day's settlement price	
Silver	Quoted in dollars and cents per troy oz, with a min fluctuation of 10/100 of a cent per troy oz ($5 per contract), basis Chicago	Consult broker	
Soya Beans	Quoted in cents and quarter-cents per bu, with a min fluctuation of ¼ cent per bu ($12.50 per contract)	Consult broker	
Soybean Meal	Quoted in dollars and cents per short ton, with min fluctuations of 10 cents per short ton ($10 per contract), basis fob rail cars, bulk, Decatur, Illinois	Consult broker	
Soybean Oil	Quoted in dollars and cents per 100 lb (cents and hundredths of a cent per lb), with min fluctuation of	Consult broker	

one cent per 100 lb ($6 per
contract), basis Decatur,
Illinois, with freight
adjusted to Decatur — New
York City

Wheat   Quoted in cents and quarter-   Consult broker
cents per bu, with a min
fluctuation of ¼ cent per
bu ($12.50 per contract)

Contract particulars:
Corn —
Quality: No 2 Yellow corn and substitutions at differentials established by the Exchange

Delivery Months: December, March, May, July, September

Delivery: Delivery of corn may be made by registered warehouse receipts issued against stocks in warehouses that have been declared regular for delivery by the Chicago Board of Trade, located in the Chicago Switching District. Delivery may also be made from warehouses that have been declared regular for delivery located in the Toledo, OH, Switching District, and the St Louis, MO, Switching District (which includes East St Louis and Alton, IL), at a discount of 4 cents per bu under the (Chicago) contract price.

Gold —
Quality: Three bars of refined gold cast in gross weights of one kg min, 32.150 troy oz, assaying not less than 995 fineness and bearing brands and markings officially approved by the exchange. Settlement shall be on the basis of the fine oz of gold delivered. Refined gold of fineness above 9999 shall be considered to be 9999 pure for the purposes of calculating the fine gold content. Each bar may not weigh less than one kg. A bar weighing more than one kg shall be considered to weigh one kg gross.

Delivery months: January, March, May, July, September, November

Delivery: Deliveries on gold futures contracts shall be made by the delivery of depository vault receipts issued by vaults which have been approved and designated as regular vaults by the Exchange.

Iced Broilers —
Quality: USDA Grade A, whole, eviscerated, broiler-fryer chickens iced packed and ready to cook, in the 2.5 to 3.5-lb range in natural proportion

Delivery months: As much as ten months ahead, according to a schedule determined by the Exchange

Delivery: Deliveries on the iced broiler contract are made by delivery of demand certificates issued by plants approved by the Chicago Board of Trade and having inspection and grading services of the Poultry Division of the USDA. Shippers are limited to issuing no more demand certificates in a single day than their registered daily loading capacity, which is defined as not less than 25 per cent nor no more than 100 per cent of the shipper's maximum daily production capacity with an obvious maximum of three shifts or 24 hours. Deliveries must be made no later than the last business day of the month. No redelivery of broiler demand certificates is permitted. Tender is made one business day prior to delivery. If a long takes delivery against the demand certificate, he must

189

furnish loading orders and final detailed shipping instructions no later than 14.00 (Central Time) on the date of delivery. The shipment of broilers is to arrive at the destination specified by the owner on the fourth business day after delivery of the demand certificate. The long receiving delivery of a demand certificate has the right to sell his certificate back to the issuer. He must notify the issuer of his intention to sell back on the business day prior to the date of delivery of the certificate (ie the notice day). The price the long receives is the weighted average published by the USDA for Grade A poultry delivered into the Chicago area the following week.

Oats —
Quality: No 2 Heavy White, No 1 White and substitutions at differentials established by the Exchange

Delivery months: July, September, December, March, May

Delivery: Delivery of oats is made by delivering registered warehouse receipts issued against stocks in warehouses approved by the Exchange in the Chicago Switching District or the Minneapolis or St Paul, Minnesota, Switching Districts. Deliveries from Minneapolis or St Paul are made at a discount of 7½ cents per bu under contract prices.

Plywood —
Quality: Group 1, standard 32/16, 48 inches by 96 inches, 4 or 5 ply, half-inch thick CD, exterior glue

Delivery months: January, March, May, July, September, November

Delivery: Delivery on plywood futures contracts is made by shipping certificates issued by either plywood mills approved as regular by the Chicago Board of Trade or by warehouses approved by the Exchange. The certificate obligates the shipper to ship a boxcar of contract grade plywood ten business days after receipt of an initial loading order.

Silver —
Quality: Refined silver, assaying not less than .999 fineness and made up of one or more brands and markings officially listed by the Exchange, in bars cast in basic weights of 1,000 or 1,100 troy oz (each bar may vary no more than ten per cent more or less); delivery against contracts shall be in units of 5,000 troy oz (six per cent more or less)

Delivery months: As much as 15 months ahead, according to a schedule determined by the Exchange

Deliveries: Deliveries of silver are made by vault receipts drawn on deposits made in vaults in Chicago approved by the Exchange.

Soya Beans —
Quality: No 2 Yellow Soya Beans and substitutions at differentials established by the Exchange

Delivery months: September, November, January, March, May, July, August

Delivery of Soya Beans is made by registered warehouse receipts issued by warehousemen against stocks in warehouses that have been declared regular by the Chicago Board of Trade.

Soybean Meal —
Quality: One grade of meal only, with minimum protein of 44 per cent;

Exchange regulations give exact specifications and are available on request.

Delivery months: October, December, January, March, May, July, August, September

Delivery of soybean meal is made by a shipping certificate issued by shippers (processors or nonprocessing shippers) approved as regular by the Chicago Board of Trade.

Soybean Oil —
Quality: One grade only — see regulations for specifications

Delivery months: October, December, January, March, May, July, August, September

Delivery of soybean oil will normally be made by delivering registered warehouse receipts issued by warehousemen against stocks in warehouses that have been declared regular by the Chicago Board of Trade.

Wheat —
Quality: No 2 Soft Red, No 2 Dark Hard Winter, No 2 Hard Winter, No 2 Yellow Hard Winter, No 2 Dark Northern Spring, No 1 Northern Spring, No 2 Heavy Northern Spring, and substitutions at differentials established by the Exchange

Delivery months: July, September, December, March, May

Delivery: Delivery of wheat is made by delivering registered warehouse receipts issued against stocks in warehouses approved by the Exchange in the Chicago Switching District or Toledo, OH, Switching District. Deliveries from Toledo are made at a discount of two cents per bu under contract price.

Are rules and regulations available? Yes, with approval of Secretary's Office

Can they be purchased? Yes

Arbitration rules: See Federal Regulations.

Currency dealt in: US dollars

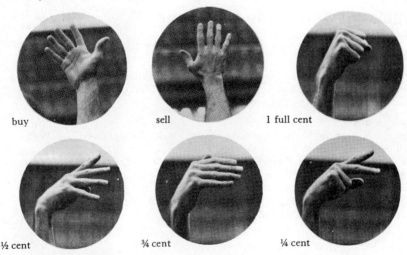

buy   sell   1 full cent

½ cent   ¾ cent   ¼ cent

Hand signals used by pit traders to clarify verbal bids and offers

Average volume of trading over past two years:

	Contracts traded		Estimated dollar value*	
	1975	1974	1975	1974
Corn	4,835,049	4,679,042	70,896.3	74,279.7
Gold	54,331	1,143**	878.2	21.2**
Gulf Wheat	—	1,455	—	31.9
Iced Broilers	179,393	221,128	2,210.1	2,380.6
Oats	154,067	199,486	1,201.7	1,593.4
Plywood	285,486	383,322	2,590.7	3,257.4
Silver	1,952,703	1,462,195	47,987.6	37,432.1
Soya Beans	3,913,804	2,731,297	116,388.7	100,956.9
Soybean Meal	792,227	878,182	11,130.7	13,884.0
Soybean Oil	1,489,720	1,620,316	23,668.6	33,103.0
Stud Lumber	2,320	3,258	28.3	37.6
Wheat	2,262,841	2,376,611	43,785.9	57,929.8

* *Estimated dollar value of commodities is reported in millions and is derived from the average unit price at which that commodity traded during the period reported and represents, for comparison purposes only, one measurement of the value of the respective commodities underlying CBT futures contracts. The estimated dollar value of commodities traded does not represent the monetary value of futures contracts nor cash participation in the Chicago Board of Trade futures market*

** *1974 figures represent only one trading day, 31 December 1974*

Recommended commission rates and margins: Consult broker.

Membership, types of: Individual — 1,402; registered member firms — approx 320

Date of establishment of market: 1848

Chicago Mercantile Exchange

444 W Jackson Blvd, Chicago, Illinois 60606

Telephone: 312-648 1000

The Exchange is organized into two divisions — International Monetary Market Division of CME and Associate Mercantile Market Division of CME — with the CME being the umbrella.

Commodities:
Chicago Mercantile Exchange — Live Cattle, Feeder Cattle, Live Hogs, Pork Bellies, Boneless Beef, Frozen Skinned Hams
IMM Division — British Pound, Canadian Dollar, Deutsche Mark, Dutch Guilder, French Franc, Mexican Peso, Japanese Yen, Swiss Franc, Gold, Copper, US Silver Coins, US Treasury Bills
AMM Division — Shell Eggs, Frozen Eggs, Nest Run Eggs, Frozen Turkeys, Lumber, Grain Sorghum (Milo), Potatoes, Butter

Titles of appointments: President; Executive Vice-President; Vice-President — Public Information and Marketing; Vice-President — Research, and Chief Economist; Vice-President — Compliance and Audits; Vice-President — Internal Operations

Name of President: Everette B Harris

Hours of trading:

Boneless Beef	09.05 to 12.45	Lumber	09.00 to 13.05
Butter	09.25 to 12.35	Potatoes	09.00 to 12.50
Fresh Eggs	09.20 to 13.00	Skinned Hams	09.10 to 13.00
Nest Run Eggs	09.20 to 13.00	Turkeys	09.10 to 12.45
Frozen Eggs	09.20 to 13.00	Feeder Cattle	09.05 to 12.45
Frozen Pork Bellies	09.10 to 13.00	Milo	09.30 to 13.15
Live Cattle (New and Old)	09.05 to 12.45	Gold	08.25 to 13.30
Live Hogs	09.15 to 12.55	Copper	08.45 to 13.15

Trading unit:

Boneless Beef	36,000 lb	Lumber	100,000 bd ft
Butter	38,000 lb	Potatoes	80,000 lb
Fresh Eggs	22,500 doz	Skinned Hams	36,000 lb
Nest Run Eggs	22,500 doz	Turkeys	36,000 lb
Frozen Eggs	36,000 lb	Feeder Cattle	42,000 lb
Frozen Pork Bellies	36,000 lb	Milo	400,000 lb
Live Cattle (New and Old)	40,000 lb	Gold	100 troy oz
Live Hogs	30,000 lb	Copper	12,500 lb

Trading limits:

Commodity	Minimum fluctuation equals In price	Per contract	Limit
Boneless Beef	2½/100¢/lb	$9	1½¢/lb (150 pt) ($540)
Butter	2½/100¢/lb	$9.50	1½¢/lb (150 pt) ($570)
Fresh Eggs	5/100¢/doz	$11.25	2¢/doz (200 pt) ($450)
Nest Run Eggs	5/100¢/doz	$11.25	2¢/doz (200 pt) ($450)
Frozen Eggs	2½/100¢/lb	$9	1½¢/lb (150 pt) ($540)
Frozen Pork Bellies	2½/100¢/lb	$9	2¢/lb (200 pt) ($720)
Live Cattle (New and Old)	2½/100¢/lb	$10	1½¢/lb (150 pt) ($600)
Live Hogs	2½/100¢/lb	$7.50	1½¢/lb (150 pt) ($450)
Lumber	10¢/1000 bd ft	$10	$5/mb ft (500 pt) ($500)
Potatoes	1¢/cwt	$8	50¢/cwt* (50 pt)** ($400)
Skinned Hams	2½/100¢/lb	$9	1½¢/lb (150 pt) ($540)
Turkeys	2½/100¢/lb	$9	1½¢/lb (150 pt) ($540)
Feeder Cattle	2½/100¢/lb	$10.50	1½¢/lb (150 pt) ($630)
Milo	2½/100¢/cwt	$10	15¢/cwt (15 pt) ($600)
Gold	.10 (10 pt)	$10	$5/oz (500 pt)†φ ($500)
Copper	.0010 (10 pt)	$12.50	.05† (500 pt) ($625)

*   *This information subject to CFTC approval*
** *Potatoes limit on last two days of trading shall be $1/cwt*
†   *Except on last day of trading, where there will be no limit, or when expanded limit rule is in effect*
φ   *Gold limits will be $5/oz if gold price is below $150/oz; if above, gold limit will be $10/oz*

Contract particulars:

Commodity	Quality	Delivery points
Boneless Beef	90 per cent lean	92
Butter	92 score	89
Fresh Eggs	90 per cent A and AA	157
Nest Run Eggs	20 per cent AA	117
Frozen Eggs	24.7 per cent egg solids	84
Frozen Pork Bellies	12/14 lb bellies	56
Live Cattle (New and Old)	Choice	5 each
Live Hogs	USDA Grade 1,2,3,4	7
Lumber	Hem-fir random 2x4s	11
Potatoes	Russet Burbank	10
Skinned Hams	14/17 lb frozen	56
Turkeys	100 per cent A	90
Feeder Cattle	80 per cent USDA Choice	11
Milo	US No 2	15
Gold	.995 fine	IMM Approved Depositories
Copper	Electrolytic	IMM Approved Warehouses

Are rules and regulations available? Yes

Can they be purchased? Yes — cost $25 to Chicago Mercantile Exchange, 444 W Jackson Blvd, Chicago, IL 60606

Arbitration rules: It is declared to be contrary to the objects and policy of the Exchange that members should engage in litigation over disputes involving a transaction upon the Exchange. When any such dispute occurs between members, it shall be promptly reported to the president by the party claiming to be aggrieved. The president shall then determine whether or not the dispute involves a transaction or transactions upon the Exchange which shall be arbitrated, shall so notify the parties in writing and submit a form of arbitration agreement for their signatures. A member receiving notice from the president that the matter is to be arbitrated shall have ten days in which to file an appeal with the Board. The appeal shall be in writing and shall state the member's reasons for refusing to arbitrate. The Board shall, after hearing, reverse or affirm the ruling of the president. Any member who refuses to arbitrate after ruling of the president or ruling of the Board after appeal, or any member who refuses to comply with a final arbitration award, shall be guilty of a major offence.

Each year, promptly after his election, the chairman of the Board, with the approval of the Board, shall appoint an Arbitration Committee, to consist of ten members, none of whom shall be a member of the Board, and each of whom shall serve for one year and until his successor has been appointed.

Upon execution of an arbitration agreement, the president shall select five members of the Arbitration Committee to conduct the hearing. Each of the parties to the arbitration may strike one member of the panel designated by the president, in which event that member shall be excused from hearing the matter. The president shall then select alternate members from the Arbitration Committee to constitute a panel of five members for that hearing and shall designate one of the five members to act as chairman, with the right to vote only in the event of a tie vote. The matter submitted to arbitration shall be heard within ten days from the date of submission unless good cause can be shown to the panel.

After such hearing, the arbitration panel shall file its award in writing and signed by the members joining in the award with the president who shall deliver copies thereof by certified mail to all interested parties. The award shall be signed in the name of the arbitration panel by the chairman and at least three sitting members. If an appeal has been waived or if the original claim was for $1,000 or less, the award shall be final.

An arbitration fee of $125 and an appeal fee of $125 shall be paid to the Exchange as part of the cost of arbitration. The party requesting arbitration shall deposit in advance the sum of $175 and the party requesting an appeal shall deposit in advance the sum of $250. All fees and costs, including the cost of the stenographic transcript of the testimony and panel members' fees, shall be paid as provided in the final award.

Is there an appeal? Yes. Where the amount in controversy exceeds $1,000, any party to the arbitration may appeal the decision of the panel to the Board. Such appeal shall be perfected by filing a written notice with the President within ten days after notice of the award. The award shall become final if no notice is filed within said period. In the following cases the Board may enter an order vacating the award of the arbitration panel: (a) Where the award was procured by corruption or fraud; (b) Where there was evident partiality or corruption in the arbitrators or any of them; (c) Where the arbitrators were guilty of misconduct in refusing to hear pertinent evidence; or of any other behaviour by which the rights of any party have been prejudiced; (d) Where the arbitrators exceeded their jurisdiction; (e) Where the arbitrators acted in manifest disregard of the applicable law.

The Board may consider the record made before the arbitration panel and any other pertinent evidence submitted by the parties in support of or opposition to the award. In the event that the Board determines to vacate the award, it shall be resubmitted to a new panel of arbitration for rehearing.

The Board may modify or correct an award upon the application of any party where there has been an obvious material miscalculation or misdescription; or where the award is imperfect in a matter of form not affecting the merits of the controversy. All such modifications or corrections shall be final and binding upon the parties.

Currency dealt in: US dollars

Average volume of trading over past two years: 5,700,000 contracts (one side only)

Recommended commission rates and margins:

Commodity	Minimum margin*	Delivery month margins	Minimum commission**
Boneless Beef	I $600	I $800	D $25
	M $400	M $500	O $40
Butter	I $750	I $750	D $25
	M $450	M $450	O $40
Fresh Eggs	I $700	I $1,200	D $25
	M $500	M $900	O $40
Nest Run Eggs	I $700	I $1,200	D $25
	M $500	M $900	O $40
Frozen Eggs	I $600	I $900	D $25
	M $400	M $600	O $40

Commodity	Minimum margin*	Delivery month margins	Minimum commission**
Frozen Pork Bellies	I $1,200	I $2,000	D $26
	M $900	M $1,500	O $45
Live Cattle (New)	I $900	I $1,500	D $25
	M $700	M $1,000	O $40
Live Cattle (Old)	I $1,200	I $1,500	D $25
	M $800	M $1,000	O $40
Live Hogs	S H		
	I $700/700	I $1,200	D $22
	M $500/500	M $900	O $35
Lumber	S H		
	I $700/500	I $1,000	D $25
	M $500/500	M $700	O $40
Potatoes	I $800	I $1,500	D $20
	M $600	M $1,000	O $30
Skinned Hams	I $500	I $500	D $26
	M $300	M $300	O $45
Turkeys	I $600	I $1,000	D $25
	M $400	M $600	O $40
Feeder Cattle	S H		
	I $800/600	I $1,200	D $25
	M $600/400	M $900	O $40
Milo	S H		
	I $400/300	—	D $20
	M $300/300	—	O $30
Gold	I $500	—	D $27
	M $300	—	O $45
Copper	I $500	—	D $22
	M $350	—	O $35

* Minimum margins are as follows: (I) refers to initial margins, (M) refers to maintenance margins

** Minimum commissions are based on non-member rates: (D) refers to initial transactions offset same day, (O) refers to initial transactions offset any subsequent day

Membership, types of: Chicago Mercantile Exchange Membership entitles one to trade in all divisions of CME; International Monetary Market Division Membership, Associate Mercantile Market Division Membership. Approximate cost (as of 4/12/76) — CME $144, IMM $41, AMM $32

Floor members, as at December 1976: 500 CME Members, 650 IMM Members, of which approximately 500 are also CME members, and 150 AMM Members

Date of establishment of market: Chicago Mercantile Exchange was established on 1 December 1919; International Monetary Market on 16 May 1972, and Associate Mercantile Market on 1 February 1976.

Membership of other organizations: Futures Industry Association, among many others

KANSAS CITY

The Board of Trade of Kansas City, Missouri, Inc

4800 Main St, Suite 274, Kansas City, Missouri 64112

Telephone: 816-753 7363

Commodities: Wheat, Sorghum — futures contracts. Spot cash market for many grains

Titles of appointments: President, First Vice-President, Second Vice-President, Executive Vice-President and Secretary, and 12 other Directors

Name of Executive Vice-President and Secretary: W N Vernon III

Branches and affiliates: Grain Clearing Co

Hours of trading: 09.30 to 13.15 Central Time

Trading unit: 5,000 bu (futures contracts)

Daily trading limits: Wheat — 25 cents per bu from previous close; Sorghum — 10 cents per bu from previous close. Price changes may not be less than ¼ cent per bu ($12.50).

Contract particulars:
Quality: No 2 US Grade (Nos 1 and 3 are also deliverable at 1½ cents premium or discount for hard winter wheat).

Delivery points: Wheat and sorghum deliveries may be made by warehouse receipts issued by regular approved elevators within the Kansas City switching limits, and track deliveries in the Kansas City rail switching district.

Delivery months traded: July, September, December, March, May

Are rules and regulations available? Yes, they are furnished to members.

Can they be purchased? Yes; $15 each

Arbitration rules: Arbitration is authorized for members and non-members in accordance with rules.

Is there an appeal? Yes — to Appeals Committee in cash cases, (to CFTC on futures arbitration appeals)

Currency dealt in: US dollars

Average volume of trading over past two years: 519,098 contracts per year

Recommended commission rates and margins: *(See following table.)*

197

Minimum commission rates:

	Wheat	**Corn**	**Sorghum**	**Gulf Wheat**
Price range:	One rate	One rate	One rate	One rate
Regular trades:				
Resident member*	$7.50	$7.50	$7.50	$15
Non-resident member	$11	$11	$11	$15
Non-member	$22	$22	$22	$30
Spreads or straddles: **				
Member	$7.50	$7.50	$7.50	$7.50
Non-member	$15	$15	$15	$15
Day trades:				
Resident member	$1.40	$1.40	$1.40	$1.40
Non-member	None	None	None	None
Foreign rates:	None	None	None	None

* *Resident clearing member transfer fee $3.75*
** *Intra-market*

Note: *All rates were subject to negotiation above 19 contracts. This dropped to those above 14, on 6 September 1975; above 9, on 6 September 1976; and will drop to above 4, on 6 September 1977; and to all on 6 March 1978, per settlement of antitrust suit*

Minimum customer margins on grain futures contracts, three cent reduction in intra-market spreads:

	Cents per bushel			
Type of transaction	**KC Gulf Wheat**	**Corn**	**Soybeans**	**Sorghum**
Initial margins:				
Hedging	20	10	10	10
Inter-market spreads	5*	15*	–	15
Intra-market spreads	2	2	2	2
All other trades	25	15	15	15

Maintenance margins:
Customers' margins on all commitments shall be maintained at the following minimum levels, or the Clearing House requirements, whichever is higher:

Hedging	20	10	10	10
Inter-market spreads	5*	15*	–	15
Intra-market spreads	2	2	2	2
All other trades:				
1,000,000 bu or less	20	10	12	10
1,000,000 to 2,000,000	20	10	12	10
2,000,000 to 3,000,000	20	10	14	10
3,000,000 to 4,000,000	20	10	16	10
Over 4,000,000	20	10	18	10

Stop loss orders shall not be acceptable in place of the minimum maintenance margins set forth above.

* *On Kansas City side of spread*

Membership, type of: There is only one class of members, those duly elected to membership.

Trading members, as at January 1976: *See page 247.* (No separate category; about 150 [of 214 total] are in Kansas City, and about 80 to 100 are on the floor during the market sessions.)

Date of establishment of market: 1856; futures trading began 1876

MINNEAPOLIS
Minneapolis Grain Exchange
4th Ave and 4th St S, Room 150, Minneapolis, Minnesota 55415

Telephone: 612-338 6212

Commodities: Spring Wheat, Durum Wheat, Feed Barley and Oat Futures Contracts. Actively traded in the Exchange's cash market are Spring Wheat, Durum Wheat, Barley, Oats, Corn, Rye, Flaxseed and Soya Beans.

Titles of appointments: Executive Vice-President, Secretary, Treasurer

Name of Executive Vice-President and Secretary: Alvin W Donahoo

Hours of trading: 09.30 to 13.15 Central Time

Trading unit: All futures contracts are traded in multiples of 5,000 bu; job lots of 1,000 bu are permissible.

Trading limits: Spring Wheat and Durum Wheat Futures — 20 cents per bu above or below the previous day's close. Barley Futures — 10 cents per bu above or below the previous day's close. Oat Futures — 6 cents per bu above or below the previous day's close. Variable limits of 150 per cent of the original level go into effect under special conditions.

Contract particulars:

Commodity	Contract grade	Delivery points
Spring Wheat	US no 2 Northern Spring Wheat, 13.5 per cent protein or higher	Minneapolis—St Paul, Duluth—Superior, Red Wing
Durum Wheat	US No 3 Hard Amber Durum	Duluth—Superior, Minneapolis—St Paul
Barley	US No 3 Barley	Duluth—Superior, Minneapolis— St Paul
Oats	US No 2 Heavy Oats	Duluth—Superior, Minneapolis—St Paul

Are rules and regulations available? Yes

Can they be purchased? Yes, $6 per copy

Arbitration rules: The Rules and Regulations of the Exchange provide for the arbitration of disputes between members and between a member and a non-member if the non-member consents in writing to the jurisdiction of the Board of Arbitration. The Board of Arbitration has the jurisdiction to hear and decide all disputes and differences submitted to it arising out of trades, contracts, agreements or other transactions which are governed by or made subject to the Charter, Rules, Regulations, customs or usages of the Association.

Is there an appeal? The right of appeal exists within the Rules and Regulations of the Exchange.

Currency dealt in: US dollars

Average volume of trading over two years:

	Jan—Dec 1974	Jan—Dec 1975
Spring Wheat Futures	872,873,000 bu	985,488,000 bu
Durum Wheat Futures	19,870,000 bu	11,155,000 bu

Recommended commission rates: Negotiable

Membership, type of: Any person of legal age whose character, credit and reputation for fair dealing are such as to satisfy the Directors' Membership Committee and Board of Directors that the applicant will be a suitable person to entrust with the privileges and responsibilities of membership, and only such persons, shall be eligible to membership in this Association.

Trading members, as at December 1975: *See Appendix 1 (page 257).*

Date of establishment of market: 1881

Membership of other organizations: National Grain and Feed Dealers Association, National Grain Trade Council

NEW YORK

Citrus Associates of the New York Cotton Exchange, Inc

37 Wall St, New York, NY 10005

Telephone: 212-269 7880

Commodity: Frozen Concentrated Orange Juice

Titles of appointments: President, First Vice-President, Second Vice-President, Treasurer, Executive Director and Secretary, Assistant Secretary

Hours of trading: Each weekday 10.15 to 14.45

Trading unit: 15,000 lb

Trading limits: Min .05 cents per lb ($7.50 per contract), max three cents above or below the previous close, three cents limit in any one day except either on or after the eighth day of the current month at which time there is no limit

Contract particulars:
Quality: US Grade A, Brix value not less than 51° with acid ration not less than 13 to 1 and not more than 19 to 1. Min component elements fixed at 37 for colour, 37 for flavour, 19 for defects.

Delivery points: Licensed Warehouses in the State of Florida

Delivery months: January, March, May, July, September, November

Currency dealt in: US dollars

Membership, types of: Class A Members who are members of the New York Cotton Exchange, and 200 Associate Members

Commodity Exchange Inc

81 Broad St, New York, NY 10004

Telephone: 212-269 9450; **Telex:** 127066; **Cable address:** Comexinc

Commodities: Copper, Gold, Silver

Titles of appointments: President, Vice-President, Secretary, Assistant Secretary, Director of Compliance

Name of President: Lee H Berendt

Hours of trading: Copper — 09.50 to 14.00, Gold — 09.25 to 14.30, Silver — 10.00 to 14.15, Eastern Standard Time

Trading units:
Copper — 25,000 lb/avoir (12.5 short tons) (two per cent more or less)
Gold — 100 troy oz (five per cent more or less)
Silver — 5,000 troy oz (six per cent more or less)

Trading limits:
Copper — three cents per lb above or below the lowest price of the closing range of such month of the preceding business session. No limits imposed on trading in current (spot) delivery month.
Gold — ten dollars per oz above or below the lowest price of the closing range of such month of the preceding business session. No limits imposed on trading in current (spot) delivery month.
Silver — 20 cents per oz above or below the lowest price of the closing range of such month of the preceding business session. No limits imposed on trading in current (spot) delivery month.

Contract particulars:
Quality:
Copper — The contract calls for delivery of 25,000 lb (two per cent more or less) of copper. Each contract must be made up exclusively of: (1) one of the deliverable grades; (2) one of the deliverable shapes of the grade; (3) one of the Brands officially listed by the Exchange. (Cathodes must bear a distinguishing mark and be the product of a refiner on the Exchange's official list of approved refiners of cathodes.) Delivery is at the seller's option and may take place at any time during the period specified in the contract from one of the warehouses licensed by the Exchange.
Gold — The gold futures contract calls for delivery of 100 troy oz (five per cent more or less) of refined gold, assaying not less than 995 fineness, cast either in one bar or in three one-kg bars and bearing a serial number and identifying stamp of an approved refiner. Delivery is at the seller's option and may take place during normal business hours of any business day within the period specified in the contract from one of the depositories or vaults licensed by the Exchange.
Silver — The silver futures contract calls for delivery of 5,000 troy oz (six per cent more or less) of refined silver, assaying not less than 999 fineness, in bars cast in weights of 1,000 or 1,100 troy oz (with tolerances above or below said weights customary in the trade). The bars must be made up of one or more of the brands or markings listed by the Exchange. Delivery is at the seller's option and may take place during normal business hours of any business day within the

period specified in the contract from one of the depositories or vaults licensed by the Exchange.

Delivery points:

Copper — licensed warehouses:

Port of New York

	Facilities at:
Continental Terminals, Inc 724 Clinton St, Brooklyn, NY 11231	724 Clinton St, Brooklyn, NY 611 Smith St, Brooklyn, NY
Greenpoint Terminal Warehouse, Inc Foot of Noble and West Sts, Brooklyn, NY 11222	Noble and West Sts, Brooklyn, NY 43-17 Queens St, Long Island City, NY 57-02 48th St, Maspeth, NY 98 Frelinghuysen Ave, Newark, NJ 1 Railroad Ave, Jersey City, NJ
Harborside Terminal Management Co 34 Exchange Place, Jersey City, NJ 07302	34 Exchange Place, Jersey City, NJ
Held Warehouse & Transportation Corp 99 Hook Rd, Bayonne, NJ 07002	471 Van Brunt St, Brooklyn, NY Bldg 201, Export and Calcutta Sts, Port Newark, NJ Bldg 266, Marlin and Transit Sts, Port Newark, NJ
Mid-Hudson Warehouse of New Jersey, Inc 29-51 Pavonia Ave, Jersey City, NJ 07302	29-51 Pavonia Ave, Jersey City, NJ
Municipal Warehouse Co, Inc 130 Third St, Brooklyn, NY 11231	130 Third St, Brooklyn, NY 112 Third St, Brooklyn, NY 137 Third St, Brooklyn, NY 409-411 Bond St, Brooklyn, NY
Van Brunt Port Jersey Warehouses, Inc 112 Port Jersey Blvd, Jersey City, NJ	112 Port Jersey Blvd, Jersey City, NJ

Amarillo, Texas

Dalby Transfer & Storage Co Inc 401-11 North Arthur St, Amarillo, TX 79105	401-11 North Arthur St, Amarillo, TX

Chicago, Illinois

Griswold & Bateman Warehouse Co 3322 North Alta St, Franklin Park, IL 60131	3322 North Alta St, Franklin Park, IL

Philadelphia, Pennsylvania

Tacony Industrial Storage Co One Brown St, Philadelphia, PA 19123	One Brown St, Philadelphia, PA
H W R Corp 217 Atlantic Ave, Camden, NJ 08104	217 Atlantic Ave, Camden, NJ

New Orleans, Louisiana

Madison Warehouse Corp 1200 South Peters St, New Orleans, LA 70130	1200 South Peters St, New Orleans, LA

Reading, Pennsylvania

O'Brien's Storage Co, Inc 500 South Fifth St, Reading, PA 19602	500 South Fifth St, Reading, PA

St Louis, Missouri

Mississippi Avenue Warehouse, Inc 3914 Union Blvd, St Louis, MO 63115	1401 Mississippi Ave, East St Louis, IL

Tacoma, Washington

Inter City Auto Freight, Inc
1821 Dock St, Tacoma, WA 98401

Pacific Storage Co
PO Box 1757, Tacoma, WA 98401

Facilities at:

1821 Dock St, Tacoma, WA
459 East 15th St, Tacoma, WA
1216 St Paul Ave, Tacoma, WA
2018 Canal St, Tacoma, WA
440 East 19th St, Tacoma, WA
535 Dock St, Tacoma, WA
1729 North 30th St, Tacoma, WA
2602 Part of Tacoma Rd, Tacoma, WA

El Paso, Texas

El Paso Terminal Warehouse, Inc
421 Frederick Rd, El Paso, TX 79983

421 Frederick Rd, El Paso, TX

Gold — licensed depositories:

City of New York

Chase Manhattan Bank
One Chase Manhattan Plaza, New York
NY 10005

Citibank
55 Wall St, New York, NY 10005

Iron Mountain Depository
26 Broadway, New York, NY 10004

Irving Trust Co
One Wall St, New York, NY 10005

Republic National Bank of New York
452 Fifth Ave, New York, NY 10018

Swiss Bank Corp
15 Nassau St, New York, NY 10005

Facilities at:

One Chase Manhattan Plaza,
New York, NY

2 Broadway, New York, NY
55 Wall St, New York, NY
399 Park Ave, New York, NY
26 Broadway, New York, NY

One Wall St, New York, NY

115 Broadway, New York, NY

120 Broadway, New York, NY

Silver — licensed depositories:

City of New York

Chase Manhattan Bank
One Chase Manhattan Plaza, New York
NY 10005

Citibank
55 Wall St, New York, NY 10005

Iron Mountain Depository
26 Broadway, New York, NY 10004

Irving Trust Co
One Wall St, New York, NY 10005

Republic National Bank of New York
452 Fifth Ave, New York, NY 10018

Facilities at:

One Chase Manhattan Plaza,
New York, NY

2 Broadway, New York, NY
686 Broadway, New York, NY
399 Park Ave, New York, NY
26 Broadway, New York, NY

One Wall St, New York, NY

115 Broadway, New York, NY
393 Seventh Ave, New York, NY

Are rules and regulations available? Yes

Can they be purchased? Yes

Arbitration rules: A party desiring to initiate an arbitration proceeding shall file with the Secretary a concise statement of claim or controversy, together with a copy of an agreement to arbitrate disputes under the Rules of the Exchange, or a copy of a court order directing such an arbitration, or if such party is not a member of the Exchange, a statement that such party elects to have the claim or controversy arbitrated before the Exchange.

A copy of the statement filed by the party initiating the proceeding shall be furnished by the Secretary to the opposing party for reply. Said reply shall be filed with the Secretary within ten days of the receipt by such opposing party of said statement, or such longer period as may be granted by the Exchange.

The Board of Governors or the Chairman of the Arbitration Committee may decline to permit the use of the arbitration facilities of the Exchange.

The arbitrators may at any time during the proceeding and shall, upon the joint request of the parties thereto, dismiss the proceeding and refer the parties to their remedies at law.

The maximum amount chargeable to the parties as costs to cover the expense of the arbitration proceeding shall not exceed the following:

(a) The party initiating a proceeding shall deposit with the Exchange upon the institution of the proceeding the sum of $100.

(b) If there is more than one hearing, the sum of $75 for each subsequent hearing.

(c) The Arbitration Committee may engage a court reporter to make a stenographic record and transcript of the arbitration proceeding in any situation where the Committee deems such record and transcript to be desirable. The cost of such stenographic record and transcript shall be borne by the parties to the arbitration as the arbitrators shall determine.

All controversies shall be heard by three arbitrators who are members of the Exchange unless the amount in controversy is less than $2,000 or the parties so agree, in which event the controversy may be heard before one arbitrator who is a member of the Exchange.

Upon receipt of a submission, agreement or court order, the Chairman of the Arbitration Committee shall designate an arbitrator or three arbitrators, as the case may be. The Secretary shall promptly notify the parties in writing of the name and business affiliation of each designee, and within five business days after the date of mailing of such notice any party may file written objection with the Secretary to any one or more of the arbitrators designated. The Arbitration Committee shall sustain or reject the objections made and if any objection is sustained, the Chairman of the Arbitration Committee shall designate an additional arbitrator or arbitrators as the case may be.

The Chairman of the Arbitration Committee shall also designate one of the arbitrators to act as chairman in the proceeding.

The hearing shall be private, unless otherwise directed by the Arbitration Committee. Such direction must be made when requested by the parties.

At any time during the hearings or before the hearings are declared closed, any party may move the amendment of his claim or counterclaim, and, if the arbitrators shall permit, such amendment shall be incorporated forthwith in an amendment to the submission, or, where a submission was not required, in an amendment to the statement of claim or counterclaim, as the case may be.

The award of the arbitrators shall be made in writing and shall be acknowledged in like manner as a deed to be recorded.

The arbitrators and any attorney of record in the arbitration proceeding shall have such powers of subpoena as may be provided by law, but so far as it is possible for them to do so, the parties shall produce witnesses and present proofs without the issuance of subpoena.

The Arbitration Committee shall have the power to interpret and apply the Rules. Any such decisions of the Arbitration Committee shall be made in writing, filed with the Secretary, and be available to the arbitrators in any proceeding.

The award of the arbitrators may be confirmed, enforced, vacated, modified or corrected pursuant to the Civil Practice Law and Rules of the State of New York.

An award rendered in an arbitration pursuant to the By-Laws and Rules shall be binding on and enforceable against the member or member firm with respect to whom it has been rendered in accordance with the laws of the State of New York.

A fee of $25 shall be paid by the Exchange to each arbitrator for each hearing attended by such arbitrator. If in the judgment of the Arbitration Committee such arbitrators have performed unusual or extraordinary services, the arbitrators shall be awarded extra fees in an amount determined by the Arbitration Committee and may direct payment thereof by the parties or any of them as they may deem proper.

Is there an appeal? No

Currency dealt in: US dollars

Average volume of trading over past two years:
Total volume (in contracts)
Copper —   1974 — 411,071; 1975 — 494,019; 1976 (8 mths) — 884,598
Gold —   1974 (31 Dec) — 2,550; 1975 — 393,517; 1976 (8 mths) — 240,275
Silver —   1974 — 1,365,915; 1975 — 2,902,315; 1976 (8 mths) — 1,984,463

Recommended commission rates and margins:

	Margins	
	All contracts (per contract)	Straddle transactions (per straddle)
Copper	$750	None
Gold	$300	None
Silver	$1,000	None

For transactions entered into on or after the first notice day of a current delivery month (including straddles involving the current delivery month) add $200, $100 and $250 respectively to the above amounts.

The Board of Governors has amended a previous regulation, and accordingly, the Commodity Exchange, Inc original margin requirements, at any time, may be lower than the original margin requirements as set by the Comex Clearing Association, Inc. This applies to Copper, Gold and Silver.

Commission rates and charges

	Copper	Gold	Silver
Non-member:			
Straight trade — round turn	$36.00	$45.00	$22.50
Day trade — round turn	$18.00	$22.50	$11.25
Straddle — round turn	$50.40	$63.00	$31.50
Member:			
Straight trade — round turn	$18.00	$22.50	$15.00
Day trade — round turn	$9.00	$11.25	$11.25
Straddle — round turn	$25.20	$31.50	$16.00

	Copper	Gold	Silver
Members and non-members residing outside the United States and Canada:	$1.00 commission charge for each contract bought or sold in addition to the above rates	$1.25	—
Floor members:			
Day clearance — round turn	$2.00	$2.00	$2.00
30-day rate — round turn	$3.50	$3.50	$3.50
Floor brokerage — per contract	$2.00	$2.50	$1.75
Floor brokerage — per straddle	$2.80	$3.50	$2.75

Membership, types of: There are 386 registered memberships on Commodity Exchange, Inc. Members are registered in one of the following groups: Commission House Group; General Group; Hide Group; Metal Group; Rubber Group. All memberships are held in the names of individuals.

Trading members, as at March 1976: *See Appendix 1 (page 268).*

Date of establishment of market: The market opened with Silver in 1933. Gold — 31 December 1974

New York Cocoa Exchange, Inc

127 John St, New York, NY 10038

Telephone: 212-422 5984; **Cable address:** CocoaChange

Commodity: Cocoa

Titles of appointments: President, Secretary

Name of President: Walter L Perkins

Branches and affiliates: Affiliate — New York Cocoa Clearing Association, Inc

Hours of trading: 10.00 to 15.00

Trading units: 30,000 lb

Trading limits: Four cents above or below the previous day's settling price. However, trading during any one day is limited to a max of four cents trading range.

Contract particulars:
Quality: All grades of cocoa are deliverable against Exchange contracts with certain additions and deductions applicable to the various grades and growths. The standard growths of cocoa beans are as follows: Ghana of the main crop; Bahia; San Tome, above or superior; Ivory Coast main crop, fermented; Costa Rican, fermented; Panama, fermented; Nigeria of the main crop
Delivery points: Port of New York District, Delaware River Port District

Are rules and regulations available? Yes

Can they be purchased? Yes — $15 per copy

Arbitration rules: It shall be the duty of the Arbitration Committee to hear and decide any controversy which may arise between persons, firms and/or corporations whether or not members of the Exchange; all claims, disputes, differences and controversies between or among members of the Exchange arising out of their relations or obligations to one another as members of the Exchange; any claims and grievances of customers, whether or not members of the Exchange, against any member of the Exchange or employee thereof, provided that (i) the use of the arbitration procedure shall be voluntary, (ii) such precedure shall not be applicable to any claim in excess of $15,000, (iii) such procedure shall not result in any compulsory payment except as agreed upon between parties, and (iv) the term 'customer' shall not include a futures commission merchant or a floor broker. Complaints shall be instituted in writing. At the conclusion of the hearing upon an arbitration held under Section 50(a) or Sections 50(b) or 50(c) of the By-Laws, and after due deliberation upon all the allegations, claims, charges, defences and proofs of all parties to such arbitration, the panel shall make an award thereupon. An award by a majority of the members of the panel of arbitrators shall be deemed the award of the panel concurring therein, in as many counterparts as may be necessary in order to supply one to each party and one to the Secretary of the Exchange. An arbitration fee not in excess of $500 as fixed by the panel is payable into the Treasury of the Exchange.

Currency dealt in: US dollars

Average volume of trading over past two years: Fiscal year ended 30 September 1975 – 330,219 Contracts. Fiscal year ended 30 September 1976 – 320,642 Contracts

Recommended commission rates and margins:

Commission rates		Margin
Member	*Non-member*	
$30 round turn	$60 round turn	$3,000 per contract

Trading members, as at February 1976: *See Appendix 1 (page 278).*

Date of establishment of market: 1 October 1925

New York Cocoa Exchange, Inc
Trading in Natural Rubber Futures Contracts

127 John St, New York, NY 10038

Telephone: 212-422 5985; **Cable address:** CocoaChange

Commodity: Natural Rubber

Titles of appointments: President, Secretary

Name of President: Walter L Perkins

Branches and affiliates: Affiliate – New York Cocoa Clearing Association, Inc

Hours of trading: 09.45 to 14.45

Trading unit: 33,000 lb (15 tonnes)

Trading limits: Two cents above or below the previous day's settling price. However, trading during any one day is limited to a max of two cents trading range.

Contract particulars:

Quality: Deliverable Grades (Hevea Braziliensis) and Conditions: International No 1 Ribbed Smoked Sheets at the tender price. The seller may also deliver a contract unit of Ribbed Smoked Sheets which is inferior to International No 1 Ribbed Smoked Sheets provided the inferiority as determined by the Exchange does not exceed one half of the quality difference between International No 1 Ribbed Smoked Sheets and International No 2 Ribbed Smoked Sheets. If the inferiority is determined not to exceed one quarter of this difference the unit shall be eligible for delivery at a discount equivalent to two per cent of the tender price; if the inferiority is determined to exceed one quarter but not one half of this difference at a discount equivalent to four per cent of the tender price. Technically Specified Rubber of constant viscosity (5CV) at the tender price. Technically Specified Rubber 5L at the tender price. Technically Specified Rubber 5 at discount equivalent to four per cent of the tender price. Rubber from government stockpile shall not be eligible for certification.

Delivery points: Port of Boston (MA), Port of New York (NY), Port of Norfolk (VA), Port of New Orleans (LA).

Are rules and regulations available? Yes

Can they be purchased? Yes — $15 per copy

Arbitration rules: Same rules apply as in the case of Cocoa.

Is there an appeal? Same rules apply as in the case of Cocoa.

Currency dealt in: US dollars

Average volume of trading over past two years: 1975 — 4,199 contracts, 1976 — 613 contracts

Recommended commission rates and margins: Rubber commission rates are fully negotiable; margin — $750

Membership, type of: There is only one class of Member. *(See membership of New York Cocoa Exchange Inc, Appendix 1 (page 278).*

Date of establishment of market: 22 January 1975

New York Coffee and Sugar Exchange, Inc

79 Pine St, New York, NY 10005

Telephone: 212-422 1800; **Telex:** 12-9176; **Cable address:** NYCOFSUGEX

Commodities: Coffee and Sugar Futures

Titles of appointments: Chairman, Vice-Chairman, Secretary-Treasurer, 12 Members-at-large of the Board of Managers, President and Vice-President

Name of President: Bennett J Corn

Hours of trading:

	Coffee	Sugar
Opening call	09.45	10.00
General trading until	14.28	14.43
Closing call begins	14.30	14.45

Trading unit:
Coffee B — 32,500 lb (in about 250 bags)
Coffee C — 37,500 lb (in about 250 bags)
Sugar   — 50 long tons

Trading limits:
Units — Cents and hundredths of cents per lb
Limits — Subject to action by Board of Managers
Present Limits — Sugar: one cent per lb up or down from preceding day's close
Coffee: three cents per lb up or down from preceding day's close
Three successive limit moves in the same direction triggers automatic increase in limit until limit moves cease.

Contract particulars:
Quality:
Coffee B — Unwashed Arabica from Brazil
Coffee C — Mild washed Arabica from most producing countries
Sugar   — Raw centrifugal sugar, basis 96° polarization, premiums for polarization to 98°, discounts for polarization below 96°

Delivery points:
Coffee — in warehouse approved by the Exchange in the Port of New York
Sugar No 11 — Most cane sugar-producing areas of the world — delivery fob loading port on Receiver's vessel

Are rules and regulations available? Yes, to members and other approved persons

Can they be purchased? Yes, terms will be stated on request.

Arbitration rules: For disputes between members, arbitration is mandatory. For disputes between a member and a non-member, arbitration is available through Arbitration Committee if both parties agree to be bound by award.

Is there an appeal? Arbitration procedures and usage subject to regulation by Commodity Futures Trading Commission, a US Government agency.

Currency dealt in: US dollars

Average volume of trading over past two years: 1974 — 750,000 lots approx, 1975 — 850,000 lots approx

Recommended commission rates and margins: Minimum commissions apply to first nine lots in any transaction; negotiable after that. Minimum commission per round turn at present prices:

	Member	Non-member
Coffee per lot	$40	$80
Sugar No 11 per lot	$31	$62
Sugar No 12 per lot	No minimum	

Margin levels subject to determination by Board of Managers.

Membership, types of: About 320 members. A member may obtain floor trading privileges if he maintains specified net liquid assets and demonstrates his capacity for trading to the satisfaction of the Floor Committee. About 60 members of the Exchange are also members of the New York Coffee & Sugar Clearing Association which guarantees performance under all contracts. A member may extend privileges of membership to a corporation of which he is an executive upon application and approval by the Board of Managers.

Date of establishment of market: Coffee trading commenced in 1882; sugar trading in 1916.

New York Cotton Exchange

37 Wall St, New York, NY 10005

Telephone: 212-269 7880; **Telex:** 235068 PACE UR

Commodity: Cotton

Titles of appointments: Chairman of the Board, Vice-Chairman of the Board, Treasurer

Names of Chief Executives: J William Donaghy, Executive Director and Secretary; Joseph J O'Neill, Assistant Secretary

Branches and affiliates: Citrus Associates of the New York Cotton Exchange, Inc; Wool Associates of the New York Cotton Exchange, Inc; Petroleum Associates of the New York Cotton Exchange, Inc

Hours of trading: 10.30 to 15.00

Trading unit: 50,000 lb, 100 bales of cotton, 500 lb to a bale with quality in Strict Low Middling 1-1/16 inch

Trading limits: (1) Trades for future delivery shall not, during any one day, be made at prices varying more than two cents per lb above or below the settlement price of such month of the preceding session of the Exchange. (2) The provisions of this rule shall not apply to trading in the current month on or after the first notice day for such month. (3) At the discretion of the Board of Managers, any limit of trading herein provided for may from time to time and without previous notice, be changed or suspended or temporarily modified.

Contract particulars:
Quality: The base quality deliverable on Contract No 1 is Middling 15/16 inch. The base quality deliverable on Contract No 2 is Strict Low Middling 1-1/16 inch. Staples deliverable: 29/32nds of one inch and longer on Contract No 1. 1-1/32nd of one inch and longer on Contract No 2
Micronaire test: Cotton must Micronaire not less than 3.5 nor more than 4.9 to be tenderable on contract.

Grades and code numbers for tenderable grades of United States Upland Cotton:

White Grades	Code No	Light Spotted Grades	Code No
Good Middling	11	Good Middling Lt Spotted	12
Strict Middling	21	Strict Middling Lt Spotted	22
Middling Plus	30	Middling Lt Spotted	32
Middling	31		
Strict Low Middling Plus	40		
Strict Low Middling	41		
Low Middling Plus	50		
Low Middling	51		

Staple lengths:

Contract No 1 –	29/32	15/16	31/32	Inch and up
Code Nos	29	30	31	32 and up
Contract No 2 –	1-1/32	1-1/16	1-3/32 and up	
Code Nos	33	34	35 and up	

Rain-Grown and Non-Rain-Grown: Non-Rain-Grown cotton shall be tenderable on contract without discrimination, but must be so identified as such in conformity with general trade practice when filing your request for inspection and certification. When so declared, the EIA will stamp the information on Form CN–331 and on the warehouse receipts.

Delivery points: Charleston, SC; Mobile, AL; New Orleans, LA; Houston, TX; Galveston, TX; Memphis, TN; Greenville, SC

Are rules and regulations available? Yes

Arbitration rules: The Arbitration Committee, which shall consist of six members of the Exchange, shall elect one of its members as Chairman and one as Vice-Chairman to act in the absence of the Chairman. The Chairman of the Committee shall from time to time choose from members of the Committee a Subcommittee of three members to head and determine each controversy submitted for arbitration and shall designate one of said members as Chairman of the Subcommittee and one as Vice-Chairman to act in the absence of the Chairman.

Any controversy between parties who are members of the Exchange shall, at the request of any such party, be submitted to arbitration in accordance with the Arbitration By-Laws.

Any controversy between a party who is a member of the Exchange, on the one hand, and a party who is a non-member, on the other hand, shall, at the request of the non-member, be submitted to arbitration in accordance with the Arbitration By-Laws provided the non-member executes and delivers to the Exchange an agreement in such form as the Exchange prescribes agreeing to be bound by the provisions of the Arbitration By-Laws and by the award of the arbitrators.

Any controversy between a member of the Exchange and a Warehouseman shall, at the request of either party, be submitted to arbitration in accordance with the Arbitration By-Laws.

An arbitration proceeding may be instituted under this section by the mailing to the Secretary of the Exchange of a request for arbitration setting forth a concise statement of the controversy and the date on which it arose. The Secretary shall refer the request for arbitration to the Chairman of the Arbitration Committee who shall designate a Subcommittee to hear the controversy and shall deliver said request to the Chairman of said Subcommittee.

A copy of the request for arbitration shall be mailed by the Chairman of the Subcommittee to the other party to the controversy. The party against whom the arbitration is sought shall mail to the Chairman of the Subcommittee and to the party requesting the arbitration, within seven business days after the mailing to it of a copy of the request for arbitration, an answer in writing setting forth a concise statement of its position with respect to the controversy.

Neither a member nor a Warehouseman shall be required to submit to arbitration hereunder unless the request for arbitration is mailed within 90 days after the date on which the controversy arose. If there is a dispute as to whether the request for arbitration was made within the time required by this subsection, such dispute shall be determined by the Subcommittee, after hearing, prior to the hearing on the merits.

The Chairman of the Subcommittee shall decide all questions of procedure respecting the hearing. The Subcommittee shall have the power to subpoena parties to the controversy, witnesses, and books, records and documents to the extent permitted by law. All members of the Subcommittee shall be present at the hearing and at any adjournment thereof.

After the hearing, the Subcommittee shall render its award which shall be in such form as may be required for filing in a court proceeding for the enforcement of the award. The award shall be made by the decision of a majority of the Subcommittee and shall be final and binding on the parties. The award shall be delivered to the Secretary who shall mail a copy thereof to each of the parties.

The arbitrators shall determine and include in the award a direction as to how costs of the arbitration shall be borne by the parties. Such costs shall include the fees of the arbitrators and the cost of the stenographic record of the proceeding, if made.

Where an arbitration is requested by a non-member other than a Warehouseman, the Subcommittee may require a deposit to cover costs in an amount not exceeding $150 before proceeding with the hearing.

The award of the arbitrators may be entered in any court having jurisdiction, in accordance with the laws of the State of New York.

Failure of a member to comply with an award of the arbitrators shall be grounds for disciplinary action against such member as in the case of a violation of the By-Laws.

Is there an appeal? No

Currency dealt in: US dollars

Average volume of trading over past two years: 1974 — 396,434 Contracts, 1975 — 525,103 Contracts, Average — 460,769 Contracts

Recommended commission rates and margins: The following rates of commission are the lowest that may be charged on transactions for future delivery:

For each 100 bales bought or sold for any person residing in the United States, Canada or Mexico who is not a member of the Exchange, $25 when the price of such transaction does not exceed 50 cents per lb; and when the price of such transaction exceeds 50 cents per lb, an additional $5 shall be charged.

Rates for members shall be $15 for each 100 bales bought or sold when the price of such transaction does not exceed 50 cents per pound and when the price of such transaction exceeds 50 cents per pound, an additional $2.50 shall be charged.

212

(Day Clearance) $2.25 for each 100 bales bought and sold on the same day when cleared for a member making such transaction for his own personal account; provided that such member is eligible under the By-Laws and Rules to make contracts on the floor of the Exchange. Orders for such transactions may be given by the member only when actually present on the floor of the Exchange. Any purchase or sale by another member shall carry a floor brokerage charge.

(Straddles) (a) On non-member business, $37.50 per straddle when the prices do not exceed 50 cents per lb; and when the price of one side exceeds 50 cents per lb, $45 per straddle; on member business, $22.50 per straddle when the prices do not exceed 50 cents per lb, and when the price of one side exceeds 50 cents per lb, $27.50; provided that orders shall be clearly designated as straddle orders; that such transactions shall be carried in a separate account designated 'Straddle Account', consisting of a like number of New York contracts on each side carried by any one commission house; that contracts in a straddle account may be liquidated at straddle rates by the transfer of one side from one month to another; that straddle rates shall not apply to transfers of contracts from one month to another in any accounts other than straddle accounts; and further provided that when any part of a straddle is broken by a subsequent transaction liquidating one side only, or by delivery or receipt of cotton on one side, the straddle rate shall apply to such side and the non-straddle rate shall then automatically apply to an equal number of contracts on the opposite side, which must be transferred from 'Straddle Account' to a non-straddle account.

(b) Straddles between New York market and any foreign market made for a non-member may carry a rate on the New York contracts equal to but not less than two-thirds of the straight rate for non-member business, provided that both sides of the straddle are effected through the same member or member firm on the same day or during the next succeeding session. These rates do not apply to contracts made for members.

(Day Trades) For each 100 bales entered into and liquidated upon the same day for a single account for which the buying and selling orders both originate from the party for whom the account is carried: for non-members, 50 per cent of the straight rate for non-members, and on member business, 50 per cent of the straight rate for members. The special rates of this paragraph shall not apply to omnibus accounts.

For each 100 bales bought or sold for any person residing outside of the United States, Canada and Mexico, the foregoing rates plus $1.50.

(Floor Brokerage) For each 100 bales bought or sold by one member for another, giving up his principal on the day of the transaction, $2.50, when the price of such transaction does not exceed 50 cents, and $3 shall be charged when the price of such transaction exceeds 50 cents per lb.

(15 Day Trades) The commission rate on contracts entered into by members, executing the orders themselves for their own personal account, shall be $12.50 for each 100 bales bought and sold, provided such contracts entered into shall be closed out within 15 calendar days. On these contracts no floor brokerage may be charged. The above rate does not apply to a member who has conferred his membership rate privileges upon a corporation.

The above-mentioned rates shall be in each case the minimum commission that may be charged by any member of the Exchange and shall be absolutely net and free of all and any rebate, in any way, shape, or manner; nor shall any bonus or *pro rata* percentage of commission be given or allowed to persons other than those covered by Commission Law Rules 6.03 and 6.06.

However, the Board of Managers may grant to a member of the Exchange entering the armed forces of the United States (or entering upon service for the United States which, in the opinion of the Board, is the equivalent of entering the armed forces) the privilege of effecting with another member or members of the Exchange, an arrangement for such time as the Board may determine, wherein stipulated floor brokerage business of such member qualifying under this By-Law may be handled by such other member or members on the basis of a fixed return to the qualifying member. This privilege shall not be granted unless and until all the particulars of the proposed arrangement have been first submitted in writing to and approved by the Board and, if granted, may thereafter be revoked by the Board in its discretion. The aforesaid privilege under the conditions named is also extended to executive officers and Committee members who absent themselves for the purpose of representing the Exchange on Exchange business.

The penalty for violating or evading, or seeking, offering, proposing, promising, or agreeing to violate or evade the provisions of this Section in any way, shape or manner whatsoever, whether by an agreement, arrangement, or understanding, expressed or implied, either directly or indirectly, in person or through any firm or co-partnership of which a member may be or may appear to be a partner, or through any agent or agents, or otherwise, shall be, upon conviction for the first offence, suspension for a period not exceeding 12 months, the term of suspension to be fixed at the discretion of a majority of the entire Board, and for the second offence, expulsion.

Restrictions on minimum commission rates: From the effective date of this Section, the provisions of any By-Law or Rule respecting non-member rates of commission shall be superseded as follows:
(I) Futures Trading: (a) the provisions of the By-Laws respecting non-member rates of commission for futures trading shall not apply: (i) in the first year after the effective date to that part of a non-member transaction exceeding 24 contracts; (ii) in the second year after the effective date, to that part of a non-member transaction exceeding 19 contracts; (iii) in the third year after the effective date, to that part of a non-member transaction exceeding 14 contracts; (iv) in the fourth year after the effective date, to that part of a non-member transaction exceeding nine contracts; (v) in the first six months of the fifth year after the effective date, to that part of a non-member transaction exceeding four contracts; and (vi) in the last six months of the fifth year and thereafter, to any non-member transaction irrespective of size. (b) The term 'non-member transaction' means the total of all purchase contracts or the total of all sale contracts (both new positions and liquidations) executed on the Exchange on the same day pursuant to a single non-member order for one account. For purposes of this subparagraph (b), straddles shall be treated as two orders (one for the purchase and one for the sale). (c) Commissions on futures trading shall be calculated, and may be billed, on each purchase and each sale. The minimum commission on each purchase or sale contract in that portion of a non-member transaction remaining subject to minimum rates shall be one-half the round turn rate specified in the By-Laws.
(II) Spot Transactions: The provision of subparagraph (a) of paragraph I shall apply to spot transactions on the Exchange.
(III) Interpretation: All By-Laws, Rules, Regulations, rulings and official actions of the Exchange shall be interpreted to conform to this Section, and any

requirement or action in conflict with this Section shall be superseded hereby. No member or member firm shall conduct business on the Exchange with a non-member at a rate less than the minimum rate of commission, except as provided in this Section.

(IV) Effective Date: This Section has been adopted to carry out the provisions of a settlement agreement with respect to class actions instituted against various commodity exchanges and their members, which settlement agreement is to become effective when certain conditions have been met. This Section shall become effective 60 days after the effective date of the settlement agreement, which date shall be announced by the Exchange.

Minimum initial margin requirements effective on all new business from 8 July 1976:

Speculative (per contract)
All prices $4,000

Hedge (per contract)
All prices $1,500

Straddles (per straddle)
Speculative $1,200
Hedge $500

Membership, types of: 450 seats available on the Exchange

Trading members, as at June 1976: *See Appendix 1 (page 283).*

Date of establishment of market: September 1870

New York Mercantile Exchange

6 Harrison St, New York, NY 10013

Telephone: 212-966 2600

Commodities: Maine Potatoes, Butter (Spot), Imported Boneless Beef, Platinum, Palladium, US Silver Coins, Gold, Heating Oil, Industrial Fuel Oil, Silver Dollars (Spot)

Titles of appointments: President, Executive Vice-President and Controller, Vice-President for Research and Education, Secretary

Names of Chief Executives: Richard B Levine — President, Jean LeBreton — Secretary

Trading units:

Commodity	Contract
Maine Potatoes	Car = 50,000 lb
Imported Boneless Beef	Pounds = 36,000
Platinum	Ounces = 50 Troy
Palladium	Ounces = 100 Troy
US Silver Coins	10 bags of $1,000 each
Gold	Ounces = 32.151 (1 kg)
Spot Silver Dollars	$1,000 face value
Heating Oil	Tonnes = 100
Industrial Fuel Oil	Tonnes = 100

Guide to World Commodity Markets

Trading limits:

Commodity	Minimum Fluctuation	Minimum Value Change per Contract	Maximum Fluctuation
Maine Potatoes	1¢ per 100 lb	$5	$250 ae
Imported Boneless Beef	2¢ per 100 lb	$7.20	$540 be
Platinum	10¢ per oz	$5	$500 ae
Palladium	5¢ per oz	$5	$400 ace
US Silver Coins	$1 per bag	$10	$1,500 ae
Gold	20¢ per oz	$6.40	$320 de
Spot Silver Dollars	$5 per contract	$5	—
Heating Oil	10¢ per tonne	$10	$200 ae
Industrial Fuel Oil	10¢ per tonne	$10	$200 ae

a — no limit on last trading day
b — $720 during delivery month
c — $500 during delivery month
d — no limit during delivery month
e — consult appropriate Rules for expanded limits

Hours of trading and Delivery months:

Commodity	Hours of trading	Closing range	Termination of trading	Delivery months
Maine Potatoes	10.00 to 13.30	13.28 to 13.30	5th business day of month	Nov, Mar, Apr, May
Butter (Spot)	Friday only 11.30 to 11.45	—	—	—
Imported Boneless Beef	10.15 to 13.45	13.43 to 13.45	15th day of month*	Jan, Mar, May, July, Sept, Nov
Platinum	09.45 to 14.10	14.05 to 14.10	14th day of month*	Jan, Apr, July, Oct
Palladium	10.20 to 12.55	12.53 to 12.55	14th day of month*	Mar, June, Sept, Dec
US Silver Coins	09.35 to 14.15	14.13 to 14.15	14th day of month*	Jan, Apr, July, Oct
Gold	09.25 to 14.30	14.28 to 14.30	3rd from last business day of delivery month	Jan, Mar, May, July, Sept, Dec + 3 current months
Heating Oil, Industrial Fuel Oil	10.25 to 14.00	13.58 to 14.00	Last business day preceeding spot month	Jan, Mar, May, July, Sept, Nov
Silver Dollars (Spot)	12.00 to 13.00	—	—	—

* Or the first Exchange business day immediately prior thereto

Contract particulars:
Quality:
Maine Potatoes — The Grade Standards are US Department of Agriculture Standards for Grades of Potatoes in effect on day of delivery. Contract specifications in this contract are presently subject to revision.
Platinum — Minimum specifications 99.8 per cent pure platinum and platinum metals with a minimum of 99.5 per cent pure platinum.
Palladium — Minimum specifications 99.8 per cent pure palladium.

Gold — Fineness of at least 9995.0. Exchange quotations shall be on the basis of 1,000 fine but payment shall be based upon the actual fineness of the gold delivered.

US Silver Coins — US Silver dimes, quarters or half-dollars bearing date of 1964 or earlier, with gross weight (including bag, seal and tag) of not less than 54.5 lb for each $1,000 face amount. Coins must be of specified quality and may have been reduced in weight by natural abrasion only.

Imported Boneless Beef — Basically, the beef delivered under this contract shall be hard frozen ($0°$F or less), fresh boneless, manufacturing quality beef, full carcass, less briskets and all or part of the plates, but the lot delivered may include shanks or tenderloins or both.

Delivery points:
Maine Potatoes — Presently subject to revision
Platinum, Palladium, Gold and US Silver Coins — In an Exchange approved depository located within the New York Metropolitan area having a 50-mile radius from Columbus Circle as the central point
Imported Boneless Beef — Basically, the negotiable warehouse receipts used in making deliveries must have been issued by an Exchange approved warehouse situated in the Ports of New York, Philadelphia or Tampa.

Are rules and regulations available? Yes

Can they be purchased? Yes, $30 to non-members, plus postage

Arbitration rules: The Arbitration Committee shall consist of 12 Exchange members appointed by the Board, four of whom shall be members of the Board, chosen as equitably as possible from all diversified interests of the Exchange membership. The Board shall appoint a Chairman and a Vice-Chairman to act in the absence of the Chairman. Any controversy between a member on the one hand, and a non-member on the other hand, shall be submitted to arbitration pursuant to this Section at the request of the non-member provided the non-member executes and delivers to the Exchange an agreement in such form as the Exchange prescribes agreeing to be bound by the provisions of this Section and by the award of the arbitrators.

An arbitration proceeding may be instituted under this Section by the mailing to the President of the Exchange a request for arbitration setting forth a concise statement of the controversy and the date on which it arose. The President shall refer the request for arbitration to the Chairman of the Arbitration Committee who shall designate a Subcommittee to hear the controversy and shall deliver said request to the Chairman of said Subcommittee. A member shall not be required to submit to arbitration under this Section unless the request for arbitration is mailed within 180 days after the date on which the controversy arose. If there is a dispute as to whether the request for arbitration was made within the time required by this subsection, such dispute shall be determined after a hearing by the Subcommittee prior to the hearing on the merits. The party against whom the arbitration is sought shall mail to the Chairman of the Subcommittee and to the party requesting the arbitration, within seven business days after the mailing to it of a copy of the request for arbitration, an answer in writing setting forth a concise statement of its position with respect to the controversy. The Subcommittee shall hold a hearing on the controversy after reasonable notice of the time and place of hearing has been given to the parties by the Chairman of the Subcommittee. The Chairman of the Subcommittee shall

Recommended commission rates and margins — New York Mercantile Exchange

	Maine Potatoes		Platinum	Palladium	Gold	Coins	Beef	Heating and Industrial Fuel Oils	Spot Silver Dollars
	XH	JK							
Margins									
Customer	$500	$750	$750	$800	$500	$2,500	$1,200	$500	—
Clearing Member	$350	$500	$500	$600	$350	$2,000	$1,000	$300	—
		(1976 Contract)							
Extra Margins	$125		$500	$600	$350	$600	$200	—	—
Straddle									
Customer	$500		$300	$150	$150	$150	$600	$200	—
Clearing Member	$300		$200	$150	$100	$100	$500	$100	—
Floor Brokerage Fees	$2/$1/buy and sell on spread		$3.00	$2.50	$2.00	$2.00	$2.50	$2.50	$2.00
Clearing Fees	*		*	*	*	*	**	***	$2.00
Commission (Members/Non-Members)									
Round Turn	$15/30		$22.50/45	$25/50	$15/30	$17.50/35	$20/40	$25/45	$25/50
Day Trade	$10/15+		$11.25/22.50	$12.50/25	$7.50/15	$8.75/17.50+	$10/20+	$12.50/25	—
Day Clear	$2.00		$2.75	$2.50	$2.00	$2.75	$2.00	$5.00	—
Pass Outs	$1.25		$1.25	$1.00	$1.25	$1.25	$1.25	$2.50	—
Spreads	$15/30		$22.50/45	$25/50	$15/30	$17.50/35	$20/40	$30/55	—
Roll Over	$7.50/15		$11.25/22.50	$12.50/25	$7.50/15	$8.75/17.50	$10/20	$15/27.50	—

Ten Day Brokerage Rate = one-half rate for qualified floor traders within ten days

+ *Applies when two or more contracts are bought and sold on the same day*
* *Clearing Fees per contract (included in commission) Cust Day $0.50, Cust Ovrnt $1.00, House Day $0.12½, House Ovrnt $0.50*
** *Clearing Fees per contract (included in commission) Cust Day $0.75, Cust Ovrnt $1.50, House Day $0.12½, House Ovrnt $0.75*
*** *Clearing Fees per contract (included in commission) Cust Day $1.25, Cust Ovrnt $2.00, House Day $0.50, House Ovrnt $1.25*

decide all questions of procedure respecting the hearing. The Subcommittee shall have the power to subpoena parties to the controversy, witnesses, and books, records and documents to the extent permitted by law. All members of the Subcommittee shall be present at the hearing and at any adjournment thereof. After the hearing, the Subcommittee shall render its award which shall be in such form as may be required for filing in a court proceeding for the enforcement of the award. The award shall be made by the decision of a majority of the Subcommittee and shall be final and binding on the parties. Each member of the Subcommittee shall receive a fee of $25 for his service as arbitrator. The arbitrators shall determine and include in the award a direction as to how costs of the arbitration shall be borne by the parties. Such costs shall include the fees of the arbitrators and the cost of the stenographic record of the proceedings, if made. Where an arbitration is requested by a non-member, the Subcommittee may require a deposit to cover costs not exceeding $100 before proceeding with the hearing. The award of the arbitrators may be entered in any court having jurisdiction in accordance with the laws of the State of New York. Failure of a member to comply with an award of the arbitrators shall be grounds for disciplinary action against such member as in the case of a violation of the By-Laws.

Is there an appeal? No. The decision of the Committee shall be final and binding on the parties.

Currency dealt in: US dollars

Average volume of trading over two years:

	1974	1975
Maine Potatoes	770,781	795,732
Platinum	199,623	90,287
US Silver Coins	90,852	50,659
Imported Boneless Beef	4,803	3,396
Palladium	2,277	1,349
Heating Oil	11	8
Industrial Fuel Oil	6	98
Gold	1,230	36,733
Total	1,069,583	978,262

Recommended commission rates and margins: *See Table opposite.*

Membership, types of: Regular Membership, Commercial Associate Membership (category no longer open), Petroleum Associate Membership

Trading members, as at January 1976: *See Appendix 1 (page 285).*

Date of establishment of market: 1872 as 'Butter and Cheese Exchange of New York'; name 'New York Mercantile Exchange' adopted in 1882

Petroleum Associates of the New York Cotton Exchange, Inc

37 Wall St, New York, NY 10005

Telephone: 212-269 7880; **Telex:** 235068 PACE UR

Wool Associates of the New York Cotton Exchange, Inc

37 Wall St, New York, NY 10005

Telephone: 212-269 7880

Commodity: Wool

Titles of appointments: President, First Vice-President, Second Vice-President, Treasurer, Secretary, Assistant Secretary

Hours of trading: Each weekday 10.00 to 14.30

Trading unit: 6,000 lb

Trading limits: Min .10 cents per lb ($6 per contract), max 10 cents per lb above or below except on or following the eighth day of a current month at which time there is no limit.

Contract particulars:
Quality: Standard 64's quality 2-¾ inches in length. Allowances as permitted by the Exchange

Delivery points: From Licensed Warehouses in Charleston, SC; Columbus, OH; Craig, CO; Greater Boston, MA; Kansas City, MO; Minneapolis, MN; Rawlings, WY; Salt Lake City, UT; San Angelo, TX; San Francisco-Stockton, CA

Delivery months: March, May, July, October, December

Currency dealt in: US dollars

Membership, types of: Class A Members, who are members of the New York Cotton Exchange, and a Class B membership

Uruguay

Agricultural Commodity Exchange
(Camara Mercantil de Productos del Pais)
Avenida Gral Rondeau 1908, Montevideo

Telephone: Montevideo 88191/87661; **Cable address:** Camertil

Commodities: Grain, Oil Seed, Wool and other agricultural products

Titles of appointments: President, Secretary

Membership, types of: Regular Members, of which there are 300; Member Organizations, ten

Date of establishment of market: 1891. The Exchange is a federation of dealers and producers. It publishes a weekly 'Informacion Semanal'.

Appendices

Appendices

Appendix 1:
Commodity Market Trading Members

AUSTRALIA: *Sydney*
Sydney Futures Exchange Ltd, trading members, as at December 1975

Bailey Herbaux & Masurel Pty Ltd
252 George St, Sydney 2000. Tel: 2-27 7884

Booth Newman Pty Ltd
44 Bridge St, Sydney 2000. Tel: 2-27 7881

K V Chapman & Co Pty Ltd
29 Reiby Pl, Sydney 2000. Tel: 2-27 8878

Clive Hall Pty Ltd
26 O'Connell St. Sydney 2000.
Tel: 2-233 5533

Dalgety Australia Ltd
38 Bridge St, Sydney 2000. Tel: 2-20 524

A Dewavrin Futures Pty Ltd
189-193 Kent St, Sydney 2000.
Tel: 2-27 1221

Robert Howes & Associates Pty Ltd
4th Floor, Bank of Adelaide Building,
275 George St, Sydney 2000. Tel: 2-29 2911

C Itoh & Co (Aust) Ltd
1 Alfred St, Sydney 2000. Tel: 2-27 7611

Jackson, Graham, Moore & Partners
56 Pitt St, Sydney 2000. Tel: 2-20 561

Kanematsu-Gosho (Australia) Pty Ltd
39-41 York St, Sydney 2000. Tel: 2-29 3021

Michell-Marriner Futures (Sydney) Pty Ltd
10th Floor, Kindersley House, 33 Bligh St,
Sydney 2000. Tel: 2-231 3975

Nichols (Futures) Pty Ltd
155 Belmore Rd, Randwick 2031.
Tel: Randwick 39 2002

Ross, McConnel, Kitchen & Co Pty Ltd
26 O'Connell St, Sydney 2000.
Tel: 2-232 2466

Simonius Vischer & Co
1 York St, Sydney 2000. Tel: 2-27 2906

FRANCE:
Le Havre/Paris: **International Market of Robusta Coffees;** *Paris:* **Cocoa Terminal Market on the Paris Commodity Exchange; International Market of White Sugar of Paris; Paris Toasted Soyabeans International Market; trading members, as at 18 October 1976.**

Bache Halsey Stuart Commodities SA
6 Rue Royale, 75008 Paris.
Rep: Villada, G. Tel: 1-260 32 45

Bauche-Terme
4 Rue Jean-Nicot, 75007 Paris.
Rep: Bauche, G. Tel: 1-551 76 70

Borione, Pierre-Elie
8 Rue Amiral-de-Coligny, 75001 Paris.
Tel: 1-260 33 13

CICOMAP (Compagnie Internationale de Commission sur les Matières Premières)
4 Ave Marceau, 75008 Paris.
Rep: Charbit, R. Tel: 1-723 78 67

CFCC (Compagnie Française et Continentale de Commerce)
Siège Social: 32 Rue d'Argout, 75022 Paris.
Bureaux: 18 Rue de la Banque, 75002 Paris.
Reps: Fopma, F; Mikes, M. Tel: 1-232 87-75/
1-508 08 66/1-233 84 47/1-260 06 13/
1-260 00 93

Compagnie Française du Sucre et des Produits du Sol
18 Ave Matignon, 75008 Paris.
Reps: Ribac, A; Legrand, C. Tel: 1-266 92 22

Debayser (Société G)
32 Ave Kléber, 75116 Paris.
Reps: Lafuge, J-P; Bernard, A. Tel: 1-502 14 43

Debman SA
32 Ave Kléber, 75116 Paris.
Reps: Lafuge, J-P; Bernard, A.
Tel: 1-553 53 35/1-727 60 41

Desbief & Wiart
24, Ave de l'Opéra, 75001 Paris.
Rep: Desbief M. Tel: 1-742 33 84

Etlafric (France)
15, Rue du Louvre, 75001 Paris.
Rep: Etlin, R. Tel: 1-233 21 25

GENECO (Compagnie Générale de
Commerce et de Commission)
15 Rue du Louvre, 75001 Paris.
Rep: Bachelier, J. Tel: 1-231 50 07

General Cocoa (France)
15 Rue du Louvre, 75001 Paris.
Rep: Des Cloizeaux, R. Tel: 1-233 61 27

Michel Goldschmidt & Fils (SACF)
16 Rue du Louvre, 75001 Paris.
Reps: Goldschmidt, M; Goldschmidt, F.
Tel: 1-260 25 57/1-260 23 36

Harborn Commodities
1 Place des Deux-Ecus, 75001 Paris.
Rep: Brandt, W.
Tel: 1-508 07 10/1-231 28 71

Huet, Claude SA
15 Rue du Louvre, 75001 Paris.
Rep: Huet, C. Tel: 1-260 39 62

Hurtebize-Terme SA
15 Rue du Louvre, 75001 Paris.
Rep: Hurtebize, A. Tel: 1-261 53 11

LB (Société Anonyme)
4 Rue Ventadour, 75001 Paris.
Reps: Lafosse, P; Boumendil, J.
Tel: 1-266 03 41

Loiret-Terme
33 Rue du Louvre, 75002 Paris.
Rep: Ruffin, P. Tel: 1-233 21 42/
1-233 48 43

LUC-Terme SA
11 Rue du Bouloi, 75001 Paris.
Rep: Luck, E. Tel: 1-236 26 52

Maiseries de la Mediterranée (Société
Nouvelle des)
Siège Social: 4 Rue Montesquieu, 75001
Paris.
Bureaux: 15 Rue du Louvre, 75001 Paris.
Rep: Gaveau, R. Tel: 1-233 44 12/
1-231 26 82

Maurer (Société Anonyme Georges)
27 Rue J-J-Rousseau, 75001 Paris.
Reps: Maurer, J; Maurer, P.
Tel: 1-236 39 31/1-508 44 41/1-508 45 30

Node Langlois Matieres Premieres SA
3 Rue de Provence, 75009 Paris.
Rep: Node Langlois, P. Tel: 1-523 03 08/
1-523 17 79/1-523 05 70

Nouvelle Primateria SA
36 Ave Hoche, 75008 Paris.
Rep: Richard J. Tel: 1-924 97 10

Pacol SA
51 Rue d'Amsterdam, 75008 Paris.
Reps: Spencer, A; Weil, R.
Tel: 1-874 06 24/1-526 63 69

Peeters, Pierre; Bourse de Commerce No. 14
2 Rue de Viarmes, 75040 Paris.
Tel: 1-508 54 94/1-233 82 65

Rameau Jean
51 Rue J-J-Rousseau, 75001 Paris.
Tel: 1-233 97 56

SETI (Société d'Exportation de Tourteaux
et Issues)
20 Rue de la Ville-l'Evêque, 75008 Paris.
Tel: 1-742 30 80

SOCOMCO (Société Internationale de
Commerce et de Commission)
43 Rue de Maubeuge, 75009 Paris.
Reps: Fricquegnon, J-J; Duclau P.
Tel: 1-526 95 09/1-285 15 38

Sucres et Denrees-Terme SA
55 Ave Kléber, 75784 Paris.
Reps: Varsano, M; Maurel, E.
Tel: 1-704 75 00/1-727 61 89

Sucre-Union SA
14 Rue de Bassano, 75783 Paris.
Rep: Lafuge, J-P. Tel: 1-720 85 26/
1-723 43 53

Uni-Terme
41-43 Rue de Varenne, 75007 Paris.
Rep: Debourse, J. Tel: 1-544 38 08

Wiart Jean-Georges SA
24 Ave de l'Opéra, 75001 Paris.
Reps: Wiart, M; Negre, C. Tel: 1-742 55 83/
1-742 33 84

JAPAN: *Osaka*
The Osaka Sampin Exchange, trading members, as at April 1977

Daiichi Shohin Co Ltd
5 Shinmeicho, Kita-ku, Osaka

Daito Tsusho Co Ltd
5-1 Minami-Ohgimach, Kita-ku, Osaka

Doi Shoji Co Ltd
10 Minami-Kyutaro-Machi 3 chome,
Higashi-ku, Osaka

Eguchi Shoji Co Ltd
5 Koraibashi 1 chome, Higashi-ku, Osaka

Fuji Shohin Co Ltd
12-1 Shinmeicho, Kita-ku, Osaka

Gomi Sangyo Co Ltd
9-2 Minami-Kyutaro-Machi 3 chome,
Higashi-ku, Osaka

Hayashi Shoji Co Ltd
5 Minami-Hommachi 3 chome,
Higashi-ku, Osaka

Hiro Shoji Co Ltd
14 Awaza-Minami-Dori 2 chome, Nishi-ku,
Osaka

Hirota Shoji Co Ltd
76 Kitahama 2 chome, Higashi-ku, Osaka

Hokushin Shohin Co Ltd
10 Shiomachi-Dori 2 chome, Minami-ku,
Osaka

Kanetsu Shoji Co Ltd
48-1 Kyobashi 3 chome, Higashi-ku, Osaka

Kawachi Co Ltd
26 Minami-Hommachi 2 chome, Higashi-ku,
Osaka

Kishi Shoten Co Ltd
4-1 Hommachi 4 chome, Higashi-ku, Osaka

Kojima Shoji Co Ltd
39 Kita-Kyuhoji-Machi 2 chome, Higashi-ku,
Osaka

Koyo Shoji Co Ltd
4 Azuchi-Machi 3 chome, Higashi-ku, Osaka

Kyoei Bussan Co Ltd
144 Umegaecho, Kita-ku, Osaka

Marubeni Co Ltd
3 Hommachi 3 chome, Higashi-ku, Osaka

Marugo Shoji Co Ltd
33 Koraibashi 2 chome, Higashi-ku, Osaka

Matsu Shoji Co Ltd
1 Hommachi 5 chome, Higashi-ku, Osaka

Nakai Seni Co Ltd
27 Kitahama 1 chome, Higashi-ku, Osaka

Nishida Saburo Shoten Co Ltd
77 Kitahama 2 chome, Higashi-ku, Osaka

Okachi Co Ltd
21 Kita-Kyutaro-Machi 5 chome, Higashi-ku,
Osaka

Okata Shoji Co Ltd
24 Hommachi 3 chome, Higashi-ku, Osaka

Okayasu Shoji Co Ltd
53 Kitahama 2 chome, Higashi-ku, Osaka

Osaka Ohishi Co Ltd
24 Shiomachi-Dori 2 chome, Minami-ku,
Osaka

Osaka Oroshio Iryo Co Ltd
20 Koraibashi 2 chome, Higashi-ku, Osaka

Osaka Toyoshima Co Ltd
40 Minami-Hommachi 2 chome, Higashi-ku,
Osaka

Suzuya Shoji Co Ltd
10-2 Tanimachi 3 chome, Higashi-ku, Osaka

Tayama Co Ltd
1-1 Minami-Hommachi 1 chome,
Higashi-ku, Osaka

Yagi Shoten Co Ltd
10-1 Minami-Kyutaro-Machi 2 chome,
Higashi-ku, Osaka

Yutaka Shoji Co Ltd
4 Ryogae 2 chome, Higashi-ku, Osaka

MALAYSIA: *Kuala Lumpur*
**Malaysian Rubber Exchange and
Licensing Board, trading members, as
at 2 December 1975**

Producers — Class 5(1)(a)

Alma Rubber Estates Sdn Bhd
17 Pangkor Rd, Penang

Chee Tat Realty Pte Ltd
Ladan Han Yang, Peti Surat 105, Masai,
Johore

Compagnie des Caoutchoucs de Padang,
c/o Socfin Co Bhd
PO Box 330, Kuala Lumpur 23-01

Compagnie du Cambodge, c/o Socfin Co Bhd
PO Box 330, Kuala Lumpur 23-01

Dunlop Estates Bhd
PO Box 55, Bastion House, Malacca

Eng Thye Plantations Bhd
Ladang Gula, Kuala Kurau, Perak

Federal Land Development Authority
Jalan Maktab, Kuala Lumpur 15-02

Gan Teng Siew Realty Sdn Bhd
Room 202, Kwong Yik Bank Building,
2nd Floor, Jalan Bandar, Kuala Lumpur
01-20

Hock Lee Enterprises (M) Sdn Bhd
Sungei Pulong, Sungei Buloh, Selangor

Khaw Gim Leong Sdn Bhd
47-J Weld Quay, Penang

Kuala Lumpur-Kepong Bhd
2nd Floor, The Regent of Kuala Lumpur,
54A Jalan Imbi, Kuala Lumpur 06-23

Plantations des Terres Rouges,
c/o Socfin Co Bhd
PO Box 330, Kuala Lumpur 23-01

Pontian United Plantations Ltd
Kuku Estate, PO Box 501, Kukup, Johore

Rahman Hydraulic Tin Berhad
25 Beach St, Penang

Saw Choo Theng
23 Beach St, Penang

Selangor Plantations Co Ltd,
c/o Socfin Co Bhd
PO Box 330, Kuala Lumpur 23-01

Syarikat Lim Theng Hin Ltd.
211 Victoria St, Penang

Syarikat Perba (Sdn) Bhd
5th Floor, Room 506, Bangunan Kwang
Tung Association, 44 Jalan Pudu,
Kuala Lumpur

Taiko Plantations Sdn Bhd
6 Jalan Tambun, PO Box 167, Ipoh, Perak

Tan Sri Senator Gan Teck Yeow
14-16 Jalan Klyne, Kuala Lumpur 01-21

Tee Teh
14-16 Jalan Klyne, Kuala Lumpur 01-21

Uniroyal Malaysian Plantation Sdn Bhd
Hongkong Bank Chambers, PO Box 350,
Penang

Unitac Ltd
96 Jalan Hang Jebat, PO Box 117, Malacca

West Country Sdn Bhd
Kajang, Selangor

Manufacturers' Buying Agents —
Class 5(1)(b)

Dunlop Malayan Rubber Supply Co Sdn Bhd
7th Floor, Hwa-Li Building, Jalan Ampang,
Kuala Lumpur 01-17

Dunlop Rubber Purchasing Co Pte Ltd
PO Box 1257, Singapore

Firestone Malaya Sdn Bhd
PO Box 58, Butterworth, Province Wellesley

Societe des Matieres Premieres Tropicales
188 Sungai Besi Rd, Kuala Lumpur 07-02

Estates' Selling Agents — Class 5(1)(c)

Barlow Boustead Estates Agency Sdn Bhd
52 Jalan Ampang, PO Box 1070,
Kuala Lumpur 01-16

Harrisons & Crosfield (M) Sdn Bhd
70 Jalan Ampang, Peti Surat 1007,
Kuala Lumpur 04-05

Kumpulan Guthrie Sdn Bhd
7th Floor, Wisma Damansara, Jalan
Semantan, Kuala Lumpur 23-03

Plantation Agencies Sdn Bhd
Chartered Bank Chambers, PO Box 706,
Beach St, Penang

Sime Darby Plantations Bhd
3rd Floor, President House, 54A Jalan Imbi,
PO Box 157, Kuala Lumpur 01-16

Brokers — Class 5(1)(d)

Green & Collier Pte Ltd
Asia Insurance Building, Jalan Weld,
Kuala Lumpur 05-02

Green & Collier (M) Sdn Bhd
4th Floor, Asia Insurance Building,
Kuala Lumpur 05-02

Hock Tong Rubber Brokers Pte Ltd
91 Jalan Ampang, Kuala Lumpur 01-17

Holiday, Bath Sdn Bhd
Lee Yan Lian Building, Jalan Mountbatten,
Kuala Lumpur 01-21

Lewis & Peat (Malaya) Sdn Bhd
8th Floor, Lee Yan Lian Building, Jalan Tun
Perak, Kuala Lumpur 01-21

Union Rubber Brokers (Malaysia) Sdn Bhd
Room 508, Lee Yan Lian Building, Jalan
Mountbatten, Kuala Lumpur 01-21

Dealers — Class 5(1)(e)

Ace Commercial Enterprise Sdn Bhd
Lot 16, Wisma Central, Jalan Ampang,
Kuala Lumpur

ACLI (M) Sdn Bhd
Room 401, Asia Insurance Building,
Kuala Lumpur

Aik Ming Realty Sdn Bhd
8H 15 Main Road, Pakan Nanas, Johore

Aik Seng & Co Ltd
91 Jalan Ampang, Kuala Lumpur 01-17

Alcan Getah Malaysia Sdn Bhd
2nd Floor, Wisma Bunga Raya, Jalan
Ampang, Kuala Lumpur

Anglo-American Corp Ltd
PO Box 2536, Kuala Lumpur 01-21

Chop Ban Lee
12 Loke Yew Street, Bentong, Pahang

Ban Lee Sdn Bhd
Lee Yan Lian Building, Jalan Mountbatten,
Kuala Lumpur 01-21

Ban Seng Hong Sdn Bhd
47 Jalan Maharani, Muar, Johore

Ban Seng Rubber Co Ltd
24 Pekan Melayu, PO Box 103, Alor Star,
Kedah

Bee Seng & Co
14-16 Jalan Klyne, Kuala Lumpur 01-21

Bee Seng Co Sdn Bhd
14-16 Jalan Klyne, Kuala Lumpur 01-21

CC Commodities Sdn Bhd
Bangunan Yee Seng, Jalan Weld,
Kuala Lumpur

Central Trading Corp (M) Sdn Bhd
30 Jalan Tiga, off Jalan Chan Sow Lin,
Kuala Lumpur 07-03

Chong Hin Rubber Factory Sdn Bhd
Jalan Sungai Jati, via Jalan Kota Raja,
PO Box 25, Kelang, Selangor

Chuan Keat Chan Sdn Bhd
13 Station St, Klang, Selangor

The Colombo Commercial Co (Malaysia)
Sdn Bhd
9 Weld Quay, PO Box 309, Penang

Dominion Rubber Co (M) Ltd
23 Jalan Melayu, Kuala Lumpur 01-03

East Asiatic Co Ltd
Denmark House, PO Box 354,
Kuala Lumpur 04-05

Eastern Rubber Factory Sdn Bhd
1 Mile Stone, Jalan Paloh, Yong Peng,
Johore

Eng Aik Rubber Sdn
16 Jalan Besar, Tongkang Pechah,
Batu Pahat, Johore

Eng Lam Co Sdn Bhd
134 Jalan Rahmat, Batu Pahat, Johore

Eversharp Rubber Industries, Sdn Bhd
7 Jalan Muar, Jementah, Johore

Faure Fairclough Malaysia Sdn Bhd
3rd Floor, President House, 54A Jalan Imbi,
PO Box 157, Kuala Lumpur

Foh Chong & Sons Sdn Bhd
PO Box 97, Johore Bahru

Freudenberg & Co (Malaysia) Sdn Bhd
Asia Insurance Building, Singapore 1,
Kuala Lumpur

General Produce Agency Ltd
66-B Penang St, Penang

Harper, Gilfillan & Co Ltd
Rubber Department, PO Box 156, Penang

H & C Latex Sdn Bhd
Petaling PO, Petaling, Selangor

Hock Bee Trading Co Sdn Bhd
67 Beach St, PO Box 468, Penang

Hock Chin Aun Sdn Bhd
287-B Jalan Asaad, Kulim, Kedah

Hock Heng Co Ltd
Railway Goodsyard, PO Box 355,
Kuala Lumpur

Hock Hin (Muar) Rubber Co Sdn Bhd
43 Jalan Maharani, Muar, Johore

Hoe Hock Sdn Bhd
9 Jalan Rugayah, Batu Pahat, Johore

Hoe Peng Co Ltd
3030 Main Rd, Nibong Tebal, Province,
Wellesley

Hong Giap Sdn Bhd
6½ Mile Stone, Jalan Muar, Segamat, Johor

Hong Joo & Co
1 Jalan Bandar, Kuala Lumpur 01-18

Hong Seng Co Ltd
5 Jalan Bendahara, Ipoh, Perak

Joo Seng Rubber Co Sdn Bhd
14 Taiping Rd, Kuala Kangsar, Perak

Joo Seng Rubber Co (Selangor) Ltd
Joo Seng Building, Weld Quay, Penang

Kautschuk — Gesellschaft (M) Sdn Bhd
21 Jalan Gelenggang, PO Box 2486,
Kuala Lumpur

Keck Seng (M) Sdn Bhd
2G Foh Chong Building, Johore Bharu

Kennedy Burkhill & Co Sdn Bhd
Chartered Bank Chambers, Penang

Kheng Lip Co Sdn Bhd
178-A Beach St, Penang

Kian Ann Chan
9 Jalan Rugayah, Batu Pahat, Johore

Kian Lee SMR Factory Sdn Bhd
87 Kampong Hulu, Malacca

Chop Kim Bee
15 Bibby Rd, Raub, Pahang

Klang Rubber Co Sdn Bhd
1 Jalan Pulasan, Kelang, Selangor

Kota Trading Co Sdn Bhd
2nd Floor, Room 204, OCBC Building,
Johore Bahru, Johore

Kuek Ho Yao
4 Jalan Bukit Chagar, Johore Bahru, Johore

Lam Eng Rubber Factory (M) Sdn Bhd
PO Box 62, Sungai Petani, Kedah

Lam Joo Sdn Bhd
34 & 36 Jalan Bachang, Malacca

Lam Seng Manufacturing Enterprises Sdn Bhd
4 Jalan Tuan Sheikh, Seremban

Lam Seng Rubber (M) Sdn Bhd
3rd Floor, Room 309, Bangunan Lee Yan
Lian, Kuala Lumpur 01-21

Lean Hoe Rubber Factory Sdn Bhd
1st Floor, A-14, OUB Building,
33-C Beach St, Penang

Lee Latex Ltd
PO Box 967, Kuala Lumpur 14-17

Lee Rubber Co Ltd
Lee Rubber Building, 145 Jalan Bandar,
Kuala Lumpur 01-27

Lee Rubber (Selangor) Ltd
Lee Rubber Building, 145 Jalan Bandar,
PO Box 356, Kuala Lumpur 01-27

Lembaga Tabung Getah Sabah
PO Box 361, Koto Kinabalu, Sabah

Lewis & Peat Group (Malaysia) Sdn Bhd
8th Floor, Lee Yan Lian Building, Jalan
Mountbatten, Kuala Lumpur

Lian Aik (Chuang Kee) Sdn Bhd
30 Jalan Rahmat, Batu Pahat, Johore

Lian Hin Rubber Co Sdn Bhd
17-19 Jalan Silang, Kuala Lumpur 01-21

Lian Seng Co Sdn Bhd
13 Jalan Silang, Kuala Lumpur 01-21

Maclaine, Watson & Co (Pte) Ltd
PO Box 695, Singapore

Malay Rubber Plantations (Malaysia) Bhd
Pinji Estate, Lahat, Perak

Malaysia Commodity Sdn Bhd
25 Jalan Temerloh, Mentakab, Pahang

Malaysian Rubber Development Corp Bhd
7 Jalan Eaton, Kuala Lumpur 04-08

Malaysian Rubber Research and
Development Board
PO Box 193, Kuala Lumpur 01-01

Manilal & Sons (M) Ltd
3 Penang St, Penang

Melaka Tong Bee Sdn Bhd
87 Kampong Hulu, Malacca

Nam Cheong Co
59 Jalan Klyne, Kuala Lumpur 01-21

Nam Hong Trading Co Sdn Bhd
41 Jalan Tunku Hassan, Seremban,
North Sembilan

Nanyang Co (Pte) Ltd
Ayer Merah, Kulim, South Kedah

New Fountain Enterprises (M) Sdn Bhd
PO Box 103, Yong Peng, Johore

Pacol Sdn Bhd
5th Floor, Lee Yan Lian Building,
Jalan Mountbatten, Kuala Lumpur 01-21

Patel Hldgs Sdn Bhd
76 Bishop St, (1st Floor), Penang

Pernas MRDC Sdn Bhd
1st Floor, Bangunan Bakti, 91 Jalan
Campbell, Kuala Lumpur

Revertex (M) Sdn Bhd
PO Box 508, Kluang, Johore

Saw Brothers Realty Ltd
23 Beach St, Penang

Chop Seng Hin
189-191 Jalan Limbongan, Pasir Puteh,
Kelantan

Sin Aik Joo
4 Jalan Klyne, Kuala Lumpur 01-21

Socfin Co Bhd
3rd Mile, Damansara, PO Box 330,
Kuala Lumpur 23-01

Soon Cheong Rubber Co Ltd
21¼ Miles, Kulai, Johore   xx

Southern Corp (Nibong Tebal) Sdn Bhd
3030 Main Road, Nibong Tebal, Province
Wellesley

Southern Rubber Works Sdn Bhd
178-A Beach St, Penang

South Malaya Co Sdn Bhd
39 Jalan Mersing, Kluang, Johore

Su Hock Co Ltd
178-A Beach St, Penang

Suka (Johore) Sdn Bhd
61 & 62 Main Rd, Scudai, Johore

Swee Hin Rubber Sdn Bhd
Jalan Sungai Jati, via Jalan Kota Raja,
Klang, Selangor

Synn Lee Co Sdn Bhd
167-A Kota Rd, Taiping, Perak

Tai Teong Rubber Factory Sdn Bhd
67 Beach St, Penang

Teong Huat Co Sdn Bhd
15 China St, Ghaut, Penang

Thye Chiang & Co
21 & 23 Sungai Mati, Muar, Johore

Tian Teck Sdn Bhd
C8282 Batu Berendam, Malacca

Tong Teik Co Ltd
B3, 2nd Floor, Elceetee Building,
33-C Beach St, Penang

Ulu Tiram Manufacturing Co Ltd
Ulu Tiram Estate, PO Box 705,
Johore Bahru, Johore

Union Co Sdn Bhd
3603 Jalan Ismail, Kota Bharu, Kelantan

United Polymer Sdn Bhd
13th Floor, Lee Yan Lian Building,
Jalan Mountbatten, Kuala Lumpur 01-21

Yee Foong & Co Ltd
Godown No 2, Railway Goods Yard,
Seremban, North Sembilan

Yee Seng Rubber Co Sdn Bhd
Bangunan Yee Seng (4th Floor)
15 Jalan Weld, Kuala Lumpur

Yew Chuan Sdn. Bhd
Room 301 (3rd Floor), 44 Jalan Pudu,
Kuala Lumpur

Yong Hing Trading Co (M) Ltd
33-C Beach St, PO Box 772, Penang

Associate Members

Alcan Far East (Pte) Ltd
PO Box 215, Killiney Rd, Post Office,
Singapore 9

Chautard & Co (Rubber) Ltd
Riber Bank House, 67 Upper Thames St,
London EC4

Corrie, MacColl & Sons Ltd
Dunster House, 37 Mincing Lane,
London EC3

C Czarnikow Ltd
Plantation House, Mincing Lane,
London EC3

S Figgis & Co Ltd
Dunster House, Mincing Lane, London EC3

The Goodyear Orient Co Pte Ltd
105 Lorong 3, Geylang, Singapore 14

Gow, Wilson Ltd
Market Building, 29 Mincing Lane,
London EC3

Holiday, Cutler, Bath & Co Pte Ltd
Denmark House, Raffles Quay, Singapore 1

Hooglandt & Co
139/149-A Market St, PO Box 245,
Singapore 1

AC Israel Rubber Co Delaware
11D Wall St, New York, NY 10005

AC Israel Woodhouse Co Ltd (London)
21 Mincing Lane, London EC3R 7DN

Kasho Co Ltd
7th Floor Bangunan Yee Seng, 15 Jalan
Weld, Kuala Lumpur

Kobayashi Yo-ko Co Ltd
5, 1 Chome Nihonbashi Kakigaracho,
Chuo-Ku, Tokyo, Japan

Lam Seng Rubber Co Ltd
9-E Asia Insurance Building, Singapore 1

Lewischn & Heilbut Ltd
71 St Mary Axe, London EC3P 3ED

Marubeni Corp
PO Box 865, Kuala Lumpur

Nomura Trading Co Ltd
9 Jalan Gereja (4th Floor), Kuala Lumpur

Pacol Ltd
47 Mark Lane, London EC3

South Union Co (Pte) Ltd
4A & 4B, Far Eastern Bank Building,
156 Cecil St, Singapore

Wm Jas & Hy Thompson (Hldg) Ltd
48 Fenchurch St, London EC3

Edward Till & Co Ltd
Plantation House, Mincing Lane,
London EC3

Trading Co Guntzel & Schumacher,
(England) Ltd
St Olaf House, Tooley Street, London SE1

Tropical Produce Co (Pte) Ltd
10th Floor, Rooms 1002-1006,
Supreme House, PO Box 278, Singapore 9

Union Rubber Brokers Pte Ltd
46A Chartered Bank Chambers, Singapore

United Baltic Corp Ltd
21 Mincing Lane, London EC3

THE NETHERLANDS: *Amsterdam/
Rotterdam*
**The Egg Terminal Market, trading
members, as at April 1977**

Nieuwenhuis Termijnmarkt Service BV
IJweg 997, Hoofddorp

Sameico
Wolbeslanden 1, Postbox 1, Bornerbroek

Kon G de Vries P Zonen BV
Centraal Station, Amsterdam

**The Pork Terminal Market, trading
members, as at April 1977**

Dopromij BV
Postbox 11507, Amsterdam

JWC Glasbergen
Prins Hendrikstraat 26, Doetinchem

H Nieuwenhuis Termijnmarkt Service BV
IJweg 997, Hoofddorp

Kon G de Vries P Zonen BV
Centraal Station, Amsterdam

W F Westerman & Co BV
Postbox 3445, Amsterdam

J van Zalinge
Koninginneweg 1, Bussum

**The Potato Terminal Market, broker
members, as at April 1977**

Makelaardij W M Kreeuwen BV
Postbox 3733, Amsterdam

Manger Intermedia BV
Postbox 10030, Amsterdam

Proterma BV
Postbox 102215, Amsterdam

Kon G de Vries & Zonen BV
Centraal Station — Amsterdam

W F Westerman & Co BV
Postbox 3445, Amsterdam

Van Santen & Van Westen BV
Postbox 55, Barendrecht

SINGAPORE: *Singapore*
**Rubber Association of Singapore,
trading members, as at April 1976**

Class A — Estates' Selling Agents

John Buttery & Co Ltd
100C, Pasir Panjang Rd, Singapore 5.
Tel: 65-636722

Harrisons & Crosfield (Singapore) Pte Ltd
7th Floor, MacDonald House, Orchard Rd,
Singapore 9. Tel: 65-323261

Guide to World Commodity Markets

Sime Darby (Singapore) Ltd (Rubber Dept)
32nd Floor, UIC Building, 5 Shenton Way,
Singapore 1, PO Box 1772. Tel: 65-2200577

Ross Taylor & Co Pte Ltd
3B, 3rd Floor, Crosby House, Robinson Rd,
PO Box 1249, Singapore 1. Tel: 65-93542

Class B — Brokers

General Rubber Trading House Pte Ltd
301, 3rd Floor, GRTH Building, 66/68 East
Coast Rd, Singapore 15. Tel: 65-466555/
65-465410

Green & Collier Pte Ltd
PO Box 170, President Building, 3rd Floor,
320 Serangoon Rd, Singapore 8.
Tel: 65-362022/65-363044/65-322914

Hock Tong Rubber Brokers Pte Ltd
Rooms 605/606, 6 Cecil St, Singapore 1.
Tel: 65-77511/65-77515

Holiday, Cutler, Bath & Co (Pte) Ltd
8th Floor, Denmark House, Raffles Quay,
Singapore 1. Tel: 65-75066

Lewis & Peat (Singapore) Pte Ltd
3rd Floor, Finlayson House, Raffles Quay,
Singapore 1. Tel: 65-96727

Malaysia Brokers (1963) Pte Ltd
8th Floor, Room 805, Tat Lee Building,
63 Market St, Singapore 1. Tel: 65-92151/6

Union Rubber Brokers (Pte) Ltd
46-A Chartered Bank Chambers, Battery Rd,
Singapore 1.
Tel: European Brokers 65-92341/Chinese
Brokers 65-94411/General Office 65-94418

H M Wyllie
PO Box 1952, 46A Chartered Bank
Chambers, Singapore 1

Class C — Manufacturers' Buying Agents

Dunlop Trading (Pte) Ltd

Firestone Singapore Pte Ltd

Goodrich Co Pte Ltd

Goodyear Orient Co Pte Ltd

Societe des Matieres Premiers Tropicales

Class D — Dealers

Aik Hoe & Co (Pte) Ltd
Suite 1001, 10th Floor, Ocean Building,
Collyer Quay, Singapore 1. Tel: 65-919233

Aik Hwa Trading Co (Pte) Ltd
3rd Floor, 20 Peck Seah St, Singapore 2.
Tel: 65-96655

Aik Leong Co (Pte) Ltd
6th Floor, Union Building, 173-F Tras St,
Singapore 2. Tel: 65-2200154

Alcan Far East (Pte) Ltd
5th Floor, Room A, Yen San Building,
268 Orchard Rd, PO Box 215, Killiney Rd
Post Office, Singapore. Tel: 65-371533

Anglo-American Corporation Sdn Bhd
7th Floor, Denmark House, PO Box 658,
Singapore 1. Tel: 65-75001

Ann Bee Rubber Co Pte Ltd
2602, 26th Floor, International Plaza,
Singapore 10. Tel: 65-2201868/
65-2201903

Anson Co (Pte) Ltd
46-B, Boat Quay, Singapore 1.
Tel: 65-94931/65-94932

Asian Produce Trading Co
Room 5G, 5th Floor, Far Eastern Bank
Building, 156 Cecil St, Singapore 1.
Tel: 65-982435/65-981109/65-981191/
65-984618

Asiatic Produce Co Pte Ltd
Shenton House, 1809, 18th Floor,
2 Shenton Way, Singapore 1.
Tel: 65-2204783

Ban Hin Leong Co (Pte) Ltd
3rd Floor, 35-36 Philip St, Singapore 1.
Tel: 65-95514/65-77407

Ban Joo Trading Co
7B Amoy St, Singapore 1. Tel: 65-92932/
65-73723/65-981647

Ban Seng Rubber Co (Pte) Ltd
34-B Philip St, (2nd Floor), Singapore 1.
Tel: 65-71625

Bian Bee Co Pte Ltd
34-36 Cecil St, Singapore 1. Tel: 65-917155

Bian Hin Rubber Co (Pte) Ltd
134 Havelock Rd, Singapore 3.
Tel: 65-74725/65-96433/
65-74708/65-97773

Bian Thye Rubber Co (Pte) Ltd
134 Havelock Rd, Singapore 3.
Tel: 65-97773/65-96433/65-74725/
65-74708

Brilliance Industrial & Investment Co (Pte)
Ltd
Room 820, 8th Floor, People's Park Centre,
101 Upper Cross St, Singapore 1.
Tel: 65-981220

C C Commodities Pte Ltd
4th Floor, Rooms 5 & 6, Malayan Bank
Chambers, Singapore 1. Tel: 65-984011/3

Central Processes Pte Ltd
Suite 803, 8th Floor, Ocean Building,
Collyer Quay, Singapore 1.
Tel: 65-983516/7

Chan Tong & Co (Pte) Ltd
43 Boat Quay, Singapore 1. Tel: 65-95872

Chee Tat Realty (Pte) Ltd
Unit 325, 3rd Floor, Textile Centre,
200 Jalan Sultan, Singapore 7.
Tel: 65-2589677

Chin Hock Chiang & Co
58 Boat Quay, Singapore 1. Tel: 65-92747/
65-92748

Chin Hock Rubber Co (Pte) Ltd
4th Floor, Tat Lee Building, 63 Market St,
Singapore 1. Tel: 65-94811/7

Chong Lee Co (Pte) Ltd
45 Telok Ayer St, Singapore 1.
Tel: 65-79512

Commodity Traders Sdn Bhd
Maritime Building, Singapore 1.
Tel: 65-92161

Daarnhouwer & Co (FE) Pte Ltd
179-F, Union Building, Tras St, Singapore 2.
Tel: 65-982810

Dunn Trading Co (Pte) Ltd
39-39A Pekin St, Singapore 1.
Tel: 65-77221/3

The East Asiatic Co Ltd
PO Box 158, Singapore. Tel: 65-76011

Eng Keok Teck Rubber Factory
47-B, 2nd Floor, Boat Quay, Singapore 1.
Tel: 65-95381/3, 65-93843

Ewart Properties (M) Sdn Bhd
Lowson Building, 396 Alexandra Rd,
Singapore 5. Tel: 65-631811

Freudenberg & Co (Far East) Pte Ltd
11-A & B, Asia Insurance building,
Finlayson Green, Singapore 1.
Tel: 65-93786

Gama Trading Co Pte Ltd
9 North Canal Rd, Singapore 1.
Tel: 65-92781/65-94291

E B Goh Pte Ltd
113 Market St, Singapore 1. Tel: 65-70794/
65-94694

Good Line Pte Ltd
Tower 2502, DBS Building, 6 Shenton Way,
Singapore 1. Tel: 65-2209888 (3 lines)

Goodman Rubber Factory Pte Ltd
51 Lorong 21, Geylang, Singapore 14.
Tel: 65-463888/65-464006

Guan Seng Rubber Co (Pte) Ltd
24 Philip St, Singapore 1. Tel: 65-910053

Han Huat & Co. Pte Ltd
3 Lorong Telok, Singapore 1. Tel: 65-93549

Heap Hoe Co Pte Ltd
Suite 1001, 10th Floor, Ocean Building,
Collyer Quay, Singapore 1. Tel: 65-919233

Heap Huat Rubber Co Ltd
4-A & B, 4th Floor, Far Eastern Bank
Building, 156 Cecil St, Singapore 1.
Tel: 65-92111/7

Hock Soon & Co (Pte) Ltd
4th Floor, Tat Lee Building, 63 Market St,
Singapore 1. Tel: 65-94811/7

Hoe Joo Co Pte Ltd
4-A & B, 4th Floor, Far Eastern Bank
Building, 156 Cecil St, Singapore 1.
Tel: 65-92111/7

Hoe Lee Rubber Co (Pte) Ltd
14 Seah St, Singapore 7. Tel: 65-31629

Hooglandt & Co
34 Boon Leat Terrace, Off Pasir Panjang Rd,
Singapore 5. Tel: 65-625446

Indonesian Rubber Co Pte Ltd
Tower 2603, 26th Floor, DBS Building,
6 Shenton Way, Singapore 1.
Tel: 65-2206163/65

International Polymer Pte Ltd
45-A, Robinson Rd, Singapore 1.
Tel: 65-983521

International Rubber Co (Pte) Ltd
54-A Boat Quay, (1st Floor), Singapore 1.
Tel: 65-97379/65-92733/65-75491

C Itoh & Co Ltd
11th & 12th Floor, Unit Nos. 1101 & 1202,
Hong Leong Building, 16 Raffles Quay,
Singapore 1. Tel: 65-2202755

Jayapura Pte Ltd
33-C Hongkong St, Singapore 1.
Tel: 65-910603

Joo Cheong Co Pte Ltd
42 Middle Rd, Singapore 7.
Tel: 65-329884/65-30101/65-328646

Kah Hin Rubber Co Ltd
Orchard Towers, Front Block, 17th Floor,
Unit 1705, 400 Orchard Rd, Singapore 9.
Tel: 65-2353166

Kallang Rubber Co (Pte) Ltd
377 C & D, Kallang Rd, Singapore 12.
Tel: 65-2586187/65-2587404

Kasho Co Ltd
Room No 5AB, 5th Floor, Asia Insurance
Building, Finlayson Green, Singapore 1.
Tel: 65-94345/6 & 65-75729

Keck Seng (S) Pte Ltd
21 New Bridge Rd, Singapore.
Tel: 65-78732

Kheng Leong Co (Pte) Ltd
15 Pekin St, Singapore 1. Tel: 65-78651

Kian Lee SMR Factory & Co
527 & 528, 5th Floor, Plaza Singapura,
Orchard Rd, Singapore 9. Tel: 65-335091

Koon Seng Trading Co (Pte) Ltd
60-A Telok Ayer St, Singapore 1.
Tel: 65-74564

Ko Rubber Plantations Ltd
Orchard Towers, Front Block, 17th Floor,
Unit 1705, 400 Orchard Rd, Singapore 9.
Tel: 65-2353166

Kota Trading Co Sdn Bhd
45-C Boat Quay, Singapore 1.
Tel: 65-917355

Lam Chuan Co Pte Ltd
54-B Boat Quay, 2nd Floor, Singapore 1.
Tel: 65-913211/5

Lam Seng Rubber Co Pte Ltd
14th Floor, Room 1403, Shenton Way,
Singapore 1. Tel: 65-2208944/6

Lee Latex (Pte) Ltd
290 Orchard Rd, Singapore 9.
Tel: 65-374334/65-374977

Lee Rubber Co (Pte) Ltd
290 Orchard Rd, Singapore 9.
Tel: 65-374334/65-374977

Lian Seng & Co
27/28 Nunes Building, Malacca St,
Singapore 1. Tel: 65-71749/65-74951

Lian Siang Pte Ltd
Sindo House, 37 Robinson Rd, Singapore 1.
Tel: 65-919611

Lim Hup Choon (S) Pte Ltd
44 Cecil St, Singapore 1. Tel: 65-917266

Lyton Corp Sdn Bhd
7th Floor, Denmark House, PO Box 658,
Singapore 1. Tel: 65-75001

Maclaine Watson & Co Pte Ltd
3rd Floor, Maritime Building, Collyer Quay,
Singapore 1. Tel: 65-95921

Manilal & Sons Pte Ltd
11-A, Malacca St, Singapore 1.
Tel: 65-70307

Marubeni Corp
2801 & 2901, 28th & 29th Floor, Hong
Leong Building, 16 Raffles Quay,
Singapore 1. Tel: 65-2200971

Mequip (S) Pte Ltd
Suite 803, 8th Floor, Ocean Building,
Collyer Quay, Singapore 1.

Mercantile Enterprises Pte Ltd
75-A Boat Quay, Singapore 1.
Tel: 65-74844/65-982146/65-982503

Mercator (Pte) Ltd
4-B, 4th Floor, Far Eastern Bank Building,
156 Cecil St, Singapore 1. Tel: 65-92111/7
& 65-70508

Mitsui & Co Ltd
6th Floor, Industrial & Commercial Bank
Building, 2 Shenton Way, Singapore 1.
Tel: 65-982510/11

M A Namazie (Pte) Ltd
227 Telok Ayer St, Singapore 1.
Tel: 65-76449

Namazie Shipping & Trading Co Pte Ltd
Suite 804, Straits Trading Building,
Battery Rd, Singapore 1. Tel: 65-72449/
65-96889

New Fountain Enterprises (Pte) Ltd
42-B South Bridge Rd, Singapore 1
Tel: 65-94431

New Fountain Realty Pte Ltd
Room 804, 8th Floor, Shenton House,
3 Shenton Way, Singapore 1.
Tel: 65-2200989/65-2200993

New Products Trading Co Pte Ltd
73-B Boat Quay, Singapore 1.
Tel: 65-914460

New Spring (Pte) Ltd
134-A Amoy St, Singapore 1.
Tel: 65-74538

Nichimen Co Ltd
Room 1401, 14th Floor, Hong Leong
Building, 16 Raffles Quay, Singapore 1.
Tel: 65-2208233

Nilakandi International Pte Ltd
16 Pekin St, Singapore 1. Tel: 65-912283

Nomura Trading Co Ltd
43 Bank of China Building, Battery Rd,
Singapore 1. Tel: 65-94975/65-94976

Pacol Pte Ltd
Suite 2102, 21st Floor, Ocean Building,
Collyer Quay, Singapore 1. Tel: 65-97425

Paterson, Simons & Co (S) Pte Ltd
Maritime Building, Collyer Quay,
Singapore 1. Tel: 65-92321

Patriot (Pte) Ltd
94-A Robinson Rd, Singapore 1.
Tel: 65-981310

Peck Seng Co
Room 2006, 20th Floor, High St Centre,
North Bridge Rd, Singapore 6.
Tel: 65-360377

Quek Shin & Sons Pte Ltd
Room 723, 7th Floor, Colombo Court,
Singapore 6. Tel: 65-321932/65-321993

Sahabat Co Pte Ltd
Room 804, 8th Floor, Tat Lee Building,
63 Market St, Singapore 1. Tel: 65-917218

Seng Hong Chan (S) Pte Ltd
42 Market St, Singapore 1. Tel: 65-70983/
65-76441

Seng Soon Hock Co (Pte) Ltd
4th Floor, Tat Lee Building, 63 Market St,
Singapore 1. Tel: 65-94811/7

Shin Teck Co (Pte) Ltd
44 Boat Quay, Singapore 1.
Tel: 65-95831/2 & 65-78587

Sim Lim Co (Pte) Ltd
14th Floor, Selegie Complex, Selegie Rd,
Singapore 7. Tel: 65-327771

Singapore Eastern Supplies Pte Ltd
18th Floor, UIC Building, Shenton Way,
Singapore 1. Tel: 65-2200666

Singapore Tong Teik (Pte) Ltd
1401, 14th Floor, Shenton House,
3 Shenton Way, Singapore 1.
Tel: 65-2200211

Sin Lian Rubber Co (Pte) Ltd
118-B Cross St, Singapore 1.
Tel: 65-79038/65-912038

Sinsar Trading & Co
55-A China St, Singapore 1. Tel: 65-983930

S & L (Produce) Pte Ltd
Room 2, 3rd Floor, Finlayson House,
Singapore 1. Tel: 65-93911

Soon Cheong Rubber Co Ltd
31 Seah St, Singapore 7. Tel:65-360595/
65-362608/65-363959

South Asia Rubber Co
75-A Boat Quay, Singapore 1.
Tel: 65-982503/65-982146/65-74884 (office)
65-663813/65-660045 (factory)

South Central Rubber (Pte) Ltd
Room 502, 5th Floor, Tat Lee Building,
63 Market St, Singapore 1.
Tel: 65-912415/6 & 65-911977

Southern Co (Malaya) Pte Ltd
1404, 14th Floor, Shenton House, Shenton
Way, Singapore 1. Tel: 65-2207390/
65-2207408

Southseas Commodities (Pte) Ltd
Room 1002, Supreme House, Penang Rd,
Singapore 9. Tel: 65-322211/4

South Union Co Pte Ltd
4A & 4B, 4th Floor, Far Eastern Bank
Building, 156 Cecil St, Singapore 1.
Tel: 65-92111/7

Sum Huat Hang Trading (Pte) Ltd
28-A Pekin St, Singapore 1. Tel: 65-919591

Superluck Rubber Co Pte Ltd
3rd Floor, 35-36 Philip St, Singapore 1.
Tel: 65-95165/6

Swee Kee Rubber Pte Ltd
9 Clarke Quay, Singapore 6.
Tel: 65-322110

Tai Tak Estates Sdn Bhd
1301-1302, 13th Floor, UOB Building,
1 Bonham St, Singapore 1.
Tel: 65-96114/65-96087

Tat Lee Co (Pte) Ltd
63 Market St, Singapore 1. Tel: 65-79461/4

Teck Lay (Pte) Ltd
Orchard Towers, Front Block, 17th Floor,
Unit 1705, 400 Orchard Rd, Singapore 9.
Tel: 65-2353166

Terusan Corp Pte Ltd
801/802 Tat Lee Building, 63 Market St,
Singapore 1. Tel: 65-97921

Thai Lee & Co
3rd Floor, Bank of China Building,
Singapore 1. Tel: 65-95051/5

Thong Guan Co (Pte) Ltd
94 Telok Ayer St, Singapore 1.
Tel: 65-914962

Tjiat Lee Rubber Co Pte Ltd
39-B Market St, Singapore 1.
Tel: 65-918958/9

Tjiat Seng & Co Pte Ltd
39 Market St, Singapore 1. Tel: 65-73130/
65-73191

Toho Rubber Processing Co Pte Ltd
8th Floor, Tat Lee Building, 63 Market St,
Singapore 1. Tel: 65-95212/4

Tong Fong Co (1974) Pte Ltd
Tong Fong Building, 52-H Chin Swee Rd,
Singapore 3. Tel: 65-75147/65-75149

Tropical Produce Co (Pte) Ltd
Supreme House, 10th Floor, Rooms 1002-
1006, Penang Rd, Singapore 9. PO Box 278.
Tel: 65-322211/4

United Rubber Millers Co (Pte) Ltd
Far Eastern Bank Building, 6th Floor,
156-H Cecil St, Singapore 1.
Tel: 65-71288/9

Vipin Co
22-A/B Robinson Rd, Singapore 1.
Tel: 65-77645

Waringin (Pte) Ltd
Suite 2408/9, 24th Floor, Ocean Building,
Singapore 1. Tel: 65-912633

William Jacks & Co (Singapore) Sdn Bhd
PO Box 197, 8M, Asia Insurance Building,
Singapore 1. Tel: 65-95862/65-94841

Yew Lian (Pte) Ltd
38 Bank of China Building, Singapore 1.
Tel: 65-93657/8

Zlin Co (Pte) Ltd
Tower 3101 & 3102, (31st Floor),
DBS Building, 6 Shenton Way, Singapore 1.
Tel: 65-2208366

UNITED KINGDOM: *Liverpool*
The Liverpool Cotton Association Ltd, trading members, as at December 1975

United Kingdom Members' Registered Firms

Abercrombie, Bramble & Co Ltd,
506 Cotton Exchange Buildings,
Liverpool L3 9LJ. Tel: 051-236 0547
Directors: *Large, A; *Robinson, T A F;
Newbold, C R

B F Babcock & Co
418 Cotton Exchange Buildings,
Liverpool L3 9LQ. Tel: 051-236 8304
Partners: *Williamson, J M; *Keenan, B H;
*Cassir, G K

Bache & Co (London) Ltd
Plantation House, Mincing Lane,
London EC3. Tel: 01-623 4646
and at 5, The Wool Exchange, Bradford
Directors: Coffin, J D; *Thornton, O D;
Edgeley, B R; Bidgood, J; DiGaetano, F;
Kurtz, J; Safran, H; Grey-Edwards, C;
Hubbard, R D.C

Baumann, Hinde & Co Ltd
Silkhouse Court, Tithebarn St,
Liverpool, L2 2NJ. Tel: 051-236 6200
Directors: Gaunt, J H; *Brown, R A;
*Hinde, P A; Stripling, K S; Vernon, Sir N,
Bart; Wishart, J T

Wm Birtwistle Allied Mills Ltd
Osprey House, Aqueduct Rd, Blackburn,
Lancs. Tel: 0254-54272
Directors: Beggs, W J; Doige, W G;
Menaged, A; Cudworth, G H; Whittaker, H C;
Wilson, D W. Member: *Beard, J E

John Bright & Brothers Ltd
Fieldhouse Mill, P.O. Box 26, Rochdale,
Tel: 0706 48421. Cotton Exchange
Buildings, Liverpool, L3.
Directors: Marcroft, A W; Taylor, J S H;
Crowther, T R; Fullard, R; Heaton, J;
Joy, J; Young, T V. Members: *Roberts,
W F; *Reaney, K F

S M Bulley & Son Ltd
Cotton Exchange Buildings, Liverpool L3
9LJ. Tel: 051-236 3741

Bunge & Co Ltd
Bunge House, St. Mary Axe, London, EC3
Tel: 01-283 3429
101 Cotton Exchange Buildings,
Liverpool, L3 9JR. Tel: 051-236 6345
Directors: Hugaerts, W; Pendered, R G;
Johnston, H E; Nott, A J; *O'Connell, P;
Ross, A H; Slater, K J; Bloome, J L;
Dryburgh, G. Other Members: *Glen, J S;
*Howard, C W

Bunzl & Biach (British) Ltd
Crown House, North Circular Rd,
London NW10 7ST. Tel: 01-965 8222
Directors: Mann, W; Arie, E; Hirsch, F;
Kunze, K; Klotz, G; *Boyagis, G L;
Kerpner, G; Jenkinson, B A; Wilkinson, A

Carrington Viyella Yarns Ltd
Gloucester St, Atherton, Manchester.
Tel: 05234 2351
606/7 Cotton Exchange Buildings,
Liverpool L3 9LQ. Tel: 051-236 6245
Directors: Battersby, G; *McKittrick, G S;
*Isherwood, F A; Pomfret, W R; Sharrock, N;
Slack, J; Chadwick, D. Other Member:
*Hewson, C P

Cassir & Co
418 Cotton Exchange Buildings,
Liverpool L3 9LQ. Tel: 051-236 7625
Partners: Cassir, A; Cassir, G; *Cassir, G K;
*Fairbrother, M J. Other Member. *Radia V V

Alfred Cheetham & Co Ltd
507/513 Corn Exchange Building,
Manchester M4 3EY. Tel: 061-831 1367/8045
Directors: Cheetham, A; *Cheetham, J B;
Cheetham, Mrs D B; Cheetham, Mrs A J

Clover Croft & State (Spinners) Ltd
Croft Mill, Hamer, Rochdale, Lancs OL16 2UU.
Tel: 0706 44317
and at Cotton Exchange Buildings,
Liverpool L3 9LH.
Directors: Whittaker, J; Wiggins S;
*Bridge, J G; Smith, L. Other Member:
*Unsworth, L H

Cook & Thorp Ltd
138/144 Corn Exchange Buildings,
Hanging Ditch, Manchester, M4 3BN.
Tel: 061-834 6002.
and at M & B Stern Ltd
506 Cotton Exchange Buildings,
Liverpool L3 9LJ. Tel: 051-236 1364.
Directors: *Stern, D M; *Large, A;
*Boumphrey, A F W; *Stern, P J M;
Johnson, A L; Kenyon, J D

Cosmos Raw Produce Co
87/89 Aldgate High St, London EC3N 1LN.
Tel: 01-709 2361
Partners: *Moxon, F; Moxon, A; Ingr, G A

Courtaulds Ltd
Northern Spinning Division, P.O. Box 100,
Rodwell Tower, Piccadilly, Manchester
M60 3AP. Tel: 061-236 8466
107, Cotton Exchange Buildings,
Liverpool L3 9JR. Tel: 051-236 0691
Head Office: 18 Hanover Sq, London W1
Directors: Kearton, Lord; Knight, A W;
Koppel, J P; Bond, T K; Bushell, W J;
Clarke, Sir R; Entwistle, D; Field, A P;
Hartley, G A R; Hogg, C A. Morris, J R S;
Parker, M R; Smith, N H; Villiers, C H;
Wooding, N S. Members: *Dixon, P S;
*Salcedo, C

Louis Dreyfus & Co Ltd
City-Gate House, Finsbury Sq, London
EC2A 1QA. Tel: 01-628 9600
404 Cotton Exchange Buildings,
Liverpool L3 9LQ. Tel: 051-236 7957
Directors: Louis-Dreyfus, P G;
Louis-Dreyfus, J; Louis-Dreyfus, G. Sas, P;
Bowerman, I N; Brady, J; *Khosla, L K;
Allen, Sir P. Alternates: Turpault, P A;
Garrett, D P. Other Members:
*Battersby, E H; *Sparrow, J A

Alexander Eccles & Stern
506 Cotton Exchange Buildings,
Liverpool L3 9LJ. Tel: 051-236 0503
Partners: *Stern, D M; *Griffiths, J H S;
*Stern, P J M; Kenyon, J D. Other
Member: *Aldcroft, A

Alexander Eccles Ltd
506 Cotton Exchange Buildings,
Liverpool L3 9LJ. Tel: 051-236 0503
Directors: *Boumphrey, A F W; *Stern, D M;
*Stern, P J M; *Griffiths, J H S; Kenyon, J D;
Boumphrey, Mrs B L; Stern, Mrs P A

Evans & Co
G01 Cotton Exchange Buildings,
Liverpool L3 9JR. Tel: 051-236 2778
Partners: *Anderson, R N; *Anderson, R J

Fatcotco Ltd
205 Cotton Exchange Buildings,
Liverpool L3 9LA. Tel 051-236 0249
Directors: *Boutros, N F; *Boutros, N F

Frank Fehr & Co Ltd
64 Queen Street, London EC4R 1ER.
Tel: 01-248 5066
Directors: *Fehr, B H F; Madsen, R H;
Astell, G W; Fehr, R J F

L M Fischell & Co Ltd
Dunster House, Mincing Lane, London EC3.
Tel: 01-626 9692
Directors: *Fischel, J R; MacCol, D F;
Symington, M McL; Bout, W C

Forbes Reiss Ltd
Berey's Buildings, George St, Liverpool
L3 9LU. Tel: 051-236 8332
Directors: *Jeffries, R C; Jeffries, K R L

R & C Gill
45 The Albany, Old Hall St, Liverpool L3 9EJ.
Tel: 051-236 4712/3
Partners: *Chapple Gill, D P; *Mallinson, J K

Gollin Europe Ltd
N L A Tower, 12/16 Addiscombe Rd,
Croydon CR9 6AX. Tel: 01-681 0071
Directors: Gale, K C; Clarke, E J G;
Nesbitt, P E; Rayson, W A; Hadley, W H.
Member: *Burwood, D

A Hannay & Co
522 Cotton Exchange Buildings,
Liverpool L3 9LH. Tel: 051-236 3563
Partners: *Mills, B; *Jones, N M

H Hentz & Co Ltd
Gillett House, 55 Basinghall St, London EC2.
Tel: 01-606 3803
Directors: Greene, E M; Auer, J F; Crease,
Mrs I; *Govett, P J; Mundy, M

Hindley & Co Ltd
32 St Mary at Hill, London EC3.
Tel: 01-623 9333
Directors: Kissen, H; *Burt, D L;
Cowing, R D; King, J M; Shawcross, C H;
Cope, J A; Perry, V W; Saddleton, B S

Holco Trading Co Ltd
8 Lloyds Ave, London EC3N 3AB.
Tel: 01-480 7951
Directors: Schenk, H F; Morris, C C B;
*Foster, I E J; Davis, W A

Arthur Hughes Ltd
30 Brown St, Manchester M2 2JF.
Tel: 061-834 1134
Directors: *Hughes, A L; Hughes, E A;
Rider, K

G W Joynson & Co Ltd
14 Trinity Sq, London EC3N 4BN.
Tel: 01-488 6921
605 Cotton Exchange Buildings,
Liverpool L3 9LH. Tel: 051-236 6203
Directors: Ritchie, J W; *Campbell-Gray, Hon
C D; Carrodus, P S; Russ, E M; Cattell, D K

Lewis Lloyd & Co
13 Irwell Chambers East, 4 Fazakerley St,
Liverpool 3. Tel: 051-236 0108
Partner: *Herd, A G

Liverpool Cotton Services Ltd
G-01 Cotton Exchange Buildings,
Liverpool L3 9JR. Tel: 051-236 7632
Directors: *Garner, J C; Galletly, Mrs H;
*Anderson, R J; *Watmough, W R

Melladew & Clarke
401 Cotton Exchange Buildings,
Liverpool L3 9LQ. Tel: 051-236 0822
Partners: *Mallinson, E W; *Hughes, B H.
Other Member: *Dunn, W

A Meredith Jones & Co Ltd
522 Cotton Exchange Buildings, Liverpool
L3 9LH. Tel: 051-236 3563
Directors: *Meredith Jones, N; *Meredith
Jones, M; *Mills, B. Other Member:
*Turner, J W

Merrill Lynch, Pierce, Fenner & Smith
(Brokers & Dealers) Ltd
Plantation House, Mincing Lane, London EC3.
Tel: 01-623 2400
Directors: Anderson, H B; Ball, N B;
Cassady, T J; Gray, S; Sears, F J; *Romney, H

Morris & Wilson
Woodend Mills, Lees, Oldham, Lancs.
Tel: 061-652 2426/7
Partners: *Thorp, W C; *Wilson, J D M

Frank Moxon Ltd
Longlands Mill, Queen St, Mossley,
Ashton-under-Lyne, Lancs. OL5 9AH.
Tel: 045-75 2441
Directors: Brooks, R; Brooks, J H;
*Moxon, E D V

Oversea Buyers Ltd
Bath House, Holborn Viaduct, London
EC1A 2AP. Tel: 01-236 6311/6601
Directors: Wachter, Dr A; Sarasin, A;
Preiswerk, R; Ogden, J T; *Spry, E W

Palmer & Wall Ltd
Orleans House, Edmund St,
Liverpool L3 9NG. Tel: 051-236 4725
Directors: *Chapple Gill, D P; *Jemmett,
W M; *Bill, A; *Nottingham, C R E;
*Preston, L F;

Pennefather (Liverpool) Ltd
519 Cotton Exchange Buildings,
Liverpool L3 9LH. Tel: 051-236 4261
Directors: *Wadeson, G D; *Childs, R C

James Platt & Co Ltd
208 Cotton Exchange Buildings,
Liverpool L3 9LA. Tel: 051-236 2636/7
Directors: *Williams, B J; *Tunnicliffe, A D;
*Figueiredo, E W de. Other Member:
*Gorrin, G

Ralli Brothers & Coney Ltd
Stanley Hall, Edmund St,
Liverpool L3 9NN. Tel: 051-236 3651
Directors: *The Earl of Carrick, *McBride,
A K J; *Preston, L F; *Reynolds, A G;
*Bernhardt, C H; *Morris, G C H; *Davies,
R B; Southworth, P; Stead, J B A; Evans,
J B M; Carter, R J. Other Members:
*White, R; *Rimmer, F B; *Jones, H V R

Ralli Brothers & Coney (Cotton) Ltd
Stanley Hall, Edmund St, Liverpool
L3 9NN. Tel: 051-236 3651
Directors: *The Earl of Carrick, *Preston,
L F; Bodger, A L; Creed, A G. Heaton, H;
Paul, K; *Rimmer, F B; Moore, P D;
*White, R

Reynolds & Gibson Ltd
209 Cotton Exchange Buildings,
Liverpool L3 9LD. Tel: 051-236 3721
Directors: *Stead, B F; *The Earl of
Carrick; *Williams, J M K; *Cope, F B

R J Rouse & Co Ltd
Dunster House, Mincing Lane,
London EC3R 7TH. Tel: 01-623 4171
Directors: Nathaniel, N; Leighton, R S;
*Miller, D N; Scrase, A W E; Baum, J;
Lord Colgrain; Lord Aldenham

M & B Stern Ltd
506 Cotton Exchange Buildings,
Liverpool L3 9LJ. Tel: 051-236 1364
Directors: *Boumphrey, A F W; *Stern,
D M; *Large, A; *Stern, P J M;
Kenyon, J D

Volkart Brothers (U.K.) Ltd
522 Cotton Exchange Buildings,
Liverpool L3 9LH. Tel: 051-236 3563
and Market Buildings, 29 Mincing
Lane, London EC3R 7BT
Directors: Reinhart, P; Klinger, R;
Buechi, H U; *Meredith Jones, M

A L Whittington & Co
Berey's Buildings, George St,
Liverpool L3 9LU. Tel: 051-236 0930
Partner: *Whittington, A L

Windel & Co
216 Cotton Exchange Buildings,
Liverpool L3 9LA. Tel: 051-236 6879
Partner: *Windel, H

Winstanley & Co
318 Cotton Exchange Buildings, Liverpool
L3 9LF. Tel: 051-236 1426
Partners: *Farrar, J D; *Harrison, H E;
*Farrar, W D

London:

**The London Cocoa Terminal Market,
trading members, as at December 1976**

Broker Members

Austin T, C Czarnikow Ltd
P.O. Box 602, 66 Mark Lane,
London EC3R 8DH

Hon Campbell-Gray, C D, G W Joynson
& Co Ltd
14 Trinity Sq, London EC3N 4BN

Clatworthy, D G, E. D. & F. Man
30/34 Mincing Lane, London EC3R 7DS

Cowing, G L, Marshall, French & Lucas Ltd
34 Lime St, London, EC3H 7LA

Culme-Seymour, M A, E.F. Hutton &
Co (London) Ltd
Cereal House, 58 Mark Lane,
London EC3R 7EJ

*The names of Directors or Partners who are members of the Association

Feasby D, Woodhouse, Drake & Carey Ltd
Three Quays, Tower Hill, London, EC3R 6EP

Figgis D S J, S Figgis & Co Ltd
53/54 Aldgate High Street,
London EC3N 1LU

Hutchins J C, L M Fischel & Co Ltd
Dunster House, Mincing Lane,
London EC3R 7SY

Keeble L E, F. Fontannaz & Co Ltd
Fontannaz House, 19 Earl St,
London EC2A 2AH

Knight R D, E D & F Man
30/34 Mincing Lane, London EC3R 7DS

Oosterhuis J, Wilson, Smithett & Cope Ltd
32 St Mary-at-Hill, London EC3R 8DH

Patterson J A, Woodhouse, Drake &
Carey Ltd
Three Quays, Tower Hill, London EC3R 6EP

Plummer W A, Bache Halsey Stuart
(London) Ltd
Plantation House, Fenchurch St,
London EC3M 3EP

Reynolds M W T, Wilson, Smithett &
Cope Ltd
32 St Mary-at-Hill, London EC3R 8DH

Simmonds E G, Woodhouse, Drake &
Carey Ltd
Three Quays, Tower Hill, London EC3R 6EP

Williams J L, ACLI International
Commodity Services Ltd
Plantation House, Fenchurch St,
London EC3M 3DX

Home Members

E Bailey & Co Ltd
18 London St, London EC3R 7SX

Cadbury-Schweppes Ltd
1-6, Connaught Place, London W2

Cocoa Merchants Ltd
Plantation House, 'C' Wing, Mincing Lane,
London EC3M 3HX

Commodity Analysis Ltd
194/200 Bishopsgate, London EC2M 4PE

Daarnhouwer & Co Ltd
Market Buildings, 29 Mincing Lane,
London EC3R 7PD

Drexel Burnham & Co Ltd
Winchester House, 77 London Wall,
London EC2P 2HX

Duche & Sons (UK) Ltd
Berisford House, 50 Mark Lane,
London EC3R 7QJ

F Fehr & Co Ltd
Prince Rupert House, 64 Queen St,
London EC4R 1ER

Fendrake Ltd
20 Fenchurch St, London EC3M 3DB

Fergusson, Wild & Co Ltd
3 St Helen's Place, London EC3A 6BD

Gardner Lohmann Ltd
Pountney Hill House, 6 Laurence Pountney
Hill, London EC4

Gill & Duffus Ltd
St Dunstan's House, 201 Borough High St,
London SE1 1HW

Gillespie Bros & Co Ltd
Ling House, Dominion St,
London EC2M 2RT

Goldschmidt & Charteris Ltd
Dunster House, Mincing Lane,
London EC3R 7BL

M Golodetz
29 Mincing Lane, London EC3R 7EU

Harborn Ltd
Borneo House, 62-63 Mark Lane,
London EC3R 7DD

Holco Trading Co Ltd
8 Lloyd's Ave, London EC3N 3AB

A C Israel Woodhouse & Co
21 Mincing Lane, London EC3M 3DX

S N Kurkjian
1 Leadenhall St, London EC3V 1JD

G J McCaul (Overseas) Ltd
Kempson House, 35/37, Camomile St,
London EC3A 7AJ

Merrill Lynch, Pierce, Fenner & Smith
(Brokers & Dealers) Ltd
Merrill Lynch House, 3 Newgate St,
London EC1A 7DA

Moutafian Commodities Ltd
2/4 Eastcheap, London EC3M 1AL

The Nestle Co Ltd
St George's House, Croydon,
Surrey CR9 1NR

Pacol Ltd
47 Mark Lane London EC3R 7QX

Paterson, Simons & Ewart Ltd
Riverbank House, 67 Upper Thames St,
London EC4

J H Rayner (Mincing Lane), Ltd
50 Mark Lane, London EC3R 7RJ

R J Rouse & Co Ltd
Dunster House, Mincing Lane,
London EC3R 7BJ

Rowntree Mackintosh Ltd
York YO1 1XY

S N W Commodities Ltd
Rayner House, 39 Hatton Gdn,
London EC1N 8BX

Shearson Hayden Stone Ltd
Gillett House, 55 Basinghall St,
London EC2V 5ED

Sime Darby Commodities Ltd
4th Floor, 19 Leadenhall St,
London EC3V 1NN

W G Spice & Co Ltd
32 St Mary-at-Hill, London EC3R 8DH

H Stephens & Son (London) Ltd
Henry Stephens House, 12 Minories,
London EC3N 1BJ

Sugar Industry Auxiliaries Ltd
29 Mincing Lane, London EC3R 7EU

Wallace Bros Commodities Ltd.
108 Fenchurch St, London EC3M 5HP

R Wolff & Co Ltd
Knolly's House, 11 Byward St, London EC3

The Coffee Terminal Market Association of London, trading members, as at January 1977

Bache Halsey Stuart (London) Ltd
Plantation House (Block A), Fenchurch St,
London EC3M 3EP

E Bailey & Co Ltd, 69-70 Mark Lane,
London EC3R 7SX

Brooke Bond Liebig Ltd
Sir John Lyon House, 5 High Timber St,
London EC4V 3LB

Cocoa Merchants Ltd
Plantation House, Fenchurch St,
London EC3M 3HX

Commodity Analysis Ltd
194-200 Bishopsgate, London EC2M 4PE

M L Doxford & Co Ltd
10 St James St, London SW1A 1EF

Drexel Burnham & Co Ltd
Winchester House, 77 London Wall,
London EC2P 2HX

F Fehr & Co Ltd
Prince Rupert House, 64 Queen St,
London EC4R 1ER

L M Fischel & Co Ltd
Dunster House, Mincing Lane, London EC3

F Fontannaz & Co Ltd
Fontannaz House, 19 Earl St, London EC2

Foreign Trading Agency Ltd
2-4 Eastcheap, London EC3

Goldschmidt & Charteris Ltd
Dunster House, Mincing Lane,
London EC3R 7BL

M Golodetz
29 Mincing Lane, London EC3R 7EU

H Hentz & Co Ltd
Gillett House, 55 Basinghall St, London EC2

Holco Trading Co Ltd
8 Lloyds Ave, London EC3N 3AP

A C Israel Woodhouse Co Ltd
21 Mincing Lane, London EC3M 3DX

G W Joynson & Co Ltd
14 Trinity Sq, London EC3N 4BN

D & F Man (Produce) Ltd
Colonial House, Mincing Lane,
London EC3R 7DS

Marshall French & Lucas Ltd
34 Lime St, London EC3

Merrill Lynch, Pierce, Fenner & Smith
(Brokers & Dealers) Ltd
Merrill Lynch House, 3 Newgate St,
London EC1A 7DA

Pacol Ltd
47 Mark Lane, London EC3R 7QX

J H Rayner (Mincing Lane) Ltd
50 Mark Lane, London EC4R 7RJ

A J Ridge & Co Ltd
95-97 Fenchurch St, London EC3M 5AJ

Rolls & Son (Produce) Ltd
UCM House, 3-5 Swallow Place, Princes St,
London W1

Malcolm Ross & Co Ltd
46 Berkeley Sq, London W1X 5DB

R J Rouse & Co Ltd
Dunster House, Mincing Lane,
London EC3R 7TH

S N W Commodities Ltd
Rayner House, 39 Hatton Gdn,
London EC1N 8BX

Socomex Ltd
7th Floor, 10 Old Jewry, London EC2

Henry Stephens & Son (London) Ltd
Henry Stephens House, 12 Minories,
London EC3N 1BJ

Truxo Ltd
2 Whittington Ave, London EC3V 1JY

Volkart Bros (UK) Ltd
Market Buildings, 29 Mincing Lane,
London EC3

Wallace Bros Commodities Ltd
108 Fenchurch St, London EC3M 5HP

Wilson, Smithett & Cope Ltd
32 St Mary-at-Hill, London EC3R 8DH

R Wolff & Co Ltd
Knolly's House, 11 Byward St,
London EC3R 5ED

Woodhouse, Drake & Carey Ltd
Three Quays, Tower Hill, London EC3R 6EP

The London Rubber Terminal Market Association, trading members, as at December 1976

Dealer Members

E Bailey & Co Ltd
18 London St, London EC3R 7SX.
Tel: 01-481 1712

Chautard & Co (Rubber) Ltd
Riverbank House, 67 Upper Thames St,
London EC4 3AH. Tel: 01-248 5711

Corrie Maccoll & Son Ltd
Dunster House, 37 Mincing Lane,
London EC3R 7AX. Tel: 01-623 2691

C Czarnikow Ltd
PO Box 602, 66 Mark Lane,
London EC3P 3EA. Tel: 01-480 6677

F Fehr & Co Ltd
Prince Rupert House, 64 Queen St,
London EC4R 1ER. 01-248 5066

Fincham & Smith Ltd
26 St Martins Lane, London EC4R 0DS.
Tel: 01-626 1731

Harborn Ltd
Borneo House, 62-63 Mark Lane,
London EC3R 7DD. Tel: 01-481 8841

Hecht Heyworth & Alcan Ltd
Myrtil House, 70 Clifton St,
London EC2A 4SP. Tel: 01-626 7820

Holco Trading Co Ltd
8 Lloyd's Ave, London EC3N 3AB.
Tel: 01-480 7951

A C Israel Woodhouse Co Ltd
21 Mincing Lane, London EC3R 7DN.
Tel: 01-623 3131

Lewisohn & Heilbut Ltd
71 St Mary Axe, London EC3A 8HR.
Tel: 01-283 3251

Lewis & Peat (Rubber) Ltd
32 St Mary-at-Hill, London EC3R 8DH.
Tel: 01-623 9333

Macadam & Co
Monument House, 16 Monument St,
London EC3R 8AJ. Tel: 01-626 8634

Malcolm Maclaine Ltd
46 Hays Mews, London W1X 8LR.
Tel: 01-499 9577

Nordmann Rassmann (UK) Ltd
Peek House, 20 Eastcheap,
London EC3M 1BJ. Tel: 01-623 2108

Pacol Ltd
47 Mark Lane, London EC3R 7QX.
Tel: 01-623 1000

Revertex Sales Ltd
Temple Fields, Harlow, Essex.
Tel: 0279-29555

A Runge & Co Ltd
1-4 Gt Tower St, London EC3R 5AB.
Tel: 01-626 4333

Sime Darby Commodities Ltd
19 Leadenhall St, London EC3V 1NN.
Tel: 01-626 9822

W Symington & Son Ltd
Bath House, 53-60 Holborn Viaduct,
London EC1A 2ES. Tel: 01-248 6554

Trading Co Guntzel & Schumacher
Hambro House, Vintner's Place,
London EC4V 3BA. Tel: 01-248 1147

United Baltic Corp Ltd
24-26 Baltic St, London EC1Y 0TB.
Tel: 01-253 3456

Wallace Bros Commodities Ltd
108 Fenchurch St, London EC3M 5HP.
Tel: 01-481 8231

Broker Members

S Figgis & Co Ltd
Dunster House, Mincing Lane, London EC3.
Tel: 01-626 3460

Gow Wilson Ltd
6 Lloyd's Ave, London EC3N 3AX.
Tel: 01-481 9771

G W Joynson & Co Ltd
14 Trinity Sq, London EC3N 4ES.
Tel: 01-480 6921

J H Rayner & Co Ltd
Rayner House, 39 Hatton Gdn,
London EC1N 8BX. Tel: 01-242 5491

R J Rouse & Co Ltd
Dunster House, Mincing Lane,
London EC3R 7TA. Tel: 01-626 3064

South Asia Co (London) Ltd
Vintry House, Queen St, London EC4R 1BA.
Tel: 01-248 6385

W Jas & H Thompson (Rubber) Ltd
Ibex House, Minories, London EC3N 1LR.
Tel: 01- 488 1551

E Till & Co Ltd
Corn Exchange Chambers, 2 Seething Lane,
London EC3N 4HB. Tel: 01-626 9212

Wilson, Smithett & Cope Ltd
32 St Mary-at-Hill, London EC3R 8DH.
Tel: 01-623 9333

R Wolff & Co Ltd
Knollys House, 11 Byward St,
London EC3 5ED. Tel: 01-626 8765

The London Grain Futures Market, trading members, as at December 1976

ACLI International Commodity Services Ltd
Plantation House, Fenchurch St,
EC3. Tel: 01-623 5811

Alexanders Partners Ltd
4/7 Chiswell St, London EC1Y 4XH.
Tel: 01-588 3201

Animal Feeds Ltd
3-4 St Andrews Hill, London EC4.
Tel: 01-236 3383

Bache, Halsey & Stuart (London) Ltd
Plantation House, Fenchurch St,
London EC3. Tel: 01-623 4646

Berk Commodities Ltd
Cereal House, 58 Mark Lane, London EC3.
Tel: 01-488 2825

Berry Barclay & Co Ltd
8/13 Chiswell St, London EC1.
Tel: 01-628 4422

E Billington (Commodities) Ltd
Cunard Building, Liverpool L3 1EL
Tel: 051-236 1222

Billington Group London Office
4 Cow Cross St, London EC1.
Tel: 01-253 3113

Blood Holman & Co Ltd
28 Queen Sq, Bristol 1. Tel: 0272 22392
1 Fenchurch Buildings, Fenchurch St,
London EC3M 5HR. Tel: 01-488 4236

BOCM Silcock Ltd
St Bridget's House, Bridewell Place,
London EC4P 4BP. Tel: 01-353 7474

Bunge & Co Ltd
Bunge House, St Mary Axe,
London EC3A 8AT. Tel: 01-283 3429

Coley & Harper Ltd
14 Creechurch Lane, London EC3A 5AY.
Tel: 01-283 6198

Commodity Analysis Ltd
194/200 Bishopsgate, London EC2M 4PE.
Tel: 01-283 6767

Continental (London) Ltd
Creechurch House, Creechurch Lane,
London EC3A 5DR. Tel: 01-283 4222

Cook International Commodities (UK) Ltd
Marine Engineers Memorial Building,
18 London St, London EC3R 7JP.
Tel: 01-709 8871

Dalgety International Trading Ltd
The Corn Exchange Building, 52 Mark Lane,
London EC3R 7NE. Tel: 01-709 9701

J Darling Proprietary Ltd
8/13 Chiswell St, London EC1.
Tel: 01-638 8613

Drexel Burnham & Co Ltd
Winchester House, 77 London Wall,
London EC2N 1BE. Tel: 01-628 2491

Louis Dreyfus & Co Ltd
City Gate House, 39/45 Finsbury Sq,
London EC2A 1QA. Tel: 01-628 9600

Eurocommodities Ltd
18/19 Fish Street Hill, London EC3R 6BY.
Tel: 01-283 7642

European Grain & Shipping Ltd
16 Finsbury Circus, London EC2M 7BY.
Tel: 01-628 9844

Eurograin (GB) Ltd
23/25 Eastcheap, London EC3.
Tel: 01-626 0076

F Fehr & Co Ltd
Prince Rupert House, 64 Queen St,
London EC4R 1ER. Tel: 01-248 5066

L M Fischel & Co Ltd
Dunster House, 37 Mincing Lane,
London EC3R 7QQ. Tel: 01-626 9692

C Goldschmidt Ltd
61/62 Crutched Friars, London EC3N 2DL.
Tel: 01-480 7631

Goldschmidt & Charteris Ltd
Dunster House, Mincing Lane,
London EC3. Tel: 01-623 2621

Granfin Trading Ltd
City Gate House, Finsbury Sq, London EC2.
Tel: 01-628 9600

H Hentz & Co Ltd
Gillett House, 55 Basinghall St,
London EC2V 5ED. Tel: 01-606 3803

Holco Trading Co Ltd
8 Lloyds Ave, London EC3N 3AB.
Tel: 01-480 7951

A A Hooker & Co Ltd
24 St Mary Axe, London EC3.
Tel: 01-283 9681

Howle Marketing Ltd
Wrinehill Mill, Betley, Nr Crewe, Cheshire.
Tel: 09362-367
110 Tooley St, London SE1 2TH.
Tel: 01-403 0611

Inter Commodities Ltd
29/31 Mitre St, London EC3.
Tel: 01-283 6691

T A Jones & Co Ltd
Cotts House, 25/29 Camomile St,
London EC3P 3AJ. Tel: 01-283 3188

G W Joynson & Co Ltd
14 Trinity Sq, London EC3N 4BN.
Tel: 01-480 6921

Macleod Frentzel Ltd
Corn Exchange Chambers, 2 Seething Lane,
London EC3N 4EP. Tel: 01-481 1993

G J McCaul (Overseas) Ltd
Kempson House, 35/37 Camomile St,
London EC3A 7AJ. Tel: 01-283 1255

Nitrovit Ltd
Brook House, 48 Upper Thames St,
London EC4V 3DE. Tel: 01-248 5266

J Oates Ltd
18/19 Fish Street Hill, London EC3R 6BY.
Tel: 01-623 7301

H W Peabody Grain Ltd
St Clare House, 28/35 Minories,
London EC3N 1DA. Tel: 01-481 1288

Powell Union Produce Ltd
71 St Mary Axe, London EC3A 5AX.
Tel: 01-283 3202

Rayner Hatton Garden Ltd
Rayner House, 39 Hatton Gdn,
London EC1N 8BX. Tel: 01-242 3377

R H M Flour Mills Ltd
R H M Centre, PO Box 551,
152 Grosvenor Rd, London SW1V 3JL.
Tel: 01-821 1444

J Richardson & Sons (Overseas) Ltd
Lowndes House, 1/9 City Rd,
London EC1Y 1BH. Tel: 01-638 8501

T G Roddick & Co Ltd
India Building, Water St, Liverpool L2 0RA.
Tel: 051-227 4561
Europe House, World Trade Centre,
London E1 9AA. Tel: 01-480 7371

P Rominger & Co
Capel House, 54 New Broad St, London EC2.
Tel: 01-638 0245

Schwarz & Co (Grain) Ltd
Battlesbridge House, 87/89 Tooley St,
London SE1. Tel: 01-407 6221

Shipping & Produce Co Ltd
62/63 Queen St, London EC4.
Tel: 01-248 0521

R Simon & Co Ltd
5 Philpot Lane, London EC3M 8AH.
Tel: 01-623 0041

R T Smyth & Co Ltd
3 Lloyds Ave, London EC3N 3DS.
Tel: 01-480 6699

Spillers Grain & Feed Ltd
St Giles House, 1 Drury Lane,
London WC2B 5RD. Tel: 01-836 8030

Thompson, Lloyd & Ewart
Sir John Lyon House, 5 High Timber St,
Upper Thames St, London EC4V 3LU.
Tel: 01-248 6631

Tradax, England, Ltd
Kempson House, 35/37 Camomile St,
London EC3A 7AT. Tel: 01-283 5272

Upper Thames Commodities Ltd
10-12 Creechurch Lane, London EC3A 5AD.
Tel: 01-283 6211

Usborne & Son (London) Ltd
24 St Mary Axe, London EC3.
Tel: 01-283 6141

Wallace Bros Commodities Ltd
108 Fenchurch St, London EC3M 5HP.
Tel: 01-481 8231

Whitson, Nielson & Francis Ltd
63/65 Crutched Friars, London EC3N 2DN.
Tel: 01-488 3656

G Wills & Sons Ltd
Epworth House, 25/35 City Rd,
London EC1Y 1AN. Tel: 01-628 2535

E Willstaedt Ltd
50 Mark Lane, London EC3.
Tel: 01-709 9144

The London Metal Exchange, trading members, as at December 1976

Amalgamated Metal Trading Ltd
2 Metal Exchange Buildings, Leadenhall Ave,
London EC3V 1LD

Ametalco Trading Ltd
29 Gresham St, London EC2V 7DA

Anglo Chemcial Metals Ltd
Gillett House, 55 Basinghall St,
London EC2V 5HN

Associated Lead Manufacturers Ltd
Clements House, 14-18 Gresham St,
London EC2P 2JS

H Bath & Son Ltd
Market Buildings, Mincing Lane,
London EC3R 7EE

Billiton-Enthoven Metals Ltd
Colonial House, Mincing Lane,
London EC3 7EE

Brandeis Goldschmidt & Co Ltd
30 Gresham St, London EC2P 2EB

Cerro Metals Ltd
66 Warnford Court, Throgmorton St,
London EC2

Cominco (UK) Ltd
4 Coleman St, London EC2R 5AX

The Commercial Metal Co Ltd
Plantation House, Mincing Lane,
London EC3M 3DX

Continental Ore Europe Ltd
5 Whittington Ave, London EC3V 1LJ

C Davis (Metal Brokers) Ltd
Whittington House, Whittington Ave,
London EC3V 1LE

Entores (Metal Brokers) Ltd
79-83 Chiswell St, London EC2Y 9BA

Gerald Metals Ltd
Europe House, World Trade Centre,
St Catherine by the Tower, London E1

Gill & Duffus (Metals) Ltd
St Dunstan's House, 201 Borough High St,
London SE1 1HY

Intsel Ltd
Worldwide House, 25-29 Worship St,
London EC2A 2DT

Leopold Lazarus Ltd
Gotch House, 20-34 St Bride St,
London EC4A 4DL

Lonconex Ltd
29 Mincing Lane, London EC3R 7EU

Maclaine Watson & Co Ltd
2-4 Idol Lane, London EC3R 5DL

Metallgesellschaft Ltd
19-21 Gt Tower St, London EC3R 5AQ

Metdist Ltd
Barrington House, 59-67 Gresham St,
London EC2V 7EY

Philipp & Lion
Chile House, 20 Ropemaker St,
London EC2Y 9AR

J H Rayner (Mincing Lane) Ltd
50 Mark Lane, London EC3R 7RJ

Tennant Trading Metals Ltd
9 Harp Lane, Lower Thames St,
London EC3R 6DR

H P Thompson & Sons Ltd
8 Lloyds Ave, London EC3N 3AB

Triland Metals Ltd
Bow Bells House, Bread St,
London EC4M 9BQ

Wilson, Smithett & Cope Ltd
32 St Mary-at-Hill, London EC3R 8DH

R Wolff & Co Ltd
Knollys House, 11 Byward Street,
London EC3R 5ED

The London Soya Bean Meal Futures Market, trading members, as at December 1976

ACLI International Commodity Services Ltd
Plantation House, Fenchurch St,
London EC3M 3DX. Tel: 01-623 5811

Anscom Brokers Ltd
6 Lloyds Ave, London EC3N 3AX.
Tel: 01-481 4711

Bache Halsey Stuart (London) Ltd
Plantation House, Fenchurch St,
London EC3M 3EP. Tel: 01-623 4646

BOCM Silcock Ltd
St Bridget's House, Bridewell Place,
London EC4P 4BP. Tel: 01-353 7474

Coley & Harper Ltd
14 Creechurch Lane, London EC3A 5AY.
Tel: 01-283 6198

Commodity Analysis Ltd
194/200 Bishopsgate, London EC2M 4PE.
Tel: 01-283 6767

P Cremer (UK) Ltd
43 London Wall, London EC2M 5TB.
Tel: 01-628 0276

C Czarnikow Ltd
66 Mark Lane, London EC3P 3EA.
Tel: 01-480 6677

Dalgety International Trading Ltd
52 Mark Lane, London EC3R 7SR.
Tel: 01-709 9701

Drexel Burnham & Co Ltd
77 London Wall, London EC2P 2HX.
Tel: 01- 628 2491

European Grain & Shipping Ltd
16 Finsbury Circus, London EC2M 7BY.
Tel: 01-628 9844

L M Fischel & Co Ltd
Dunster House, Mincing Lane,
London EC3R 7SY. Tel: 01-626 9692

F Fehr & Co Ltd
64 Queen St, London EC4R 1ER.
Tel: 01-248 5066

Goldschmidt & Charteris Ltd
Dunster House, Mincing Lane,
London EC3R 7BL. Tel: 01-623 2621

H Hentz & Co Ltd
Gillett House, 55 Basinghall St,
London EC2V 5ED. Tel: 01-606 3803

Holco Trading Co Ltd
8 Lloyds Ave, London EC3N 3AB.
Tel: 01-480 7951

G W Joynson & Co Ltd
14 Trinity Sq, London EC3N 4ES.
Tel: 01-480 6921

Lewis & Peat (Produce) Ltd
32 St Mary-at-Hill, London EC3R 8DH.
Tel: 01-623 3111

Macleod Frentzel Ltd
2 Seething Lane, London EC3N 4EP.
Tel: 01-481 1993

Pacol Ltd
47 Mark Lane, London EC3R 7QX.
Tel: 01-623 1000

Powell Union Produce Ltd
71 St Mary Axe, London EC3A 8AX.
Tel: 01-283 3202

Rayner Hatton Garden Ltd
39 Hatton Gdn, London EC1N 8BX.
Tel: 01-242 3377

A Reinstein (London) Ltd
24 Bedford Sq, London WC1 3HH.
Tel: 01-481 1993

T G Roddick & Co Ltd
Europe House, World Trade Centre,
London E1 9AA. Tel: 01-480 7371

Sime Darby Commodities Ltd
Royal Mail House, 19 Leadenhall St,
London EC3V 1NN. Tel: 01-626 9822

W V B (Brokers) Ltd
64 Queen St, London EC4R 1AD.
Tel: 01-248 0951

The London Vegetable Oil Terminal Market Association, trading members, as at December 1976

ACLI International Commodities Ltd
Plantation House, Mincing Lane,
London EC3

Bache Halsey Stuart (London) Ltd
Plantation House, Fenchurch St,
London EC3M 3EP

Colombo Commercial Co (Produce) Ltd
21 Mincing Lane, London EC3

Commodity Analysis Ltd
194-200 Bishopsgate, London EC2N 4PE

Continental (London) Ltd
Creechurch House, Creechurch Lane,
London EC3

C Czarnikow Ltd
PO Box 602, 66 Mark Lane,
London EC3R 7QX

Dalgety International Trading Ltd
52 Mark Lane, London EC3

Drexel Burnham & Co Ltd
Winchester House, 77 London Wall,
London EC2

Eurocommodities Ltd
18/19 Fish Street Hill, London EC3R 6BY

F Fehr & Co Ltd
Prince Rupert House, 64 Queen St,
London EC4 1ER

L M Fischel & Co Ltd
Dunster House, Mincing Lane, London EC3

F Fontahnaz & Co Ltd
Fontannaz House, 19 Earl Street,
London EC2A 2AH

D Geddes & Son Ltd
Norden House, Basingview, Basingstoke,
Hampshire RG21 2NG

Goldschmidt & Charteris Ltd
Dunster House, Mincing Lane,
London EC3R 7BL

M Golodetz,
29 Mincing Lane, London EC3R 7EU

Holco Trading Co Ltd
8 Lloyds Ave, London EC3N 3AB

G W Joynson & Co Ltd
14 Trinity Sq, London EC3N 4BN

Lewis & Peat (Produce) Ltd
32 St Mary-at-Hill, London EC3R 8DH

E D & F Man (Produce) Ltd
Colonial House, Mincing Lane,
London EC3R 7DS

Merrill Lynch, Pierce Fenner & Smith
(Brokers & Dealers) Ltd
Merrill Lynch House, 3 Newgate St,
London EC1A 7DA

Moutafian Commodities Ltd
2-4 Eastcheap, London EC3M 1AL

Overseas Buyers Ltd
Bath House, Holborn Viaduct,
London EC1A 2AP

Pacol Ltd
47 Mark Lane, London EC3R 7QX

The Produce Brokers Co Ltd
Produce House, Wickham Court Rd,
West Wickham, Kent

J H Rayner (Mincing Lane) Ltd
50 Mark Lane, London EC3R 7RJ

T G Roddick & Co Ltd
Europe House, World Trade Centre,
London E1 9AA

R J Rouse & Co Ltd
Dunster House, Mincing Lane, London EC3

SNW Commodities Ltd
Rayner House, 39 Hatton Gdn,
London EC1N 8BX

Shearson Hayden Stone Ltd
Gillett House, 55 Basinghall St,
London EC2V 5ED

Sime Darby Commodities Ltd
19 Leadenhall St, London EC3

Trading Co Guntzel & Schumacher
(England) Ltd
Hambro House, Vintner's Place,
London EC4V 3BA

Vantol Ltd
29 Mincing Lane, London EC3

R Wolff & Co Ltd
Knollys House, 1 Byward St,
London EC3R 5ED

Woodhouse, Drake & Carey Ltd
Three Quays, Tower Hill, London EC3

The London Wool Terminal Market Association, trading members, as at December 1976

ACLI International Commodity Services Ltd
Plantation House, Fenchurch St,
London EC3M 3DX

Bache Halsey Stuart (London) Ltd
Plantation House (Block A), Fenchurch St,
London EC3M 3EP

Bailey, Herbaux & Masurel & Co Ltd
38 Piccadilly, Bradford BD1 3LN

Chapman Modiano & Co Ltd
80 Clifton St, London EC2A 4RS

Commodity Analysis Ltd
194/200 Bishopsgate, London EC2M 4PE

A Dewavrin Ltd
ADL House, 14 Mill St, Bradford BD1 4AE

Drexel Burnham & Co Ltd
Winchester House, 77 London Wall,
London EC2P 2HX

Gardner Lohmann Ltd
Pountney Hill House, 6 Laurence Pountney
Hill, London EC4R 0BL

Sir James Hill & Sons Ltd
Melbourne Mills, Dalton Lane,
Keighley BD21 4LQ

Hirsch Son & Rhodes (Futures) Ltd
Cumberland House, Greenside Lane,
Bradford BD8 9RX

G W Joynson & Co Ltd
14 Trinity Sq, London EC3N 4BN

Kanematsu-Gosho (Commodities) Ltd
Tribute House, 120 Moorgate,
London EC2P 2JY

Kreglinger & Masurel (Futures) Ltd
Chronicle House, 72/78 Fleet St,
London EC4Y 1HY

Merrill Lynch Pierce, Fenner & Smith
(Brokers & Dealers) Ltd
Merrill Lynch House, 3 Newgate St,
London EC1A 7DA

Prouvost & Lefebvre Ltd
National House, Sunbridge Rd,
Bradford BD1 2QQ

R J Rouse & Co Ltd
Dunster House, Mincing Lane,
London EC2R 7TH

SNW Commodities Ltd
Rayner House, 39 Hatton Gdn,
London EC1N 8BX

Wallace Bros (Commodities) Ltd
108 Fenchurch St, London EC3M 5HP

Tea Brokers Association of London, trading members, as at December 1976

Gow, White
84 Middlesex St, London E1 7EZ

Haines & Co (London) Ltd
Sir John Lyon House, Upper Thames St,
London EC4V 3LR

T Cumberlege & Inskipp
Sir John Lyon House, Upper Thames St,
London EC4V 3LD

Thompson, Lloyd & Ewart
Sir John Lyon House, Upper Thames St,
London EC4V 3LU

Wilson, Smithett & Co
Sir John Lyon House, Upper Thames St,
London EC4V 3LS

The United Terminal Sugar Market Association, trading members, as at December 1976

Allfrey P
Woodhouse, Drake & Carey Ltd
Three Quays, Tower Hill, London EC3R 6EP

Burt D L
Wilson, Smithett & Cope Ltd
32 St Mary-at-Hill, London EC3R 8DH

Campbell-Gray C D
G W Joynson & Co Ltd
14 Trinity Sq, London EC3N 4BN

The Earl of Carrick
Maclaine, Watson & Co Ltd
46 Berkely Sq, London W1X 5DD

Clatworthy A E
E D & F Man Ltd
30-34 Mincing Lane, London EC3R 7DS

Clatworthy D G
E D & F Man Ltd
30-34 Mincing Lane, London EC3R 7DS

Dumas T C C
E D & F Man Ltd
30-34 Mincing Lane, London EC3R 7DS

Evans G D
E Bailey Sugar Ltd
18 London St, London EC3R 7SX

Fischel J R
L M Fischel (Sugar) Ltd
Dunster House, Mincing Lane,
London EC3R 7SY

Fisher R E
Woodhouse, Drake & Carey Ltd
Three Quays, Tower Hill, London EC3R 6EP

Gittins M B
Wallace Bros Commodities Ltd
108 Fenchurch St, London EC3M 3DB

Golodetz A, Golodetz M
29 Mincing Lane, London EC3R 7EU

Harcourt D St C
C Czarnikow Ltd
PO Box 602, 66 Mark Lane,
London EC3P 3EA

Harding A J S
Goldschmidt & Charteris Ltd
Dunster House, Mincing Lane,
London EC3R 7BL

Hecks J P
R. Anderson & Co Ltd
Three Quays, Tower Hill, London EC3R 6EP

Johnson E H
M Golodetz Ltd
29 Mincing Lane, London EC3R 7EU

Laughlin A C D
E A de Pass & Co Ltd
58 Borough High St, London SE1 1XF

Lawson T
Wilson, Smithett & Cope Ltd
32 St Mary-at-Hill, London EC3R 8DH

Leon G
R Wolff & Co Ltd
11 Byward St, London EC3R 5ED

McFall R G
Jardine Gill & Duffus (UK) Ltd
201 Borough High St, London SE1 1HW

Margulies E S
Margulies (Sugar) Ltd
Berisford House, 50 Mark Lane,
London EC3R 7QS

Miller C M
C Czarnikow Ltd
PO Box 602, 66 Mark Lane,
London EC3P 3EA

Moutafian A N
Moutafian Commodities Ltd
2-4 Eastcheap, London EC3M 1AL

Oxley N L
B L Oxley & Co Ltd
29 Mincing Lane, London EC3R 7EE

Schenk A P
C Czarnikow Ltd
PO Box 602, 66 Mark Lane,
London EC3P 3EA

Scrase A W E
R J Rouse & Co Ltd
Dunster House, Mincing Lane,
London EC3R 7TH

Stone M J C
E D & F Man Ltd
30-34 Mincing Lane, London EC3R 7DS

Taylor R J
Woodhouse, Drake & Carey Ltd
Three Quays, Tower Hill, London EC3R 6EP

Weldon M
Cocoa Merchants Ltd
Plantation House, Rood Lane,
London EC3M 3HX

Whiting D A
Comfin (Commodity & Finance) Co Ltd
18 London St, London EC3R 7JP

United States: *Kansas City*
The Board of Trade of Kansas City, Missouri, Inc, trading members, as at January 1976

Adams M K
Wolcott & Lincoln Inc
Suite 460, Kansas City Board of Trade Bldg,
Kansas City, MO. Tel: 816-753 6750

Allis C D Jr
L Dreyfus Corp
PO Box 437, Shawnee Mission, KS 66205.
Tel: 913-362 7700

Amstutz D G (President)
Cargill Investor Services Inc
141 West Jackson Blvd, Chicago, IL 60604.
Tel: 312-341 9330

Anderson R J
1210 West 51st St, Kansas City, MO 64112.
Tel: 816-931 7720

Anderson R Z
Suite 239, Kansas City Board of Trade Bldg,
Kansas City, MO. Tel: 816-931 8100

Attebury S L
PO Box 2707, Amarillo, TX 79105.
Tel: 806-335 1639

Balthrop J E (Vice President)
Bunge Corp
PO Box 431, Fort Worth, TX 76101.
Tel: 817-926 7916

Bartlett P D Jr (President)
Bartlett & Co, Grain (inc)
Suite 600, Kansas City Board of Trade Bldg,
Kansas City, MO. Tel: 816-753 6300

Batte R E (Asst Vice President)
Bunge Corp
300 Southwest Blvd, Kansas City, KS 66103.
Tel:913 236 6500

Baumgartner J F (Vice President)
Simonds-Shields-Theis Grain Co Inc
Suite 401, Kansas City Board of Trade Bldg,
Kansas City, MO. Tel: 816-561 4155

Beeson M M (Vice President)
International Multifoods Corp
1200 Multifoods Bldg, Minneapolis,
MN 55402. Tel: 612-339 8444

Beyer P T
General Mills Inc
Suite 363, Kansas City Board of Trade Bldg,
Kansas City, MO. Tel: 816-753 2200

Bisang F A
Midwestern Grain Co, Division of Garnac
Grain Co Inc
Suite 436, Kansas City Board of Trade Bldg,
Kansas City, MO. Tel: 816-753 5464

Bradley C (Vice President)
Kansas City Terminal Elevator Co Inc
Suite 260, Kansas City Board of Trade Bldg,
Kansas City, MO. Tel: 816-931 1762

Brown C A
W M Farmer
Suite 239, Kansas City Board of Trade Bldg,
Kansas City, MO. Tel: 816-931 8100

Brown L A Jr
PO Box 307, Louisburg, KS 66053.
Tel: 816-561 5522

Buckman M S
Far-Mar-Co Inc
Suite 303, Kansas City Board of Trade Bldg,
Kansas City, MO. Tel: 816-756 2050

Burdett, T V
ADM Milling Co Inc
Suite 359, Kansas City Board of Trade Bldg,
Kansas City, MO. Tel: 913-381 7400

Burns W J
Cargill Inc
Suite 565, Kansas City Board of Trade Bldg,
Kansas City, MO. Tel: 816-756 0587

Callier V C
Cook Grain Co Inc
Suite 251, Kansas City Board of Trade Bldg,
Kansas City, MO. Tel: 816-753 5441

Capps J G (Vice President)
Paine, Webber, Jackson & Curtis Inc
208 South LaSalle St, Chicago,IL 60604.
Tel: 313-346 2900

Cartmill R S (Vice President)
Cook Grain Co Inc
Suite 251, Kansas City Board of Trade Bldg,
Kansas City, MO. Tel: 816-753 5441

Cernich E T
Suite 239, Kansas City Board of Trade Bldg,
Kansas City, MO. Tel: 816-931 8100

Cernich T G
E T Cernich
Suite 239, Kansas City Board of Trade Bldg,
Kansas City, MO. Tel: 816-931 8100

Christiansen C (Asst Secretary)
Ralston Purina Co Inc
Suite 249, Kansas City Board of Trade Bldg,
Kansas City, MO. Tel: 816-756 3700

Christopher H
B C Christopher & Co
Suite 100, Kansas City Board of Trade Bldg,
Kansas City, MO. Tel: 816-932 7200

Coleman J C
ContiCommodity Services Inc
Suite 246, Kansas City Board of Trade Bldg,
Kansas City, MO. Tel: 816-753 5544

Collett J H
B C Christopher & Co
Suite 100, Kansas City Board of Trade Bldg,
Kansas City, MO. Tel: 816-932 7100

Cooper B O
Rickel Inc
Suite 430, Kansas City Board of Trade Bldg,
Kansas City, MO. Tel: 816-561 5912

Cottier B O (Executive Vice President)
Bartlett & Co Grain Inc
Suite 600, Kansas City Board of Trade Bldg,
Kansas City, MO. Tel: 816-753 6300

Coughenour J R
Cook Grain Co Inc
Suite 251, Kansas City Board of Trade Bldg,
Kansas City, MO. Tel: 816-753 5441

Cox H A Jr (Vice President)
Reynolds Securities Inc
120 Broadway, New York, NY 10005.
Tel: 212-558 6000

Cramblit A J (Vice President)
Geldermann & Co Inc
141 West Jackson Blvd, Chicago, IL 60604.
Tel: 312-663 0400

Crawford D P
Shay Grain Co Inc
Suite 358, Kansas City Board of Trade Bldg,
Kansas City, MO. Tel: 816-531 5320

Daly P R (Asst Vice President)
Cargill Inc
Suite 565, Kansas City Board of Trade Bldg,
Kansas City, MO. Tel: 816-756 0587

Davidson W E (Vice President)
MFA Commodities Co Inc
Suite 262, Kansas City Board of Trade Bldg,
Kansas City, MO. Tel: 816-753 7475

Davis W R
Myers & Co Inc
Suite 110, Kansas City Board of Trade Bldg,
Kansas City, MO. Tel: 816-931 8517

Dawson R L
Missouri Farmers Association Inc
Suite 262, Kansas City Board of Trade Bldg,
Kansas City, MO. Tel: 816-753 7475

Dean R L (Vice President)
Seaboard Allied Milling Corp
PO Box 19148, Kansas City, MO 64141.
Tel: 816-561 9200

Deeds C N
Shay Grain Co Inc
Suite 358, Kansas City Board of Trade Bldg,
Kansas City, MO. Tel: 816-531 5320

DeGraw G F (Vice President)
Far-Mar-Co Inc
Suite 303, Kansas City Board of Trade Bldg,
Kansas City, MO. Tel: 816-756 2050

Dittmer T H (President)
R E Friedman & Co Inc
222 South Riverside Plaza, Chicago,
IL 60606. Tel: 312-648 1060

Dreiling A R
Far-Mar-Co Inc
Suite 303, Kansas City Board of Trade Bldg,
Kansas City, MO. Tel: 816-756 2050

Edelblute G F
Far-Mar-Co Inc
Suite 303, Kansas City Board of Trade Bldg,
Kansas City, MO. Tel: 816-756 2050

Edwards H C (Chairman of Board)
Dixie Portland Flour Mills Inc
Suite 266, Kansas City Board of Trade Bldg,
Kansas City, MO. Tel: 816-561 5131

Egan E J
The Pillsbury Co Inc
Suite 230, Kansas City Board of Trade Bldg,
Kansas City, MO. Tel: 816-753 1605

Eiszner J R (Vice President)
CPC International Inc
International Plaza, Englewood Cliffs,
NJ 07632. Tel: 201-894 4000

Ellis J F
Continental Grain Co Inc
Suite 310, 4901 Main, Kansas City,
MO 64112. Tel: 816-756 2550

Elsham I E
Cargill Inc
Suite 565, Kansas City Board of Trade Bldg,
Kansas City, MO. Tel: 816-756 0587

Epling H R
Geisel Grain Co Inc
Suite 204, Kansas City Board of Trade Bldg,
Kansas City, MO. Tel: 816-753 4466

Evans S D Sr
Evans Grain Co
PO Box 1388, Salina, KS 67401.
Tel: 913-827 4484

Farley I E
Seaboard Allied Milling Corp
PO Box 19148, Kansas City, MO 64141.
Tel: 816-561 9200

Farmer W Michael
Suite 239, Kansas City Board of Trade Bldg,
Kansas City, MO. Tel: 816-931 8100

Farnen J F (Vice President)
F J Farnen & Co Inc
Suite 501, Kansas City Board of Trade Bldg,
Kansas City, MO. Tel: 816-531 5528

Farnen W W (President)
F J Farnen & Co Inc
Suite 501, Kansas City Board of Trade Bldg,
Kansas City, MO. Tel: 816-531 5528

Felts C B Jr (President)
Garvey Elevators Inc
PO Box 1688, Fort Worth, TX 76101.
Tel: 817-625 1611

Ferguson W E (Chairman of Board)
Thomson & McKinnon Auchincloss
Kohlmeyer Inc
1 New York Plaza, New York NY 10004.
Tel: 212-482 7000

Fink D T
Ralston Purina Co Inc
Suite 249, Kansas City Board of Trade Bldg,
Kansas City, MO. Tel: 816-756 3700

Fisher O E (Vice President)
Topeka Mill & Elevator Co Inc
PO Box 400, Topeka, KS 66601.
Tel: 816-842 6771

FitzPatrick F J
Simonds-Shields-Theis Grain Co Inc
Suite 401, Kansas City Board of Trade Bldg,
Kansas City, MO. Tel: 816-561 4155

Fivian R C (First Vice President)
Bache & Co Inc
141 West Jackson Blvd, Chicago, IL 60604.
Tel: 312-346 4300

Fleming W A
Union Equity Cooperative Exchange Inc
Suite 255, Kansas City Board of Trade Bldg,
Kansas City, MO. Tel: 816-931 6210

Fox W B (President)
C B Fox Co Inc
1620 National Bank of Commerce Bldg,
New Orleans, LA 70112. Tel: 504-524 0782

Franzen R E (Asst Secretary)
Midwestern Grain Co, Division of Garnac
Grain Co Inc
Suite 436, Kansas City Board of Trade Bldg,
Kansas City, MO. Tel: 816-753 5464

Frazier G D (Executive Vice President)
Union Equity Cooperative Exchange Inc
PO Box 3408, Enid OK 73701.
Tel: 405-237 5151

French J C
Kansas City Terminal Elevator Co Inc
Suite 260, Kansas City Board of Trade Bldg,
Kansas City, MO. Tel: 816-931 1762

Frost J A
Continental Grain Co Inc
Suite 310, 4901 Main, Kansas City,
MO 64112. Tel: 816-756 2550

Fullmer J D
Bunge Corp
300 Southwest Blvd, Kansas City KS 66103.
Tel: 913-236 6500

Geisel J S Jr (President)
Geisel Grain Co Inc
Suite 204, Kansas City Board of Trade Bldg,
Kansas City, MO. Tel: 816-753 4466

Gelbort R B (President)
Mayer-Gelbort Inc
141 West Jackson Blvd, Chicago, IL 60604.
Tel: 312-427 1044

Gibson D L (Secretary)
Wolcott & Lincoln Inc
Suite 460, Kansas City Board of Trade Bldg,
Kansas City, MO. Tel: 816-753 6750

Gibson D W (Vice President)
Wolcott & Lincoln Inc
Suite 460, Kansas City Board of Trade Bldg,
Kansas City, MO. Tel: 816-753 6750

Goldschmidt W M (President)
ContiCommodity Services Inc
141 West Jackson Blvd, Chicago, IL 60604.
Tel: 312-786 0800

Goss J L
L Dreyfus Corp
PO Box 437, Shawnee Mission, KS 66205.
Tel: 913-362 7700

Gound J C (Asst Vice President)
Lincoln Commodites Inc
Suite 254, Kansas City Board of Trade Bldg,
Kansas City, MO. Tel: 816-561 0610

Greenman J N (President)
Flour Mills of America Inc
PO Box 511, Fort Worth, TX 76101.
Tel: 817-926 9221

Greer M L
L Dreyfus Corp
PO Box 437, Shawnee Mission, KS 66205.
Tel: 913-362 7700

Gregg J B
Morrison-Gregg-Mitchell Grain Co
Suite 458, Kansas City Board of Trade Bldg,
Kansas City, MO. Tel: 816-931 7756

Gregg J P
Morrison-Gregg-Mitchell Grain Co
Suite 458, Kansas City Board of Trade Bldg,
Kansas City, MO. Tel: 816-931 7756

Gregg S B
Morrison-Gregg-Mitchell Grain Co
Suite 458, Kansas City Board of Trade Bldg,
Kansas City, MO. Tel: 816-931 7756

Grinberg D
Smith Barney, Harris Upham & Co Inc
Suite 234, Kansas City Board of Trade Bldg,
Kansas City, MO. Tel: 816-842 6622

Grismore S D
Clayton Brokerage Co of St Louis Inc
Suite 335, Kansas City Board of Trade Bldg,
Kansas City, MO. Tel: 816-931 8691

Grosch J T (Executive Vice President)
Garvey Commodities Corp
141 West Jackson Blvd, Chicago, IL 60604.
Tel: 312-427 5285

Gundelfinger C J
ADM Milling Co Inc
Suite 255, Kansas City Board of Trade Bldg,
Kansas City, MO. Tel: 816-931 6652

Gwin J D
International Multifoods Corp
Suite 258, Kansas City Board of Trade Bldg,
Kansas City, MO. Tel: 816-931 2875

Hale H D (President)
ADM Milling Co Inc
PO Box 7007, Shawnee Mission, KS 66207.
Tel: 913-381 7400

Halloran E T
Hennessy & Associates
Suite 200, Kansas City Board of Trade Bldg,
Kansas City, MO. Tel: 816-756 3450

Handley A L (Vice President)
Wolcott & Lincoln Inc
Suite 460, Kansas City Board of Trade Bldg,
Kansas City, MO. Tel: 816-753 6750

Harper W H Jr
ContiCommodity Services Inc
Suite 246, Kansas City Board of Trade Bldg,
Kansas City, MO. Tel: 816-753 5544

Harrington J R
General Mills Inc
Suite 363, Kansas City Board of Trade Bldg,
Kansas City, MO. Tel: 816-753 2200

Hartzell R B
Bartlett & Co Grain Inc
Suite 600, Kansas City Board of Trade Bldg,
Kansas City, MO. Tel: 816-753 6300

Heard M M
E T Cernich
Suite 358, Kansas City Board of Trade Bldg,
Kansas City, MO. Tel: 816-753 8462

Heermann K A
The Smoot Grain Co Inc
Suite 359, Kansas City Board of Trade Bldg,
Kansas City, MO. Tel: 816-931 7144

Hesemann H F
Geisel Grain Co Inc
Suite 204, Kansas City Board of Trade Bldg,
Kansas City, MO. Tel: 816-753 4466

Hogan J W (Vice President)
Ralston Purina Co Inc
Checkerboard Sq, St Louis MO 63188.
Tel: 314-982 3335

Holmquist C H (President)
Holmquist Elevator Co Inc
433 Grain Exchange Building, Omaha,
NE 68102. Tel: 402-341 5891

Hoover G L
Checkerboard Grain Co, Division of Ralston
Purina Co Inc
Suite 249, Kansas City Board of Trade Bldg,
Kansas City, MO. Tel: 816-756 3700

House D M
Peavey Co Inc
Suite 273, Kansas City Board of Trade Bldg,
Kansas City, MO. Tel: 816-931 7620

Jensen H N
B C Christopher & Co
Suite 100, Kansas City Board of Trade Bldg,
Kansas City, MO. Tel: 816-932 7107

Johnson G A (President)
Wolcott & Lincoln Inc
Suite 460, Kansas City Board of Trade Bldg,
Kansas City, MO. Tel: 816-753 6750

Johnson L W (President)
L W Johnson Co Inc
Suite 241, Kansas City Board of Trade Bldg,
Kansas City, MO. Tel: 816-561 0772

Johnson R T (Vice President)
L W Johnson Co Inc
Suite 241, Kansas City Board of Trade Bldg,
Kansas City, MO. Tel: 816-561 0772

Johnson W N (Treasurer)
Topeka Mill & Elevator Co Inc
Suite 203, Kansas City Board of Trade Bldg,
Kansas City, MO. Tel: 816-931 6119

Johnson W W (Vice President)
Bartlett and Co Grain Inc
Suite 600, Kansas City Board of Trade Bldg,
Kansas City, MO. Tel: 816-753 6300

Johnston H W
Hennessy & Associates
Suite 200, Kansas City Board of Trade Bldg,
Kansas City, MO. Tel: 816-756 3450

Johnston W R (Vice President)
The Smoot Grain Co Inc
Suite 359, Kansas City Board of Trade Bldg,
Kansas City, MO. Tel: 816-931 7144

Jordan J B (Vice President)
Union Equity Cooperative Exchange Inc
Suite 255, Kansas City Board of Trade Bldg,
Kansas City, MO. Tel: 816-931 6210

Kakinuma S (Vice President)
Mitsui & Co (USA) Inc
200 Park Ave, New York, NY 10017.
Tel: 212-973 4600

Killion D D
B C Christopher & Co
Suite 100, Kansas City Board of Trade Bldg,
Kansas City, MO. Tel: 816-932 7109

Kingan T R
Shay Grain Co Inc
Suite 358, Kansas City Board of Trade Bldg,
Kansas City, MO. Tel: 816-531 5320

Kishida T (Senior Vice President)
Sumitomo Shoji America Inc
345 Park Ave, New York, NY 10022.
Tel: 212-935 7000

Klein J (Senior Vice President)
ACLI International Commodity Services Inc
141 West Jackson Blvd, Chicago IL 60604.
Tel: 312-786 0520

Knadle R D (Vice President)
Bartlett and Co Grain Inc
Suite 600, Kansas City Board of Trade Bldg,
Kansas City, MO. Tel: 816-753 6300

Kovar W R Jr (Asst·Secretary)
Scoular-Bishop of Missouri Inc
439 Grain Exchange Bldg, Omaha,
NE 68102. Tel: 402-342 1656

Kroeger K H
Continental Grain Co Inc
Suite 310, 4901 Main, Kansas City,
MO 64112. Tel: 816-756 2550

Kublin G A
Suite 310, 4901 Main, Kansas City,
MO 64112. Tel: 816-756 2550

Kuehl T F (Vice President)
L Dreyfus Corp
PO Box 437, Shawnee Mission, KS 66205.
Tel: 913-362 7700

Laesch J H
Continental Grain Co Inc
Suite 310, 4901 Main, Kansas City,
MO 64112. Tel: 816-756 2550

Latshaw J (Executive Vice President)
E F Hutton & Co Inc
920 Baltimore Ave, Kansas City, MO 64105.
Tel: 816-221 7800

Leathers L H (Vice President)
Shearson Hayden Stone Inc
767 Fifth Ave, New York, NY 10022.
Tel: 212-350 0500

Lock J P
Bunge Corp
300 Southwest Blvd, Kansas City, KS 66103.
Tel: 913-236 6500

Lyman R E
CPC International Inc
Suite 236, Kansas City Board of Trade Bldg,
Kansas City, MO. Tel: 816-531 4600

Marchand R
Midwestern Grain Co, Division of Garnac
Grain Co Inc
Suite 436, Kansas City Board of Trade Bldg,
Kansas City, MO. Tel: 816-753 5464

Martin R C (Vice President)
United Grain Corp
3628 First National Bank Tower, Portland,
OR 97201. Tel: 503-228 6424

Masters H W (Vice President)
Masters Grain Co Inc
Suite 540, Kansas City Board of Trade Bldg,
Kansas City, MO. Tel: 816-531 9317

Masters S C (President)
Masters Grain Co Inc
Suite 540, Kansas City Board of Trade Bldg,
Kansas City, MO. Tel: 816-531 9317

Matthies S L (Asst Secretary)
General Mills Inc
PO Box 2003, Commerce Station,
Minneapolis, MN 55415. Tel: 612-540 3309

Mayer R J
Hennessy & Associates
141 West Jackson Blvd, Chicago, IL 60604.
Tel: 312-341 0444

McAuliffe J G
General Mills Inc
Suite 363, Kansas City Board of Trade Bldg,
Kansas City, MO. Tel: 816-753 2200

McCoy B C
Checkerboard Grain Co, Division of Ralston
Purina Co Inc
Suite 249, Kansas City Board of Trade Bldg,
Kansas City, MO. Tel: 816-756 3700

McGreevy T J (First Vice President)
Smith Barney, Harris Upham & Co Inc
One Crown Center, 2400 Pershing Rd,
Suite 150, Kansas City, MO 64108.
Tel: 816-842 6622

McIntosh J F
Shay Grain Co Inc
Suite 358, Kansas City Board of Trade Bldg,
Kansas City, MO. Tel: 816-531 5320

McMahon W J (Vice President)
Klecan Grain Co Inc
Suite 235, Kansas City Board of Trade Bldg,
Kansas City, MO. Tel: 816-561 8488

McWhite R B (Vice President)
Peavey Co Inc
730 Second Ave South, Minneapolis,
MN 55402. Tel: 612-370 7660

Meaney J E
Hennessy & Associates
Suite 200, Kansas City Board of Trade Bldg,
Kansas City, MO. Tel: 816-756 3450

Merrill F L (President)
Cereal Food Processors Inc
4901 Main, Suite 218, Kansas City,
MO 64112. Tel: 816-561 4271

Mesker D W (Vice President)
A G Edwards & Sons Inc
One North Jefferson Ave, St Louis,
MO 63103. Tel: 314-289 3000

Middlecamp W J Jr (Vice President)
Merrill Lynch, Pierce, Fenner & Smith Inc
Commerce Tower, Kansas City, MO 64199.
Tel: 816-421 5700

Middlekamp J W
The Pillsbury Co Inc
Suite 230, Kansas City Board of Trade Bldg,
Kansas City, MO. Tel: 816-753 1605

Miller R F (President)
Miller Grain Co Inc
PO Box 1228, Salina, KS 67401.
Tel: 913-827 9311

Mills B D
Cargill Inc
Suite 565, Kansas City Board of Trade Bldg,
Kansas City, MO. Tel: 816-756 0587

Mitchell J B
Morrison-Gregg-Mitchell Grain Co
Suite 458, Kansas City Board of Trade Bldg,
Kansas City, MO. Tel: 816-931 7756

Mooney D B
R Z Anderson
10304 Howe Drive, Leawood, KS 66207.
Tel: 913-649 7547

Morrison R F (Vice President)
ConAgra Inc
200 Kiewit Plaza, Omaha, NE 68131.
Tel: 402-346 8004

Muldrow K (President)
Goodpasture Inc
902 West Broadway, Brownfield, TX 79316.
Tel: 806-637 2541

Mullin M J
International Multifoods Corp
1200 Multifoods Bldg, Minneapolis,
MN 55402. Tel: 612-339 8444

Myers A H Jr (President)
Myers & Co Inc
Suite 110, Kansas City Board of Trade Bldg,
Kansas City, MO. Tel: 816-931 8517

Myers G K L (Vice President)
K X Grain Inc
Suite 110, Kansas City Board of Trade Bldg,
Kansas City, MO. Tel: 816-531 0915

Myers R G (Executive Vice President)
Seaboard Allied Milling Corp
PO Box 19148, Kansas City, MO 64141.
Tel: 816-561 9200

Nelson K E (Vice President)
First MidAmerica Inc
4901 Main, Suite LL 105, Kansas City,
MO 64112. Tel: 816-756 2265

Nichols O H (First Vice President)
Mitchell, Hutchins Inc
Two First National Plaza, Chicago IL 60670.
Tel: 312-782 1700

Overman J E
A S Polonyi Co Inc
2211 West 120th Terr, Leawood, KS 66209.
Tel: 913-381 0835

Payne N S
Morrison-Gregg-Mitchell Grain Co
Suite 458, Kansas City Board of Trade Bldg,
Kansas City, MO. Tel: 816-931 7756

Pease A M
Far-Mar-Co Inc
Suite 303, Kansas City Board of Trade Bldg,
Kansas City, MO. Tel: 816-756 2050

Phariss F M (Executive Vice President)
Producers Grain Corp
PO Box 111, Amarillo, TX 79105.
Tel: 806-374 0331

Pilz C R (Vice President)
Nabisco Inc
PO Box 1002, East Hanover, NJ 07936.
Tel: 201-884 0500

Polonyi A S (President)
A S Polonyi Co Inc
Suite 268, Kansas City Board of Trade Bldg,
Kansas City, MO. Tel: 816-931 6785

Polson C W (Vice President)
Continental Grain Co Inc
Suite 310, 4901 Main, Kansas City,
MO 64112. Tel: 816-756 2550

Putnam E F
Suite 266, Kansas City Board of Trade Bldg,
Kansas City, MO. Tel: 816-531 6458

Ralph W T Jr (Vice President)
Bartlett & Co Grain Inc
Suite 600, Kansas City Board of Trade Bldg,
Kansas City, MO. Tel: 816-753 6300

Ramsland R S (Vice President)
The Quaker Oats Co Inc
Merchandise Mart Plaza, Chicago, IL 60654.
Tel: 312-222 6940

Rentshler D F (Asst Secretary)
A E Staley Manufacturing Co Inc
141 West Jackson Blvd, Chicago, IL 60604.
Tel: 312-427 1691

Richardson G T
Richardson Securities of Canada
One Lombard Place, Winnipeg R3B OY2,
Canada. Tel: 204-988 5858

Rickel E J (President)
Rickel Inc
Suite 430, Kansas City Board of Trade Bldg,
Kansas City, MO. Tel: 816-561 5912

Risko S A
Lincoln Commodities Inc
Suite 254, Kansas City Board of Trade Bldg,
Kansas City, MO. Tel: 816-561 0610

Ritten J P (Vice President)
Louis N Ritten & Co Inc
109 Grain Exchange Building, Minneapolis,
MN 55415. Tel: 612-333 6231

Robins C A
Union Equity Cooperative Exchange Inc
Suite 255, Kansas City Board of Trade Bldg,
Kansas City, MO. Tel: 816-931 6210

Rockwell J H
Suite 245, Kansas City Board of Trade Bldg,
Kansas City, MO. Tel: 816-753 7557

Roddy J W
Peavey Co Inc
Suite 273, Kansas City Board of Trade Bldg,
Kansas City, MO. Tel: 816-931 7620

Romain E D (President)
Romain Grain Co Inc
Suite 240, Kansas City Board of Trade Bldg,
Kansas City, MO. Tel: 816-531 6780

Rothwell B J 2nd (Chairman of Board)
Bay State Milling Co Inc
1776 Heritage Drive, North Quincy,
MA 02171. Tel: 617-328 4400

Sanderson P M
Peavey Co Inc
Suite 273, Kansas City Board of Trade Bldg,
Kansas City, MO. Tel: 816-931 7620

Saunders W B (Vice President)
Cargill
Cargill Bldg, Minneapolis, MN 55402.
Tel: 612-473 8811

Schlunk K H (President)
A C Toepfer Inc
21 West St, New York, NY 10006.
Tel: 212-425 0119

Schmid H R (Executive Vice President)
Midwestern Grain Co, Division of Garnac
Grain Co Inc
Suite 436, Kansas City Board of Trade Bldg,
Kansas City, MO. Tel: 816-753 5464

Schorie J M (Asst Vice President)
Tabor Milling Co Inc
PO Box 12567, North Kansas City,
MO 64116. Tel: 816-221 2005

Schram D C
Missouri Farmers Association Inc
Suite 262, Kansas City Board of Trade Bldg,
Kansas City, MO. Tel: 816-753 7475

Shay D H (President)
Shay Grain Co Inc
Suite 358, Kansas City Board of Trade Bldg,
Kansas City, MO. Tel: 816-531 5320

Shultheiss R (Vice President)
Missouri Farmers Association Inc
Suite 262, Kansas City Board of Trade Bldg,
Kansas City, MO. Tel: 816-753 7475

Sigourney D F (Vice President)
Lincoln Grain Inc
Suite 238, Kansas City Board of Trade Bldg,
Kansas City, MO. Tel: 816-753 2819

Sosland M I (President)
Sosland Press Inc
Suite 650, Kansas City Board of Trade Bldg,
Kansas City, MO. Tel: 816-756 1000

Soukup D A
Lincoln Grain Inc
Suite 238, Kansas City Board of Trade Bldg,
Kansas City, MO. Tel: 816-753 2819

Spaulding S I (Asst Secretary)
Bay State Milling Co Inc
Suite 204, Kansas City Board of Trade Bldg,
Kansas City, MO. Tel: 816-561 8338

Spielman J M (Vice President)
Merrill Lynch, Pierce, Fenner & Smith Inc
141 West Jackson Blvd, Chicago, IL 60604.
Tel: 312-446 5036

Strongin P N
Bartlett & Co Grain Inc
Suite 600, Kansas City Board of Trade Bldg,
Kansas City, MO. Tel: 816-753 6300

Stucky R R (Executive Vice President)
Garvey Elevators Inc
PO Box 1948, Hutchinson, KS 67501.
Tel: 316-662 3339

Sudduth W W
Suite 245, Kansas City Board of Trade Bldg,
Kansas City, MO. Tel: 816-753 7557

Swisher C H Jr
ADM Milling Co Inc
Suite 359, Kansas City Board of Trade Bldg,
Kansas City, MO. Tel: 816-381 7400

Teetor N L
Far-Mar-Co Inc
Suite 303, Kansas City Board of Trade Bldg,
Kansas City, MO. Tel: 816-756 2050

Theis S O (Asst Vice President)
Simonds-Shields-Theis Grain Co Inc
Suite 401, Kansas City Board of Trade Bldg,
Kansas City, MO. Tel: 816-561 4155

Theis W C (President)
Simonds-Shields-Theis Grain Co Inc
Suite 401, Kansas City Board of Trade Bldg,
Kansas City, MO. Tel: 816-561 4155

Tominaga T (President)
Toshoku America Inc
551 Fifth Ave, New York, NY 10017.
Tel: 212-661 5400

Uhlmann R H (Chairman of Board)
Standard Milling Co Inc
1009 Central St, Kansas City, MO 64105.
Tel: 816-221 8200

Umbert E M
Continental Grain Co Inc
Suite 310, 4901 Main, Kansas City,
MO 64112. Tel: 816-756 2550

Vannerson F L Sr (Vice President)
Commodities Corp
Mount Lucas Rd, Princeton, NJ 08540.
Tel: 609-924 6500

Vetsch K (Vice President)
Midwestern Grain Co, Division of Garnac
Grain Co Inc
Suite 436, Kansas City Board of Trade Bldg,
Kansas City, MO. Tel: 816-753 5464

Voth G (Executive Vice President)
Far-Mar-Co Inc
PO Box 1667, Hutchinson, KS 67501.
Tel: 316-663 3321

Wallin W R (Vice President)
The Pillsbury Co Inc
608 Second Ave South, Minneapolis,
MN 55402. Tel: 612-330 5254

Welsh J L III
Cook Grain Co Inc
Suite 251, Kansas City Board of Trade Bldg,
Kansas City, MO. Tel: 816-753 5441

Wheeler E O (President)
Wheeler Bros Grain Co Inc
PO Box 29, Watonga, OK 73772.
Tel: 405-623 7223

Wholf M E
Bunge Corp
300 Southwest Blvd, Kansas City, KS 66103.
Tel: 913-236 6500

Willoughby S L
B C Christopher & Co
Suite 100, Kansas City Board of Trade Bldg,
Kansas City, MO. Tel: 816-932 7105

Witham L R
Far-Mar-Co Inc
Suite 303, Kansas City Board of Trade Bldg,
Kansas City, MO. Tel: 816-756 2050

Withrow R M
Lamson Bros & Co
111 West Jackson Blvd, Chicago, IL 60604.
Tel: 312-435 4700

Wolcott C D
Cook Grain Co Inc
Suite 251, Kansas City Board of Trade Bldg,
Kansas City, MO. Tel: 816-753 5441

Wright T B (Vice President)
Ross Industries Inc
PO Box 2696, Wichita, KS 67201.
Tel: 316-267 2281

Young, E J Jr (Vice President)
Clayton Brokerage Co of St Louis Inc
7701 Forsyth Blvd, Clayton, MO 63105.
Tel: 314-727 8000

*Firms and Corporations and Individuals who
do business in their own names*

ACLI International Commodity Services Inc
Chicago, IL 60604

ADM Milling Co Inc
PO Box 7007, Shawnee Mission, KS 66207

Anderson R J
1210 West 51st St, Kansas City, MO 64112

Anderson R Z
Suite 239, Kansas City Board of Trade Bldg,
Kansas City, MO.

Attebury S L
Amarillo, TX 79105

Bache & Co Inc
Chicago, IL 60604

Bartlett & Co Grain Inc
Suite 600, Kansas City Board of Trade Bldg,
Kansas City, MO.

Bay State Milling Co Inc
North Quincy, MA 02171
Local Address: Suite 204, Kansas City Board
Board of Trade Bldg, Kansas City, MO

Brown L A Jr
PO Box 307, Louisburg KS 66053

Bunge Corp
Fort Worth, TX 76101
Local Address: 300 Southwest Blvd,
Kansas City, KS 66103

CPC International Inc
Englewood Cliffs, NJ 07632
Local Address: Suite 236, Kansas City
Board of Trade Bldg, Kansas City, MO

Cargill Inc
Minneapolis, MN 55402
Local Address: Suite 565, Kansas City
Board of Trade Bldg, Kansas City, MO

Cargill Investor Services Inc
Chicago, IL 60604

Cereal Food Processors Inc
Suite 218, 4901 Main, Kansas City,
MO 64112

Cernich E T
Suite 239, Kansas City Board of Trade Bldg,
Kansas City, MO

Checkerboard Grain Co, Division of Ralston
Purina Co Inc
Suite 249, Kansas City Board of Trade Bldg,
Kansas City, MO

B C Christopher & Co
Suite 100, Kansas City Board of Trade Bldg,
Kansas City, MO

Clayton Brokerage Co of St Louis Inc
Clayton MO 63105
Local Address: Suite 335, Kansas City
Board of Trade Bldg, Kansas City, MO

Commodities Corp
Princeton, NJ 08540

ConAgra Inc
Omaha, NE 68131

ContiCommodity Services Inc
Chicago, IL 60604
Local Address: Suite 246, Kansas City
Board of Trade Building, Kansas City, MO

Continental Grain Co Inc
Suite 310, 4901 Main, Kansas City,
MO 64112

Cook Grain Co Inc
Suite 251, Kansas City Board of Trade Bldg,
Kansas City, MO

Dixie Portland Flour Mills Inc
Suite 266, Kansas City Board of Trade Bldg,
Kansas City, MO

L Dreyfus Corp
PO Box 437, Shawnee Mission, KS 66205

A G Edwards & Sons Inc
St Louis, MO 63103

Evans Grain Co
Salina, KS 67401

Far-Mar-Co Inc
Hutchinson, KS 67501
Local Address: Suite 303, Kansas City
Board of Trade Bldg, Kansas City, MO

Farmer W Michael
Suite 239, Kansas City Board of Trade Bldg,
Kansas City, MO

Farmer Winfried M
Suite 239, Kansas City Board of Trade Bldg,
Kansas City, MO

F J Farnen & Co Inc
Suite 501, Kansas City Board of Trade Bldg,
Kansas City, MO

First MidAmerica Inc
Suite LL 105, 4901 Main, Kansas City,
MO 64112

Flour Mills of America Inc
Fort Worth, TX 76101

C B Fox Co
New Orleans, LA 70112

R E Friedman & Co
Chicago, IL 60606

Garvey Commodities Corp
Chicago, IL 60604

Garvey Elevators Inc
Hutchinson, KS 67501
Fort Worth, TX 76101

Geisel Grain Co Inc
Suite 204, Kansas City Board of Trade Bldg,
Kansas City, MO

Geldermann & Co Inc
Chicago, IL 60604

General Mills Inc
Minneapolis, MN 55415
Local Address: Suite 363, Kansas City
Board of Trade Bldg, Kansas City, MO

Goodpasture Inc
Brownfield, TX 79316

Hennessy & Associates
Chicago, IL 60604
Local Address: Suite 200, Kansas City
Board of Trade Bldg, Kansas City, MO

Holmquist Elevator Co Inc
Omaha, NE 68102

E F Hutton & Co Inc
920 Baltimore Ave, Kansas City, MO 64105

International Multifoods Corp
Minneapolis, MN 55402
Local Address: Suite 258, Kansas City
Board of Trade Building, Kansas City, MO

L W Johnson Co Inc
Suite 241, Kansas City Board of Trade Bldg,
Kansas City, MO

K X Grain Inc
Suite 110, Kansas City Board of Trade Bldg,
Kansas City, MO

Kansas City Terminal Elevator Co Inc
Suite 260, Kansas City Board of Trade Bldg,
Kansas City, MO

Klecan Grain Co Inc
Suite 235, Kansas City Board of Trade Bldg,
Kansas City, MO

Kublin G A
4901 Main, Kansas City, MO 64112

Lamson Bros & Co
Chicago, IL 60604

Lincoln Commodities Inc
Suite 254, Kansas City Board of Trade Bldg,
Kansas City, MO

Lincoln Grain Inc
Suite 238, Kansas City Board of Trade Bldg,
Kansas City, MO

MFA Commodities Co Inc
Suite 262, Kansas City Board of Trade Bldg,
Kansas City, MO

Masters Grain Co Inc
Suite 540, Kansas City Board of Trade Bldg,
Kansas City, MO

Mayer-Gelbort Inc
Chicago, IL 60604

Merrill Lynch, Pierce, Fenner & Smith Inc
Chicago, IL 60604
Kansas City, MO 64199

Midwestern Grain Co, Division of Garnac
Grain Co Inc
Suite 436, Kansas City Board of Trade Bldg,
Kansas City, MO

Miller Grain Co Inc
Salina, KS 67401

Missouri Farmers Association Inc
Suite 262, Kansas City Board of Trade Bldg,
Kansas City, MO

Mitchell, Hutchins Inc
Chicago, IL 60670

Mitsui & Co (USA) Inc
New York, NY 10017

Morrison-Gregg-Mitchell Grain Co
Suite 458, Kansas City Board of Trade Bldg,
Kansas City, MO

Myers & Co Inc
Suite 110, Kansas City Board of Trade Bldg,
Kansas City, MO

Nabisco Inc
East Hanover, NJ 07936

Paine, Webber, Jackson & Curtis Inc
Chicago, IL 60604

Peavey Co Inc
Minneapolis, MN 55402
Local Address: Suite 273, Kansas City
Board of Trade Bldg, Kansas City, MO

The Pillsbury Co Inc
Minneapolis, MN 55402
Local Address: Suite 230, Kansas City
Board of Trade Building, Kansas City, MO

A S Polonyi Co Inc
Suite 268, Kansas City Board of Trade Bldg,
Kansas City, MO

Producers Grain Corp
Amarillo, TX 79105

Putnam E F
Suite 266, Kansas City Board of Trade Bldg,
Kansas City, MO

The Quaker Oats Co Inc
Chicago, IL 60654

Ralston Purina Co Inc
St Louis, MO 63188
Local Address: Suite 249, Kansas City
Board of Trade Bldg, Kansas City, MO

Reynolds Securities Inc
New York, NY 10005

Richardson Securities of Canada
Winnipeg, Canada

Rickel Inc
Suite 430, Kansas City Board of Trade Bldg,
Kansas City, MO

L N Ritten & Co Inc
Minneapolis, MN 55415

Rockwell J H
Suite 245, Kansas City Board of Trade Bldg,
Kansas City, MO

Romain Grain Co Inc
Suite 240, Kansas City Board of Trade Bldg,
Kansas City, MO

Ross Industries Inc
Wichita, KS 67201

Scoular-Bishop of Missouri Inc
Omaha, NE 68102

Seaboard Allied Milling Corp
PO Box 19148, Kansas City, MO 64141

Shay Grain Co Inc
Suite 358, Kansas City Board of Trade Bldg,
Kansas City, MO

Shearson Hayden Stone Inc
New York, NY 10022

Simonds-Shields-Theis Grain Co Inc
Suite 401, Kansas City Board of Trade Bldg,
Kansas City, MO

Smith Barney, Harris Upham & Co Inc
2400 Pershing Rd, Suite 150, Kansas City,
MO 64108

The Smoot Grain Co Inc
Suite 359, Kansas City Board of Trade Bldg,
Kansas City, MO

Sosland Press Inc
Suite 650, Kansas City Board of Trade Bldg,
Kansas City, MO

A E Staley Manufacturing Co Inc
Chicago, IL 60604

Standard Milling Co Inc
1009 Central St, Kansas City, MO 64105

Sudduth W W
Suite 245, Kansas City Board of Trade Bldg,
Kansas City, MO

Sumitomo Shoji America Inc
New York, NY 10022

Tabor Milling Co Inc
PO Box 12567, North Kansas City, MO

Thomson & McKinnon Auchincloss
Kohlmeyer Inc
New York, NY 10004

A C Toepfer Inc
New York, NY 10006

Topeka Mill & Elevator Co Inc
Topeka, KS 66601
Local Address: Suite 203, Kansas City
Board of Trade Bldg, Kansas City, MO

Toshoku America Inc
New York, NY 10017

Union Equity Cooperative Exchange Inc
Enid, OK 73701
Local Address: Suite 255, Kansas City
Board of Trade Building, Kansas City, MO

United Grain Corp
Portland, OR 97201

Wheeler Bros Grain Co Inc
Watonga, OK 73772

Wolcott & Lincoln Inc
Suite 460, Kansas City Board of Trade Bldg,
Kansas City, MO

Minneapolis:
**Minneapolis Grain Exchange, trading
members, as at October 1976**
*Unless City or Town is specified addresses
are Minneapolis*

Abbott R E
ContiCommodity Services Inc, subsidiary
Continental Grain Co
715 Grain Exchange

Ackerman F F
Thompson Farmers Cooperative Elevator Co
Thompson, ND

Adams D R
Farmers Union Grain Terminal Association
1667 North Snelling, St Paul, MN

Ainsworth M C
International Multifood Corp
1200 Multifoods Bldg

Aim G V
Pabst Brewing Co
548 Grain Exchange

Alsip J F 3rd
General Mills, Inc
666 Grain Exchange

Ambrose A J
Continental Grain Co
815 Grain Exchange

Amstutz D G
Cargill Investor Services Inc
Chicago IL

Andreas L W
ADM Grain Co
Decatur IL

Asper R E
Walsh Grain Co
900 Grain Exchange

Austin W
Barnesville Farmers Elevator Co
Barnesville, MN

Bafitis P T
L Dreyfus Corp
680 Grain Exchange

Bagley R C
Bagley Grain Co
654 Grain Exchange

Bahn M K
Peavey Co
730, 2nd Ave, Sth

Bailey A E
922 Grain Exchange

Bailey A F
General Mills Inc
666 Grain Exchange

Baumgartner J W
The Quaker Oats Co
1019 Grain Exchange

Becker E H
Cargill Inc
Cargill Bldg

Belski C F
Benson-Quinn Co
1075 Grain Exchange

Belski G C
Farmers Grain Co
Porter, MN

Benson J B
Reynolds Securities Inc
629, 2nd Ave, Sth

Benthin K
The Pillsbury Co
451 Grain Exchange

Bergman B R
Farmers Union Grain Terminal Association
1667 North Snelling, St Paul, MN

Berman M A
Northbrook, IL

Berman W J
Northbrook, IL

Birdsall B L
Birdsall Elevators
New Leipzig, ND

Bischoff G
Land O'Lakes Inc
Ford Dodge, IA

Blanco M F Jr
The McMillan Co
376 Grain Exchange

Blank S
Benson-Quinn Co
1075 Grain Exchange

Blewett J S
Farmers Union Grain Terminal Association
1667 North Snelling, St Paul, MN

Bloom J R
Peavey Co
730, 2nd Ave, Sth

Bock, C
Farmers Equity Exchange
New England, ND

Boe K P
The Pillsbury Co
720 Grain Exchange

Bolton J A
Atwood-Larson Co
876 Grain Exchange

Bolton R W
Atwood-Larson Co
876 Grain Exchange

Boos G J
Farmers Union Grain Terminal Association
1667 North Snelling, St Paul, MN

Borom P M
The Pillsbury Co
451 Grain Exchange

Bourn R L
Geldermann & Co Inc
416 Grain Exchange

Bowen J C
International Multifoods Corp
1200 Multifoods Bldg

Boyce M S
Merrill Lynch, Pierce, Fenner & Smith Inc
39th Floor, IDS Tower

Boyko K W
1920 Sth 1st St

Brown J R
Kellogg Commission Co
600 Grain Exchange

Bruce R III
ADM Grain Co
960 Grain Exchange

Brummer D
The Pillsbury Co
451 Grain Exchange

Bry A P
Minnesota Farm Bureau Marketing Corp
466 Grain Exchange

Buirge G R
Kellogg Commission Co
600 Grain Exchange

Burdick A L
Burdick Grain Co
375 Grain Exchange

Burgum A T
Farmers Elevator Co
Arthur, ND

Campbell H D
Dixie Portland Flour Mills Inc
Memphis, TN

Capinegro A
Lincolnwood Inc
Chicago, IL

Cargill R M
Victoria Grain Co of Minneapolis
915 Grain Exchange

Carlson D
L Dreyfus Corp
680 Grain Exchange

Caron T M
Bunge Corp
919, 13th Ave, Sth East

Carroll A R Jr
922 Grain Exchange

Case J P
Kellogg Commission Co
600 Grain Exchange

Cashman E C
Chicago, IL

Christensen D P
Cook Grain of Minnesota Inc
480 Grain Exchange

Chulik E E
Anheuser-Busch Inc
580 Grain Exchange

Clemenson R
Nash Grain & Trading Co
Nash, ND

Confer O P
Hubbard Milling Co
Mankato, MN

Cook E W
Cook Grain Co Inc
Memphis, TN

Corrigan F H
Peavey Co
730, 2nd Ave, Sth

Cottier B O
Bartlett & Co Grain
Kansas City, MO

Cramblit A J
Geldermann & Co Inc
Chicago, IL

Davis C M
Continental Grain Co
815 Grain Exchange

Dean R L
Seaboard Allied Milling Corp
Kansas City, MO

DeLaittre C D
Piper, Jaffray & Hopwood Inc
115 Sth 7th St

Della Selva A J
Benson Quinn Joseph Export Co
561 Grain Exchange

DeSmet T J
Farmers Union Grain Terminal Association
1667 North Snelling, St Paul, MN

DeWitt L F
Cargill Inc
Cargill Bldg

Dill J G Jr
Dill Co
1024 Grain Exchange

Dittmer T H
R E Friedman & Co
Chicago, IL

Doherty R T
Victoria Grain Co of Minneapolis
915 Grain Exchange

Donoho M E
General Mills Inc
666 Grain Exchange

Dunlap C
Oahe Grain Corp
Onida, SD

Dunn J T
922 Grain Exchange

Earl G R
White Bear Lake, MN

Earnest H H
Arvada, CO

Ebent G M
Ladish Malting Co
507 Grain Exchange

Engel R P
Peavey Co
730, 2nd Ave, Sth

Enright W M
Benson-Quinn Co
1075 Grain Exchange

Erickson D J
Peavey Co
730, 2nd Ave, Sth

Erickson F K Jr
Cook Grain of Minnesota Inc
480 Grain Exchange

Ewing H C
Kellogg Commission Co
600 Grain Exchange

Farkas H L
Denver, CO

Fassett R E
Fleischmann Malting Co Inc
410 Grain Exchange

Fedje D L
Fleischmann Malting Co Inc
410 Grain Exchange

Fields W B Jr
Burdick Grain Co
375 Grain Exchange

Fields W B III
Atwood-Larson Co
876 Grain Exchange

Finch L R
PO Box 15005, Commerce Station

Fivian C C
Continental Grain Co
715 Grain Exchange

Foster G D
Fleischmann Malting Co Inc
410 Grain Exchange

Fox W B
C B Fox Co
New Orleans, LA

Frank H O
563 Grain Exchange

Franko D G
Farmers Union Grain Terminal Association
1667 North Snelling, St Paul, MN

Fredrikson W A
ADM Grain Co
960 Grain Exchange

Friedman R E
Sioux City, IA

Fritz R A
Rahr Malting Co
567 Grain Exchange

Fudali J P
Hiawatha Grain Co
581 Grain Exchange

Fudali J F
Hiawatha Grain Co
581 Grain Exchange

Fuscsick M L
Boiling Springs, PA

Gagner W
Standard Milling Co
514 Grain Exchange

Garding T M
Atwood-Larson Co
876 Grain Exchange

Garrigan T
466 Grain Exchange

Gauger G
2126 IDS Center

Gaus M J
Milwaukee, WI

Geiger V C
Burdick Grain Co
375 Grain Exchange

Gerszewski P P
Farmers Cooperative Elevator Co of Oslo
Oslo, MN

Gibbons V M
Crookston Grain Co
Crookston, MN

Goldberg R W
Goldberg Feed & Grain Co
West Fargo, ND

Grambsch D
International Multifoods Corp
1200 Multifoods Bldg

Gravenish J L
ADM Grain Co
960 Grain Exchange

Grebner D
Bunge Corp
919, 13th Ave, Sth East

Grebner W G
The South Dakota Wheat Growers Association
Aberdeen, SD

Greene D M
Cargill Inc
Cargill Bldg

Greenslit T B
Searle Grain Co
1254 Grain Exchange

Gustafson A E
Brawley, CA

Gustafson W
Heinold Commodities Inc
472 Grain Exchange

Gwin J D
International Multifoods Corp
1200 Multifoods Bldg

Haberman D A
International Multifoods Corp
1200 Multifoods Bldg

Hackett S
General Mills Inc
666 Grain Exchange

Hagen T C
5649, 22nd Ave, Sth

Hajek R J
Farmers Elevator Co of Horace
Horace, ND

Hale H D
ADM Milling Co
Shawnee Mission, KA

Halperin S M
Nth Miami Beach, FL

Halpert M P
Philadelphia, PA

Hammer C R
ADM Grain Co
960 Grain Exchange

Handke G D
8616 Central Ave, Nth East

Hankinson H N
Burdick Grain Co
375 Grain Exchange

Hans P W
Burdick Grain Co
375 Grain Exchange

Hansen D E
Cargill Inc
Cargill Bldg

Hanson A D
Farmers Union Grain Terminal Association
1667 North Snelling, St Paul, MN

Hanson K N
Peavey Co
730, 2nd Ave, Sth

Harvey M E
Cargill Inc
Cargill Bldg

Haug D A
Cargill Inc
Cargill Bldg

Haugen A
Portland Farmers Elevator Co
Portland, ND

Hauser W H
Chicago, IL

Hayenga R V
Honeymead Products Co, division Farmers
Union Grain Terminal Association
25, 44th Ave, Nth East

Hays T B Jr
416 Grain Exchange

Hegman R H Sr
R Hegman Co
470 Grain Exchange

Herman K R
Kellogg Commission Co
600 Grain Exchange

Heubrock A L
ACLI International Commodity Services Inc
801 Grain Exchange

Hoff J M
Bunge Corp
919, 13th Ave, Sth East

Hoff O H
Farmers Elevator Co Inc
East Grand Forks, MN

Hogan J W
Ralston Purina Co
St Louis, MO

Hoggarth G
Wimbledon Grain Co
Courtenay, ND

Holt C J Jr
Farmers Union Grain Terminal Association
1667 North Snelling, St Paul, MN

Horazdovsky V A
The Quaker Oats Co
1019 Grain Exchange

Horn D G
Ladish Malting Co
507 Grain Exchange

Howard R L
Northwest Grain Co Inc
416 Grain Exchange

Howe R H
3411 Holmes Ave, Sth

Hoyt C R
Tennant & Hoyt Co
Lake City, MN

Hudson R J
Ralston Purina Co
406 Grain Exchange

Hughes J L
Bay State Milling Co
707 Grain Exchange

Hvidsten E N
Farmers Grain Co
Stephen, MN

Jacobson H H
ADM Grain Co
960 Grain Exchange

Jacobson T
Finley Farmers Grain & Elevator Co
Finley, ND

261

Jacoby P E
Farmers Union Grain Terminal Association
1667 North Snelling, St Paul, MN

Jensen N E
The Pillsbury Co
720 Grain Exchange

Johnson C B
Exchange Room

Johnson C M
Farmers Cooperative Marketing Association
East Grand Forks, MN

Johnson D G
J P Ritten Co
109 Grain Exchange

Johnson F W
Burdick Grain Co
375 Grain Exchange

Johnson J A R
PO Box 15263, Commerce Station

Johnson M K
Cargill Inc
Cargill Bldg

Johnson R J
Garnac Grain Co Inc
980 Grain Exchange

Johnson R G
Atwood-Larson Co
876 Grain Exchange

Johnston D T
E F Hutton & Co Inc
New York, NY

Joiner J B
4300 West Broadway

Joseph B M
I S Joseph Co Inc
777 Grain Exchange

Kaehler E E
Burdick Grain Co
375 Grain Exchange

Kaiser R M
Cargill Inc
Cargill Bldg

Kalgren R L
Atwood-Larson Co
876 Grain Exchange

Kalitowski H J
Mullin & Dillon Co
850 Grain Exchange

Kaplan M J
Mankato, MN

Katz J W
Bunge Corp
919, 13th Ave, Sth East

Kautz N J
Bay State Milling Co
North Quincy, MA

Keeler C E
Benson-Quinn Co
1075 Grain Exchange

Kelm E E
Cargill Inc
Cargill Bldg

King Dr J D
Iowa Grain Inc
Chicago, IL

Kingsbeck H I
Farmers Union Grain Terminal Association
1667 North Snelling, St Paul, MN

Kingsbeck N G
Benson-Quinn Co
1075 Grain Exchange

Kingstrom R D
Central Soya of Minnesota Inc
910 Grain Exchange

Kirschbaum D E
International Multifoods Corp
1200 Multifoods Bldg

Klein J
ACLI International Commodity Services Inc
Chicago, IL

Kneen K K
The Pillsbury Co
451 Grain Exchange

Knox J E
Benson-Quinn Co
1075 Grain Exchange

Koenig D
International Multifoods Corp
1200 Multifoods Bldg

Kohl A M
Chicago, IL

Kohler P W
Garnac Grain Co Inc
New York, NY

Kopperud D L
Midland Cooperatives Inc
2021 East Hennepin Ave

Kordell P J
I S Joseph Commodity Futures Inc
765 Grain Exchange

Kozinski J W
Glen Ellyn, IL

Krug P
Continental Grain Co
815 Grain Exchange

Kubiak R E
Farmers Union Grain Terminal Association
1667 North Snelling, St Paul, MN

Kulijewicz A
ADM Grain Co
960 Grain Exchange

Kunitz J W
Peavey Co
730, 2nd Ave, Sth

Kuziak D P
Burnsville, MN

LaBelle J C
Benson-Quinn Co
1075 Grain Exchange

Ladish J H
Ladish Malting Co
Milwaukee, WI

Lakness O R
Hammer Grain Co
Hammer, SD

Lambert J W
Northern States Grain Co
Fairmont, MN

Langen W
Kennedy Farmers Elevator Co
Kennedy, MN

Lappen J T
Schreier Malting Co
900 Grain Exchange

Larsen G R
Farmers Union Grain Terminal Association
25, 44th Ave, Nth East

Larson C W Jr
General Mills Inc
666 Grain Exchange

Larson P E
Ralston Purina Co
406 Grain Exchange

Laurel M J
Hopkins, MN

Layton L F
L Dreyfus Corp
680 Grain Exchange

Leathers L H
Shearson Hayden Stone Inc
New York, NY

Lind R G
ConAgra Fruen Inc
301 Thomas Ave, Nth

Loomis S K
ContiCommodity Services Inc, subsidiary
Continental Grain Co
715 Grain Exchange

Loonan T L
Central Soya of Minnesota Inc
910 Grain Exchange

Lund L J
ADM Grain Co
960 Grain Exchange

McCaull J D
McCaull Grain Co
650 Grain Exchange

McCaull P R
McCaull Grain Co
650 Grain Exchange

McCauslin J M
Merrill Lynch, Pierce, Fenner & Smith Inc
39th Floor, IDS Tower

McIntyre R T
Cargill Inc
Cargill Bldg

McMillan H I Jr
The McMillan Co
376 Grain Exchange

McWhite R B
Peavey Co
730, 2nd Ave, Sth

McWhite R B Jr
Exchange Room

Macdonald W H
Coast Trading Co Inc
Portland, OR

Maduff M L
Maduff & Sons
Chicago, IL

Mahl D E
Benson-Quinn Co
1075 Grain Exchange

Malusky B J
Farmers Union Grain Terminal Association
1667 North Snelling, St Paul, MN

Manne J
River Forest, IL

Martin J J
LaCrosse Milling Co, division Ward
Foods Inc
Cochrane, WI

Mastel C J
Cook Grain of Minnesota Inc
Grand Forks, ND

Master J A
Peavey Co
730, 2nd Ave, Sth

Matthies S L
General Mills Inc
666 Grain Exchange

Meldahl C
Farmers Elevator Co
Hatton, ND

Mensing T D
Minnesota Malting Co
Cannon Falls, MN

Merrill F L
Cereal Food Processors Inc
Kansas City, MO

Meyer J H
Hayward, WI

Miller H I
Bunge Corp
919, 13th Ave, Sth East

Miller J K
Valley City, ND

Mills M W
ADM Grain Co
960 Grain Exchange

Moe M J
Peavey Co
730, 2nd Ave, Sth

Moline C L
Atwood-Larson Co
876 Grain Exchange

Monson R G
Bunge Corp
919, 13th Ave, Sth East

Moquist C J
The Farmers Elevator Co
Crystal, ND

Morris E N
Chicago, IL

Morrison R F
ConAgra Inc
Omaha, NE

Moskalik J J
Farmers Union Grain Terminal Association
1667 North Snelling, St Paul, MN

Moyer K C
Cook Grain of Minnesota Inc
Jamestown, ND

Mullin J F
Exchange Room

Mullin M J
International Multifoods Corp
1200 Multifoods Bldg

Mullin W E
Mullin & Dillon Co
850 Grain Exchange

Murlowski I P
J P Ritten Co
109 Grain Exchange

Mykleby H
Farmers Elevator Co
Eldred, MN

Nedbalek J R
Central Soya of Minnesota Inc
910 Grain Exchange

Nelson R A
Peavey Co
730, 2nd Ave, Sth

Neumann L N
Cook Grain of Minnesota Inc
480 Grain Exchange

Newton M
ADM Grain Co
960 Grain Exchange

Nicholls W H
Froedtert Malt Corporation, division
Farmers Union Grain Terminal Association
462 Grain Exchange

Noble D S
Atwood-Larson Co
876 Grain Exchange

Nolan R W
109 Grain Exchange

Norman R L
Farmers Union Grain Terminal Association
25, 44th Ave, Nth East

O'Connor W F
Chicago, IL

Ohzourk J J
Park Ridge, IL

Olausen H J
Farmers Union Grain Terminal Association
1667, North Snelling, St Paul, MN

Oler W J
Benson-Quinn Joseph Export Co
561 Grain Exchange

Olsen R G
465 Grain Exchange

Olson F C
Red Oak, IA

Olson L B
Continental Grain Co
815 Grain Exchange

Olson R D
Continental Grain Co
815 Grain Exchange

Olson W C
The McMillan Co
376 Grain Exchange

O'Neill J E
Kellogg Commission Co
600 Grain Exchange

Ordos G M
Spencer Kellogg, division Textron Inc
25th Ave, Sth East 4th St

Ostroot C R
Peavey Co
730, 2nd Ave, Sth

Owens A C
950 Grain Exchange

Owens J W
922 Grain Exchange

Paliulis A P
Cargill Inc
Cargill Bldg

Paquette G J
The McMillan Co
376 Grain Exchange

Pedersen W F
The McMillan Co
376 Grain Exchange

Pederson E B
Atwood-Larson Co
876 Grain Exchange

Pelzl C C
United Grain Corp
280 Grain Exchange

Percy E C Jr
Bunge Corp
919, 13th Ave, Sth East

Peterson B E
Colfax Grain Co
Box 608, Moorhead, MN

Peterson R L
Central Soya of Minnesota Inc
910 Grain Exchange

Pierce F C
Scranton Equity Exchange
Scranton, ND

Pillsbury J S III|
First National Bank of Minneapolis
120 South 6th St

Pittelkow R T
Bunge Corp
919, 13th Ave, Sth East

Prindiville R A
Thomson & McKinnon Auchincloss
Kohlmeyer Inc
New York, NY

Pritchard Mrs M J
M J Pritchard Inc
854 Grain Exchange

Putz Dr H
New York, NY

Quain R J
Minnetonka, MN

Quain W A
Exchange Room

Quinn E E
Benson-Quinn Co
1075 Grain Exchange

Quinn R G
Benson-Quinn Co
1075 Grain Exchange

Quist S Q
Atwood-Larson Co
876 Grain Exchange

Rasmussen D G
Farmers Union Grain Terminal Association
1667 North Snelling, St Paul, MN

Reagan M P
International Multifoods Corp
1200 Multifoods Bldg

Rednor P J
Golden, CO

Reeves R S II
Kurth Malting Corp
Milwaukee, WI

Remele L A
Peavey Co
730, 2nd Ave, Sth

Revell J N
ADM Grain Co
960 Grain Exchange

Rhea E B Jr
Paine, Webber, Jackson & Curtis Inc
Chicago, IL

Richardson G T
James Richardson & Sons Ltd
Winnipeg, Manitoba, Canada

Riley S W
Atwood-Larson Co
876 Grain Exchange

Ringer J M
The McMillan Co
376 Grain Exchange

Ritten J P
L N Ritten & Co Inc
109 Grain Exchange

Roarke J A
Farmers Union Grain Terminal Association
1667 North Snelling, St Paul, MN

Roberts E R Jr
General Mills Inc
666 Grain Exchange

Robinson N A
Victoria Grain Co of Minneapolis
915 Grain Exchange

Roloff N C
Bay State Milling Co
707 Grain Exchange

Rompage H S
LaCrosse Milling Co division Ward Foods Inc
912 Grain Exchange

Rud W M
Stephen Farmers Cooperative Elevator Co
Stephen, MN

Salonen D W
Benson-Quinn Co
1075 Grain Exchange

Sander D R
Peavey Co
730, 2nd Ave, Sth

Sando D
Farmers Cooperative Elevator Co
Rosholt, SD

Sauter W L
Farmers Union Grain Terminal Association
1667 North Snelling, St Paul, MN

Sawyer G L
466 Grain Exchange

Schaefer L C
Peavey Co
730, 2nd Ave, Sth

Scheu H A
Spencer Kellogg division of Textron Inc
Exchange Room

Schirmang O J
Bloomington, MN

Schlotfeldt T D
Benson-Quinn Co
1075 Grain Exchange

Schlunk K-H
A C Toepfer Inc
New York, NY

Schuler G M Jr
Schuler Grain Co
Breckenridge, MN

Schuler O J
Schuler Elevator Inc
Munich, ND

Schultz L G
Peavey Co
730, 2nd Ave, Sth

Scroggins J M
The Scroggins Grain Co
475 Grain Exchange

Scroggins T J
The Scroggins Grain Co
475 Grain Exchange

Scully M B
LaCrosse Milling Co division Ward Foods Inc
912 Grain Exchange

Searles R L
Exchange Room

Seidl S F
Rahr Malting Co
567 Grain Exchange

Selover J M
Northwestern National Bank
Northwestern National Bank Bldg

Sexauer E H
The Sexauer Co
Brookings, SD

Shaffer B G Jr
Dependable Feed Services Inc
2120 IDS Center

Shapiro J H
2925 Aquila Ave, Sth

Shell R S
Chicago, IL

Shima W J
900 Grain Exchange

Sims F L
Cargill Inc
Cargill Bldg

Skaj D J
Peavey Co
730, 2nd Ave, Sth

Skinner N L
General Mills Inc
666 Grain Exchange

Skotty R J Jr
Saul Stone & Co
Chicago, IL

Smith H K
Atwood-Larson Co
876 Grain Exchange

Smith R J
Continental Grain Co
815 Grain Exchange

Smith R A
Cargill Inc
Cargill Bldg

Sonnesyn E N
International Multifoods Corp
1200 Multifoods Bldg

Sorby D E
Benson-Quinn Co
1075 Grain Exchange

Sorvillo M E
Chicago, IL

Staege D A
465 Grain Exchange

Stanbury A M
PO Box 15232, Commerce Station

Stanley J T
Osseo, MN

Steele R L
L Dreyfus Corp
680 Grain Exchange

Stich D F
Bunge Corp
919, 13th Ave, Sth East

Stoker H B Jr
Atwood-Larson Co
876 Grain Exchange

Stokes P T
Anheuser-Busch Inc
St Louis, MO

Stone T H
Saul Stone & Co
Chicago, IL

Strauss K M
Pabst Brewing Co
Milwaukee, WI

Strong D R
Peavey Co
730, 2nd Ave, Sth

Subak W J
Cook Grain of Minnesota Inc
480 Grain Exchange

Sueltz D
Ferney Farmers Elevator Co
Groton, SD

Sullivan W P
Chicago, IL

Summers R Jr
Kellogg Commission Co
600 Grain Exchange

Sutton R L
ACLI International Commodity Services Inc
801 Grain Exchange

Swisher C H Jr
ADM Milling Co
960 Grain Exchange

Tearse H H Jr
Searle Grain Co
1254 Grain Exchange

Thayer E B
Montana Merchandising Inc
Great Falls, MT

Theisen V M
Kurth Malting Corp
PO Box 15245, Commerce Station

Thompson A
Benson-Quinn Co
1075 Grain Exchange

Tracey R L
922 Grain Exchange

Tregillis J
Farmers Union Grain Terminal Association
1667 North Snelling, St Paul, MN

Trelstad S J
Rahr Malting Co
567 Grain Exchange

Trimble E E
Charlotte, NC

Turner M
Benson-Quinn Co
1075 Grain Exchange

Underwood G
Cargill Inc
Cargill Bldg

Urista P
Benson-Quinn Co
1075 Grain Exchange

Van Dyke W D III
Smith Barney, Harris Upham & Co Inc
Milwaukee, WI

Wald C L
L Dreyfus Corp
680 Grain Exchange

Walen A M
Benson-Quinn Co
1075 Grain Exchange

Wallin W R
The Pillsbury Co
451 Grain Exchange

Walsh M R
Walsh Grain Co
900 Grain Exchange

Walsh W S
Walsh Grain Co
900 Grain Exchange

Ware L
ADM Grain Co
960 Grain Exchange

Watson R W
Cargill Inc
Cargill Bldg

Wayne J G Jr
L Dreyfus Corp
680 Grain Exchange

Weiner J
Mt Airy, MD

Weitzer E J
Ladish Malting Co
Milwaukee, WI

Welch R B
Froedtert Malt Corp division Farmers Union
Grain Terminal Association
Milwaukee, WI

Werner M J
Farmers Union Grain Terminal Association
1667 North Snelling, St Paul, MN

Whelan L
Whelan Bros
St Thomas, ND

White R G
376 Grain Exchange

Wicklund P E
PO Box 15012, Commerce Station

Wilson C G
Minnesota Farm Bureau Marketing Corp
3110 Wooddale Drive, St Paul, MN

Wilson D W
United Grain Corp
280 Grain Exchange

Wilson J E
Atwood-Larson Co
876 Grain Exchange

Wittich V D
Peavey Co
730, 2nd Ave, Sth

Wolden R I
Atwood-Larson Co
876 Grain Exchange

Workman L H
ADM Grain Co
960 Grain Exchange

Wrisley D B
A G Edwards & Sons Inc
St Louis, MO

Wylie E D
Farmers Union Grain Terminal Association
1667 North Snelling, St Paul, MN

Yost M W
The Pillsbury Co
451 Grain Exchange

Young E J Jr
Clayton Brokerage Co of St Louis Inc
Clayton, MO

Yutrzenka M R
Argyle Co-op Warehouse Association
Argyle, MN

New York:
Commodity Exchange Inc, trading members, as at March 1976

Abrams M
120 East Hartsdale Ave, Hartsdale,
NY 10530

Afram I
Afram Bros Inc
900 South Water St, Milwaukee, WI 53204

Alexandre D L
Engelhard Minerals & Chemical Corp,
Engelhard Industries Division
430 Mountain Ave, Murray Hill, NJ 07974

Arkin J
300 South Wacker Drive, Chicago, IL 60606

Aron R
The Stanton Corp
160 Water St, New York, NY 10038

Ashraf M
c/o Eastern Trade Corp, Sheikha Bldg,
PO Box 1376, Deira, Dubai, United Arab
Emirates

Auciello D F
Great American Trading Co
6 Harrison St, Room 504, New York,
NY 10013

Augello V W
674 Keil St, Elmont, NY 11003

Baer J J
Northern Investment SA
PO Box 14-330, Madrid, Spain

Baerwald H F
International Minerals & Metals Corp
919 Third Ave, New York, NY 10022

Baldini M
Baldini, Proffitt, Reilly & Co
61 Broadway, New York, NY 10006

Barnes J C
Thomson & McKinnon Auchincloss
Kohlmeyer Inc
2 Broadway, New York, NY 10004

Baur F W
Harmon, Lichtenstein & Co
26 Broadway, New York, NY 10004

Becker-Fluegel H
NRT Metals Inc
576 Fifth Ave, New York, NY 10036

Bell S
c/o Commodity Exchange Inc, 81 Broad St,
New York, NY 10004

Belmont M
c/o Commodity Exchange Inc, 81 Broad St,
New York, NY 10004

Benjamin J F
Drexel, Burnham & Co Inc
230 West Monroe St, Chicago, IL 60606

Bergman K G
Amax Copper Inc
1270 Avenue of the Americas, New York,
NY 10020

Besso V
Intsel Corp
825, 3rd Ave, New York, NY 10022

Bierrie E P
United Baltic Corp
17 Battery Place, New York, NY 10004

Bilello L
Bache Halsey Stuart Inc
c/o Commodity Exchange Inc, 81 Broad St,
New York, NY 10004

Bischoff G H
Sharps Pixley Inc
100 Wall St, New York, NY 10005

Bleecker P B
Scholtz & Co Inc
110 Wall St, New York, NY 10005

Bleichroeder R
S Montagu & Co Ltd
114 Old Broad St, London EC2

Blot E J
2 East 67th St, New York, NY 10021

Blum L J
Eisen & Blum Inc
141 West Jackson Blvd, Chicago, IL 60604

Boglione G
Boys, Investment & Trade Ltd
c/o Swiss Credit Bank, Vevey, Switzerland

Boonshoft O
Winters Bank Tower, Suite 1360, Dayton,
OH 45402

Brady H S
Brady, Schwartz & Co
8 South Michigan, Chicago, IL 60603

Branco J P
Floor Broker Associates
81 Broad St, New York, NY 10004

Brandler J J
L B Stern & Co Ltd
c/o Commodity Exchange Inc, 81 Broad St,
New York, NY 10004

Bresky R J
Thomson & McKinnon Auchincloss
Kohlmeyer Inc
2 Broadway, New York, NY 10004

Briggs S J
Floor Broker Associates
81 Broad St, New York, NY 10004

Brodsky A
c/o Commodity Exchange Inc, 81 Broad St,
New York, NY 10004

Brook I
Geldermann & Co Inc
111 East Sunrise Ave, Coral Gables,
FL 33313

Browdy E J
Chicago Investment Co
1 North LaSalle St, Chicago, IL 60602

Burchard O
The Ore & Chemical Corp
235 East 42nd St, New York, NY 10017

Buscemi M A
c/o Commodity Exchange Inc, 81 Broad St,
New York, NY 10004

Calderaro F S
Mintz, Marcus & Co
81 Broad St, New York, NY 10004

Campbell D R
Amalgamet Inc
641 Lexington Ave, New York, NY 10022

Capinegro A
Lincolnwood Inc
141 West Jackson Blvd, Chicago, IL 60604

Caruana C R
Reynolds Securities Inc
2 Broadway, New York, NY 10004

Cashman E C
Cashman & Co
141 West Jackson Blvd, Chicago, IL 60604

Cherwin S
2803 Covered Bridge Rd, Merrick, NY 11566

Chilewich S
New York Hide Trading Co
120 Wall St, New York, NY 10005

Cohen P A
Herzfeld & Stern
30 Broad St, New York, NY 10004

Collins J R
Greene & Collins Inc
175 West Jackson Blvd, 2nd Floor, Chicago,
IL 60604

Comenzo D R
c/o New York Cotton Exchange, 37 Wall St,
New York, NY 10005

Coppola F J
Merrill Lynch, Pierce, Fenner & Smith Inc
c/o Commodity Exchange Inc, 81 Broad St,
New York, NY 10004

Coyne H J
J Aron & Co Inc
160 Water St, 19th Floor, New York,
NY 10038

Coyne M L
J Aron Commodities Corp
160 Water St, 19th Floor, New York,
NY 10038

Crystal N S
Main PO Box 338, Union City, NJ 07087

Dalton P H Jr
Interstate Securities Corp
221 South Tryon St, Charlotte, NC 28202

D'Arcy R P
Amax Copper Inc
1270 Avenue of the Americas, New York,
NY 10020

Davis C
Lonconex Ltd
29 Mincing Lane, London EC3

Deak N L
Perera Co Inc
29 Broadway, New York, NY 10006

Deane C H
Deane Metal Co
77 Water St, New York, NY 10005

Decker M
Bear, Stearns & Co
55 Water St, New York, NY 10041

Del Re A
DiLiberto, DiLiberto, Del Re & Co
81 Broad St, New York, NY 10004

DeMartino R
Commodity International Co
84 William St, New York, NY 10038

DeMicoli S
c/o Commodity Exchange Inc, 81 Broad St,
New York, NY 10004

Denberg M H
c/o Commodity Exchange Inc, 81 Broad St,
New York, NY 10004

DeVellis R F
c/o Commodity Exchange Inc, 81 Broad St,
New York, NY 10004

Diamond T L
T L Diamond & Co Inc
1 Wall St, New York, NY 10005

DiLiberto C
DiLiberto, DiLiberto, Del Re & Co
79 Pine St, New York, NY 10005

DiLiberto J
E Modet & Co
79 Pine St, New York, NY 10005

Dishy B
Dishy Easton & Co
1 State Street Plaza, New York, NY 10004

Dittmer T H
R E Friedman & Co
222 South Riverside Plaza, Chicago,
IL 60606

Donchian R D
Shearson Hayden Stone Inc
2 Greenwich Plaza, Greenwich, CT 06830

Donnelly J P Jr
Balfour, MacLaine Inc
88 Pine St, New York, NY 10005

Doty G E
Goldman Sachs & Co
55 Broad St, New York, NY 10004

Dreyfuss R F
Cerro Sales Corp
300 Park Ave, New York, NY 10022

Drogoul P G
N C Trading Co Inc
450 Park Ave, New York, NY 10022

Dubie F A
c/o Commodity Exchange Inc, 81 Broad St,
New York, NY 10004

Durant A Lord Aldenham
R J Rouse & Co Ltd
23 Blomfield St, London EC2M 7NL

Dustin D R
Precious Metals Corp of America
c/o Franklin Mint Corp, Franklin Center,
PA 19063

Ehrlich S R
Mabon, Nugent & Co
115 Broadway, New York, NY 10006

Eichenberg G A
General Hide & Skin Corp
11 Park Place, New York, NY 10007

Eisenberg H G
Brandeis, Goldschmidt & Co Inc
919 Third Ave, New York, NY 10022

Ergas I
1199 Park Ave, New York, NY 10028

Etherton J H
Amalgamated Metal Corp Ltd
641 Lexington Ave, 22nd Floor, New York,
NY 10028

Ezzo J J
Mintz, Marcus & Co
81 Broad St, New York, NY 10004

Falkenrath P K
Intsel Commodities Inc
825 Third Ave, New York, NY 10022

Fashena S
Loeb, Rhoades & Co
42 Wall St, New York, NY 10005

Fellman M A
D Witter & Co Inc
2 Broadway, New York, NY 10004

Ferer H D
A D Ferer & Sons Co
909 Abbot Drive, Omaha, NE 68102

Ferretti D A
Insilco Corp
500 South Broad St, Meriden, CT

Ferriso J A
Ferriso, LaFroscia & Co
79 Pine St, New York, NY 10005

Fields S H
Loeb, Rhoades & Co
42 Wall St, New York, NY 10005

Fisher R J
81 Broad St, New York, NY 10004

Fletcher A
C Tennant Sons & Co of New York
100 Park Ave, New York, NY 10017

Fletcher T P
161-10, 32nd Ave, Flushing, NY 11358

Fochtman J P
Internatio Inc
116 John St, New York, NY 10038

Forlenza F John
F J Forlenza & Co
16 West Granada Drive, Bucktown, NJ 08723

Forlenza F Joseph
F J Forlenza & Co
81 Broad St, New York, NY 10004

Forlenza L
F J Forlenza & Co
81 Broad St, New York, NY 10004

Forlenza M
F J Forlenza & Co
81 Broad St, New York, NY 10004

Forlenza S
1525 Old Oak Rd, Los Angeles, CA 90049

Forman J F
J F Forman Canada Ltd
299 Queen St West, Toronto, Ontario,
MSV 129, Canada

Frank E L
Engelhard Minerals & Chemical Corp,
Philipp Bros Division
299 Park Ave, New York, NY 10017

Freed J N
Ultrafin International Corp
63 Wall St, New York, NY 10005

Freeman A L
Rosenthal & Co
141 West Jackson Blvd, Chicago, IL 60604

Fried A Jr
A Fried & Co
77 Water St, New York, NY 10005

Friedlander K A
Samincorp Inc
425 Park Ave, New York, NY 10022

Friedman S
120 Broadway, Room 1023, New York,
NY 10005

Frietsch H M
International Systems & Controls Corp
2727 Allen Parkway, Suite 2280, Houston,
TX 77019

Fromer M A
Lewis & Peat Trading Inc
150 East 58th St, New York, NY 10022

Fuller K S
Richardson Securities Inc
40 Wall St, New York, NY 10005

Gange J G
UV Industries Inc
437 Madison Ave, New York, NY 10022

Garbe G P
588 Rose Blvd, Baldwin, NY 11510

Gardner R L
Chartered New England Corp
90 Broad St, New York, NY 10004

Garfield G
Garfield & Co
306 Carter Rd, Princeton, NJ 08540

Garrison D J
151 Deepdale Drive, Middletown, NJ 07748

Garrity D
General Cable Corp
500 West Putnam Ave, Greenwich, CT 06830

Gill J
Case Postale 159, 1012 Lausanne Chailly,
Switzerland

Ginzberg M L
Primary Industries Corp
666 Fifth Ave, New York, NY 10019

Glassberg M
Ag-Met Inc
PO Box 523, Hazleton, PA 18201

Glenn P F
7216 Black Rock Trail, Scottsdale, AZ 85253

Golodetz A
Genco Commodities Inc
160 Water St, New York, NY 10038

Goodman H
7851 South Ashland Ave, Chicago, IL 60620

Goodman M J
54 Levering Circle, Bala Cynwyd, PA 19004

Goodman W D
Freehling & Co
120 South LaSalle St, Chicago, IL 60603

Gosberg N I
N I Gosberg & Co Inc
1 Horizon Rd, Apt 1020 Fort Lee,
NJ 07024

Granger J S
Granger & Co
111 Broadway, New York, NY 10006

Gray L
Gray International Inc
1271 Avenue of the Americas, New York,
NY 10020

Green H
44 East 67th St, New York, NY 10021

Gremald R
Ametalco Inc
530 Fifth Ave, New York, NY 10036

Griffin R S
141 West Jackson Blvd, Suite 1258, Chicago,
IL 60604

Grillo H
W Grillo Handelsgesellschaft
AM Grillo Park 5, Duisborg Hamborn,
West Germany

Grummer E M
Merrill Lynch, Pierce, Fenner & Smith Inc
1 Liberty Park Plaza, 165 Broadway,
New York, NY 10006

Haboush E R
Galaxy Diamond Corp
48 West 48th St, New York, NY 10036

Halladin P H
85 Hillcrest Drive, Upper Saddle River,
NJ 07458

Hamilton J R
25 Hickory Place, Chatham, NJ 07928

Handleman H A
Oliveri, Handleman & Co
c/o Commodity Exchange Inc, 81 Broad St,
New York, NY 10004

Hanemann J H
c/o F J Forlenza & Co, 81 Broad St,
New York, NY 10004

Harmon R B
Harmon, Lichtenstein & Co
26 Broadway, New York, NY 10004

Harris H U Jr
Smith Barney, Harris Upham & Co Inc
1345 Avenue of the Americas, New York,
NY 10019

Harris J E
150 East Palmetto Park Rd, Boca Raton,
FL 33432

Hartley T R
3351 North Knoll Drive, Los Angeles,
CA 90068

Hatten C
ACLI International Commodity Services Inc
110 Wall St, New York, NY 10005

Haydak S
Dishy Easton & Co
1 State Street Plaza, New York, NY 10004

Hayne C P
Howard, Weil, Labouisse, Friedrichs Inc
211 Carondelet St, New Orleans, LA 70130

Heilberg J C
c/o New York Coffee & Sugar Exchange,
79 Pine St, New York, NY 10005

Heinhold H J
Heinhold Commodities Inc
222 South Riverside Plaza, Room 420,
Chicago, IL 60606

Helfer R
Helfer Commodities Corp
5 World Trade Center, Suite 6367,
New York, NY 10048

Henricks R
Harmon, Lichtenstein & Co
26 Broadway, New York, NY 10004

Herman J J
c/o New York Cotton Exchange, 37 Wall St,
New York, NY 10005

Herstein R J
c/o Commodity Exchange Inc, 81 Broad St,
New York, NY 10004

Hirsch M
Republic Clearing Corp
450 Fifth Ave, New York, NY 10018

Hockstader L A II
L F Rothschild & Co
99 William St, New York, NY 10038

Hoffstatter E W Jr
Sharps, Pixley Inc
100 Wall St, New York, NY 10005

Hohenberg J J
The Hohenberg Co
266 South Front St, Memphis, TN 38013

Horn F F
D Witter & Co Inc
2 Broadway, New York, NY 10004

Howard G H
Smith Barney, Harris Upham & Co Inc
1345 Avenue of the Americas, New York,
NY 10019

Hunter J A
Peavey Co
141 West Jackson Blvd, Chicago, IL 60604

Israel A C
ACLI International Inc
110 Wall St, New York, NY 10005

Jacobson R
Reading Industries Inc
236 Green St, South Hackensack, NJ 07606

Jaffee W L
Loeb, Rhoades & Co
375 Park Ave, New York, NY 10022

Jarecki H G
Mocatta Metals Corp
25 Broad St, New York, NY 10004

Jarecki R W, MD
Brody, White & Co Inc
25 Broad St, New York, NY 10004

Jenkins D M
c/o Commodity Exchange Inc, 81 Broad St,
New York, NY 10004

Johnston D T
E F Hutton & Co Inc
1 Battery Park Plaza, New York, NY 10004

Johnston J W
Gold Fields American Corp
230 Park Ave, New York, NY 10017

Jones D
Arrow Manufacturing Co
885 Freeway Drive North, Columbus,
OH 43229

Kaplan J
International Recycling Corp
Horseshoe Rd, Sayreville, NJ 08872

Katz E
A Hirsch & Co
500 Fifth Ave, Suite 1724, New York,
NY 10036

Kessner B
67 Navajo Ave, Lake Hiawatha, NJ 07034

Kipnis H S
H S Kipnis & Co
209 South LaSalle St, Chicago, IL 60604

Klein J
ACLI International Commodity Services Inc
141 West Jackson Blvd, Chicago, IL 60604

Klein M
Klein & Co
40 Exchange Place, New York, NY 10005

Knack R L
c/o New York Cotton Exchange, 37 Wall St,
New York, NY 10005

Kohl A
A Kohl & Co Inc
141 West Jackson Blvd, Chicago, IL 60604

Kohlberg J Jr
Bear, Stearns & Co
55 Water St, New York, NY 10041

Kuhlik I W
c/o Commodity Exchange Inc, 81 Broad St,
New York, NY 10004

Kurtz J
Bache Halsey Stuart Inc
100 Gold St, New York, NY 10038

Kurzrok M D
Lehman Bros Inc
120 Broadway, New York, NY 10005

LaFroscia R G
Ferriso, LaFroscia & Co
79 Pine St, New York, NY 10005

Lakin W T
c/o Commodity Exchange, Inc, 81 Broad St,
New York, NY 10004

Lambert D M
E P Lambert Co
First National Tower, Akron, OH 44308

Lamborn A H III
Shearson Hayden Stone Inc
81 Broad St, New York, NY 10004

Langguth C B
Brascan International Inc
127 John St, New York, NY 10038

Larson W L
Cargill Investor Services Inc
2 Broadway, New York, NY 10004

Layton W C Jr
Mine Brook Rd, Far Hills, NJ 07931

Lazarus M
c/o Commodity Exchange Inc, 81 Broad St,
New York, NY 10004

Leathers L H
Shearson Hayden Stone Inc
1 Western Union International Plaza,
New York, NY 10004

Leinsdorf G J
Philipp Brothers Division of Engelhard
Minerals & Chemicals Corp
299 Park Ave, New York, NY 10017

Leist N S
6 Harrison St, Room 412, New York,
NY 10013

Lennard G L
Gerald Metals Inc
1 Battery Park Plaza, New York, NY 10004

LePore C T
c/o Commodity Exchange Inc, 81 Broad St,
New York, NY 10004

Levenson M
Miles Metal Corp
250 Park Ave, Room 915, New York,
NY 10017

Levine M H
c/o Commodity Exchange Inc, 81 Broad St,
New York, NY 10004

Levy L
Oppenheimer & Co Inc
1 New York Plaza, New York, NY 10004

Levy M
Levy Commodities
222 South Riverside Plaza, Chicago,
IL 60606

Levyns G M
Continental Grain Co
277 Park Ave, New York, NY 10017

Leytess E
Leytess Metal & Chemical Corp
500 Fifth Ave. New York, NY 10036

Lichtenstein G
c/o Commodity Exchange Inc, 81 Broad St,
New York, NY 10004

Lichtman C
J Lichtman & Sons
241 Freylinghuysen Ave, Newark, NJ 07114

Liebman M
M Lib/Ras International
222 South Riverside Plaza, Chicago,
IL 60606

Lind B J
Lind-Waldock & Co
222 South Riverside Plaza, Chicago,
IL 60606

Lion N
Philipp & Lion
Moor House, London Wall,
London EC2Y 5AR

Lipper A III
A Lipper Corp
176 Broadway, New York, NY 10038

Lisi F A
81 Broad St, New York, NY 10004

Lisi N J
81 Broad St, New York, NY 10004

Lissauer F A
Associated Metals & Minerals Corp
733 Third Ave, New York, NY 10017

Lissner M W
Lissner Minerals & Metals Inc
1000 North Branch St, Chicago, IL 60622

Loeb H A
Loeb, Rhoades & Co
42 Wall St, New York, NY 10005

Loeb J L Jr
Loeb, Rhoades & Co
375 Park Ave, New York, NY 10022

Loewenberg R E
R E Loewenberg Capitol Management Corp
450 Park Ave, New York, NY 10022

London A O
c/o Commodity Exchange Inc, 81 Broad St,
New York, NY 10004

Lowenthal A G
Cowen & Co
1 Battery Park Plaza, New York, NY 10004

Maduff M L
Maduff & Sons
222 South Riverside Plaza, Chicago,
IL 60606

Malloy P E III
232 East 84th St, New York, NY 10028

Maneri C J
c/o New York Cotton Exchange, 37 Wall St,
New York, NY 10005

Manne J
839 Ashland Ave, River Forest, IL 60305

Marcus H R
Mintz, Marcus & Co
81 Broad St, New York, NY 10004

Margulies E
Lonray Inc
77 Water St, New York, NY 10005

Markoff S C
A-Mark Trading Corp
4640 Hollywood Blvd, Los Angeles,
CA 90027

Marx M
United Equities Co
160 Broadway, New York, NY 10038

Massey R W
Hornblower & Weeks-Hemphill, Noyes Inc
8 Hanover Sq, New York, NY 10004

Mattana G A
27 Partridge Drive, Roslyn, NY 11576

Mattey C
Bache Halsey Stuart Inc
100 Gold St, New York, NY 10038

Mayer L
Mayer & Schweitzer Inc
30 Montgomery St, Jersey City, NJ 07302

McDonnell R E
Commodity International Co
84 William St, New York, NY 10038

McHale J M
c/o Commodity Exchange Inc, 81 Broad St,
New York, NY 10004

Mehl M
c/o Commodity Exchange Inc, 81 Broad St,
New York, NY 10004

Merkin H
Merkin & Co
61 Broadway, New York, NY 10006

Merriman D W
151 East 80th St, New York, NY 10021

Mesker D W
A G Edwards & Sons Inc
1 North Jefferson, St Louis, MO 63103

Messenkopf E J
Donaldson, Lufkin & Jenrette Securities
Corp
140 Broadway, New York, NY 10005

Meyer H
Ayrton Metal & Ore Corp
30 Rockefeller Plaza, New York, NY 10020

Mintz H
PO Box 6817, Hollywood, FL 33021

Mintz L A
Mintz, Marcus & Co
81 Broad St, New York, NY 10004

Miskavi M F
Industrial & Trade Development Co
PO Box 130, Beyrouth, Lebanon

Mogul M D
Monarch Brass & Copper Corp
75 Beechwood Ave, New Rochelle,
NY 10801

Monaster M P
Christensen, Whalen & Monaster Ltd
141 West Jackson Blvd, Chicago, IL 60604

Moore J E
Harmon, Lichtenstein & Co
26 Broadway, New York, NY 10004

Moore J F
Harmon, Lichtenstein & Co
26 Broadway, New York, NY 10004

Morace J L
c/o Commodity Exchange Inc, 81 Broad St,
New York, NY 10004

Morosco F L
Metal Traders International Sales Corp
445 Park Ave, New York, NY 10022

Morrissey O J
F A Dubie & Co
81 Broad St, New York, NY 10004

Mountcastle K F Jr
Reynolds Securities Inc
120 Broadway, New York, NY 10005

Mugdan E
The Ore & Chemical Corp
235 East 42nd St, New York, NY 10017

Nadler E
126 East 61st St, New York, NY 10021

Napoletano A
c/o Commodity Exchange Inc, 81 Broad St,
New York, NY 10004

Nathanson N L
N L Nathanson & Co
460 North St, Greenwich, CT 06830

Nelsen N R
5 Woodland Rd, Brookside, NJ 07926

Nelson M H
c/o Commodity Exchange Inc, 81 Broad St,
New York, NY 10004

Nessim R
Philipp Bros, Division of Engelhard Minerals
& Chemical Corp
299 Park Ave, New York, NY 10017

Neu H
H Neu & Sons Inc
45 Nassau St, New York, NY 10005

Newman E G
Chilewich Sons & Co
120 Wall St, New York, NY 10005

Nichols O H
Mitchell, Hutchins Inc
2 First National Plaza, Chicago, IL 60670

Nordlicht J
c/o Pressner Trading Corp, 6 Harrison St,
New York, NY 10013

Novak J A
16-66 Bell Blvd, Bayside, NY 11360

O'Hare T P
Merrill Lynch, Pierce, Fenner & Smith Inc
1 Liberty Plaza, 165 Broadway, New York,
NY 10006

Oliveri E J
Oliveri, Handleman & Co
81 Broad St, New York, NY 10004

Oliverio C
Mintz, Marcus & Co
81 Broad St, New York, NY 10004

Ondo J M
c/o Commodity Exchange Inc, 81 Broad St,
New York, NY 10004

Ott H
Spiral Metal Co Inc
515 Madison Ave, New York, NY 10022

Parsoff M
Lee B Stern & Co Ltd
141 West Jackson Blvd, Chicago, IL 60604

Peiser D E
Kawana Securities Corp
50 Broadway, Room 1801, New York,
NY 10004

Peters R N
Peters & Co
141 West Jackson Blvd, Chicago, IL 60604

Piazza M
Mintz, Marcus & Co
81 Broad St, New York, NY 10004

Pinney R D
c/o Erie Investment Co, 2480 Commercial
Blvd, Fort Lauderdale, FL 33308

Posner S P
Commonwealth Holding Co
1143 Fifth Ave, New York, NY 10028

Poulat J R
Sociedad Financiera De Industria y
Descuento SA
Ave Fco I, Madero No 42, PB, Mexico, DF,
Mexico

Pressner B
Pressner Trading Corp
6 Harrison St, New York, NY 10013

Prockter A G W
Billiton-Enthoven Metals Ltd
Market Bldgs, 29 Mincing Lane, London EC3

Quint B
Dishy Easton & Co
c/o Commodity Exchange Inc, 81 Broad St,
New York, NY 10004

Rasher C E
McMahon Iron & Metal Co Inc
3300 Conner St, Bronx, NY 10469

Rasmussen J
M Lib/Ras International
222 South Riverside Plaza, Chicago,
IL 60606

Redel I
Redel Trading Co Inc
51 Sycamore Rd, Scarsdale, NY 10513

Redel N A
Redel Trading Co Inc
67 Broad St, New York, NY 10004

Rehders O F
c/o New York Cotton Exchange, 37 Wall St,
New York, NY 10005

Ritholtz A J
c/o New York Cotton Exchange, 37 Wall St,
New York, NY 10005

Rosa A
c/o New York Coffee & Sugar Exchange,
79 Pine St, New York, NY 10005

Rosenberg S
425 East 58th St, Apt 48E, New York,
NY 10022

Rosenblatt F
Primary Industries Corp
666 Fifth Ave, New York, NY 10019

Rosenthal M B
270-210 Grand Central Pkwy, Queens,
NY 11002

Rothberg S
North 1406 Park Towne Place, Philadelphia,
PA

Rothschild J S
M Rothschild & Co
15 Park Row, New York, NY 10038

Rowland R A
141 West Jackson Blvd, Chicago, IL 60604

Rowland R E Jr
c/o Commodity Exchange Inc, 81 Broad St,
New York, NY 10004

Rudner A J
F J Forlenza & Co
81 Broad St, New York, NY 10004

Rusnak M J
Enterex Commodities Corp
115 Beechwood Rd, Summit, NJ 07901

Sacks H
Brandeis, Goldschmidt & Co Inc
919 Third Ave, New York, NY 10022

Samuel J A
J A Samuel & Co
233 Broadway, New York, NY 10007

Santagata J N
Mintz, Marcus & Co
81 Broad St, New York, NY 10004

Santamaria E
E Santamaria & Co Inc
PO Box 2015, Manila, PI

Sarpi P
c/o New York Cocoa Exchange Inc,
127 John St, New York, NY 10038

Schmerer L
608 Fifth Ave, Suite 706, New York,
NY 10020

Schmidt-Fellner A H
Amax Inc
2 Greenwich Plaza, Greenwich, CT 06830

Schreiber F G
Minemet Metals Inc
450 Park Ave, New York, NY 10022

Schnell M
M Schnell Co
81 Broad St, New York, NY 10004

Schultz M L
c/o Bache Halsey Stuart Inc, 100 Gold St,
New York, NY 10038

Schwartz H
140 Poplar Drive, Roslyn, NY 11576

Schwieger J H
Paine, Webber, Jackson & Curtis Inc
140 Broadway, New York, NY 10005

Sepenuk M
21 Hyatt Ave, Newark, NJ

Shak N N
114 Ridge St, Cranford, NJ 07016

Shein I E
ACLI International Inc
110 Wall St, New York, NY 10005

Silk T J
c/o Commodity Exchange Inc, 81 Broad St,
New York, NY 10004

Silverberg A P
5 Sylvan Way, Short Hills, NJ 07078

Sinclair J E
Vilas & Hickey
26 Broadway, New York, NY 10004

Sirota B
Genora Commodities Inc
300, 71st St, Room 440, Miami Beach,
FL 33141

Sirota N L
Genora Commodities Inc
79 Pine St, New York, NY 10005

Smith E G
Albert Trostel & Sons Co
PO Box 743, Milwaukee, WI 53201

Smith J J
Fahnestock & Co
110 Wall St, New York, NY 10005

Snyder A S
Metal Traders Inc
445 Park Ave, New York, NY 10022

Solta J
4455 Douglas Ave, Riverdale, NY 10463

Soriano J M
Ansor Corp
1351 Washington Blvd, Stamford, CT 06902

Speyer A C Jr
1202 Benedum Trees Bldg, Pittsburgh,
PA 15222

Spiller J S
Mintz, Marcus & Co
81 Broad St, New York, NY 10004

Steib L W
1647 Burnett St, Brooklyn, NY 11229

Stein E A
c/o Commodity Exchange Inc, 81 Broad St,
New York, NY 10004

Stemland R R
Paine, Webber, Jackson & Curtis Inc
25 Broad St, 19th Floor, New York,
NY 10004

Steo A S
Mintz, Marcus & Co
81 Broad St, New York, NY 10004

Stern J
Stern & Stern Securities Inc
110 Wall St, New York, NY 10005

Stern L B
L B Stern & Co Ltd
141 West Jackson Blvd, Chicago, IL 60604

Stetler P H
Pouch Terminal
Edgewater St, Clifton, Staten Island,
NY 10305

Strauss S D
ASARCO Inc
120 Broadway, New York, NY 10005

Suskind D A
J Aron & Co Inc
160 Water St, 19th Floor, New York,
NY 10038

Tanne S
251 Central Park West, New York, NY 10024

Tant C P
Truebner & Co Inc
130 John St, New York, NY 10038

Tejani R H
Trans World Agencies
PO Box 648, Dubai, United Arab Emirates

Terrein C
Financiera Banamex SA
Isabel La Catolica No 39, Mexico 1, DF

Thaute E F
E F Hutton & Co Inc
1 Battery Park Plaza, New York, NY 10004

Thomte T
Thomte-Roper Inc
59 Commercial Wharf, Boston, MA 02110

Todd W P
95 Madison Ave, Morristown, NJ 07960

Trentham R E
Merrill Lynch, Pierce, Fenner & Smith Inc
1 Liberty Plaza, 165 Broadway, New York,
NY 10006

Tuck J D
Floor Broker Associates
2 Coenties Slip, New York, NY 10004

Tuomey P N
c/o Commodity Exchange Inc, 81 Broad St,
New York, NY 10004

Turman D C
c/o Commodity Exchange Inc, 81 Broad St,
New York, NY 10004

Varrall P D F
Johnson Matthey Bankers Ltd
43 Hatton Gdn, London EC1P 1AE

Vuillequez J
Amax Inc
1270 Avenue of the Americas, New York,
NY 10020

Wade J A Jr
155 East 73rd St, New York, NY 10021

Wagner J
1957 Kimball St, Brooklyn, NY 11234

Wagner M R
1957 Kimball St, Brooklyn, NY 11234

Wall H A
H Wall Co
600 Avenue Conde 'F', Coral Gables,
FL 33134

Walsh L S
21 Roselawn Ave, Lansdowne, PA 19050

Walton R
c/o Commodity Exchange Inc, 81 Broad St,
New York, NY 10004

Waltuch N D
Conti Commodity Services Inc
2 Broadway, New York, NY 10004

Weiner L
United Equities Co
160 Broadway, New York, NY 10038

Weinstein H
P Elbogen & Co Inc
45 North Station Plaza, Suite 215,
Great Neck, LI, NY 11021

Weiss L H
15 Percheron Lane, Roslyn Heights,
NY 11577

Weissblatt H J
Brody, White & Co Inc
25 Broad St, New York, NY 10004

Weissman P
Liberty Smelting Works (1962) Ltd
PO Box 840, Postal Station A, Montreal,
Quebec, Canada H3C 2V5

Weltzein H C Jr
209 Bear Ridge Rd, Pleasantville, NY 10570

Wemple F H
Handy & Harman
850 Third Ave, New York, NY 10022

Westheimer G J
c/o Commodity Exchange Inc, 81 Broad St,
New York, NY 10004

Westheimer S
c/o Commodity Exchange Inc, 81 Broad St,
New York, NY 10004

Westheimer V
344 East 51st St, New York, NY 10022

Wetzell H M
c/o Commodity Exchange Inc, 81 Broad St,
New York, NY 10004

Willstatter R
c/o Gerald Metals Inc, 1 Battery Park Plaza,
New York, NY 10004

Winzap R
Bullion Exchange & Trading Co Ltd
4 Place Pepinet, PO Box 2353, Lausanne,
Switzerland

Withrow R M
Lamson Bros & Co
111 West Jackson Blvd, Chicago, IL 60604

Witkin I
113 Campfire Rd, Chappaqua, NY 10514

Witkin W I
General Cocoa Co
160 Water St, New York, NY 10038

Wolff F F
Rudolph Wolff & Co Ltd
Knollys House, 11 Byward St,
London EC3

Woodburn G E
Precious Metals Corp of America
20 Exchange Place, New York, NY 10005

Yalkowsky S
445 East 161st St, Bronx, NY 10456

Young E J Jr
Clayton Brokerage Co of St Louis Inc
7701 Forsyth Blvd, Suite 300, Clayton,
MO 63105

Zins B C
Chartered New England Corp
90 Broad St, New York, NY 10004

New York Cocoa Exchange Inc, trading members, as at February 1976

Adams A A
c/o Woodhouse Drake & Carey Inc
127 John St, New York, NY 10038

Aitken T P
c/o Gill & Duffus Inc
130 John St, New York, NY 10038

Aron J R
c/o J Aron & Co Inc
160 Water St, New York, NY 10038

Avallone K H
c/o J F Dengel Jr Co Inc
127 John St, New York, NY 10038

Becker S M
Fahnestock & Co
110 Wall St, New York, NY 10005

Benjamin J F
c/o Drexel, Burnham & Co Inc
60 Broad St, New York, NY 10004

Berry W A
6435-4 Bay Club Drive, Fort Lauderdale,
FL 33308

Blank V A
c/o Muller & McDonnell Inc
116 John St, New York, NY 10038

Blaisse O B
c/o Wessanen Cacao BV
Zaanweg 51 (PO B11), Wormerveer,
1420, The Netherlands

Bleecker P B
c/o Scholtz & Co Inc
110 Wall St, New York, NY 10005

Blommer H
c/o The Blommer Chocolate Co
600 West Kinzie St, Chicago, IL 60610

Blumenthal B S
c/o Ward Chocolate Co Inc
Margaret & James Sts, Philadelphia,
PA 19137

Bogart L C
c/o Jell-o Division General Foods Corp
PO Box 600, West North St, Dover,
Delaware 19901

Bollard E C
c/o J J Donohue Co Inc
127 John St, New York, NY 10038

Boucher J H P
c/o Smith Barney, Harris Upham & Co Inc
120 Broadway, New York, NY 10005

Bradley E C
c/o IECO Commodities Inc
116 John St, New York, NY 10038

Brand W J M
c/o Harborn BV
Sophialaan 8-10, Amsterdam, Z, Holland

Brandt H
c/o ACLI International Inc
110 Wall St, New York, NY 10005

Bridge A
c/o E J Brach & Sons, Division of American
Home Products Corp
4656 West Kinzie St, Box 802, Chicago,
IL 60690

Brody E A Dr
c/o Brody, White & Co Inc
25 Broad St, New York, NY 10004

Brown R C
c/o The Nestle Co Inc
100 Bloomingdale Rd, White Plains,
NY 10605

Buckley J C K
c/o The Nestle Co Inc
100 Bloomingdale Rd, White Plains,
NY 10605

Burdman B R
2770 Tibbette-Wick Rd, Hubbard, OH

Buzzard J A
c/o Wilbur Chocolate Co
48-54 North Broad St, Lititz, PA 17543

Cahill J P
c/o J F Dengel Jr Co Inc
127 John St, New York, NY 10038

Capinegro A
c/o Lincolnwood Inc
141 West Jackson Blvd, Chicago, IL 60604

Carlee J L
127 John St, New York, NY 10038

Cobb R L
c/o General Foods Corp
250 North St, White Plains, NY 10625

Collins J S
c/o Paul Sarpi & Co
127 John St, New York, NY 10038

Cook E W
c/o Cook Grain Co Inc
PO Box 16902, Memphis, TN 38116

Coppola M
c/o Genco Commodities Inc
160 Water St, New York, NY 10038

Coyne H J
c/o J Aron Commodities Corp
160 Water St, New York, NY 10038

Coyne M L
c/o J Aron & Co Inc
160 Water St, New York, NY 10038

Coyne S Y
c/o J Aron & Co Inc
160 Water St, New York, NY 10038

DeMartino R
c/o Commodity International
84 William St, New York, NY 10038

Dengel J F Jr
c/o J F Dengel Jr Co Inc
127 John St, New York, NY 10038

Diamond I H
c/o I H Diamond & Co Inc
116 John St, New York, NY 10038

Diez V J
c/o Machado & Co Inc
120 Wall St, New York, NY 10005

DiLiberto J B
c/o Genora Commodities Inc
79 Pine St, New York, NY 10005

Dittmer T H
c/o R E Friedman & Co
222 South Riverside Plaza, Chicago,
IL 60606

Donohue J J
c/o J J Donohu Co Inc
127 John St, New York, NY 10038

Doty G E
Goldman, Sachs & Co
55 Broad St, New York, NY 10004

Dragonetti H H
c/o Fendrake Ltd
20 Fenchurch St, London

Edwards T H
c/o Lonray Inc
77 Water St, New York, NY 10005

Evans G D
c/o E Bailey & Co Ltd
69-70 Mark Lane, London EC3R 7SX

Fehr B H F
c/o F Fehr & Co Ltd
Prince Rupert House, 64 Queen St,
London EC4R 1ER

Fischel A N
c/o ACLI International Inc
110 Wall St, New York, NY 10005

Fischel J R
c/o L M Fischel & Co Ltd
Dunster House, Mincing Lane,
London EC3

Flanagan R M
c/o Dean Witter & Co Inc
2 Broadway, New York, NY 10004

Fletcher T P
c/o Paul Sarpi & Co
127 John St, New York, NY 10038

Fopma F
c/o BV Continentale en Afrikaanse
Handelsvereniging, 'CONTINAF'
Jacob Obrechtstraat 55, Amsterdam, Holland

Freeburg R G
c/o Merrill Lynch, Pierce, Fenner & Smith
Smith Inc
1 Liberty Plaza, 165 Broadway, New York,
NY 10006

Freeman A L
Rosenthal & Co
141 West Jackson Blvd, Chicago, IL 60604

Fromer M A
c/o Lewis & Peat Trading Inc
150 East 58th St, New York, NY 10022

Fuller K S
c/o Richardson Securities Inc
40 Wall St, New York, NY 10005

Garfield G
Garfield & Co
Carter Rd, R D 2, Princeton, NJ 08540

Gettinger H
c/o Mars, Inc
High St, Hackettstown, NJ 07840

Ginzberg J
M Golodetz & Co
666, 5th Ave, New York, NY 10019

Goldstein L
c/o Genco Commodities Inc
160 Water St, New York, NY 10038

Golodetz A
General Cocoa Co
160 Water St, New York, NY 10038

Golodetz L
c/o Sugar Industry Auxiliaries Ltd
29 Mincing Lane, London EC3R 7EU,

Grayson H B
c/o I H Diamond & Co Inc
116 John St, New York, NY 10038

Halpert L S
c/o Cocoline Chocolate Co Inc
689-697 Myrtle Ave, Brooklyn, NY 11205

Harari J
80 Broad St, New York, NY 10004

Harsha W N
c/o Pet Inc
PO Box 6070, Philadelphia, PA 19114

Heilbron W
c/o Imperial Commodities Corp
110 Wall St, New York, NY 10005

Heinold H J
c/o Heinold Commodities Inc
222 South Riverside Plaza, Chicago,
IL 60606

Hemphill J
c/o Hershey Foods Corp
127 John St, New York, NY 10038

Hilpert E
c/o Hilpert Trading Co Ltd
23 Adlerstrasse, Basle, Switzerland

Hoch J E
c/o ACLI International Inc
110 Wall St, New York, NY 10005

Hockstader L A II
L F Rothschild & Co
99 William St, New York, NY 10038

Howard R G
c/o Reynolds Securities Inc
120 Broadway, New York, NY 10005

Imregi B A
c/o Lonray (Sugar) Inc
77 Water St, New York, NY 10005

Israel A C
c/o ACLI International Commodity
Services Inc
110 Wall St, New York, NY 10005

Israel T C
c/o ACLI International Inc
110 Wall St, New York, NY 10005

Jamieson J H
c/o PACOL (Canada) Ltd
2 Bloor St West, Suite 1000, Toronto,
Ontario M4W 3E2, Canada

Jiskoot L J
c/o Thomson & McKinnon Auchincloss
Kohlmeyer Inc
1 New York Plaza, New York, NY 10004

Johnston D T
c/o E F Hutton & Co Inc
1 Battery Park Plaza, New York, NY 10004

Joseph E S
c/o IECO Commodities Inc
116 John St, New York, NY 10038

Karouni A J
87 Kingston House, London SW7,

Kipnis H S
H S Kipnis & Co
209 South LaSalle St, Chicago, IL 60604

Kooyker W
c/o Holco Trading Co Inc
116 John St, New York, NY 10038

Kurzrok M D
c/o Lehman Bros Inc
1 William St, New York, NY 10004

Langenberg O M
c/o A G Edwards & Sons Inc
1 North Jefferson St, St Louis, MO 63101

Lamborn A H Jr
c/o Shearson Hayden Stone Inc, Sugar Div.
2 Greenwich Plaza, Greenwich, CT 06830

Larson W L
c/o Cargill Investor Services Inc
2 Broadway, New York, NY 10004

Law B R
c/o Mars Ltd
Dundee Rd, Slough, Bucks, England

Leathers L H
c/o Shearson Hayden Stone Inc
1 Western Union International Plaza,
New York, NY 10004

Letsinger J A
c/o Merrill Lynch, Pierce, Fenner &
Smith Inc
1 Liberty Plaza, 165 Broadway, New York,
NY 10006

Levi H
c/o Hollander Confectionery & Cocoa Corp
80 Pine St, New York, NY 10005

Lieben S B
285 Fountain Rd, Englewood, NJ 07631

Lindberg E H
c/o Curacao Trading Co Inc
75 Maiden Lane, New York, NY 10038

Loeb P K
Loeb, Rhoades & Co
42 Wall St, New York, NY 10005

Loewy E
c/o Bauer & Loewy Trading Corp
111 John St, New York, NY 10038

Lorenze G D
c/o Gill & Duffus Inc
130 John St, New York, NY 10038

Ludlow C S (Estate of)
c/o Dean Witter & Co Inc
42 Broadway, New York, NY 10004

MacLeod W N
c/o Mincing Trading Corp
25 Broadway, New York, NY 10004

Mahler P
6 Harrison St, New York, NY 10013

Margulies E S
c/o J H Rayner (Mincing Lane) Ltd
50 Mark Lane, London EC3R 7RJ,

Marx M
United Equities (Commodities) Co
160 Broadway, New York, NY 10038

Maspons V
c/o Cia de Intercambio y Credito, C Ltda,
Guayaquil, Ecuador

Massey R W
c/o Hornblower & Weeks—Hemphill,
Noyes, Inc
8 Hanover St, New York, NY 10004

Mattey C
c/o Bache Halsey Stuart Inc
100 Gold St, New York, NY 10038

McClure K H
c/o K H McClure & Co Inc
1100 High Ridge Rd, Stamford, CT 06905

McCormack R M
c/o J F Dengel Jr Co Inc
127 John St, New York, NY 10038

McDonnell R E
Commodity International
84 William St, New York, NY 10038

McFadden E V Jr
c/o IECO Commodities Inc
116 John St, New York, NY 10038

McFall R G
c/o PACOL Ltd
47 Mark Lane, London EC3R 7QX

McInroy I A
c/o Paterson, Simons & Ewart Ltd
Riverbank House, 67 Upper Thames St,
London EC4

McNeil R S
c/o US Cocoa Corp
1615 Suckle Highway, Pensauken, NJ 08110

Messina L
c/o Genco Commodities Inc
160 Water St, New York, NY 10038

Mintz L A
Mintz-Marcus & Co
New York, NY 10004

Morton W A
c/o Truebner & Co Inc
130 John St, New York, NY 10038

Moutafian A N
c/o Moutafian Commodities Ltd
2-4 Eastcheap, London EC3

Muldorf R
c/o I H Diamond & Co Inc
116 John St, New York, NY 10038

Muller W
c/o Muller & McDonnell Inc
116 John St, New York, NY 10038

Nichols O H
c/o Mitchell, Hutchins Inc
2 First National Plaza, Chicago, IL 60603

Nugent B J
127 John St, New York, NY 10038

Nugteren A
c/o Balfour MacLaine Inc
88 Pine St, New York, NY 10005

O'Connell D J
c/o Ambrosia Chocolate Co
1133 North Fifth St, Milwaukee, WI 53209

Opler E
c/o World's Finest Chocolate Inc
2521 West 48th St, Chicago, IL 60632

Park J W
c/o Christman Associates
77 Water St, New York, NY 10005

Parry L A
c/o Brascan International Inc
127 John St, New York, NY 10038

Paulson R W
c/o Barretto Cocoa Products Inc,
61 Broadway, New York, NY 10006

Perkins W L
c/o Curacao Trading Co Inc
75 Maiden Lane, New York, NY 10038

Peters R N
Peters & Co
141 West Jackson Blvd, Chicago, IL 60604

Pilz C R
c/o Nabisco Inc
PO Box 1002, East Hanover, NJ 07936

Piper A R III
c/o Paine, Webber, Jackson & Curtis Inc
25 Broad St, New York, NY 10004

Poons M C
c/o Poons Co Inc
45 North Station Plaza, Great Neck,
Long Island, NY 11021

Preston G E
c/o SNW Commodities Ltd
Rayner House, 39 Hatton Gdn,
London EC1N 8BX

Reeders A J
c/o General Cocoa Co Holland, BV
Het Havengebouw de Ruyterkade 7,
Amsterdam, Holland

Roelli W
c/o Volkart Bros Inc
120 Wall St, New York, NY 10005

Sanders R M
c/o ACLI International Commodity
Services Inc
110 Wall St, New York, NY 10005

Sarpi P
c/o P Sarpi & Co
127 John St, New York, NY 10038

Scarano L L
c/o P Sarpi & Co
127 John St, New York, NY 10038

Schenk H F
c/o Holco Trading Co Ltd
8 Lloyd's Ave, London EC3N 3AB

Scheu J J
c/o Cocoa Products Division, W R Grace & C
1114 Avenue of the Americas, New York,
NY 10036

Scheuer A F
c/o Internatio Inc
116 John St, New York, NY 10038

Scholtz J H Jr
c/o Scholtz & Co Inc
110 Wall St, New York, NY 10005

Schur M H
c/o J Aron & Co Inc
160 Water St, New York, NY 10038

Scrase A W E
c/o R J Rouse & Co Ltd
Dunster House, 37 Mincing Lane,
London EC3R 7TH

Sirota N L
c/o Genora Commodities Inc
79 Pine St, New York, NY 10005

Smith R N
c/o Lonray Inc
77 Water St, New York, NY 10005

Snyder A S
c/o Agrimet Inc, 445 Park Ave, New York,
NY 10022

Spielman J M
c/o Merrill Lynch, Pierce, Fenner &
Smith Inc
1 Liberty Plaza, 165 Broadway, New York,
NY 10006

Stam K
c/o Catz International BV
Westersingel 96, PO Box 180, Rotterdam

Stark R M
c/o P Paul Inc
New Haven Rd, Naugatuck, CT 06771

Steimer J H
22B Celtis Plaza, Clearbrook, Cranbury,
NJ 08512

Stern W
General Cocoa Co
160 Water St, New York, NY 10038

Storyk L
c/o Fehr Bros Inc
110 Wall St, New York, NY 10005

Sweeney J F Jr
c/o The F Sweeney Corp, 50 Merrick Rd,
Rockville Center, NY 11570

Tominaga T
c/o Toshoku America Inc
551 Fifth Ave, New York, NY 10017

Truebner L H
c/o Truebner & Co Inc
130 John St, New York, NY 10038

Uhrich R L
c/o Hershey Foods Corp
19 East Chocolate Ave, Hershey, PA 17083

Van Gilder F D
c/o J F Dengel Jr Co Inc
127 John St, New York, NY 10038

Vartany M
c/o Cacao Barry Inc
540 Madison Ave, New York, NY 10022

Vietor H W
c/o Cocoa Products Corp
309 Sunset Drive, Fort Lauderdale,
FL 33301

Viguerie S C
c/o Howard, Weil, Labouisse, Friedrichs Inc
211 Carondelet St, New Orleans, LA 70130

Vollmer F W
c/o C Schroeter Inc
116 John St, New York, NY 10038

Vollmer H O
c/o C Schroeter Inc
116 John St, New York, NY 10038

Wahrsager S
Bear, Stearns & Co
55 Water St, New York, NY 10041

Waltuch N D
c/o ContiCommodity Services Inc
2 Broadway, New York, NY 10004

Wehrli W A
c/o C Schroeter Inc
116 John St, New York, NY 10038

Weldon A H D
c/o Cocoa Merchants Ltd
Plantation House, Fenchurch St,
London EC3M 3HX

Weldon M
c/o Cocoa Merchants Ltd
Plantation House, Fenchurch St,
London EC3 3HX

Weymar F H
c/o Commodities Corp
Mount Lucas Rd, Princeton, NJ 08540

Whitestone A
c/o Woodhouse, Drake & Carey Inc
127 John St, New York, NY 10038

Wincott P
c/o Philip Wincott, Inc
127 John St, New York, NY 10038

Witkin I
c/o General Cocoa Co Inc
160 Water St, New York, NY 10038

Witkin W I
113 Campfire Rd, Chappaqua, NY 10514

Woodhouse C H
c/o Woodhouse, Drake & Carey Ltd
Three Quays, Tower Hill, London EC3R 6EP

Young E J Jr
c/o Clayton Brokerage Co of St Louis Inc
7701 Forsyth Blvd, Suite 300, St Louis,
MO 63105

New York Cotton Exchange, member firms servicing individual accounts, as at June 1976

ACLI International Commodity Services Inc
20th Floor, 110 Wall St, New York, NY

Allenberg Brokerage Co
Exchange Floor (1), 37 Wall St, New York,
NY

J Aron Commodities Corp
19th Floor, 160 Water St, New York, NY

Bache Halsey Stuart Inc
5th Floor, Room S-5, 100 Gold St,
New York, NY

Bear, Stearns & Co
Room 105B, 48th Floor, 55 Water St,
New York, NY

Brody, White & Co Inc
First Floor, 25 Broad St, New York, NY

Cancellare, Rocca G
Exchange Floor (1), 37 Wall St, New York,
NY

Cargill Investor Services Inc
28th Floor, 2 Broadway, New York, NY

Clayton Brokerage Co of St Louis, Inc
Suite 1525, 1 World Trade, New York, NY

Comenzo D R
Exchange Floor (1), 37 Wall St, New York,
NY

Commodity International
6th Floor, 84 William St, New York, NY

Conti Commodity Services Inc
21st Floor, 2 Broadway, New York, NY

Cook Cotton Co Inc
Exchange Floor (1), 37 Wall St, New York,
NY

Drexel, Burnham & Co Inc
10th Floor, 60 Broad St, New York, NY

Dunavant Commodity Corp
Exchange Floor (1), 37 Wall St, New York,
NY

A G Edwards & Sons Inc
14th Floor, 20 Exchange Place, New York,
NY

Fahnestock & Co
Room 804, 110 Wall St, New York, NY

Flyn J J
Cotton Exchange Floor (1), 37 Wall St,
New York, NY

R E Friedman & Co
Suite 1411, 61 Broadway, New York, NY

Friedman R I
Cotton Exchange Floor (1), 37 Wall St,
New York, NY

Genora Commodities Inc
Room M-100, 79 Pine St, New York, NY

Gill & Duffus Inc
20th Floor, 130 John St, New York, NY

Hamilton J R
Exchange Floor (1), 37 Wall St, New York,
NY

Hehmeyer P L
Exchange Floor (1), 37 Wall St, New York,
NY

Heinold Commodities Inc
3rd Floor, 74 Pearl St, New York, NY

Herman J
Exchange Floor (1), 37 Wall St, New York,
NY

Hornblower & Weeks-Hemphill, Noyes Inc
4th Floor, Commodity Dept, 8 Hanover St,
New York, NY

E F Hutton & Co Inc
6th Floor, Commodity Dept, 1 Battery Park
Plaza, New York, NY

H S Kipnis & Co
18th Floor, 40 Rector St, New York, NY

Klein & Co
Exchange Floor (1), 37 Wall St, New York,
NY

Knack R L
Cotton Exchange Floor (1), 37 Wall St,
New York, NY

Knell F
Exchange Floor (1), 37 Wall St, New York,
NY

Layton W C Jr
Exchange Floor (1), 37 Wall St, New York,
NY

M Lazarus Co
Exchange Floor (1), 37 Wall St, New York,
NY

Loeb, Rhoades & Co
12th Floor, Commodity Margin Dept,
40 Wall St, New York, NY

Lincolnwood Inc
32nd Floor, 127 John St, New York, NY

C J Maneri Associates
Exchange Floor (1), 37 Wall St, New York,
NY

Merrill Lynch, Pierce, Fenner & Smith Inc
Commodity Operations, 10th Floor,
1 Liberty Plaza, 165 Broadway, New York,
NY

Morace J L
Cotton Exchange Floor (1), 37 Wall St,
New York, NY

Nelson M H
Exchange Floor (1), 37 Wall St, New York,
NY

Novak J A
Room 6411, 5 World Trade, New York, NY

O'Cone P M
Exchange Floor (1), 37 Wall St, New York,
NY

Paine, Webber, Jackson & Curtis Inc
Room 1437, Commodity Dept, 25 Broad St,
New York, NY

Peters & Co
32nd Floor, 127 John St, New York, NY

Phillips J H
Exchange Floor (1), 37 Wall St, New York,
NY

Preston C E
Exchange Floor (1), 37 Wall St, New York,
NY

Pressner Trading Corp
Cotton Exchange Floor (1), 37 Wall St,
New York, NY

Raul Y B
Exchange Floor (1), 37 Wall St, New York, NY

Redel Trading Co Inc
Commodity Exchange Floor, 81 Broad St, New York, NY

Rehders O F
Exchange Floor (1), 37 Wall St, New York, NY

Reynolds Securities Inc
8th Floor, Commodity Dept, 42 Broadway, New York, NY

Ritholtz A
Cotton Exchange Floor (1), 37 Wall St, New York, NY

Rosenthal & Co
Suite 6411, 5 World Trade, New York, NY

Shearson Hayden Stone Inc
Commodity Dept, 18th Floor, 17 Battery Plaza North, New York, NY

Silverberg A P
Balfour Maclaine, 24th Floor, 67 Broad St, New York, NY

Smith Barney, Harris Upham & Co Inc
24th Floor, 120 Broadway, New York, NY

Thomson & McKinnon Auchincloss, Kohlmeyer Inc
47th Floor, Commodity Dept, 1 New York Plaza, New York, NY

Valmac Industries Inc
Exchange Floor (1), 37 Wall St, New York, NY

Wade J A Jr
Exchange Floor (1), 37 Wall St, New York, NY

Wagner & Co
Exchange Floor (1), 37 Wall St, New York, NY

Weil Bros & Butler
Room 1209, 82 Wall St, New York, NY

Weis A M
Exchange Floor (1), 37 Wall St, New York, NY

Wetzell H M
Exchange Floor (1), 37 Wall St, New York, NY

Williams J M
Exchange Floor (1), 37 Wall St, New York, NY

D Witter & Co Inc
15th Floor, 2 Broadway, New York, NY

New York Mercantile Exchange, trading members (partial listing), as at January 1976

A-Mark Precious Metals Inc
4640 Hollywood Blvd, Los Angeles, CA 90027. Tel: 213-660 3434

Bache & Co Inc
100 Gold St, New York, NY 10038.
Tel: 212-791 4948

Barad-Shaff Sales Co
90 West Broadway, New York, NY 10007.
Tel: 212-964 0118

Bear, Stearns & Co
55 Water St, New York, NY 10041.
Tel: 212-952 5044

Beaver Brook Commodities
PO Box 628, Caribou, ME 04736.
Tel: 207-496 3411

Brandeis, Goldschmidt & Co Inc
919 Third Ave, New York, NY 10022.
Tel: 212-486 8685

Brody, White & Co Inc
25 Broad St, New York, NY 10004.
Tel: 212 785 1214

Bushwick Commission Co Inc
1 North West Drive, Farmingdale, NY 11735.
Tel: 516-249 6030

Cargill Investor Services Inc
2 Broadway, New York, NY 10004.
Tel: 212-825 0450

Chartered New England Corp
90 Broad St, New York, NY 10004.
Tel: 212-425 5348

Clayton Brokerage Co of St Louis Inc
7701 Forsyth Blvd, Suite 300, Clayton, MO 63105. Tel: 314-627 8000

Commodity International
84 William St, New York, NY 10038.
Tel: 212-344 4333

ContiCommodity Services Inc
2 Broadway, New York, NY 10004.
Tel: 212-344 7640

Delos Commodities
6 Harrison St, New York, NY 10013.
Tel: 212-431 5814

Delphi Commodities Inc
150 Broadway, New York, NY 10038.
Tel: 212-267 3270

Drexel Burnham & Co Inc
60 Broad St, New York, NY 10004.
Tel: 212-344 1400

Edelstein & Co Inc
6 Harrison St, New York, NY 10013.
Tel: 212-966 4900

A G Edwards & Sons Inc
20 Exchange Place, New York, NY 10005.
Tel: 212-952 7200

Fahnestock & Co
110 Wall St, New York, NY 10005.
Tel: 212-943 8900

Sam Fishberg & Co
6 Harrison St, New York, NY 10013.
Tel: 212-925 5862

Freehling & Co
120 South LaSalle, Chicago, IL 60603.
Tel: 312-346 2680

R E Friedman & Co
222 South Riverside Plaza, Chicago,
IL 60606. Tel: 312-454 4900

G S Commodities
6 Harrison St, New York, NY 10013.
Tel: 212-925 8330

Genora Commodities Inc
79 Pine St, New York, NY 10005.
Tel: 212-269 8220

Gerald Metals Inc
1 Battery Park Plaza, New York, NY 10004.
Tel: 212-425 4160

Grappel Trading Co Inc
6 Harrison St, New York, NY 10013.
Tel: 212-925 2808

Greene & Collins Inc
175 West Jackson Blvd, Chicago, IL 60604.
Tel: 800-621 5419

Harris, Upham & Co Inc
120 Broadway, New York, NY 10005.
Tel: 212-374 7143

Heinold Commodities Inc
74 Pearl St, New York, NY 10004.
Tel: 212-248 3130

Helfer Commodities
5 World Trade Center, New York, NY 10048.
Tel: 212-938 1350

Hornblower & Weeks-Hemphill, Noyes Inc
72 West Adams St, Chicago, IL 60603.
Tel: 312-641 5000

E F Hutton & Co Inc
1 Battery Park Plaza, New York, NY 10004.
Tel: 212-742 5000

International Trading Group Ltd
29201 Telegraph Rd, Southfield, MI 48076.
Tel: 1-800-482 8400

H S Kipnis & Co
40 Rector St, New York, NY 10006.
Tel: 212-482 5560

Lincolnwood Inc
127 John St, New York, NY 10038.
Tel: 212-747 1950

Loeb, Rhoades & Co
40 Wall St, New York, NY 10005.
Tel: 212-483 7345

MFX Commodities
PO Box 773, Presque Isle, ME 04769.
Tel: 207-764 4433

MPG Commodities Inc
PO Drawer 271, Presque Isle, ME 04769.
Tel: 207-768 5611

Maduff & Sons
Mercantile Exchange Bldg, Chicago,
IL 60606. Tel: 312-648 1234

Marc Commodities Corp
6 Harrison St, New York, NY 10013.
Tel: 212-925 2360

Merrill Lynch, Pierce, Fenner & Smith Inc
165 Broadway, New York, NY 10005.
Tel: 212-766 7064

Murlas Bros Commodities
110 North Franklin St, Chicago,
IL 60606. Tel: 312-641 5800

Paine, Webber, Jackson & Curtis Inc
25 Broad St, New York, NY 10004.
Tel: 212-437 6660

Paris Securities Corp
6 Harrison St, New York, NY 10013.
Tel: 212-966 1066

Peters & Co Inc
32nd Floor, 127 John St, New York,
NY 10038. Tel: 212-747 1979

H A Pollak & Co Inc
6 Harrison St, New York, NY 10013.
Tel: 212-966 2114

H B Pollak & Co
6 Harrison St, New York, NY 10013.
Tel: 212-966 2114

Primary Industries Corp
666 Fifth Ave, New York, NY 10019.
Tel: 212-581 9200

RAM Commodities Inc
6 Harrison St, New York, NY 10013.
Tel: 212-925 1030

Reynolds Securities Inc
120 Broadway, New York, NY 10005.
Tel: 212-558 6000

Richardson Securities Inc
40 Wall St, New York, NY 10005.
Tel: 212-483 0750

Rosenthal & Co
5 World Trade Center, New York,
NY 10048. Tel: 212-775 1080

Shearson Hayden Stone Inc
1 Western Union International Plaza,
New York, NY 10004. Tel: 212-623 8000

Siegel Trading Co Inc
100 North LaSalle, Chicago, IL 60602.
Tel: 312-236 6789

Sinclair & Co Inc
PO Box C, Twin Falls, ID 83301.
Tel: 208-733 6013

Stern & Stern Securities Inc
110 Wall St, New York, NY 10005.
Tel: 212-422 6717

Thomson & McKinnon-Auchincloss,
Kohlmeyer Inc
1 New York Plaza, New York, NY 10004.
Tel: 212-482 6383

D Witter & Co Inc
2 Broadway, New York, NY 10004.
Tel: 212-437 3266

Appendix 2:
Glossary of Commodity Market Terms

Actuals: Physical commodities, also commodities readily available. The commodity itself as opposed to a futures contract

Afloats: Commodities on board, underway, ready to sail

Arbitrage: Purchase of contract in one market while simultaneously selling the same commodity futures in another to take advantage of price differentials between the two exchanges

Backwardation: Market description of the situation when the spot or nearby prices are higher than those for future delivery months. Usually caused by delays in shipment thus creating shortages in available supplies. Opposite of contango

Basis/Basis grade: Difference between cash price and futures price

Basis price: Agreed price between buyer and seller of an option at which the option may be taken up. Also called the 'striking price'

Basis quote: Offer/sale of cash commodity as a difference above or below a futures price

Bear: Person expecting a decline in prices

Bear covering: Closing of short positions

Best orders: These are buy or sell orders executed by the broker at what is considered to be the best price

Bid: The price which the buyer is willing to pay

Board trading: Verbal bids in futures trading not conducted in the ring or pit but recorded on blackboards

Borrowing: Purchase of a nearby delivery date and simultaneous sale of a forward date. Used only in London Metal Exchange

Broker: Establishes contact between buyer and seller, for a fee. In the USA, ring dealing members of futures markets are frequently called brokers

Bull: Person expecting a rise in prices

Buying basis: Difference between cost of a cash commodity and a future sold as a hedge. See Selling Basis

Call: A period for trading. Conducted by a chairman to establish a price for a specific time. During a call, trading is confined to one delivery month

Call option: The option buyer/taker pays a premium and holds the right to decide at a later stage whether or not to buy at the price agreed at the time the premium was paid. The right may be exercised at any time from the point of purchase to the expiry of the option

Carrying: General term covering both Borrowing and Lending

Carrying costs: Costs connected with warehouse storage, insurance etc. On occasion includes interest and estimated changes in weight

Certified stocks: Supplies rated as deliverable

C & F: Cost and freight

CIF: Cost, insurance and freight (included in price)

Clearances: Aggregate shipments of a commodity made by sea on a specified date

Clearing house: The organization that provides clearing facilities for some futures markets

Commission house: A company, often of international coverage, which introduces client business to a floor dealing broker on the futures market. The Commission House only handles clients' business and does not trade on its own account

Commodity Futures Trading Commission: A newly introduced US regulatory agency that replaces the Commodity Exchange Commission and absorbs the Agriculture Department's Commodity Exchange Authority. It exercises control over US commodity futures market trading

Commodity Price Index: Index, or average, of commodity price movements

Contango: A situation where prices are higher in the forward delivery months than in the nearby delivery month. Opposite of backwardation. Normally in evidence when supplies are adequate or in surplus. The contango reflects either wholly or in part the costs of holding and financing

Contract: An agreement to buy or sell a specified amount of a particular commodity. It details the amount and grade of the product and the date on which the contract will mature and become deliverable, if not previously liquidated

Contract grades: That which is deliverable on a futures contract. Basic contract grade is the one deliverable at par. There may be more than one basic grade

Contract month: Month in which a given contract becomes deliverable, if not liquidated or traded out before the date specified

Contract weights: Deliverable weights of contract, as shown on warehouse receipts

Cost of tender: Total of various charges incurred when having a commodity certified and delivered

Cover: The balancing of an open position by buying or selling in the market

Crop year: Period starting from the harvesting of a crop to the corresponding period of the following year, as used statistically

Custom smelter: A smelter which relies on concentrate purchased from independent mines instead of its own captive sources

Day order/trading: Order valid throughout trading hours during day on which it is placed

Day trading: Buying and selling one or more futures contracts on the same day

Declaration date: Date when buyer's right to exercise an option expires

Delivery: There are three types of delivery: current — delivery during the present month; nearby — delivery during the nearest active month; distant — delivery in a month further off

Delivery basis: Specified locations to which the commodity in a futures contract may be physically delivered in order to terminate the contract

Delivery date: Or Prompt Date, on which the commodity must be delivered to fulfil the terms of the contract

Delivery month: Calendar month stipulated as month of delivery in a futures contract

Delivery notice: Notification of intention to deliver a certain amount of a commodity to settle a futures contract

Delivery price: Price fixed by clearing house where futures deliveries are invoiced. Also, price at which a commodities futures contract is settled when deliveries are made

Deposit: Sum of money required by the broker from his client, usually ten per cent of the value of the contract, to justify opening of a futures position

Differentials: Premiums paid for grades better than basic grade, or discounts allowed for grades below basic grade. Differentials are usually fixed by contract terms; however, commercial forces apply in cotton

Double option: This is an option which gives the buyer or person taking the option the right either to buy from or sell to the seller of the option or the person who gives it, at the basis price

EFP (Exchange for Physical): Trade between two parties — one buys physicals and sells futures contracts, the other sells physicals and buys futures contracts. Such an EFP is composed of four parts: the purchase and sale of futures contracts and the simultaneous sale and purchase by the same two parties of an equal quantity of the physical commodity

Exchange of spot or cash commodity for futures: Simultaneous exchange of a cash commodity for the equivalent in futures. This is used when the two parties carry opposite hedges in the same delivery month. Also known as 'against actuals'

Fabricator: A company which makes semi-fabricated products from refined metal and on occasion from scrap

First notice day: The first day on which notices are issued indicating delivery in a specific delivery month

Fixation: Fixing price in the future, and used in commodity call purchases and call sale trades

FOB: Free on Board

Force Majeure: This is a clause in a supply contract which permits either party not to fulfil the contractual commitments due to events beyond their control. These events may range from strikes to export delays in producing countries

Forward shipment: Contract covering actual commodity shipments at a future date which is specified

Futures contract: Contract which requires the delivery of a commodity in a specified future month, if not liquidated before the contract matures

Good Till Cancelled Order (GTC): Order which is valid at any time during market hours until executed or cancelled by the client

Grades: Standards set for judging the quality of a commodity

Grading certificates: Certificates which verify the commodity quality

Hedge: A temporary futures market sale which is made against a spot purchase, or alternatively a temporary futures market purchase made against a spot sale. The purpose is to reduce risk from price fluctuations on the physical transaction until the reverse futures market operation cancels the hedge, or liquidates the original operation

Integrated producer: A producer who owns mines, smelters and refineries and also, in some instances, fabricating plants

Inverted market: Futures market in which distant-month contracts are selling below near-month contracts

Job lot: Unit of trading smaller than the regular contract unit

Kerb trading: Unofficial trading when the market has closed. The term 'kerb' dates from the time when dealers continued trading on the kerb outside the exchanges after these had closed

Last trading day: Final day for trading a particular delivery. Positions which have not been closed by the last trading day must be fulfilled by making, or taking, delivery of the physical commodity or metal

Lending: Sale of a nearby delivery date coupled with the simultaneous purchase of a more distant date (LME term)

Life of delivery: Interval between first and last transaction in a futures contract

Limit order: An order to buy or sell at a specified price

Limit price: Largest permitted price fluctuation in a futures contract during a trading session, as fixed by contract market's rules

Liquidation: Sale of long contract to offset previous purchase. Operation which cancels an earlier position

Loan prices: These are prices at which the US Government will lend producers money for their crops

Long: An open purchased futures contract. Buying forward on the market

Long hedge: Purchase of futures which are made as a hedge against the sale of a cash commodity

Long liquidation: Closing of long positions

Long of the basis: Position of a commodity trader who has bought cash or spot goods and hedged them with sales of futures. See Hedge

Lot: Minimum contract unit in a hedge or futures market

Margin: This is the amount deposited as a guarantee for the fluctuations on a futures purchase or sale. If the contract fluctuates against the holder of the contract, he is required to provide for the difference between his contract price and the current market price by paying 'variation margin' differences. Thus the original margin continues to guarantee fully the performance of the contract at any market price level

Margin call: A commodity broker's request to a client for additional funds to secure the original deposits

Market order: To buy or sell a futures contract at prices on the market or the first obtainable price

Maximum price fluctuation: Set by the rules of a commodity exchange, this is the limit of fluctuation in the price of a futures contract during any one trading session

Minimum price fluctuation: The minimum unit by which the price of a commodity can fluctuate per trade

Nearby delivery: The nearest active month of delivery on a futures market

Net position: Difference between the number of open commodity contracts held long and short in an account

Nominal price: An estimate of the price for a futures month or date in which no trading has taken place

Offer: The seller's price for the commodity offered

Offset: Liquidation of a long or short position by the opposite transaction: the sale offsets a long position; the purchase offsets a short position

Open contracts: Contracts bought or sold and not offset by an opposite trade

Open interest: The total number of contracts, bought or sold, but not offset by the opposite transactions

Open outcry: Trading conducted by calling out bids and offers across a ring or pit and having them accepted orally

Open position: A forward market position which has not been closed out

Option: The holder of the option has the right to buy from or sell to the granter of the option a specified quantity of the commodity at an agreed price. The cost of buying the option is known as the premium

Original margin: Deposit margin made in relation to a given commitment

Pegged price: The price at which a commodity has been fixed by agreement

Pit: Place where futures are traded on the floor of a commodity exchange. Also known as ring

Point: Minimum price unit in which a commodity price is quoted

Position trader: Someone who takes long or short positions in futures markets in consequence of an opinion that prices are about to advance or decline

Premium: The amount by which a cash commodity price sells over a futures price or another cash commodity price. The excess of one futures contract price over another

Put option: This option gives the buyer (or 'taker') of the option — in exchange for the premium which he pays — the right to decide at a later date whether or not to sell to the seller (or 'granter') at the price ('basic' or 'striking' price) agreed at the time the premium was paid. The right may be exercised at any point from the purchase of the option up to the declaration date (the date upon which the option expires)

Ring: Space on a trading floor where futures are traded. Also known as pit

Scalper: A trader whose main interest is in the immediate supply and demand situation in the pit. He operates on the narrowest of profit margins and seldom carries a position overnight

Seller's call: The purchase of a commodity, the contract for which specifies quality and fixes the price in the future

Selling basis: Term meaning that the buying basis is increased to include costs and profits

Short: The sale of a commodity not owned by the seller

Short hedges: The sale of futures made as hedges against holdings of the physical commodity

Split close: Term which refers to price discrepancies and to the range of commodity prices at the close of any market session

Spot: Term denoting immediate delivery for cash, as distinct from future delivery

Spot commodity: Actual or physical commodity, as opposed to a futures contract

Spot month: The first month in which delivery can take place and for which a quotation is made on the futures market

Spot price: The commodity cash sale price, as opposed to a futures price

Spread: An order to purchase one contract month and sell another month in the same commodity, usually done on the same exchange

Squeeze: Pressure on a delivery date which results in the price of that date becoming firmer in relation to other dates

Stop loss order: An order which can be fulfilled only when the price has reached the level specified by the client. As soon as this price has been traded, the order is executed at the next obtainable price. There is no guarantee that the order will be executed at the level specified in the original order

Straddle: The simultaneous buying and selling of the same commodity on the same market. This is designed to take advantage of differences between two options. Example: the sale of a September option and the simultaneous purchase of a January option made in the expectation that a later simultaneous purchase of the September and sale of the January options will produce a profit. See Arbitrage

Switch: To advance or postpone the original contract to a different month

Switching: Exchanging a commodity in one warehouse for a commodity in another

Tenderable grades and staples: These are grades and staples designated as deliverable to settle a futures contract

Tenders: Signifying the intent to deliver a physical commodity

Terminal market: Usually synonymous with commodity exchange or futures market, especially in the United Kingdom

Transferable notice: A notice signifying the intention to make actual delivery. This is given by the seller of a futures contract, usually specifying a day about one week hence

Warehouse receipt: A receipt for a commodity given by a licensed or authorized warehouseman and issued as tender on futures contracts

Warrant or warehouse receipt: A receipt of physical deposit which gives title to the physical commodity and which is recognized as good delivery

Appendix 3:
World Time Zones

Standard Times at noon Greenwich Mean Time

British Summer Time, which is one hour ahead of GMT, is observed from 02.00 hours on the third Sunday in March until 02.00 on the fourth Sunday in October. USA Daylight Saving Time, which is one hour ahead of local standard time, is observed in all states except Arizona, Hawaii and Michigan from 02.00 on the last Sunday in April until 02.00 on the last Sunday in October. In France, in 1977, Summer Time, which is also one hour ahead of local standard time, is observed from 24.00 hours on 3 April to 24.00 on 25 September.

Accra	12.00	Damascus	14.00	Ottawa	07.00
Adelaide	21.30	Darwin	21.30	Panama	07.00
Algiers	13.00	Delhi	17.30	Paris	13.00
Amman	14.00	Djakarta	20.00	Peking	20.00
Amsterdam	13.00	Dublin	12.00	Perth	20.00
Ankara	14.00	Gibraltar	13.00	Prague	13.00
Athens	14.00	Helsinki	14.00	Quebec	07.00
Auckland	24.00	Hobart	22.00	Rangoon	18.30
Baghdad	15.00	Hong Kong	20.00	Rawalpindi	17.00
Bangkok	19.00	Istanbul	14.00	Reykjavik	12.00
Beirut	14.00	Jerusalem	14.00	Rio de Janeiro	09.00
Belgrade	13.00	Karachi	17.00	Rome	13.00
Berlin	13.00	Kuala Lumpur	20.00	San Fransisco	04.00
Berne	13.00	Lagos	13.00	Santiago	08.00
Bombay	17.30	Leningrad	15.00	Sofia	14.00
Bonn	13.00	Lima	07.00	Singapore	19.30
Brisbane	22.00	Lisbon	13.00	Stockholm	13.00
Brussels	13.00	Luxembourg	13.00	Sydney	22.00
Bucharest	14.00	Madras	17.30	Tehran	15.30
Budapest	13.00	Madrid	13.00	Tokyo	21.00
Buenos Aires	09.00	Melbourne	22.00	Toronto	07.00
Cairo	14.00	Mexico City	06.00	Tunis	13.00
Calcutta	17.30	Montevideo	08.30	Vancouver	04.00
Canberra	22.00	Moscow	15.00	Vienna	13.00
Cape Town	14.00	Nairobi	15.00	Warsaw	13.00
Caracas	08.00	New York	07.00	Washington	07.00
Chicago	06.00	Nicosia	14.00	Wellington	24.00
Copenhagen	13.00	Oslo	13.00	Winnipeg	06.00

Note to World Time Zones map
The earth turns one complete revolution in 24 hours. The surface of the Earth is divided into 24 Time Zones, each of 15° longitude or 1 hour of time. In 24 hours it turns through 360°. The times shown are the standard times on land and sea when it is 12.00 hours on the Greenwich Meridian.

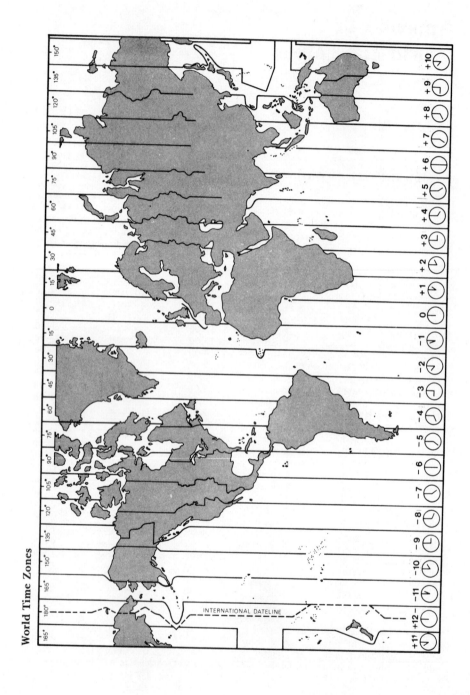

World Time Zones

Appendix 4:
Conversion Tables

Area	Hectares	Acres	Square Kilometres	Square Miles	Square Metres	Square Feet
Hectare	—	2.471	0.01	0.004	10,000	—
Acre	0.405	—	0.004	0.0015	4,046.86	—
Square Kilometre	100.0	247.1	—	0.386	—	—
Square Mile	259.0	640.0	2.590	—	—	—
Square Metre	10,000	4046.86	—	—	—	10,764
Square Foot	—	—	—	—	0.093	—

Mass	Metric Tonnes	Long Tons	Short Tons	Pounds	Kilograms
Metric Tonne	—	0.984	1.102	2205	1000
Long Ton	1.016	—	1.120	2240	—
Short Ton	0.907	0.893	—	2000	—
Pound	0.000453	0.000446	0.0005	—	2.20469
Kilogram	0.001	—	—	2.204	—

Volume	Barrels	Imperial Gallons	US Gallons	Kilolitres	Cubic Feet	Cubic Metres
Barrel	—	34.973	42	0.159	5.614	0.1589
Imperial Gallon	0.028	—	1.201	0.004	0.1605	0.0045
US Gallon	0.0238	0.833	—	0.003	0.134	0.0037
Kilolitre	6.289	219.97	264.17	—	—	—
Cubic Foot	0.178	6.2288	7.4805	—	—	0.028
Cubic Metre	6.289	219.97	264.17	—	35.315	—

Measure	Country	Class	Imperial Conversion	Metric Conversion
Bag	US	Weight	Variable	—
Bag	Brazil	Weight (coffee)	132 lb	60 kg
Bag	Cuba	Weight (sugar)	325 lb	147.4 kg
Bale	Argentina	W Wool, Skins, Hay	Variable	—
Bale	Australia	W Wool	320-330 lb	145-150 kg
Bale	Brazil	W Cotton, Wool	220 lb	99.8 kg
Bale	Britain, Egypt	Vol weight Cotton	719 lb	325.7 kg
Bale	India	Vol weight	396 lb	179.6 kg
Bale	Netherlands	W Coffee	132-136.5 lb	59.4-62 kg
Bale	New Zealand	W Wool	390-400 lb	177-181.6 kg
Bale	US	Gross	500 lb	227 kg
Bale	US	Net	480 lb	218 kg
Bushel	Britain	Capacity, dry	2219.5 cu in 1.03206 US bu	0.3637 hl
Bushel	Canada	Wheat WRS No 1	63 lb	28.60 kg
Bushel	Canada	Wheat WRS No 2	62.5 lb	28.37 kg
Bushel	Canada	Wheat WRS No 3	60.3 lb	27.38 kg
Bushel	Canada	Wheat CU No 1	61.5 lb	27.92 kg
Bushel	Canada	Wheat CU No 2	54 lb	24.52 kg
Bushel	Canada	Wheat CU No 3	Variable	—
Bushel	Canada	Barley Feed No 1	48.3 lb	21.30 kg
Bushel	Canada	Barley Feed No 2	46.9 lb	21.29 kg
Bushel	Canada	Oats Feed No 1	36 lb	16.34 kg
Bushel	Canada	Oats Feed No 2	32 lb	14.53 kg
Bushel	Canada	Rye CW No 1	58 lb	26.33 kg
Bushel	Canada	Rye CW No 2	56 lb	25.42 kg
Bushel	Canada	Rye CW No 3	54 lb	24.52 kg
Bushel	Canada	Flaxseed CW No 1	51 lb	23.15 kg
Bushel	Canada	Flaxseed CW No 2	50 lb	22.7 kg
Bushel (Winchester or Struck bu)	US	Capacity, dry	2150.42 cu in	0.3524 hl
Bushel	US	Wheat	60 lb	27.24 kg
Bushel	US	Soya Beans	60 lb	27.24 kg
Bushel	US	Corn	56 lb	25.42 kg
Bushel	US	Sorghums	56 lb	25.42 kg
Bushel	US	Barley	38 lb	17.25 kg
Bushel	US	Oats	32 lb	14.53 kg
Picul	Borneo (Dutch)	Weight	135.64 lb	61.52 kg
Picul	China	Weight	133.33 lb	60.48 kg
Picul	Hong Kong	Weight	133.33 lb	60.48 kg
Picul	Japan	Weight	132.28 lb	60 kg
Picul	Malaysia	Weight	133.33 lb	60.48 kg
Picul	Sumatra	Weight	133.33 lb	60.48 kg

W — Weight
Vol — Volume

bu — bushel
hl — hectolitre

cu in — cubic inches
kg — kilogram

British Bushels into US Bushels
1 British bushel = 1.03205623 US bushel
1 US bushel = 0.968939 British bushel.

American bushels:
1 bushel (heaped) US = 1.25 US (struck) bushel = .4405 hectolitre
Also = 5 US pecks; 40 US dry quarts; 80 US dry pints.

1 bushel (US or Winchester Struck bushel) = 0.96894 British bushel = 0.3523808 hectolitre or 4 US pecks or 32 US dry quarts or 64 US dry pints.

British bushels:
1 British bushel = 1.03206 US bushels = 0.363677 hectolitre = 4 British pecks
= 8 British gallons = 32 British quarts = 64 British pints = 1.28435 cu ft = 2219.35 cu in
= volume of 80 lb water (at $62°$F).

Appendix 5:
The World's Currencies

Country	Basic or principal unit of currency
Afghanistan	Afghani
Albania	Lekë
Algeria	Algerian Dinar
Angola	Kwanza
Antigua	East Caribbean Dollar (EC$)
Argentina	Argentinian Peso
Australia	Australian Dollar
Austria	Schilling
Bahamas, The	Bahamian Dollar (B$)
Bahrain	Bahrain Dinar
Bangladesh	Taka
Barbados	East Caribbean Dollar (EC$)
Belgium	Belgian Franc
Belize	Belizean Dollar
Benin	CFA Franc
Bermuda	Bermudan Dollar (Canadian, UK and US currencies also in use)
Bhutan	Tikchung
Bolivia	Bolivian Peso
Botswana	Pula
Brazil	Cruzeiro
Brunei	Brunei Dollar
Bulgaria	Lev
Burma	Kyat
Burundi	Burundi Franc
Cameroun Republic	Franc de la Communauté Financière Africaine (Franc CFA)
Canada	Canadian Dollar
Central African Empire	Franc CFA
Central American Common Market	Central American Peso
Chad	Franc CFA
Chile	Chilean Escudo
China, People's Republic of	Renminbi Yuan
Colombia	Colombian Peso
Congo (Brazzaville)	Franc CFA
Costa Rica	Colon
Cuba	Cuban Peso
Cyprus	Cyprus Pound
Czechoslovakia	Koruna
Dahomey	Franc CFA
Denmark	Danish Krone

Country	Basic or principal unit of currency
Dominica	East Caribbean Dollar (EC$)
Dominican Republic	Dominican Republic Peso
Ecuador	Sucre
Egypt	Egyptian Pound (£E)
El Salvador	El Salvador Colon
Ethiopia	Ethiopian Birr
Fiji	Fijian Dollar ($F)
Finland	Markka
France	French Franc
French Guinea	French Franc
Gabon	Franc CFA
Gambia	Dalasi
German Democratic Republic	Ostmark or DDR-Mark
Germany, Federal Republic	Deutsche Mark (DM)
Ghana	Cedi
Gibraltar	Gibraltar Pound
Greece	Drachma
Grenada	East Caribbean Dollar (EC$)
Guadeloupe	French Franc
Guatemala	Quetzal
Guinea-Bissau	Escudo
Guinea, Equatorial	Guinean Peseta
Guinea, Republic of	Sili
Guyana	Guyanese Dollar ($G)
Haiti	Gourde
Honduras	Lempira (L)
Hong Kong	Hong Kong Dollar (HK$)
Hungary	Forint
Iceland	Icelandic Krona
India	Indian Rupee
Indonesia	Rupiah (Rp)
Iran	Iranian Rial
Iraq	Iraqi Dinar
Ireland	Irish Pound
Israel	Israeli Pound (I£)
Italy	Lira
Ivory Coast	Franc CFA
Jamaica	Jamaican Dollar (J$)
Japan	Yen
Jordan	Jordanian Dinar (JD)
Kenya	Kenya Shilling (Ks)
Khmer Republic	Riel
Korea, Democratic People's Republic of (North Korea)	Won
Korea, Republic of (South Korea)	Won
Kuwait	Kuwait Dinar (KD)
Laos	Kip Pot Poi
Lebanon	Lebanese Pound (£L)
Lesotho	South African Rand
Liberia	Liberian Dollar (also US Dollar)
Libya	Libyan Dinar (LD)
Liechtenstein	Franken or Swiss Franc

Country	Basic or principal unit of currency
Luxembourg	Luxembourg Franc
Macao	Pataca
Malagasy Republic	Franc Malgache (FMG)
Malawi	Kwacha (K)
Malaysia	Ringgit
Mali	Mali Franc
Malta	Maltese Pound
Martinique	Local Franc
Mauritania	Ouguiya
Mauritius	Mauritian Rupee
Mexico	Mexican Peso
Monaco	French Franc
Mongolia	Tugrik
Montserrat	East Caribbean Dollar (EC$)
Morocco	Dirham
Mozambique	Escudo
Namibia (South West Africa)	South African Rand
Nepal	Nepali Rupee (NR)
Netherlands	Netherlands Gulden or Guilder or Florin
Netherlands Antilles	Netherlands Antilles Florin (NAFI) or Guilder
New Zealand	New Zealand Dollar ($NZ)
Nicaragua	Cordoba
Niger	Franc CFA
Nigeria	Naira
Norway	Norwegian Krone
Oman	Ryal Omani
Pakistan	Pakistan Rupee
Panama	Balboa
Papua New Guinea	Kina
Paraguay	Guarani
Peru	Gold Sol
Philippines	Philippine Peso
Pitcairn Islands	Australian Dollar
Poland	Zloty
Portugal	Portuguese Escudo
Puerto Rico	US Dollar ($)
Qatar	Qatar/Dubai Ryal
Réunion	French Franc
Rhodesia	Rhodesian Dollar (R$)
Romania	Leu
Rwanda	Rwanda Franc
St Kitts	East Caribbean Dollar (EC$)
St Lucia	East Caribbean Dollar (EC$)
St Vincent	East Caribbean Dollar (EC$)
Samoa (Western)	Tala
Saudi Arabia	Saudi Arabian Ryal
Senegal	Franc CFA
Seychelles	Rupee
Sierra Leone	Leone
Sikkim	Indian Rupee
Singapore	Singapore Dollar (S$)
Somalia	Somali Shilling

Country	Basic or principal unit of currency
South Africa, Republic of	Rand (R)
South West Africa (Namibia)	South African Rand
Spain	Spanish Peseta
Sri Lanka	Sri Lanka Rupee
Sudan	Sudanese Pound
Surinam	Surinam Guilder (also Netherlands currency)
Swaziland	Lilangeni
Sweden	Swedish Krona
Switzerland	Franken or Swiss Franc
Syria	Syrian Pound (£S)
Taiwan	New Taiwan Dollar
Tanzania	Tanzanian Shilling
Thailand	Baht
Togo	Franc CFA
Tonga	Pa'anga
Trinidad and Tobago	Trinidad and Tobago Dollar
Tunisia	Tunisian Dinar
Turkey	Turkish Lira (TL)
Uganda	Ugandan Shilling
United Arab Emirates	Dirham
United Kingdom (UK)	Pound Sterling (£)
United States of America (USA)	US Dollar ($)
Upper Volta	Franc CFA
Uruguay	Uruguayan Peso
USSR	Rouble
Venezuela	Bolivar
Vietnam, Democratic Republic of (North Vietnam)	Dong
Vietnam, Republic of (South Vietnam)	Piastre
Western Samoa	Tala
West Indies Associated States	East Caribbean Dollar (EC$)
Yemen Arab Republic	Yemeni Ryal (also Indian Rupee)
Yemen, People's Democratic Republic of	South Yemen Dinar
Yugoslavia	Yugoslav Dinar
Zaire	Zaire
Zambia	Kwacha (K)

Index